HANDBOOK OF SPACE TRAVEL AND TOURISM

HANDBOOK OF SPACE TRAVEL AND TOURISM

Percy K. Singh

KANISHKA PUBLISHERS, DISTRIBUTORS
NEW DELHI-110 002

KANISHKA PUBLISHERS, DISTRIBUTORS
4697/5-21A, Ansari Road, Daryaganj
New Delhi-110 002
Phones : 2327 0497, 2328 8285
Fax : 011-2328 8285
e-mail: kanishka_publishing@yahoo.co.in

First Published 2010

ISBN 978-81-8457-239-1

PRINTED IN INDIA

Published by Madan Sachdeva for Kanishka Publishers, Distributors, 4697/5-21A, Ansari Road, Daryaganj, New Delhi-110 002; Typeset by Manas Enterprises, Delhi, and Printed at Rajdhani Printers, Delhi.

Preface

This publication titled "Handbook of Space Travel and Tourism" is a unique attempt to address all aspects of space travel and tourism. It gives both conceptual and practical aspects of this new kind of commercial activity. This handbook provides readers with an introductory overview of space tourism, exploration, habitat and advocacy with focus on related timeline of orbital launches. The modern trend of space colonization and its rapid commercialization is covered, including moon as an attractive extra-celestial body. The quasi universal intergalactic denomination is also discussed. Select case studies of space technologies, space stations and spaceports are done so as to elaborate further on related issues and leading initiative in this regard. Various typologies, elements, dimensions and records of spaceflights are presented in detail, such as orbital, sub-orbital, interplanetary, etc. A mode case study is done of a spaceflight manual. This handbook also provides an exhaustive listing of private spacecraft companies offering different types of services in space. Such major companies are discussed briefly. Global successful spacecrafts, spaceplanes and notable space tourists have been included for elaborate description in this handbook. The timeline of space travel is given so as to have a proper understanding. Select global projects related to low cost access to space for promoting space tourism have been described in an extensive way. Similarly, major global organizations associated with space travel and tourism are described. Model examples of space art, space fellowships and prizes are covered. Besides, a tourism perspective on sex in space is given, including its elements, dimensions and trends. This handbook also highlights issues related to survival, adaptation, dress, food, music and medicines used in space. In concrete terms, this is a complete referencebook on the subject.

Percy K. Singh

Contents

Preface v

1. **Introduction to Space Tourism, Exploration, Habitat and Advocacy** 1
   - Space Tourism: An Introduction
   - Outer Space: An Introductory Overview
   - Outline of Space Exploration
   - Timeline of Orbital Launches
   - Space Habitat: An Overview
   - Space Advocacy

2. **Space Colonization and Commercialization: Special Focus on Moon** 29
   - Space Colonization
   - Colonization of the Moon
   - Commercialization of Space
   - Quasi Universal Intergalactic Denomination

3. **Space Technology, Space Station and Spaceport: Select Case Studies** 62
   - Space Technology
   - Space Station
   - International Space Station
   - Spaceport
   - Mojave Air and Spaceport
   - Singapore Spaceport
   - Spaceport America

4. **Spaceflight: Typology, Elements, Dimensions and Records** 98
   - Spaceflight
   - Orbital Spaceflight
   - Sub-Orbital Spaceflight
   - Interplanetary Spaceflight

- Human Spaceflight
- Private Spaceflight
- Astronaut
- Commercial Astronaut
- Spaceflight Participant
- Spaceflight Manual: A Model Case Study
- List of Spaceflight Records

5. Private Spaceflight Companies Offering Services in Space and Space Tourism: An Exhaustive Listing 149

- Private Spaceflight Companies
- ARCASPACE
- Bigelow Aerospace
- Blue Origin
- EADS Astrium
- Excalibur Almaz
- da Vinci Project
- Interorbital Systems
- Mojave Aerospace Ventures
- Orbital Sciences Corporation
- PlanetSpace
- Rocketplane XP
- Rotary Rocket
- Virgin Galactic
- Space Adventures
- Space Transport Corporation
- Space Environment
- SpaceDev
- Lynx Rocketplane
- Xerus (Spaceplane)
- SpaceX

6. Successful Spacecrafts, Spaceplanes and Spacetourists: Model Case Studies 206

- Spacecraft
- Spaceplane
- Suborbital Spaceplane
- Genesis I
- Genesis II

- Scaled Composites SpaceShipOne
- Scaled Composites SpaceShipTwo
- Mark Shuttleworth
- Charles Simonyi
- Gregory Olsen
- Anousheh Ansari
- Dennis Tito
- Richard Garriott
- James Benson
- Timeline of Space Travel by Nationality

7. Select Global Projects Related to Low-Cost Access to Space for Promoting Space Tourism **241**

- Tier One
- Tier 1B
- Tier Two
- Rutan Voyager
- VSS Enterprise
- VSS Voyager
- VMS Eve
- The Spaceship Company
- Scaled Composites White Knight
- Scaled Composites SpaceShip Three
- Space Island Project
- Space Island Group
- Pioneer Rocketplane
- MirCorp
- Blue Origin Goddard
- Blue Origin New Shepard
- DSE-Alpha
- Cosmopolis XXI
- XCOR Aerospace

8. Major Global Organizations Associated with Space Travel and Tourism **269**

- Space Tourism Society
- Astronaute Club Européen
- LiftPort Group
- Commercial Spaceflight Federation
- Association of Autonomous Astronauts
- El Club de Los Astronautas

9. Space Art, Fellowships and Prizes: Model Examples 275

- ❑ Space Art
- ❑ Space Fellowship
- ❑ Ansari X Prize

10. Sex in Space: A Tourism Perspective 283

- ❑ Sex in Space
- ❑ 2suit
- ❑ Best "Zero Gravity Sex" Titles
- ❑ Mile High Club
- ❑ Galactic Suite

11. Space and Spaceflight: Issues Related to Survival, Adaptation, Suit, Food, Music and Medicine 292

- ❑ Space and Survival
- ❑ Human Adaptation to Spaceflight
- ❑ Flight Suit
- ❑ Space Food
- ❑ Space-themed Music
- ❑ Space Medicine

Bibliography 315

Index 321

1

Introduction to Space Tourism, Exploration, Habitat and Advocacy

SPACE TOURISM: AN INTRODUCTION

Space tourism is the recent phenomenon of tourists paying for flights into space pioneered by Russia. As of 2009, orbital space tourism opportunities are limited and expensive, with only the Russian Space Agency providing transport. The price for a flight brokered by Space Adventures to the International Space Station aboard a Soyuz spacecraft is $20-35 million.

Infrastructure for a suborbital space tourism industry is being developed through the construction of spaceports in numerous locations, including California, Oklahoma, New Mexico, Florida, Virginia, Alaska, Wisconsin, Esrange in Sweden as well as the United Arab Emirates. Some use the term "personal spaceflight" as in the case of the Personal Spaceflight Federation.

A number of startup companies have sprung up in recent years, hoping to create a space tourism industry, for a list of such companies, and the spacecraft they are currently building.

Early Dreams

After early successes in space, much of the public saw intensive space exploration as inevitable. Those aspirations are remembered in science fiction such as Arthur C. Clarke's *A Fall of Moondust* and also *2001: A Space Odyssey*, Roald Dahl's *Charlie and the Great Glass Elevator*, Joanna Russ's 1968 novel *Picnic on Paradise*, and Larry Niven's Known Space stories. Lucian in 2 A.D. in his book *True History* examines the idea of a crew of men whose ship travels to the Moon during a storm. Jules Verne also took up the theme of lunar visits in his books, *From the Earth to the Moon* and *Around the Moon*. Robert A. Heinlein's short story *The Menace from Earth*, published in 1957, was one of the first to incorporate elements of a developed space tourism industry within its framework. During the 1960s and 1970s, it was common belief that space hotels would be launched by 2000. Many futurologists around the middle of the 20th century speculated that the average family of the early 21st century would be able to enjoy a holiday on the Moon.

The end of the Space Race, however, signified by the Moon landing, decreased the emphasis placed on space exploration by national governments and therefore led to decreased demands for public funding of manned space flights.

Precedents

The Soviet space Programme was aggressive in broadening the pool of cosmonauts. The Soviet Intercosmos Programme also included cosmonauts selected from Warsaw Pact members (from Czechoslovakia, Poland, East Germany, Bulgaria, Hungary, Romania) and later from allies of the USSR (Cuba, Mongolia, Vietnam) and non-aligned countries (India, Syria, Afghanistan). Most of these cosmonauts received full training for their missions and were treated as equals, but especially after the Mir Programme began, were generally given shorter flights than Soviet cosmonauts. The European Space Agency took advantage of the Programme as well.

The U.S. space shuttle Programme included payload specialist positions which were usually filled by representatives of companies or institutions managing a specific payload on that mission. These payload specialists did not receive the same training as professional NASA astronauts and were not employed by NASA, so they were essentially private astronauts. NASA was also eager to prove its capability to Congressional sponsors, and Senator Jake Garn and (then Representative, now Senator) Bill Nelson were both given opportunities to fly on board a shuttle. As the shuttle Programme expanded, the Teacher in Space Programme was developed as a way to expand publicity and educational opportunities for NASA. Christa McAuliffe would have been the first Teacher in Space, but was killed in the Challenger disaster and the Programme was cancelled. During the same period a Journalist in Space Programme was frequently discussed, with individuals such as Walter Cronkite and Miles O'Brien considered front-runners, but no formal Programme was ever developed. McAuliffe's backup in the Teacher in Space Programme, Barbara Morgan, trained and flew aboard STS-118 as a fully trained NASA payload specialist and spoke to many students as an educator during the trip.

With the realities of the post-Perestroika economy in Russia, its space industry was especially starved for cash. The Tokyo Broadcasting System (TBS) offered to pay for one of its reporters to fly on a mission. For $28 million, Toyohiro Akiyama was flown in 1990 to Mir with the eighth crew and returned a week later with the seventh crew. Akiyama gave a daily TV broadcast from orbit and also performed scientific experiments for Russian and Japanese companies. However, since the cost of the flight was paid by his employer, Akiyama could be considered a business traveller rather than a tourist.

In 1991, British chemist Helen Sharman was selected from a pool of public applicants to be the first Briton in space. As the United Kingdom had no human space Programme, the arrangement was by a consortium of private companies who contracted with the Russian space Programme. Sharman was also in a sense a private space traveller, but she was a working cosmonaut with a full training regimen.

Orbital Space Tourism

At the end of the 1990s, MirCorp, a private venture by then in charge of the space station, began seeking potential space tourists to visit Mir in order to offset some of its maintenance costs. Dennis Tito, an American businessman and former JPL scientist, became their first candidate. When the decision to de-orbit Mir was made, Tito managed to switch his trip to the International Space Station through a deal between MirCorp and U.S.-based Space Adventures, Ltd., despite strong opposition from senior figures at NASA. Space Adventures remains the only company to have sent paying passengers to space.

In conjunction with the Federal Space Agency of the Russian Federation and Rocket and Space Corporation Energia, Space Adventures facilitated the flights for the world's first private space explorers: Dennis Tito, Mark Shuttleworth, Gregory Olsen, Anousheh Ansari and Charles Simonyi. The first three participants paid in excess of $20 million (USD) each for their 10-day visit to the ISS.

On April 28, 2001, Dennis Tito became the first "fee-paying" space tourist when he visited the International Space Station (ISS) for seven days. He was followed in 2002 by South African computer millionaire Mark Shuttleworth. The third was Gregory Olsen in 2005, who was trained as a scientist and whose company produced specialist high-sensitivity cameras. Olsen planned to use his time on the ISS to conduct a number of experiments, in part to test his company's products. Olsen had planned an earlier flight, but had to cancel for health reasons.

After the Columbia disaster, space tourism on the Russian Soyuz programme was temporarily put on hold, because Soyuz vehicles became the only available transport to the ISS. However, in 2006, space tourism was resumed. On September 18, 2006, Anousheh Ansari, an Iranian American (Soyuz TMA-9), became the fourth space tourist (she prefers spaceflight participant). On April 7, 2007, Charles Simonyi, an American billionaire of Hungarian descent, joined their ranks (Soyuz TMA-10).

In 2003, NASA and the Russian Space Agency agreed to use the term 'Spaceflight Participant' to distinguish those space travellers from astronauts on missions coordinated by those two agencies. Tito, Shuttleworth, Olsen, Ansari, and Simonyi were designated as such during their respective space flights. NASA also lists Christa McAuliffe as a"Space Flight Participant" (although she did not pay a fee), apparently due to her non-technical duties aboard the STS-51-L flight.

List of Flown Space Tourists

Six of the space tourists flew to and from the International Space Station on Soyuz spacecraft through the space tourism company, Space Adventures:

Space Tourist	*Nationality*	*Year*	*Duration of Flight*
Dennis Tito	American	2001	9 days (Apr 28-May 6)
Mark Shuttleworth	South African / British	2002	11 days (Apr 25-May 5)
Gregory Olsen	American	2005	11 days (Oct 1-Oct 11)
Anousheh Ansari	Iranian / American	2006	12 days (Sept 18-Sept 29)
Charles Simonyi	Hungarian / American	2007	15 days (Apr 7-Apr 21)
		2009	12 days (Mar 26-Apr 8)
Richard Garriott	American / British	2008	12 days (Oct 12-Oct 23)

Future Space Tourists

Space Tourist	*Nationality*	*Scheduled to Fly*
Guy Laliberté	Canadian	October 2009

Suborbital Flights

More affordable suborbital space tourism is viewed as a money-making proposition by several other companies, including Space Adventures, Virgin Galactic, Starchaser, Blue Origin, Armadillo Aerospace, XCOR Aerospace, Rocketplane Limited, the European"Project Enterprise", and others. Most are proposing vehicles that make suborbital flights peaking at an altitude of 100-160 kilometres. Passengers would experience three to six minutes of weightlessness, a view of a twinkle-free starfield, and a vista of the curved Earth below. Projected costs are expected to be about $200,000 per passenger.

As of November 2007 Virgin Galactic had pre-sold nearly 200 seats for their suborbital space tourism flights, according to the company's president.

The X Prize

On October 4, 2004, the SpaceShipOne, designed by Burt Rutan of Scaled Composites, won the $10,000,000 X Prize, which was designed to be won by the first private company who could reach and surpass an altitude of 62 miles (100 km) twice within two weeks. The altitude is beyond the Kármán Line, the arbitrarily defined boundary of space. The first flight was flown by Michael Melvill on June 21, 2004 to a height of 62 miles, making him the first commercial astronaut. The prize-winning flight was flown by Brian Binnie, which reached a height of 69.6 miles, breaking the X-15 record.

Virgin Galactic

Virgin Galactic, one of the leading potential space tourism groups, is planning to begin passenger service aboard the VSS Enterprise, a Scaled Composites SpaceShipTwo type spacecraft. The initial seat price will be $200,000, but that price is expected to eventually fall to $20,000. To date, over two hundred people have made down payments on bookings. Headed by Sir Richard Branson's Virgin Group, Virgin Galactic hopes to be the first private space tourism company to regularly send civilians into space. A citizen astronaut will only require three days of training before spaceflight. SpaceShipTwo will be a scaled up version of SpaceShipOne, the spacecraft which claimed the Ansari X Prize. Both spacecraft were designed by Burt Rutan's Scaled Composites. Launches will initially occur at the Mojave Spaceport in California, and will then be moved to Spaceport America in Upham, New Mexico. Tourists will also be flown from Kiruna, Sweden. The spacecraft will travel 360,000 feet (109.73 km/68.18 miles) high. This goes beyond the internationally defined boundary between Earth and space of 100 km. Spaceflights will last 2.5 hours, carry 6 passengers, and reach a speed of Mach 3. SpaceShipTwo will not require a space shuttle-like heat shield for atmospheric reentry as it will not experience the extreme aerodynamic heating experienced during reentry at orbital velocities (approximately Mach 22.5 at a typical shuttle altitude of 300 km, or 185 miles). The glider will employ a "feathering" technique to manage drag during the unpowered descent and landing. SpaceShipTwo will use a single hybrid rocket motor to launch from mid-air after detaching from a mother ship at 50,000 feet, instead of NASA's space shuttle's ground-based launch.

Project Enterprise

Project Enterprise was launched by the German TALIS Institute in 2004 and is the first project of its kind in Europe. The goal is to develop a rocket-propelled spaceplane by 2011 that will carry one pilot and up to five passengers into suborbital space. The plane will launch from the ground using rockets, and will return in an unpowered flight like Virgin Galactic's SpaceShipTwo. The prototypes and finished spaceplane will be launched from an airport near Cochstedt (Germany; Saxony-Anhalt).

Since 2004, the TALIS Institute has gained many industrial partners, including XtremeAir, who will manufacture the airframe, and Swiss Propulsion Laboratory SPL, who will deliver the propulsion components. XtremeAir is known for their acrobatic airplanes, and SPL has designed and tested liquid propellant rocket engines since 1998.

Current work is focusing on the first prototype, the "Black Sky": An existing acrobatic airplane that would be fitted with a single rocket engine and a new wing. The rocket engine is expected to deliver a thrust of 10 kN. The test Programme for this engine started in 2007 at SPL.

Legality

United States

In December 2005, the U.S. Government released a set of proposed rules for space tourism.

Under current US law, any company proposing to launch paying passengers from American soil on a suborbital rocket must receive a license from the Federal Aviation Administration's Office of Commercial Space Transportation (FAA/AST). The licensing process focuses on public safety and safety of property, and the details can be found in the Code of Federal Regulations, Title 14, Chapter III.

This is in accordance with the Commercial Space Launch Amendments Act passed by Congress in 2004.

Orbital Flights, Space Stations and Space Hotels

- EADS Astrium, a subsidiary of European aerospace giant EADS, announced its space tourism project on June 13, 2007.
- SpaceX is a private space company which develops their own rocket family called *Falcon* and a capsule named Dragon, capable of sending up to 7 people

to any space station, either ISS or a possible station by Bigelow Aerospace. Falcon 1 has already undertaken testflights and successfully completed its first commercial flight on July 14, 2009, deploying the Malaysian RazakSAT into orbit. Falcon 9 (which will be the rocket for the Dragon capsule) is currently in vertical position at Space Launch Complex 40 in Cape Canaveral, and will take its first testflight in late 2009. The Dragon capsule is slated to enter service in 2009.

- Constellation Services International (CSI) is working on a project to send manned spacecraft on commercial circumlunar missions. Their offer would include a week-long stay at the ISS, as well as a week-long trip around the Moon.
- Space Adventures Ltd. have also announced that they are working on circumlunar missions to the moon, with the price per passenger being $100,000,000. They are currently developing spaceports at the United Arab Emirates (Ras al-Khaimah) and in Singapore.
- Orbital space tourist flights are also being planned by Excalibur Almaz, using modernized *TKS* space capsules.

Several plans have been proposed for using a space station as a hotel. American motel tycoon Robert Bigelow has acquired the designs for inflatable space habitats from the Transhab Programme abandoned by NASA. His company, Bigelow Aerospace, already launched the first inflatable habitat module named Genesis I on 12 July 2006. The second test module, Genesis II was launched on 28 June 2007. It is also currently planning to launch a prototype space station module by late 2008, and plans to officially launch the first commercial space station by 2012 (tagged *Nautilus*) which will have 330 cubic metres (almost as big as the ISS's 425 cubic metres of usable volume).

Bigelow Aerospace is currently offering the America's Space Prize, a $50 million prize to the first US company to create a reusable spacecraft capable of carrying passengers to a Nautilus space station.

Other companies have also expressed interest in constructing "space hotels". For example, Excalibur Almaz plans to modernize and launch its Soviet-era Almaz space stations, which will feature the largest windows ever on spacecraft. Virgin's Richard Branson has expressed his hope for the construction of a space hotel within his lifetime. He expects that beginning a space tourism Programme will cost $100 million. Hilton International announced the Space Islands Project, a plan to connect together used space shuttle fuel tanks, each the diameter of a Boeing 747 aircraft. A separate organization, Space Island Group announced their distinct Space Island Project (note the singular "Island"), and plans on having 20,000 people on their "space island" by 2020, with the number of people doubling for each decade. British Airways has expressed interest in the venture. If and when Space Hotels develop, it would initially cost a passenger $60,000, with prices lowering over time.

Fashion designer Eri Matsui has designed clothing, including a wedding gown, intended to look best in weightless environments.

Advocacy, Education, and Industry Organizations

Several organizations have been formed to promote the space tourism industry, including the Space Tourism Society, and others. More information about the future of Space Tourism can be found at Space Tourism Lecture, which is a free online Space Tourism Lecture handout collection. Since 2003 Dr. Robert A. Goehlich and Pierluigi Polignano teaches the world's first and only Space Tourism class at Keio University, Yokohama, Japan. UniGalactic Space Travel Magazine is a bi-monthly educational publication covering space tourism and space exploration developments in companies like SpaceX, Orbital Sciences, Virgin Galactic and organizations like NASA. The content of UniGalactic Space Travel Magazine can be found on UniGalactic website.

Opinions of Commercial Space Tourism

A web-based survey suggested that over 70 per cent of those surveyed wanted less than or equal to 2 weeks in space; in addition, 88 per cent wanted to spacewalk (only 74 per cent of these would do it for a 50 per cent premium), and 21 per cent wanted a hotel or space station.

The concept has met with some criticism from social commentators and politicians, notably Günter Verheugen, vice-president of the European Commission, who said of the EADS Astrium Space Tourism Project "It's only for the super rich, which is against my social convictions".

Objection to "Space Tourist" Terminology

Dennis Tito, Mark Shuttleworth, Gregory Olsen, Anousheh Ansari and Richard Garriott have all preferred to be called something other than "space tourist". In each case, they explained their preferences by pointing out that they carried out scientific experiments as part of their journey; Garriott additionally emphasized that their training is identical to requirements of non-Russian cosmonauts, and that teachers or other citizens chosen to fly with NASA are called astronauts.Tito has asked to be known as an "independent researcher". Shuttleworth proposed "pioneer of commercial space travel". Olsen preferred "private researcher."Ansari prefers the term "private space explorer". Garriott prefers "cosmonaut" or "astronaut", but will accept "private" in front of either. Alone among those who have paid to go to orbit so far, Charles Simonyi seems to have no concerns about calling it "space tourism", even in reference to his own experience. Asked in an interview "Do you foresee a day when space tourism is not just the province of billionaires—when it will be as affordable as plane travel?", he did not object to the implicit categorization of his own trip, but rather answered "Yes, the only question is when ...."

Although many space enthusiasts subscribe to the notion of space tourism as a potential burgeoning industry that could further the development and settlement of space, some of these same enthusiasts object to the use of the term "space tourist". Rick Tumlinson of the Space Frontier Foundation, for example, has said:

> "I hate the word tourist, and I always will .... 'Tourist' is somebody in a flowered shirt with three cameras around his neck."

Others with perhaps less enthusiasm for space development seem to agree. Alex Tabarrok has categorized it as a kind of "adventure travel". The mere fact of people paying for a travel experience does not, in his view, make that activity "tourism". Oxford dictionary is considering entering the word Touronaut as the new word to describe a space tourist.

> "At best and for the foreseeable future space travel will remain akin to climbing Everest, dangerous and uncommon. Yes, we might see 100 flights a year but that's not space tourism—tourism is fat guys with cameras."

Space tourism is a recent phenomenon where wealthy individuals or corporations are spending up to $25 million for a chance to travel in low Earth orbit (LEO) and beyond. California multi-millionaire Dennis Tito spent $20 million on space tourism to become the first paying tourist, in 2001. Tito, the founder of Wilshire Associates and former JPL scientist, travelled aboard a Russian Soyuz capsule, launched by U.S. company, Space Adventures Ltd., where he spent 7 days aboard the International Space Station (ISS). Space tourism has become a bigger goal over the past few years as NASA has announced they are cutting down on the ventures and the Shuttle will be retired in 2010.

NASA hopes to rely on the commercial orbital transportation systems (COTS) to shuttle astronauts and cargo to the ISS thereafter and it looks like commercial craft will be available by then.

If you've ever seen Arnold Schwarzenegger's movie "Total Recall" you'll know that space tourism was a central theme to that movie. But, space tourism is not just some pipe dream as companies like Scaled Composites, Blue Origin, and SpaceX are developing craft and Programmes to do just this.

Following Dennis Tito as the second to partake of the space tourism industry, in 2002 was South African millionaire, Mark Shuttleworth, who certainly was "shuttle worthy" as he also spent around $20 million to travel aboard a Russian Soyuz TM-34 and spend 8 days aboard the ISS.

Following Shuttleworth in 2005, was Greg Olsen, who spent the same amount on tourism to travel to the ISS via a Russian Soyuz capsule. And space tourism has not stopped there, as the third fee-paying tourist, Olsen rejected the "tourist" designation noting that he had conducted several experiments while on the ISS. Olsen is co-founder and chairman of Sensors Unlimited Inc., a company developing infared cameras and sensors. In 2006, Iran-born American citizen Anousheh Ansari became the fourth in the ISS tourism lineup and the first female to buy a ticket in the space tourism industry.

Some have argued that John Glenn in 1998 was the first official extraterrestrial tourist, but others discount that claim since Glenn was a non-paying participant in the flight. If you think also that space tourism is so expensive that nobody will want to go, then think again since there is a waiting list to be launched into LEO and aboard the ISS.

Space tourism has been criticized as being a "playground for the rich." And, while there may be some current truth to this, the vision for the future is to make space tourism affordable and available to the middle class in just a few, short years. While 'N Sync singer Lance Bass may have fallen short of cash and Madonna was voted down in her request, still many companies are working on making suborbital flights affordable to the general public.

Tired of Disneyland and Magic Mountain? Been to all the major continents and want more? Done all of the extreme sports and just can't get that adrenaline rush anymore? Space tourism may just be the Next Big Thing on your agenda in the not too distant future.

Even Bigelow Aerospace and the X-Prize Foundation are getting in on the act by offering monetary awards for breakthrough technology in the space tourism industry. By most estimates, space tourism may be a reality as soon as 2009 or 2010. Just as there was a "race to space" decades ago, now there is a race to space tourism in this decade.

So, if you've got the bug to travel and have always dreamed of going beyond the confines of Earth, that possibility may just exist sooner than you think. You'll have to wait a few years to book your flight though as all of the details are being worked out. Until, then come back to this site often to see what others are doing to advance the space tourism industry.

OUTER SPACE: AN INTRODUCTORY OVERVIEW

Outer space (often simply called **space**) comprises the relatively empty regions of the universe outside the atmospheres of celestial bodies. *Outer* space is used to distinguish it from airspace and terrestrial locations.

Contrary to popular understanding, outer space is not completely empty (i.e. a perfect vacuum), but contains a low density of particles, predominantly hydrogen plasma, as well as electromagnetic radiation and neutrinos. Hypothetically, it also contains dark matter and dark energy.

The term *outer space* was first recorded by the English poet Lady Emmeline Stuart Wortley in her poem "The Maiden of Moscow" in 1842, and also later attested to the writings of HG Wells in 1901. The shorter term *space* is actually older, first used to mean the region beyond Earth's sky in John Milton's *Paradise Lost* in 1667.

Environment

Outer space is the closest approximation of a perfect vacuum. It has effectively no friction, allowing stars, planets and moons to move freely along ideal gravitational trajectories. But no vacuum is truly perfect, not even in intergalactic space where there are still a few hydrogen atoms per cubic centimetre. (For comparison, the air we breathe contains about 10^{19} molecules per cubic centimetre.) The deep vacuum of space could make it an attractive environment for certain industrial processes, for instance those that require ultraclean surfaces.

Stars, planets, asteroids, and moons keep their atmospheres by gravitational attraction, and as such, atmospheres have no clearly delineated boundary: the density of atmospheric gas simply decreases with distance from the object. The Earth's atmospheric pressure drops to about 1 Pa at 100 kilometres (62 mi) of altitude, the Kármán line which is a common definition of the boundary with outer space. Beyond this line, isotropic gas pressure rapidly becomes insignificant when compared to radiation pressure from the sun and the dynamic pressure of the solar wind, so the definition of pressure becomes difficult to interpret. The thermosphere in this range has large gradients of pressure, temperature and composition, and varies greatly due to space weather. Astrophysicists prefer to use number density to describe these environments, in units of particles per cubic centimetre.

Temperature

All of the observable universe is filled with large numbers of photons, created during the Big Bang, the so-called cosmic background radiation, and quite likely a correspondingly large number of neutrinos called the cosmic neutrino background. The current temperature of the photon radiation is about 3 K (–270.15 °C; –454.27 °F).

Effect on Human Bodies

Contrary to popular belief, a person suddenly exposed to the vacuum would not explode, freeze to death or die from boiling blood, but would take a short while to die by asphyxiation (suffocation). Air would immediately leave the lungs due to the enormous pressure gradient. Any oxygen dissolved in the blood would empty into the lungs to try to equalize the partial pressure gradient. Once the deoxygenated blood arrives at the brain, death would quickly follow.

Humans and animals exposed to vacuum will lose consciousness after a few seconds and die of hypoxia within minutes. Blood and other body fluids do boil when their pressure drops below 6.3 kPa, the vapour pressure of water at body temperature. This condition is called ebullism. The steam may bloat the body to twice its normal size and slow circulation, but tissues are elastic and porous enough to prevent rupture. Ebullism is slowed by the pressure containment of blood vessels, so some blood remains liquid. Swelling and ebullism can be reduced by containment in a flight suit. Shuttle astronauts wear a fitted elastic garment called the Crew Altitude Protection Suit (CAPS) which prevents ebullism at pressures as low as 2 kPa. Water vapour would also rapidly evaporate off from exposed areas such as the lungs, cornea of the eye and mouth, cooling the body. Rapid evaporative cooling of the skin will create frost, particularly in the mouth, but this is not a significant hazard. Space may be cold, but it's mostly vacuum and transfers heat ineffectually; as a result the main temperature regulation concern for space suits is how to get rid of naturally generated body heat.

Cold or oxygen-rich atmospheres can sustain life at pressures much lower than atmospheric, as long as the density of oxygen is similar to that of standard sea-level atmosphere. The colder air temperatures found at altitudes of up to 3 kilometres (1.9 mi) generally compensate for the lower pressures there. Above this altitude, oxygen enrichment is necessary to prevent altitude sickness, and spacesuits are necessary to prevent ebullism above 19 kilometres (12 mi). Most spacesuits use only 20 kPa of pure oxygen, just enough to sustain full consciousness. This pressure is high enough to prevent ebullism, but simple evaporation of blood can still cause decompression sickness and gas embolisms if not managed.

Rapid decompression can be much more dangerous than vacuum exposure itself. Even if the victim does not hold his breath, venting through the windpipe may be too slow to prevent the fatal rupture of the delicate alveoli of the lungs. Eardrums and sinuses may be ruptured by rapid decompression, soft tissues may bruise and seep blood, and the stress of shock will accelerate oxygen consumption leading to hypoxia. Injuries caused by rapid decompression are called barotrauma. A pressure drop as small as 13 kPa, which produces no symptoms if it is gradual, may be fatal if it occurs suddenly.

Boundary

Traditionally, there was no clear boundary between Earth's atmosphere and space, as the density of the atmosphere gradually decreases as the altitude increases. Nevertheless, several boundaries have been set, namely:

- The Fédération Aéronautique Internationale has established the Kármán line at an altitude of 100 kilometres (62 mi) as a working definition for the boundary between aeronautics and astronautics. This is used because above an altitude of roughly 100 km, as Theodore von Kármán calculated, a vehicle would have to travel faster than orbital velocity in order to derive sufficient aerodynamic lift from the atmosphere to support itself.
- The United States designates people who travel above an altitude of 50 miles (80 km) as astronauts.
- NASA's mission control uses 76 miles (122 km) as their re-entry altitude, which roughly marks the boundary where atmospheric drag becomes noticeable, (depending on the ballistic coefficient of the vehicle), thus leading shuttles to switch from steering with thrusters to maneuvering with air surfaces.

In 2009, scientists at the University of Calgary reported detailed measurements with an instrument called the Supra-Thermal Ion Imager (an instrument that measures the direction and velocity of ions), which allowed them to determine that space begins 118 kilometres (73 mi) above Earth. The boundary represents the midpoint of a gradual transition over tens of kilometres from the relatively gentle winds of the Earth's atmosphere to the more violent flows of charged particles in space, which can reach speeds well over 600 miles per hour (1,000 km/h).

This was only the second time that direct measurements of charged particle flows have been conducted at this region, which is too high for balloons and too low for satellites. It was however the first study to include all the relevant elements for this kind of determination—for example, the upper atmospheric winds.

The instrument was carried by the JOULE-II rocket on January 19, 2007, and travelled to an altitude of about 124 miles (200 km). From there it collected data while it was moving through the "edge of space".

Space Versus Orbit

To perform an orbit, a spacecraft must travel faster than a sub-orbital spaceflight. A spacecraft has not entered orbit until it is travelling with a sufficiently great horizontal velocity such that the acceleration due to gravity on the spacecraft is less than or equal to the centripetal acceleration being caused by its horizontal velocity. So to enter orbit, a spacecraft must not only reach space, but must also achieve a sufficient orbital speed (angular velocity). For a low-Earth orbit, this is about 7,900 m/s (28,440.00 km/h; 17,671.80 mph); by contrast, the fastest airplane speed ever achieved (excluding speeds achieved by deorbiting spacecraft) was 2,200 m/s (7,920.00 km/h; 4,921.26 mph) in 1967 by the North American X-15. Konstantin Tsiolkovsky was the first person to realize that, given the energy available from any available chemical fuel, a several-stage rocket would be required. The escape velocity to pull free of Earth's gravitational field altogether and move into interplanetary space is about 11,000 m/s (39,600.00 km/h; 24,606.30 mph). The energy required to reach velocity for low Earth orbit (32 MJ/kg) is about twenty times the energy required simply to climb to the corresponding altitude [10 kJ/(km·kg)].

There is a major difference between sub-orbital and orbital spaceflights. The minimum altitude for a stable orbit around Earth (that is, one without significant atmospheric drag) begins at around 350 kilometres (220 mi) above mean sea level. A common misunderstanding about the boundary to space is that orbit occurs simply by reaching this altitude. Achieving orbital speed can theoretically occur at any altitude, although atmospheric drag precludes an orbit that is too low. At sufficient speed, an airplane would need a way to keep it from flying off into space, but at present, this speed is several times greater than anything within reasonable technology.

A common misconception is that people in orbit are outside Earth's gravity because they are "floating". They are floating because they are in "free fall": they are accelerating toward Earth, along with their spacecraft, but are simultaneously moving sideways fast enough that the "fall" away from a straight-line path merely keeps them in orbit at a constant distance above Earth's surface. Earth's gravity reaches out far past the Van Allen belt and keeps the Moon in orbit at an average distance of 384,403 kilometres (238,857 mi).

Regions

Space being not a perfect vacuum, its different regions are defined by the various atmospheres and "winds" that dominate within them, and extend to the point at which those winds give way to those beyond. Geospace extends from Earth's atmosphere to the outer reaches of Earth's magnetic field, whereupon it gives way to the solar wind of interplanetary space. Interplanetary space extends to the heliopause, whereupon the solar wind gives way to the winds of the interstellar medium. Interstellar space then continues to the edges of the galaxy, where it fades into the intergalactic void.

Geospace

Geospace is the region of outer space near the Earth. Geospace includes the upper region of the atmosphere, as well as the ionosphere and magnetosphere. The Van Allen radiation belts also lie within the geospace. The region between Earth's atmosphere and the Moon is sometimes referred to as **cis-lunar space**.

Although it meets the definition of outer space, the atmospheric density within the first few hundred kilometres above the Kármán line is still sufficient to produce significant drag on satellites. Most artificial satellites operate in this region called low earth orbit and must fire their engines every few days to maintain orbit. The drag here is low enough that it could theoretically be overcome by radiation pressure on solar sails, a proposed propulsion system for interplanetary travel. Planets are too massive for their trajectories to be affected by these forces, although their atmospheres are eroded by the solar winds.

Geospace is populated at very low densities by electrically charged particles, whose motions are controlled by the Earth's magnetic field. These plasmas form a medium from which storm-like disturbances powered by the solar wind can drive electrical currents into the Earth's upper atmosphere.

During geomagnetic storms two regions of geospace, the radiation belts and the ionosphere, can become strongly disturbed. These disturbances interfere with the functioning of satellite communications and navigation (GPS) technologies. These storms increase fluxes of energetic electrons that can permanently damage satellite electronics, and can also be a hazard to astronauts, even in low-Earth orbit.

Geospace contains material left over from previous manned and unmanned launches that are a potential hazard to spacecraft. Some of this debris re-enters Earth's atmosphere periodically.

The absence of air makes geospace (and the surface of the Moon) ideal locations for astronomy at all wavelengths of the electromagnetic spectrum, as evidenced by the spectacular pictures sent back by the Hubble Space Telescope, allowing light from about 13.7 billion years ago—almost to the time of the Big Bang—to be observed.

The outer boundary of geospace is the interface between the magnetosphere and the solar wind. The inner boundary is the ionosphere. Alternately, geospace is the region of space between the Earth's upper atmosphere and the outermost reaches of the Earth's magnetic field.

Interplanetary

Outer space within the solar system is called **interplanetary space**, which passes over into interstellar space at the heliopause. The vacuum of outer space is not really empty;

it is sparsely filled with cosmic rays, which include ionized atomic nuclei and various subatomic particles. There is also gas, plasma and dust, small meteors, and several dozen types of organic molecules discovered to date by microwave spectroscopy. Interplanetary space is defined by the solar wind, a continuous stream of charged particles emanating from the Sun that creates a very tenuous atmosphere (the heliosphere) for billions of miles into space. The discovery since 1995 of extrasolar planets means that other stars must possess their own interplanetary media.

Interstellar

Interstellar space is the physical space within a galaxy not occupied by stars or their planetary systems. The interstellar medium resides—by definition—in interstellar space.

Intergalactic

Intergalactic space is the physical space between galaxies. Generally free of dust and debris, intergalactic space is very close to a total vacuum. Certainly, the space between galaxy clusters, called the voids, is nearly empty. Some theories put the average density of the universe as the equivalent of one hydrogen atom per cubic metre. The density of the universe, however, is clearly not uniform; it ranges from relatively high density in galaxies (including very high density in structures within galaxies, such as planets, stars, and black holes) to conditions in vast voids that have much lower density than the universe's average.

Surrounding and stretching between galaxies, there is a rarefied plasma that is thought to possess a cosmic filamentary structure and that is slightly denser than the average density in the universe. This material is called the *intergalactic medium (IGM)* and is mostly ionized hydrogen, i.e. a plasma consisting of equal numbers of electrons and protons. The IGM is thought to exist at a density of 10 to 100 times the average density of the universe (10 to 100 hydrogen atoms per cubic metre). It reaches densities as high as 1000 times the average density of the universe in rich clusters of galaxies.

The reason the IGM is thought to be mostly ionized gas is that its temperature is thought to be quite high by terrestrial standards (though some parts of it are only "warm" by astrophysical standards). As gas falls into the Intergalactic Medium from the voids, it heats up to temperatures of 10^5 K to 10^7 K, which is high enough for the bound electrons to escape from the hydrogen nuclei upon collisions. At these temperatures, it is called the Warm-Hot Intergalactic Medium (WHIM). Computer simulations indicate that on the order of half the atomic matter in the universe might exist in this warm-hot, rarefied state. When gas falls from the filamentary structures of the WHIM into the galaxy clusters at the intersections of the cosmic filaments, it can heat up even more, reaching temperatures of 10^8 K and above.

OUTLINE OF SPACE EXPLORATION

Space exploration is the use of astronomy and space technology to explore outer space. Physical exploration of space is conducted both by human spaceflights and by robotic spacecraft.

Essence of Exploration

Space exploration is a high technology domain in which relatively few countries have made major investments. Near-term practical applications include communications, meteorology, Earth resources exploitation and assessment, search and rescue, and military intelligence gathering. Longer-term activities, often with a mixture of practical and cultural justifications, include such areas as scientific investigation, asteroidal impact hazard assessment and its mitigation, and microgravity materials science and biology research, both pure and applied. A further strong justification, somewhat speculative and often quite controversial, is human expansion into the space environment, for solar energy and space materials utilization, exploration, and eventual colonization and habitation.

Terms that describe space exploration include:

- Big Science
- Exploration
- High tech
- Space
- Spaceflight

Branches of Space Exploration

Space exploration can be divided into two branches: manned and unmanned. Unmanned, or robotic, missions entail the use of untended satellites and probes for communications, various military purposes, observation, solar and heliospheric science, Solar System exploration, space-based astronomy, and so on. Manned missions include trained human personnel who go into space for various purposes such as constructing a space station, repair or upgrade of previously launched spacecraft (notably the HST), performing human-tended experiments as in micro-gravity or biology, and especially understanding the effects on humans of the space environment in preparation for future human exploration and possible habitation. In the past decade there have also been several fee-paying "space tourists", mostly accommodated on a space-available basis. While the utility of robotic missions seems established, the merit and value of human presence in space has been hotly debated and remains somewhat controversial in some quarters, though it does appear to have wide popular appeal.

1. Manned spaceflight
2. Unmanned spaceflight

Current Space Exploration

Space Agencies

The best funded space agencies are:

Country	*Agency*	*Budget*
United States	**NASA**	$17.3 billion
	ESA (European Space Agency)	$4.260 billion
France	**CNES** (French space agency)	$2.49 billion
Japan	**JAXA** (Japan Aerospace Exploration Agency)	$2.0 billion
Russia	**RKA** (Russian Federal Space Agency)	$1.4 billion
Germany	**DLR** (German Aerospace Center)	$1.242 billion
Italy	**ASI** (Italian Space Agency)	$978 million
India	**ISRO** (Indian Space Research Organization)	$815 million
China	**CNSA** (Chinese National Space Administration)	$500 million
United Kingdom	**BNSC** (British National Space Centre)	$414 million
Canada	**CSA** (Canadian Space Agency)	$321 million
Ukraine	**NSAU** (National Space Agency of Ukraine)	$250-300 million
Belgium	Belgian science policy and space policy	$230 million
Spain	**CDTI** (Spanish space agency)	$175 million
Netherlands	**SRON** (Netherlands Institute for Space Research)	$160 million
South Korea	**KARI** (Korea Aerospace Research Institute)	$150 million
Brazil	**AEB** (Brazilian Space Agency)	$120 million
Switzerland	**SSO** (Swiss Space Office)	$110 million
Sweden	**SNSB** (Swedish National Space Board)	$100 million

Active Space Missions

- Mars Express, ESA satellite orbitting Mars
- Mars Reconnaissance Orbiter, NASA
- Mars Exploration Rover, NASA
- MESSENGER, NASA probe to Mercury launched in 2004
- Hayabusa, JAXA unmanned space mission to asteroid
- New Horizons, probe to Pluto
- Rosetta, ESA mission to Comet 67P/Churyumov-Gerasimenko
- Venus Express, ESA satellite orbitting Venus

Future of Space Exploration

Lunar (the Moon)

- Future lunar missions
- Colonization of the Moon
- Lunar outpost (NASA)

Sun

- Sundiver (space mission)

Mercury

- Colonization of Mercury

Venus

- Current and future missions to Venus

Mars

- Colonization of Mars
- Manned mission to Mars

Outer Solar System

- Colonization of the outer Solar System
- Colonization of Titan

General Space Exploration Concepts

- Astronaut
- Space and survival
- Spacecraft
- Space science

Leaders in Space Exploration

- Neil Armstrong—first man to walk on the Moon.
- Yuri Gagarin—first man to orbit the Earth.
- John Glenn—oldest man in orbit.

TIMELINE OF ORBITAL LAUNCHES

This is a **timeline of first orbital launches by the country**. While a number of countries have built satellites, as of 2009, nine countries historically have developed the capability to send objects into orbit using their own launch vehicles. In addition, Russia and Ukraine inherited the space launchers and satellites capability from the Soviet Union, following its dissolution in 1991. Russia launches its rockets from its own and foreign (Kazakh) spaceports; Ukraine—only from foreign (Russian and Kazakh) spaceports. Another two, France and the United Kingdom, after becoming space powers independently (but by using a foreign spaceport), later joined space launcher facilities in the multi-national European Space Agency. Thus, as of 2009, eight countries currently have a proven orbital launch capability. In all cases where a country has conducted human spaceflights (as for 2009, three—USSR/Russia, USA, China), these launches were preceded by unmanned launches.

List of First Orbital Launches by Country

Order	*Country* [0]	*Satellite*	*Rocket*	*Location*	*Date (UTC)*
1	Soviet Union[1]	Sputnik 1	Sputnik-PS	Baikonur, Soviet Union (today Kazakhstan)	4 October 1957
2	**United States**	Explorer 1	Juno I	Cape Canaveral, Florida, United States	1 February 1958
3	France[2]	Astérix	Diamant A	Hammaguir, Algeria	26 November 1965
4	**Japan**	Ōsumi	Lambda-4S	Uchinoura, Japan	11 February 1970
5	**People's Republic of China**	Dong Fang Hong I	Long March 1	Jiuquan, China	24 April 1970
6	United Kingdom[3]	Prospero X-3	Black Arrow	Woomera, Australia	28 October 1971
7	**India**	Rohini 1	SLV	Sriharikota, India	18 July 1980
8	**Israel**	Ofeq 1	Shavit	Palmachim, Israel	19 September 1988
—	**Ukraine**	Strela-3 (x6, Russian)	Tsyklon-3	Plesetsk, Russia	28 September 1991
—	**Russia**[4, 5]	Kosmos 2175	Soyuz-U	Plesetsk, Russia	21 January 1992
9	**Iran**[4]	Omid	Safir-2	Semnan, Iran	2 February 2009

Notes

0. Countries and successor states indicated in bold retain orbital launch capability.
1. The Soviet Union's successor state, Russia, took over the Soviet space programme after the Soviet Union's dissolution.
2. France launched its first satellite by its own rocket from Algeria, which had been a French territory when the spaceport was built but had achieved independence before the satellite launch. Later France provided a spaceport for ESA space launchers in French Guyana.
3. The UK only self-launched a single satellite and that from a foreign (Australian) spaceport. Britain did not maintain a space launcher capability later.
4. Russia and Ukraine inherited space launcher and satellite capability from the Soviet Union rather than developing it indigenously.
5. Ukraine provides its own space launcher to Russia rather than used its own space launcher to launch satellite (first time - Sich-1 in August 31, 1995).

The race to launch the first satellite was closely contested by the Soviet Union and the United States, and was the beginning of the Space Race. The launching of satellites, while still contributing to national prestige, is a significant economic activity as well, with public and private rocket systems competing for launches, using cost and reliability as selling points.

Other Launches and Projects

The above list includes confirmed satellite launches by rockets produced by the launching country. Lists with differing criteria might include the following launches.

Unconfirmed Launches

- Iraq developed and tested the Tammouz space launch vehicle without a payload on 5 December 1989. According to a press release by the Iraqi News Agency, the warhead completed six orbits, but this was never confirmed.
- North Korea announced on 31 August 1998 that they successfully launched the Kwangmyongsong from Musudan-ri, but this was never confirmed. Another launch on 5 April 2009, with the Kwangmyongsong-2 satellite, was also reported to have reached orbit; however, US and South Korean officials stated that the launch failed to reach orbit.

Failed Launches

- Brazil has yet to launch a satellite into orbit and its space Programme suffered three satellite launch failures, the latest being the explosion of a VLS-1 rocket on 22 August 2003 at the Alcântara Launch Centre, which resulted in 21 deaths.

Launches of Non-domestic Launch Vehicles

- Some countries (Italy, Australia, Kazakhstan) have no self-developed rocket systems, but provide their spaceports (San Marco platform, Woomera, Baikonur Cosmodrome) for launches of their own satellites (San Marco 2 on 26 April 1967, WRESAT on 29 November 1967, KazSat on 17 June 2006) and foreign satellites on aboard of foreign rockets (American, European, Russian, Ukrainian).
- More than three dozen other countries (beginning with Canada on 29 September 1962) launched their satellites onboard foreign rockets (including those listed above, and Chinese, Indian, etc.) from foreign spaceports.

Abandoned Projects

- South Africa developed the space launcher RSA-3 in the 1980s. This rocket was tested 3 times without a satellite payload in 1989 and 1990. The programme was postponed and cancelled in 1994 for political reasons.
- Germany had a preliminary development of numerous rocket space launchers and re-usable launch systems (Sänger II, etc.) after WWII. These were never

realized as national or European projects. Also, in the late 1970s and early 1980s, the private German company OTRAG tried to develop low-cost commercial space launchers. Only sub-orbital tests of the first prototypes of these rockets were carried out.

- Canada had developed the gun-based space launchers Martlet and GLO as the joint Canadian-American Project HARP in the 1960s. These rockets were never tested.
- Spain developed the space launcher Capricorno (Capricorn) in the 1990s. This rocket was never tested.

Future Projects

- South Korea has completed the construction of Naro Space Center in 2008, the country's first spaceport, which is set to launch the nation's first space rocket, KSLV-1, carrying a self-developed orbital satellite in July 2009.
- Brazil announced that it plans to launch its VLS-1 rocket off from the Alcântara Launch Center in 2011.
- Romania is developing the balloon-launched Haas rocket.
- Azerbaijan announced in 2009 the beginning of tender offers in building Azerbaijan's first satellite whose launch is due December of 2011.

SPACE HABITAT: AN OVERVIEW

A **space habitat** (also called an **orbital colony**, or a **space colony**, **city**, or **settlement**) is a space station intended as a permanent settlement rather than as a simple waystation or other specialized facility. No space habitats have yet been constructed, but many design proposals have been made with varying degrees of realism by both science fiction authors and engineers.

History

About 1970, near the end of Project Apollo, Gerard K. O'Neill, an experimental physicist, was looking for a topic to tempt his physics students, most of whom were freshmen in Engineering. He hit upon the creative idea of assigning them feasibility calculations for large space habitats. To his surprise, the habitats seemed to be feasible even in very large sizes: cylinders five miles (8 km) in diameter and twenty miles (34 km) long, even if made from ordinary materials such as steel and glass. Also, the students solved problems such as radiation protection from cosmic rays (almost free in the larger sizes), getting naturalistic sun angles, provision of power, realistic pest-free farming and orbital attitude control without reaction motors. He published an article about these colony proposals in Physics Today in 1974. The article was expanded in the book *High Frontier.*

The result motivated NASA to sponsor a couple of summer workshops led by Dr. O'Neill. Several designs were studied, some in depth, with sizes ranging from 1,000 to 10,000,000 people. Attempts were made to make the habitats as self-supporting as possible, but all of the designs relied on regular shipments from Earth or the Moon, notably for raw materials and volatiles. Closed ecologies and aggressive recycling should dramatically reduce this reliance. Recent research has increased the probability of finding frozen water in deep craters on the moon's south pole, and found that certain asteroids contain significant amounts of volatiles such as water and ammonia. This suggests space habitats could rely less on Earth than these original studies indicated.

At the time, colonization was definitely seen as an end in itself. The basic proposal by O'Neill had an example of a payback scheme: construction of solar power satellites from lunar materials. O'Neill's intention was not to build solar power satellites as such, but rather to give an existence proof that orbital manufacturing from lunar materials could generate profits. He, and other participants presumed that once such manufacturing facilities were on-line, many profitable uses for them would be found, and the colony would become self-supporting, and begin to build other colonies as well.

The proposals and studies generated a notable groundswell of public interest. One effect of this expansion was the founding of the L5 Society in the U.S., a group of enthusiasts that desired to build and live in such colonies. The group was named after the space-colony orbit which was then believed to be the most profitable, a kidney-shaped orbit around either of Earth's lunar Lagrange points 5 or 4.

In this era, Dr. O'Neill also founded the quieter, and more targeted Space Studies Institute, which initially funded and constructed prototypes of much of the radically new hardware needed for a space colonization effort, as well as number of paper studies of feasibility. One of the early projects, for instance, was a series of functional prototypes of a mass driver, the essential technology to be used to economically move ores from the moon to space colony orbits.

In 1986, the L5 Society later became the National Space Society, and former members started a number of related efforts, including the Artemis Project, and the Mars Society. As well, some former L5 Society members seem to be active in radical engineering groups such as the Extropian Institute. A number of prominent modern space engineers and rocket scientists trace their motivation to this era.

The space habitats have inspired a large number of fictional societies in Science Fiction. Some of the most popular and recognizable are the Japanese Gundam universe, and Babylon 5.

Motivation

There are several prominent reasons for space colonization: security, profits, energy and raw materials.

Space habitats are likely to be less affected by disasters that damage the Earth, such as overpopulation, or ocean strikes by large bolides (e.g. meteorites, etc.). Although an individual habitat is probably less secure than Earth, many habitats together add substantially to human survivability. They provide opportunities for migration.

Space has most of the same raw materials found on Earth, and large amounts of energy. It should be possible to make profits, if the infrastructure for space mining and space manufacturing can be created. The initial investments required are large, but the profitability is potentially open-ended.

As there exists a vast amount of material to build with in the solar system, and as a space habitat is out of planetary gravity wells, allowing for relatively cheap travel and movement of materials, a vast population using multiple habitats could live and work in space permanently. The Earth can be viewed as quite small, overpopulated and restrictive compared to outer space.

Habitats outside the shadows of planets can use solar power 24 hours a day. Zero-*g* enables the creation of extremely large-yet-flimsy concentrating mirrors to gather this constant and abundant energy. As well, colonies may employ nuclear power, which wouldn't have all the same environmental and safety concerns that might be present with a nuclear installation on Earth.

Advantages

Space habitats orbiting Earth have a number of potential advantages over those on the surface of other planets:

1. Adjustable artificial gravity, via changing a colony's rotation speed. This attribute is important if humans born and raised on the colonies are to be able to return to Earth. It is expected that those born on low-gravity bodies (such as the Moon or Mars) could result in insufficient skeletal strength to function effectively in Earth's higher gravity without significant habilitation.
2. Access to vast resources, including the material of the solar system's asteroids.
3. Constant access to solar energy.
4. Immense population capacity. Using the free-floating resources of the solar system, current estimates extend into the trillions.
5. Easier trade with Earth than planetary colonies, as colonies orbiting Earth will not have a gravity well to overcome to export to Earth, and a smaller gravity well to overcome to import from Earth.

Problems

Space habitats must solve a number of problems in order to maintain healthy normal human populations:

Initial Capital Outlay

Even the smallest of the habitat designs mentioned below is more massive than the total mass of all items ever launched by mankind into earth orbit. Prerequisites to building habitats are either cheaper launch costs or a mining and manufacturing base on the Moon or other body having low delta-v from the desired station orbit.

Internal Life Support Systems

Air pressure with normal partial pressures of oxygen, carbon dioxide and nitrogen is a basic requirement of any space habitat. Basically, most colony designs are large, thin-walled pressure vessels. Oxygen is available from lunar rock. Nitrogen is available from the Earth but nitrogen is recycled nearly perfectly. Also, nitrogen may be available from comets and outer planets' moons in the form of ammonia. Nitrogen may also be available in unknown quantities on certain other bodies in the outer solar system. The air can be recycled in a number of ways. The obvious method is to use photosynthetic gardens, possibly using hydroponics or forest gardening. However, these do not remove some industrial pollutants, such as volatile oils, and excess simple molecular gases. The standard method used on nuclear submarines is to use a catalytic burner, which effectively removes most organics. Further protection might be provided by a small cryogenic distillation system to gradually remove impurities such as mercury vapour, and noble gases that cannot be catalytically burned.

Organic materials for food production must also be provided. At first, most of these would have to be imported from the moon, asteroids, or the Earth. After that, recycling would reduce the need for imports. One proposed recycling method would start by burning the cryogenic distillate, plants, garbage and sewage with air in an electric arc, and distilling the result. The resulting carbon dioxide and water would be immediately usable in the farms. The nitrates and the salts in the ash would be dissolved in water and separated into pure minerals. Most of the nitrates, potassium and sodium salts would effectively recycle as fertilizers. Other minerals containing iron, nickel, and silicon could be chemically purified in batches and reused industrially. The small fraction of remaining materials, well below 0.01 per cent by weight, could be processed into pure elements with zero-gravity mass spectrography, and added in appropriate amounts to the fertilizers and industrial stocks. This method's only current existence is a proof considered by NASA studies. It's likely that methods would be greatly refined as people begin to actually live in space habitats.

Simulated Gravity

Long-term on-orbit studies have proven that zero gravity weakens bones and muscles, and upsets calcium metabolism and immune systems. Most people have a continual stuffy nose or sinus problems, and a few people have dramatic, incurable motion sickness. Most colony designs would rotate in order to use inertial forces to simulate gravity. NASA studies with chickens and plants have proven that this is an effective physiological substitute for gravity. Turning one's head rapidly in such an environment causes a "tilt" to be sensed as one's inner ears move at different rotational rates. Centrifuge studies show that people get motion-sick in habitats with a rotational radius of less than 100 metres, or with a rotation rate above 3 rotations per minute. However, the same studies and statistical inference indicate that almost all people should be able to live comfortably in habitats with a rotational radius larger than 500 metres and below 1 RPM. Experienced persons were not merely more resistant to motion sickness, but could also use the effect to determine "spinward" and "antispinward" directions in the centrifuges.

Protection from Hostile External Environment

- **Radiation:** Space radiation has two distinct problems. One is that cosmic rays expose one to 80 millisieverts per year, well above the maximum safe occupational threshold of 50 mSv, and well above the healthy population maximum of 3 mSv. Another, separate issue is that solar flares occasionally emit very large amounts of soft x-rays, and energetic particles. When these events occur, they can exceed 4 sieverts, the lethal dose for half the population. The most interesting result of the studies was the discovery that large space habitats are effectively shielded by their structure and air, which easily exceeds the two metres of steel needed. Smaller habitats could be shielded by stationary (non-rotating) bags of rock. Sunlight could be admitted indirectly via mirrors in radiation-proof louvres, which would function in the same manner as a periscope.
- **Heat rejection:** The colony is in a vacuum, and therefore resembles a giant thermos bottle. The sunlight to radiated energy ratio can be reduced and controlled with large venetian blinds. Habitats also need a radiator to eliminate heat from absorbed sunlight and organisms. Very small habitats might have a central vane that rotates with the colony. In this design, convection would raise hot air "up" (toward the center), and cool air would fall down into the outer habitat. Some other designs would distribute coolants, such as chilled water from a central radiator. Because blinds and radiators might be a major expense, inexpensive habitats might be very warm.
- **Foreign objects:** The habitat would need to withstand potential impacts from space debris, meteoroids, dust etc.

Transportation and Maneuvering

- **Orbital stationkeeping:** The optimal habitat orbits are still debated, and so orbital stationkeeping is probably a commercial issue. The lunar L_4 and L_5 orbits are now thought to be too far away from the moon and Earth. A more modern proposal is to use a two-to-one resonance orbit that alternately has a close, low-energy (cheap) approach to the moon, and then to the Earth. This provides quick, inexpensive access to both raw materials and the major market. Most colony designs plan to use electromagnetic tether propulsion, or mass drivers used as rocket motors. The advantage of these is that they either use no reaction mass at all, or use cheap reaction mass.
- **Attitude control:** Most mirror geometries require something on the habitat to be aimed at the sun and so attitude control is necessary. The original O'Neill design used the two cylinders as momentum wheels to roll the colony, and pushed the sunward pivots together or apart to use precession to change their angle. Later designs rotated in the plane of their orbit, with their windows pointing at right angles to the sunlight, and used lightweight mirrors that could be steered with small electric motors to follow the sun.

Designs/Solutions

NASA Designs

Designs proposed in NASA studies included:

- Bernal sphere—"Island One", a spherical habitat for about 20,000 people.
- Stanford torus—A larger alternative to "Island One."
- O'Neill cylinder—"Island Three" (pictured), the largest design.
- Lewis One
- A "bolo," a spacecraft or habitat connected by a cable to a counterweight or other habitat. This design has been proposed as a Mars ship, initial construction shack for a space habitat, and orbital hotel. It has a comfortably long and slow rotational radius for a relatively small station mass. Also, if some of the equipment can form the counter-weight, the equipment dedicated to artificial gravity is just a cable, and thus has a much smaller mass-fraction than in other designs. This makes it a tempting design for a deep-space ship. For a long-term habitation, however, radiation shielding must rotate with the habitat, and is extremely heavy, thus requiring a much stronger and heavier cable.
- "Beaded habitats": This speculative design was also considered by the NASA studies, and found to have a roughly equivalent mass fraction of structure and therefore comparable costs. Small habitats would be mass-produced to standards that allow the habitats to interconnect. A single habitat can operate alone as a bolo. However, further habitats can be attached, to grow into a "dumbbell," then a "bow-tie," then a ring, then a cylinder of "beads," and finally a framed array of cylinders. Each stage of growth shares more radiation shielding and capital equipment, increasing redundancy and safety while reducing the cost per person. This design was originally proposed by a professional architect because it can grow much like Earth-bound cities, with incremental individual investments, unlike designs that require large start-up investments. The main disadvantage is that the smaller versions use a large amount of structure to support the radiation shielding, which rotates with them. In large sizes, the shielding becomes economical, because it grows roughly as the square of the colony radius. The number of people, their habitats and the radiators to cool them grow roughly as the cube of the colony radius.

Other Designs

- Bubbleworld: The Bubbleworld, or Inside/Outside concept, was originated in 1964 by Dandridge M. Cole and Donald W. Cox in a non-fiction book called *Islands in Space: The Challenge of the Planetoids*. The concept calls for a large asteroid of iron or nickel-iron composition to have a tunnel drilled through its longest axis of rotation and filled with a volatile substance, possibly water. A very large solar reflector would be constructed nearby, focusing solar heat onto the asteroid, first to weld and seal the tunnel ends, then more diffusely to slowly heat the entire outer surface. As the metal softens, the water inside expands and inflates the mass, while rotational forces help shape it into a cylindrical form. Once expanded and allowed to cool, it can be spun to produce artificial gravity, and the interior filled with soil, air and water. By creating a slight bulge in the middle of the cylinder, a ring-shaped lake can be made to form. Reflectors will allow sunlight to enter and to be directed where needed. Clearly, this method would require a significant human and industrial presence in space to be at all feasible.

The Bubbleworld concept was popularized by science fiction author Larry Niven. Niven used the idea in his fictional Known Space stories, describing these worlds as the primary habitats of the Belters, a civilization who had colonized the Asteroid Belt.

SPACE ADVOCACY

Space advocacy can be described as the general position supporting, pleading or arguing for the idea or cause of space exploration and settlements. It is a form of advocacy that specifically includes support for private space initiatives and is also a political position that favours the exploration, utilization, and colonization of outer space.

There are many different individuals and organizations dedicated to space advocacy. They are usually active in educating the public on space related subjects, lobbying governments for increased funding in space-related activities or supporting private space activities. They also recruit members, fund projects, and provide information for their membership and interested visitors. They are sub-divided into three categories depending on their primary work: practice, advocacy, and theory.

History

Historians agree that space flight and especially manned space flight was not inevitable, but rather that society was convinced of the need for it by a few revolutionaries. These "revolutionaries" were primarily members of the Russian, American, British, and German science communities and starting in the 1930s began to share their individual plans for a future in space to their respective governments and the public.

Influential books and other media began to emerge which included works containing illustrations by Chesley Bonestell (based on Wernher von Braun's designs) such as The Conquest of Space (1949) and magazine articles including the "Man Will Conquer Space Soon!" series of article in Colliers magazine between 1952 and 1954. Television shows included Walt Disney's Man in Space and Man and the Moon in 1955, and Mars and Beyond in 1957.

List of Space Advocacy Organisations

Actively-involved Organisations

Organisations that are directly involved in space exploration, having their own active projects.

Organisation	*Founded*	*Purpose and Goals*	*Pursuits*
SETI Institute	1960, America	To search for extraterrestrial intelligent life	Runs SETI
The Planetary Society	1980, America	To explore the Solar System, search for Near Earth Objects, and search for extraterrestrial life	Launched Cosmos 1
Artemis Project		Was a private venture to establish a permanent, self-supporting base on the Moon by 2002	

Lobbying Organisations

Organisations that focus mainly on lobbying government agencies and businesses to step up their efforts.

Organisation	*Founded*	*Purpose and Goals*
British Interplanetary Society	1933, United Kingdom	To support and promote astronautics and space exploration
American Astronautical Society	1954, America	Dedicated to the advancement of space science and exploration
National Space Institute	1974, America	To help maintain public support for the US space programme (later became the National Space Society)
L5 Society	1975, America	To promote the space colony ideas of Dr. Gerard K. O'Neill (later became the National Space Society)
Citizens' Advisory Council on National Space Policy	1980, America	Was a group of prominent American citizens concerned with US space policy
Students for the Exploration and Development of Space	1980, America	To promote space exploration and development through educational and engineering projects
Space Frontier Foundation	1988, America	To promote large-scale settlement of the inner solar system, under strong free market capitalism
Mars Society	1998, International	To encouraging the exploration and settlement of Mars
California Space Authority	2001, America	To foster the development of specified activities in California related to space flight
MarsDrive	2005, International	To involve the public, directly and actively, in the settlement and exploration of space

Educating and Publicising Organisations

Organisations involved in educating the public, to boast their understanding and enthusiasm about space.

Organisation	*Founded*	*Purpose and Goals*
Coalition for Space Exploration		To educate and inform the public on the value and benefits of space exploration and to help ensure the United States will remain a leader in space, science and technology
Canadian Space Society	1983, Canada	To sponsor, promote and engage in activities designed to promote increased knowledge of space
National Space Society	1987, America	An organization with the vision of "people living and working in thriving communities beyond the Earth."
El Club de los Astronautas	2004, Spain	To promote the exploration of space in a wider sense, and to experience the universe
SpaceVidcast	2008, America	A multimedia, internet based broadcaster dedicated to "...getting all of planet Earth excited about space flight and living amongst the stars."

Theorising Organisations

Organisations that focus on advocating a theory for space exploration or colonization.

Organisation	*Purpose and Goals*
Alliance to Rescue Civilization	Devoted to the establishment of an off-earth "backup" of human civilization
Living Universe Foundation	Has a detailed plan in which the entire galaxy is colonized.
Red Colony	Strives to collect and develop theories in mars colonization and terraformation via contributions and debate from the general public
The Mars Foundation	Through its mars homestead project, is developing a unified plan for building the first habitat on mars by exploiting local materials

2

Space Colonization and Commercialization: Special Focus on Moon

SPACE COLONIZATION

Space colonization (also called **space settlement, space humanization, space habitation**, etc.) is the concept of autonomous (self-sufficient) human habitation of locations outside Earth. It is a major theme in science fiction, as well as a long-term goal of various national space programmes.

While many people think of space colonies on the Moon or Mars, others argue that the first colonies will be in orbit. They have determined that there are ample quantities of all the necessary materials on the Moon and Near Earth Asteroids, and that solar energy is readily available in very large quantities.

In 2005 NASA Administrator Michael Griffin identified space colonization as the ultimate goal of current spaceflight programmes, saying:

> ... the goal isn't just scientific exploration ... it's also about extending the range of human habitat out from Earth into the solar system as we go forward in time ... In the long run a single-planet species will not survive ... If we humans want to survive for hundreds of thousands or millions of years, we must ultimately populate other planets. Now, today the technology is such that this is barely conceivable. We're in the infancy of it. ... I'm talking about that one day, I don't know when that day is, but there will be more human beings who live off the Earth than on it. We may well have people living on the moon. We may have people living on the moons of Jupiter and other planets. We may have people making habitats on asteroids ... I know that humans will colonize the solar system and one day go beyond.
>
> —*Michael D. Griffin*

As of 2009, the ISS provides a temporary, yet still non-autonomous, human presence in low earth orbit. The NASA Lunar outpost, providing a permanent human presence on the moon, is at the planning stage. There is an ongoing development of technologies that may be used in future space colonization projects.

Method

Building colonies in space would require access to water, food, space, people, construction materials, energy, transportation, communications, life support, simulated gravity, and radiation protection. Colonies would presumably be situated to help fulfil those requirements.

Materials

Colonies on the Moon, Mars and Ceres could extract local materials. The Moon is deficient in volatiles (principally hydrogen, and nitrogen), but possesses a great deal of oxygen, silicon, and metals such as iron, aluminum and titanium. Launching materials from Earth is very expensive, so bulk materials could come from the Moon, a Near-Earth Object (NEO—an asteroid or comet with an orbit near Earth), Phobos or Deimos where gravitational forces are much smaller, there is no atmosphere, and there is no biosphere to damage. Many NEOs contain substantial amounts of metals, oxygen, hydrogen and carbon. Certain NEOs may also contain some nitrogen.

Farther out, Jupiter's Trojan asteroids are thought to be high in water ice and probably other volatiles.

Energy

Solar energy in orbit is abundant, reliable, and is commonly used to power satellites today. There is no night in space, and no clouds or atmosphere to block sunlight. The solar energy available, in watts per square metre, at any distance, d, from the Sun can be calculated by the formula $E = 1366/d^2$, where d is measured in astronomical units.

Particularly in the weightless conditions of space, sunlight can be used directly, using large solar ovens made of lightweight metallic foil so as to generate thousands of degrees of heat at no cost; or reflected onto crops to enable photosynthesis to proceed.

Large structures would be needed to convert sunlight into significant amounts of electrical power for settlers' use. In highly electrified nations on Earth, electrical consumption can average 1 kilowatt/person (or roughly 10 megawatt-hours per person per year).

Energy has been suggested as an eventual export item for space settlements, perhaps using wireless power transmission e.g. via microwave beams to send power to Earth or the Moon. This method has zero emissions, so would have significant benefits such as elimination of greenhouse gases and nuclear waste. Ground area required per watt would be less than conventional solar panels.

The Moon has nights of two Earth weeks in duration and Mars has night, dust, and is farther from the Sun, reducing solar energy available by a factor of about ½-= ⅔, and possibly making nuclear power more attractive on these bodies. Alternatively, energy could be transmitted to the lunar and Martian surfaces from a solar power satellite.

For both solar thermal and nuclear power generation in airless environments, such as the Moon and space, and to a lesser extent the very thin Martian atmosphere, one of the main difficulties is dispersing the inevitable heat generated. This requires fairly large radiator areas.

Transportation

Space Access

Transportation to orbit is often the limiting factor in space endeavours. To settle space, much cheaper launch vehicles are required, as well as a way to avoid serious damage to the atmosphere from the thousands, perhaps millions, of launches required. One possibility is the air-breathing hypersonic spaceplane under development by NASA and other organizations, both public and private. There are also proposed projects such as building a space elevator or a mass driver; or launch loops.

Cislunar and Solar System Travel

Transportation of large quantities of materials from the Moon, Phobos, Deimos, and Near Earth asteroids to orbital settlement construction sites is likely to be necessary.

Transportation using off-Earth resources for propellant in conventional rockets would be expected to massively reduce in-space transportation costs compared to the present day; propellant launched from the Earth is likely to be prohibitively expensive for space colonization, even with improved space access costs.

Other technologies such as tether propulsion, VASIMR, ion drives, solar thermal rockets, solar sails, magnetic sails, and nuclear thermal propulsion can all potentially help solve the problems of high transport cost once in space.

For lunar materials, one well-studied possibility is to build mass drivers to launch bulk materials to waiting settlements. Alternatively, lunar space elevators might be employed.

Communication

Compared to the other requirements, communication is easy for orbit and the Moon. A great proportion of current terrestrial communications already passes through satellites. Yet, as colonies further from the earth are considered, communication becomes more of a burden. Transmissions to and from Mars suffer from significant delays due to the speed of light and the greatly varying distance between conjunction and opposition—the lag will range between 7 and 44 minutes—making real-time communication impractical. Other means of communication that do not require live interaction such as e-mail and voice mail systems should pose no problem.

Life Support

People need air, water, food, gravity and reasonable temperatures to survive for long periods. On Earth, a large complex biosphere provides these. In space settlements, a small, closed ecological system must recycle or import all the nutrients without "crashing."

The closest terrestrial analogue to space life support is possibly that of the nuclear submarine. Nuclear submarines use mechanical life support systems to support humans for months without surfacing, and this same basic technology could presumably be employed for space use. However, nuclear submarines run "open loop" extracting oxygen from seawater, and typically dumping carbon dioxide overboard, although they recycle existing oxygen. Recycling of the carbon dioxide has been approached in the literature using the Sabatier process or the Bosch reaction.

Alternatively, and more attractive to many, the Biosphere 2 project in Arizona has shown that a complex, small, enclosed, man-made biosphere can support eight people for at least a year, although there were many problems. A year or so into the two-year mission oxygen had to be replenished, which strongly suggests that they achieved atmospheric closure.

The relationship between organisms, their habitat and the non-Earth environment can be:

- Organisms and their habitat fully isolated from the environment (examples include artificial biosphere, Biosphere 2, life support system).
- Changing the environment to become a life-friendly habitat, a process called terraforming.
- Changing organisms to become more compatible with the environment.

97-99 per cent of the light energy provided to the plant ends up as heat and needs to be dissipated somehow to avoid overheating the habitat. A combination of the above technologies is also possible.

Radiation Protection

Cosmic rays and solar flares create a lethal radiation environment in space. In Earth orbit, the Van Allen belts make living above the Earth's atmosphere difficult. To protect life, settlements must be surrounded by sufficient mass to absorb most incoming radiation. Somewhere around 5-10 tons of material per square metre of surface area is required. This can be achieved cheaply with leftover material (slag) from processing lunar soil and asteroids into oxygen, metals, and other useful materials, however it represents a significant obstacle to maneuvering vessels with such massive bulk. Inertia would necessitate powerful thrusters to start or stop rotation; however shielding material can be stationary around a rotating interior. Hull-metals can also be polarized with electrical current to provide additional protection without adding mass.

Self-replication

Self-replication is an optional attribute, but many think it the ultimate goal because it allows a much more rapid increase in colonies, while eliminating costs to and dependence on Earth. It could be argued that the establishment of such a colony would be Earth's first act of self-replication. Intermediate goals include colonies that expect only information from Earth (science, engineering, entertainment, etc.) and colonies that just require periodic supply of light weight objects, such as integrated circuits, medicines, genetic material and perhaps some tools.

Population Size

In 2002, the anthropologist John H. Moore estimated that a population of 150-180 would allow normal reproduction for 60 to 80 generations—equivalent to 2000 years.

A much smaller initial population of as little as two female humans should be viable as long as human embryos are available from Earth. Use of a sperm bank from Earth also allows a smaller starting base with negligible inbreeding.

Researchers in conservation biology have tended to adopt the "50/500" rule of thumb initially advanced by Franklin and Soule. This rule says that a short-term effective population size (N_e) of 50 is needed to prevent an unacceptable rate of inbreeding, while a long-term N_e of 500 is required to maintain overall genetic variability. The $N_e = 50$ prescription corresponds to an inbreeding rate of 1 per cent per generation, approximately half the maximum rate tolerated by domestic animal breeders. The $N_e = 500$ value attempts to balance the rate of gain in genetic variation due to mutation with the rate of loss due to genetic drift.

Effective population size N_e depends on the number of males N_m and females N_f, in the population according to the formula:

$$N_e = \frac{4 \times N_m \times N_f}{N_m + N_f}$$

Location

Location is a frequent point of contention between space colonization advocates.

The location of colonization can be on a physical body or free-flying:

- On a planet, natural satellite, or asteroid
- In orbit around the Earth, Sun, Lagrangian point or other object

Planetary Locations

Some planetary colonization advocates cite the following potential locations:

Mars

Mars is a frequent topic of discussion. Its overall surface area is similar to the dry land surface of Earth, it may have large water reserves, and has carbon (locked as carbon dioxide in the atmosphere).

Mars may have gone through similar geological and hydrological processes as Earth and therefore contain valuable mineral ores, but this is debated. Equipment is available to extract *in situ* resources (water, air, etc.) from the Martian ground and atmosphere. There is a strong scientific interest in colonizing Mars due to the possibility that life could have existed on Mars at some point in its history, and may even still exist in some parts of the planet.

However, its atmosphere is very thin (averaging 800 Pa or about 0.8 per cent of Earth sea-level atmospheric pressure); so the pressure vessels necessary to support life are very similar to deep space structures. The climate of Mars is colder than Earth's. Its gravity is only around a third that of Earth's; it is unknown whether this is sufficient to support human beings for extended periods of time (all long-term human experience to date has been at around Earth gravity or one g).

The atmosphere is thin enough, when coupled with Mars' lack of magnetic field, that radiation is more intense on the surface, and protection from solar storms would require radiation shielding.

Mars is often the topic of discussion regarding terraforming to make the entire planet or at least large portions of it habitable.

Mercury

There is a suggestion that Mercury could be colonized using the same technology, approach and equipment that is used in colonization of the Moon. Such colonies would almost certainly be restricted to the polar regions due to the extreme daytime temperatures elsewhere on the planet. The recent discovery of ionized water has astounded scientists. This discovery significantly improves the small planet's prospects as a future colony.

Venus

While the surface of Venus is far too hot and features atmospheric pressure at least 90 times that at sea level on Earth, its massive atmosphere offers a possible alternate location for colonization. At an altitude of approximately 50 km, the pressure is reduced to a few atmospheres, and the temperature would be between 40-100 °C, depending on the altitude. This part of the atmosphere is probably within dense clouds which contain some sulfuric acid. Even these may have a certain benefit to colonization, as they present a possible source for the extraction of water.

Gas Giants

It may also be possible to colonize the three farthest gas giants with floating cities in their atmospheres. By heating hydrogen balloons, large masses can be suspended underneath at roughly Earth gravity. Jupiter would be less suitable for habitation due to its high gravity, escape velocity and radiation. Such colonies could export Helium-3 for use in fusion reactors if they ever become practical. Escape from the gas giant planets (especially Jupiter) seems well beyond current or near-term foreseeable chemical rocket technology however, due to the combination of large velocity and high acceleration needed even to achieve low orbit. A gas core reactor rocket, with a projected Isp of 3000, would be up to the task, however. The radioactive fallout would drop deep into the planets core, and so wouldn't cause a problem for colonists.

Ceres

Ceres is a dwarf planet in the main asteroid belt, comprising about one-third the mass of the whole belt and being the sixth largest body in the inner Solar System by mass and volume. Being the largest body in the asteroid belt, Ceres could become the main base and transport hub for future asteroid mining infrastructure, allowing mineral resources to be transported further to Mars, the Moon and Earth: Main Belt Asteroids. It may be possible to Paraterraform Ceres, making life easier for the colonists. Given its low gravity and fast rotation, a space elevator would also be practical.

Satellite Locations

The Moon

Due to its proximity and familiarity, Earth's Moon is also frequently discussed as a target for colonization. It has the benefits of proximity to Earth and lower escape velocity, allowing for easier exchange of goods and services. A major drawback of the Moon is its low abundance of volatiles necessary for life such as hydrogen, nitrogen, and carbon. Water ice deposits that may exist in some polar craters could serve as a source for these elements. An alternative solution is to bring hydrogen from near earth asteroids and combine it with oxygen extracted from lunar rock.

The moon's low surface gravity is also a concern (it is unknown whether 1/6 g is sufficient to support human habitation for long periods).

Jovian Moons—Europa, Callisto and Ganymede

The Artemis Project designed a plan to colonize Europa, one of Jupiter's moons. Scientists were to inhabit igloos and drill down into the Europan ice crust, exploring any sub-surface ocean. This plan also discusses possible use of "air pockets" for human inhabitation. Europa is considered one of the more habitable bodies in the solar system and so merits investigation as a possible abode for life.

Ganymede is the largest moon in the Solar System. It may be attractive as Ganymede is also the only moon with a magnetosphere and so is less irradiated at the surface. The presence of magnetosphere, likely indicates a convecting molten core within Ganymede, which may in turn indicate a rich geologic history for the moon.

NASA performed a study called *HOPE* (Revolutionary Concepts for Human Outer Planet Exploration) regarding the future exploration of the solar system. The target chosen was Callisto. It could be possible to build a surface base that would produce fuel for further exploration of the solar system.

The three out of four largest moons of Jupiter (Europa, Ganymede and Callisto) have an abundance of volatiles making future colonization possible.

Phobos and Deimos

The moons of Mars may be an appealing target for space colonization. Low delta-v is needed to reach the Earth from Phobos and Deimos, allowing delivery of material to cislunar space, as well as transport around the Martian system. The moons themselves may be suitable for habitation, with methods similar to those for asteroids.

Titan, Enceladus and other Saturnian Moons

Titan has been suggested as an appealing target for colonization, because it is the only moon in our solar system to have a dense atmosphere and is rich in carbon-bearing compounds. Robert Zubrin identified Titan as possessing an abundance of all the elements necessary to support life, making Titan perhaps the most advantageous locale in the outer Solar System for colonization, and saying "In certain ways, Titan is the most hospitable extraterrestrial world within our solar system for human colonization".

Enceladus is a small, icy moon orbiting close to Saturn, notable for its extremely bright surface and the geyser-like plumes of ice and water vapour that erupt from its southern polar region. If Enceladus has liquid water, it joins Mars and Jupiter's moon Europa as one of the prime places in the solar system to look for extraterrestrial life and possible future settlements.

Other large satellites: Rhea, Iapetus, Dione, Tethys and Mimas, all have large quantities of volatiles, which can be used to support settlement.

Moons of Uranus, Neptune's Triton and beyond

The five large moons of Uranus (Miranda, Ariel, Umbriel, Titania and Oberon) and Triton-Neptune's moon, although very cold, all have large amounts of frozen water and other volatiles and could potentially be settled, only they would require a lot of nuclear power to sustain the habitats. Triton's thin atmosphere also contains some nitrogen and even some frozen nitrogen on the surface (the surface temperature is 38 K or about –391° Fahrenheit). Pluto is estimated to have a very similar structure to Triton.

Free Space Locations

Space Habitats

Free space locations in space would necessitate a space habitat, also called space colony and orbital colony, or a space station which would be intended as a permanent settlement rather than as a simple waystation or other specialized facility. They would be literal "cities" in space, where people would live and work and raise families. Many designs have been proposed with varying degrees of realism by both science fiction authors and scientists.

A space habitat would also serve as a proving ground for a generation ship which could function as a long-term home for hundreds or thousands of people. Such a space habitat could be isolated from the rest of humanity but near enough to Earth for help. This would test if thousands of humans can survive on their own before sending them beyond the reach of any help.

Earth Orbit

Compared to other locations, Earth orbit has substantial advantages and one major, but solvable, problem. Orbits close to Earth can be reached in hours, whereas the Moon is days away and trips to Mars take months. There is ample continuous solar power in high Earth orbits, whereas all planets lose sunlight at least half the time. Weightlessness makes construction of large colonies considerably easier than in a gravity environment. Astronauts have demonstrated moving multi-ton satellites by hand. 0 g recreation is available on orbital colonies, but not on the Moon or Mars. Finally, the level of (pseudo-) gravity is controlled at any desired level by rotating an orbital colony. Thus, the main living areas can be kept at 1 g, whereas the Moon has 1/6 g and Mars 1/3 g. It's not known what the minimum g-force is for ongoing health but 1 g is known to ensure that children grow up with strong bones and muscles.

The main disadvantage of orbital colonies is lack of materials. These may be expensively imported from the Earth, or more cheaply from extraterrestrial sources, such as the Moon (which has ample metals, silicon, and oxygen), Near Earth Asteroids, comets, or elsewhere.

Lagrange Points

Another near-Earth possibility are the five Earth-Moon Lagrange points. Although they would generally also take a few days to reach with current technology, many of these points would have near-continuous solar power capability since their distance from Earth would result in only brief and infrequent eclipses of light from the Sun.

The five Earth-Sun Lagrange points would totally eliminate eclipses, but only L_1 and L_2 would be reachable in a few days' time. The other three Earth-Sun points would require months to reach.

However, the fact that Lagrange points L_4 and L_5 tend to collect dust and debris, while L_1-L_3 require active station-keeping measures to maintain a stable position, make them somewhat less suitable places for habitation than was originally believed.

Asteroids

Near Earth Asteroids: Many small asteroids in orbit around the Sun have the advantage that they pass closer than Earth's moon several times per decade. In between these close approaches to home, the asteroid may travel out to a furthest distance of some 350,000,000 kilometres from the Sun (its aphelion) and 500,000,000 kilometres from Earth.

Main Belt Asteroids: Colonization of asteroids would require space habitats. The asteroid belt has significant overall material available, the largest object being Ceres, although it is thinly distributed as it covers a vast region of space. Unmanned supply craft should be practical with little technological advance, even crossing 1/2 billion kilometres of cold vacuum. The colonists would have a strong interest in assuring that their asteroid did not hit Earth or any other body of significant mass, but would have extreme difficulty in moving an asteroid of any size. The orbits of the Earth and most asteroids are very distant from each other in terms of delta-v and the asteroidal bodies have enormous momentum. Rockets or mass drivers can perhaps be installed on asteroids to direct their path into a safe course.

Statites: Statites or "static satellites" employ solar sails to position themselves in orbits that gravity alone could not accomplish. Such a solar sail colony would be free to ride solar radiation pressure and travel off the ecliptic plane. Navigational computers with an advanced understanding of flocking behaviour could organize several statite colonies into the beginnings of the true "swarm" concept of a Dyson sphere.

Outside the Solar System

Looking beyond our solar system, there are billions of potential suns with possible colonization targets.

> The long-term survival of the human race is at risk as long as it is confined to a single planet. Sooner or later, disasters such as an asteroid collision or nuclear war could wipe us all out. But once we spread out into space and establish independent colonies, our future should be safe. There isn't anywhere like the Earth in the solar system, so we would have to go to another star.
>
> —*Stephen Hawking, Physicist*

Starship

Space colonization technology could in principle allow human expansion at high, but sub-relativistic speeds, substantially less than the speed of light, *c*. An interstellar colony ship would be similar to a space habitat, with the addition of major propulsion capabilities and independent energy generation. Hypothetical starship concepts proposed both by scientists and in hard science fiction include:

- A generation ship would travel much slower than light, with consequent interstellar trip times of many decades or centuries. The crew would go through generations before the journey is complete, so that none of the initial crew would be expected to survive to arrive at the destination, assuming current human lifespans.
- A sleeper ship, in which most or all of the crew spend the journey in some form of hibernation or suspended animation, allowing some or all who undertake the journey to survive to the end.
- An Embryo-carrying Interstellar Starship (EIS), much smaller than a generation ship or sleeper ship, transporting human embryos or DNA in a frozen or dormant state to the destination. (Obvious biological and psychological problems in birthing, raising, and educating such voyagers, neglected here, may not be fundamental.)
- A nuclear fusion or fission powered ship (e.g., ion drive) of some kind, achieving velocities of up to perhaps 10 per cent *c* permitting one-way trips to nearby stars with durations comparable to a human lifetime.

- A Project Orion-ship, a nuclear-powered concept proposed by Freeman Dyson which would use nuclear explosions to propel a starship. A special case of the preceding nuclear rocket concepts, with similar potential velocity capability, but possibly easier technology.
- Laser propulsion concepts, using some form of beaming of power from the Solar System might allow a light-sail or other ship to reach high speeds, comparable to those theoretically attainable by the fusion-powered electric rocket, above. These methods would need some means, such as supplementary nuclear propulsion, to stop at the destination, but a hybrid (light-sail for acceleration, fusion-electric for deceleration) system might be possible.

The above concepts all appear limited to high, but still sub-relativistic speeds, due to fundamental energy and reaction mass considerations, and all would entail trip times which might be enabled by space colonization technology, permitting self-contained habitats with lifetimes of decades to centuries. Yet human interstellar expansion at average speeds of even 0.1 per cent of *c* would permit settlement of the entire Galaxy (assuming it is not inhabited already) in less than one-half of a galactic rotation period of ~250,000,000 years, which is comparable to the timescale of other galactic processes. Thus, even if interstellar travel at near relativistic speeds is never feasible (which cannot be clearly determined at this time), the development of space colonization could allow human expansion beyond the Solar System without requiring technological advances that cannot yet be reasonably foreseen. This could greatly improve the chances for the survival of intelligent life over cosmic timescales, given the many natural and human-related hazards that have been widely noted.

Example

The star Tau Ceti, about eleven light years away, has an abundance of cometary and asteroidal material in orbit around it. These materials could be used for the construction of space habitats for human settlement.

Terrestrial Analogues to Space Colonies

The most famous attempt to build an analogue to a self-sufficient colony is Biosphere 2, which attempted to duplicate Earth's biosphere.

Many space agencies build testbeds for advanced life support systems, but these are designed for long duration human spaceflight, not permanent colonization.

Remote research stations in inhospitable climates, such as the Amundsen-Scott South Pole Station or Devon Island Mars Arctic Research Station, can also provide some practice for off-world outpost construction and operation. The Mars Desert Research Station has a habitat for similar reasons, but the surrounding climate is not strictly inhospitable.

Nuclear Submarines provide an example of conditions encountered in artificial space environment. Crews of these vessels often spend long periods (6 months or more) submerged during their deployments. However, the submarine environment provides a somewhat open life support system since the vessel can replenish supplies of fresh water and oxygen from seawater.

Literature

The literature for space colonization began in 1869 when Edward Everett Hale wrote about an inhabited artificial satellite.

The Russian schoolmaster and physicist Konstantin Tsiolkovsky foresaw elements of the space community in his book *Beyond Planet Earth* written about 1900. Tsiolkovsky had his space travellers building greenhouses and raising crops in space.

Others have also written about space colonies as Lasswitz in 1897 and Bernal, Oberth, Von Pirquet and Noordung in the 1920s. Wernher von Braun contributed his ideas in a 1952 *Colliers* article. In the 1950s and 1960s, Dandridge M. Cole published his ideas.

Another seminal book on the subject was the book *The High Frontier: Human Colonies in Space* by Gerard K. O'Neill in 1977 which was followed the same year by *Colonies in Space* by T.A. Heppenheimer.

M. Dyson wrote *Home on the Moon; Living on a Space Frontier* in 2003; Peter Eckart wrote *Lunar Base Handbook* in 2006 and then Harrison Schmitt's *Return to the Moon* written in 2007.

Justification

In 2001, the space news website Space.com asked Freeman Dyson, J. Richard Gott and Sid Goldstein for reasons why some humans should live in space. Their answers were:

- Spread life and beauty throughout the Universe
- Ensure the survival of our species
- Make money from solar power satellites, asteroid mining, and space manufacturing
- Save the environment of Earth by moving people and industry into space
- Provide entertainment value in order to distract from immediate surroundings
- Ensure sufficient supply of rare materials, including from the Outer Solar System—natural gas (in connection with expected worldwide hydrocarbons peak) and drinking water (in connection with expected worldwide water shortage)

Louis J. Halle, formerly of the United States Department of State, wrote in *Foreign Affairs* (Summer 1980) that the colonization of space will protect humanity in the event of global nuclear warfare.

The scientist Paul Davies also supports the view that if a planetary catastrophe threatens the survival of the human species on Earth, a self-sufficient colony could "reverse-colonize" the Earth and restore human civilization.

The author and journalist William E. Burrows and the biochemist Robert Shapiro proposed a private project, the Alliance to Rescue Civilization, with the goal of establishing an off-Earth backup of human civilization.

Another important reason used to justify space is the effort to increase the knowledge and technological abilities of humanity.

Objections

Colonizing space would require massive amounts of financial, physical and human capital devoted to research, development, production, and deployment. While the total costs may be unknown, even maintaining the current budget of NASA is politically challenging in the US.

Even if the technology were available, and the costs of deploying a programme fairly low, and the likelihood of success high, only a small number of people would directly benefit from a colony (either enthusiastic colonists or high risk commercial interests), leaving most of financing the programme to the public.

The fundamental problem of public things, needed for survival, such as space programmes, is the free rider problem. Convincing the public to fund such programmes would require additional self-interest arguments: If the objective of space colonization is to provide a "backup" in case everyone on Earth is killed, then why should someone on Earth pay for something that is only useful after they're dead? This assumes that space colonization is not widely acknowledged as a sufficiently valuable social goal.

Other objections include concern about creating a culture in which humans are no longer seen as human, but rather as material assets. The issues of human dignity, morality, philosophy, culture, bioethics, and the threat of megalomaniac leaders in these new "societies" would all have to be addressed in order to space colonization to meet the psychological and social needs of people living in isolated colonies or generation ships. Although they are not being utilized yet cultural anthropologists may have something to offer to the space programmes.

As an alternative or addendum for the future of the human race, many science fiction writers have focused on the realm of the 'inner-space', that is the computer aided exploration of the human mind and human consciousness.

Counter Arguments

The Argument of Need

The population of Earth continues to increase, while its carrying capacity and available resources do not. If the resources of space are opened to use and viable life-supporting habitats can be built, the Earth will no longer define the limitations of growth. On the other hand, extrapolations made using available figures for population growth, shows that the population of Earth will stop growing around 2070.

Furthermore, even if humanity manages to avoid devastating Earth through war, pestilence, pollution, global cooling, global warming, and even cometary impacts, the Earth will ultimately become uninhabitable by the heating of the Sun as it ages. If humanity has not made permanent habitations in space by the time any one of these incidents occurs, it may very well go extinct.

> "Maybe the reason civilizations don't get around to colonizing other planets is that there's a narrow window when they have the tools, population and will to do so, and the window usually closes on them." —*J. Richard Gott III*
>
> "If it's true that civilizations normally go extinct because they get stuck on their home planets, then the odds are against us." —*J. Richard Gott III*

The Argument of Cost

Many people overestimate how much money is spent on space and underestimate how much money is spent on defense or social programmes.

Military Spending

For example, as of 2008, over $845 billion has been spent on the current war in Iraq. In comparison, it only cost $2 billion to create the Hubble Space Telescope, and NASA's annual budget averages only about $16 billion. In other words, the money that has been spent on the Iraq war could have theoretically funded NASA for approximately 52 years.

Social Spending Programmes

The United States government spends ~$581 billion on its Social Security Programme, an additional ~$561 billion on Medicare, plus additional money on other social programmes whose budget lies within the bounds of the "Other Discretionary Spending" category of the Federal Budget. This means that the United States spends more than $1.142 trillion on social programmes per year (equal to more than $3,807 per person per year). In comparison, the United States space programme costs a mere $53 per person per year.

The Argument of Benefits

Detractors of the development of permanent space colonies and infrastructure often cite the very high initial investment costs of space colonies and permanent space infrastructure yet they ignore all potential returns on that investment. The long-term vision of developing space infrastructure is that it will provide long-term benefits far in excess of the initial start-up costs. Therefore, such a development programme should be viewed more as a long-term investment and not like current social spending programmes that incur spending commitments but provide little or no return on that investment.

Because current space launch costs are so high (on the order of $4,000 to $40,000/kg launched into orbit) any serious plan to develop space infrastructure at a reasonable cost must include developing the ability of that infrastructure to manufacture most or all of its requirements plus those for permanent human habitation in space. Therefore, the initial investments must be made in the development of the initial capacity to provide these necessities: Materials, Energy, Transportation, Communication, Life support, Radiation protection, Self-replication, and Population.

Once the needs of the permanent settlements have been met, any additional production capacity could be used to either extend that initial infrastructure (a concept commonly called "bootstrapping") or traded back to Earth in payment of the initial investment or in exchange for goods more easily manufactured on the Earth.

Although some items of the infrastructure requirements above can already be easily produced on the Earth and would therefore not be very valuable as trade items (oxygen, water, base metal ores, silicates, etc.), other high value items are more abundant, more easily produced, of higher quality, or can only be produced in space. These would provide (over the long-term) a very high return on the initial investment in space infrastructure.

Some of these high trade value goods include precious metals, gem stones, power, solar cells, ball bearings, semi-conductors, and pharmaceuticals.

> ... the smallest Earth-crossing asteroid 3554 Amun is a mile-wide (2 km) lump of iron, nickel, cobalt, platinum, and other metals; it contains 30 times as much metal as Humans have mined throughout history, although it is only the smallest of dozens of known metallic asteroids and worth perhaps US$ 20 trillion if mined slowly to meet demand at 2001 market prices.

> In the 2,900 km³ of Eros, there is more aluminium, gold, silver, zinc and other base and precious metals than have ever been excavated in history or indeed, could ever be excavated from the upper layers of the Earth's crust.

The main impediments to commercial exploitation of these resources are the very high cost of initial investment, the very long period required for the expected return on those investments (estimated to be 50 years or more by some), and because it has never been done before—the high-risk nature of the investment.

The Argument of Nationalism

Space proponents counter this argument by pointing out that humanity as a whole has been exploring and expanding into new territory since long before Europe's colonial period, going back into prehistory (the nationalist argument also ignores multinational cooperative space efforts); that seeing the Earth as a single, discrete object instills a powerful sense of the unity, connectedness of the human environment, and of the immateriality of political borders; and that in practice, international collaboration in space has shown its value as a unifying and cooperative endeavour.

Advocacy

Space advocacy organizations include

- The Alliance to Rescue Civilization plans to establish backups of human civilization on the Moon and other locations away from Earth.
- The Colonize the Cosmos site advocates orbital colonies.
- The Artemis Project plans to set up a private lunar surface station.
- The British Interplanetary Society, founded in 1933, is the world's longest established space society.
- The Living Universe Foundation has a detailed plan in which the entire galaxy is colonized.
- The Mars Society promotes Robert Zubrin's Mars Direct plan and the settlement of Mars.
- The National Space Society is an organization with the vision of "people living and working in thriving communities beyond the Earth."
- The Planetary Society is the largest space interest group, but has an emphasis on robotic exploration and the search for extraterrestrial life.
- The Space Frontier Foundation promotes strong free market, capitalist views about space development.
- The Space Settlement Institute is searching for ways to make space colonization happen in our lifetimes.
- The Space Studies Institute was founded by Gerard K. O'Neill to fund the study of space habitats.
- Students for the Exploration and Development of Space (SEDS) is a student organization founded in 1980 at MIT and Princeton.
- Foresight Nanotechnology Institute—The space challenge.

In Fiction

Although established space colonies are a stock element in science fiction stories, fictional works that explore the themes, social or practical, of the settlement and occupation of a habitable world are much rarer. The following list is restricted to works dealing primarily with the initial stages of colonization.

RPGs

- *2300 AD* (1987) by Game Designers Workshop, Mankind has colonized about 30 planets and found 8 different alien civilizations.

COLONIZATION OF THE MOON

The **colonization of the Moon** is the proposed establishment of permanent human communities on the Moon. Advocates of space exploration have seen settlement of the Moon as a logical step in the expansion of humanity beyond the Earth. National claims to the best locations on the moon may eventually lead to another space race. Polar colonies would be ideal for avoiding long cold nights and to take full advantage of the sun. Nations first to arrive at the poles might lay claim to them, similar to claims made at the Earth's north pole.

Overview

Permanent human habitation on a planetary body other than the Earth is one of science fiction's most prevalent themes. As technology has advanced, and concerns about the future of humanity on Earth have increased, the argument that space colonization is an achievable and worthwhile goal has gained momentum. Because of its proximity to Earth, the Moon has been seen as a prime candidate for the location of humanity's first permanently occupied extraterrestrial base.

Should attempts at colonization go ahead, economic concerns are likely to lead to settlements being created near mines and processing centers, or near the poles where a continuous source of solar energy can be harnessed. While it would be relatively easy to resupply a lunar base from Earth, in comparison to a Martian base, the Moon is likely to play a large role in the development of long-duration closed-loop life support systems. Duplicating the ecology of Earth so that wastes can be recycled is essential to any long-term effort of space exploration. The wealth of knowledge gained by extracting and refining resources on the Moon could significantly enhance efforts to build colonies elsewhere in the Solar System.

History

The notion of siting a colony on the Moon originated before the space age; Konstantin Tsiolkovsky (1857-1935), among others, suggested such a step. From the 1950s onwards, a number of concepts and designs have been suggested by scientists, engineers and others.

Noted science fiction author Arthur C. Clarke proposed a lunar base of inflatable modules covered in lunar dust for insulation in 1954. A spaceship, assembled in low Earth orbit, would be launched towards the Moon, and astronauts would set up the igloo-like modules and an inflatable radio mast. Subsequent steps would include the establishment of a larger, permanent dome; an algae-based air purifier; a nuclear reactor for the provision of power; and electromagnetic cannons to launch cargo and fuel to interplanetary vessels in space.

In 1959, John S. Rinehart suggested that the safest design would be a structure that could "[float] in a stationary ocean of dust," since there were, at the time this concept was outlined, theories that there could be mile-deep dust oceans on the Moon. The proposed design consisted of a half-cylinder with half-domes at both ends, with a micrometeoroid shield placed above the base.

The *Project Horizon* was a 1959 study regarding the U.S. Army's plan to establish a fort on the Moon by 1967. H.H. Koelle, a German rocket engineer of the Army Ballistic Missile Agency (ABMA) was leading the Project Horizon study. The first landing would be carried out by two "soldier-astronauts" in 1965 and more construction workers would soon follow. Through numerous launches (61 Saturn I and 88 Saturn V), 245 tons of cargo would be transported to the outpost by 1966.

Exploration Phase

Exploration of the lunar surface by spacecraft began in 1959 when the Soviet Luna 2 mission crash-landed into the surface. The same year, the Luna 3 mission radioed photographs to Earth of the Moon's hitherto unseen far side, marking the beginning of a decade-long series of unmanned lunar explorations.

Responding to the Soviet programme of space exploration, US President John F. Kennedy in 1961 told the U.S. Congress on May 25: "I believe that this nation should commit itself to achieving the goal before this decade is out of landing a man on the moon and returning him safely to the Earth." The same year the Soviet leadership made some of its first public pronouncements about landing a man on the Moon and establishing a lunar base.

In 1962, John DeNike and Stanley Zahn published their idea of a sub-surface base located at the Sea of Tranquility. This base would house a crew of 21, in modules placed 4 metres below the surface, which was believed to provide radiation shielding as well as the Earth's atmosphere does. They favoured nuclear reactors for energy production, because they are more efficient than solar panels, and would also overcome the problems with the long lunar nights. For life support system, an algae-based gas exchanger was proposed.

Manned exploration of the lunar surface began in 1968 when the Apollo 8 spacecraft orbited the Moon with three astronauts on board. This was mankind's first direct view of the far side. The following year, the Apollo 11 lunar module landed two astronauts on the Moon, proving the ability of humans to travel to the Moon, perform scientific research work and bring back sample materials.

Additional missions to the Moon continued this exploration phase. In 1969 the Apollo 12 mission landed next to the Surveyor 3 spacecraft, demonstrating precision landing capability. Following the near-disaster of Apollo 13, Apollo 14 was the last mission on which astronauts were quarantined on their return from the Moon. The use of a manned vehicle was demonstrated in 1971 with the Lunar Rover during Apollo 15. Apollo 16 made the first landing within the rugged lunar highlands. However, interest in further exploration of the Moon was beginning to wane among the American public. In 1972 Apollo 17 was the final Apollo lunar mission, and further planned missions were scrapped at the directive of President Nixon. Instead, focus was turned to the Space Shuttle and manned missions in near Earth orbit.

The Soviet Luna programme failed to send a manned mission to the Moon. However, in 1966 Luna 9 was the first probe to achieve a soft landing and return close-up shots of the lunar surface. Luna 16 in 1970 returned the first Soviet lunar soil samples, while in 1970 and 1973 during the Lunokhod Programme two robotic rovers landed on the Moon. Lunokhod 1 explored the lunar surface for 322 days, but the contact with Lunokhod 2 was lost after about 4 months of its operation. 1974 saw the end of the Soviet Moonshot, two years after the last American manned landing.

In the decades following, interest in exploring the Moon faded considerably, and only a few dedicated enthusiasts supported a return. However, evidence of lunar ice at the poles gathered by NASA's Clementine (1994) and Lunar Prospector (1998) missions rekindled some discussion, as did the potential growth of a Chinese space programme that contemplated its own mission to the Moon. Subsequent research suggested that there was far less ice present (if any) than had originally been thought, but that there may still be some usable deposits of hydrogen in other forms.

In 2004, U.S. President George W. Bush called for a plan to return manned missions to the Moon by 2020. Propelled by this new initiative, NASA issued a new long-range plan that includes building a base on the Moon as a staging point to Mars. This plan envisions a Lunar outpost at one of the moon's poles by 2024 which, if well-sited, might be able to continually harness solar power; at the poles, temperature changes over the course of a lunar day are also less extreme, and reserves of water and useful minerals may be found nearby. In addition, the European Space Agency has a plan for a permanently manned lunar base by 2025. Russia has also announced similar plans to send a man to the moon by 2025 and establish a permanent base there several years later.

A Chinese space scientist has said that the People's Republic of China could be capable of landing a human on the moon by 2022, and Japan and India also have plans for a lunar base by 2030. Neither of these plans involves permanent residents on the Moon. Instead they call for sortie missions, in some cases followed by extended expeditions to the lunar base using rotating crew members, as is currently done for the International Space Station.

Advantages and Disadvantages

Putting aside the general questions of whether a human colony beyond the Earth is feasible or scientifically desirable in light of cost-efficiency, proponents of space colonization point out that the Moon offers both advantages and disadvantages as a site for such a colony.

Advantages

Placing a colony on a natural body would provide an ample source of material for construction and other uses, including shielding from radiation. The energy required to send objects from the Moon to space is much less than from Earth to space. This could allow the Moon to serve as a construction site or fuelling station for spacecraft. Some proposals include using electric acceleration devices (mass drivers) to propel objects off the Moon without building rockets. Others have proposed momentum exchange tethers. Furthermore, the Moon does have some gravity, which experience to date indicates may be vital for fetal development and long-term human health. Whether the Moon's gravity (roughly one-sixth of Earth's) is adequate for this purpose, however, is uncertain.

In addition, the Moon is the closest large body in the solar system to Earth. While some Earth-crosser asteroids occasionally pass closer, the Moon's distance is consistently within a small range close to 384,400 km. This proximity has several benefits:

- Monetary (space tourism), security, and technological gains.

- The energy required to send objects from Earth to the Moon is lower than for most other bodies.
- Transit time is short. The Apollo astronauts made the trip in three days. Other chemical rockets such as would be used for any Moon missions in the next one to two decades at least would take a similar length of time to make the trip.
- If the Moon were colonized then it could be tested if humans can survive in microgravity. Those results could be utilized for a viable Mars colony as well.
- The short transit time would also allow emergency supplies to quickly reach a Moon colony from Earth, or allow a human crew to evacuate relatively quickly from the Moon to Earth in case of emergency. This could be an important consideration when establishing the first human colony.
- The round trip communication delay to Earth is less than three seconds, allowing near-normal voice and video conversation, and allowing some kinds of remote control of machines from Earth that are not possible from any other celestial body. The delay for other solar system bodies is minutes or hours; for example, round trip communication time between Earth and Mars ranges from about eight minutes to about forty minutes. This again would be of particular value in an early colony, where life-threatening problems requiring Earth's assistance could occur.
- On the lunar near side, the Earth appears large and is always visible as an object 60 times brighter than the Moon appears from Earth, unlike more distant locations where the Earth would be seen merely as a star-like object, much as the planets appear from Earth. As a result, a lunar colony might feel less remote to humans living there.
- A lunar base would provide an excellent site for any kind of observatory. Particular advantages arise from building observatory facilities on the Moon from lunar materials. As the Moon's rotation is so slow, visible light observatories could perform observations for days at a time. It is possible to maintain near-constant observations on a specific target with a string of such observatories spanning the circumference of the Moon. The fact that the Moon is geologically inactive along with the lack of widespread human activity results in a remarkable lack of mechanical disturbance, making it far easier to set up interferometric telescopes on the lunar surface, even at relatively high frequencies such as visible light.
- A lunar base could also hold a future site for launching rockets, to distant planets such as Mars. Launching rockets from the Moon would be an easier prospect than on Earth due to the Moon's lower gravity requiring a lower escape velocity.
- A lunar base could also feed 100 people on 0.5 hectare space farms.
- The low gravity would enable far more launches of heavy materials into space.
- It is the easiest, cheapest, and quickest way to make a colony other than on our Earth.

- A moon colony provides us with most of the experiments, skills, and knowledge we need to colonize another planet.
- A moon colony can easily be seen from the Earth, and might inspire many more humans to seriously consider the advantages and future of colonization. A clear sign or signal can be made to remind humans on Earth, inspiring future leaders, astronauts, and scientists.

Disadvantages

There are several disadvantages to the Moon as a colony site:

- The long lunar night would impede reliance on solar power and require a colony to be designed that could withstand large temperature extremes. An exception to this restriction are the so-called "peaks of eternal light" located at the lunar north pole that are constantly bathed in sunlight. The rim of Shackleton Crater, towards the lunar south pole, also has a near-constant solar illumination. Other areas near the poles that get light most of the time could be linked in a power grid.
- The Moon lacks light elements (volatiles), such as carbon and nitrogen, although there is some evidence of hydrogen near the north and south poles. Additionally, oxygen, though one of the most common elements in the regolith constituting the Moon's surface, is only found bound up in minerals that would require complex industrial infrastructure using very high energy to isolate. Some or all of these volatiles are needed to generate breathable air, water, food, and rocket fuel, all of which would need to be imported from Earth until other cheaper sources are developed. This would limit the colony's rate of growth and keep it dependent on Earth. The cost of volatiles could be reduced by constructing the upper stage of supply ships using materials high in volatiles, such as carbon fiber and other plastics, although converting these into forms useful for life would involve substantial difficulty. The 2006 announcement by the Keck Observatory that the binary Trojan asteroid 617 Patroclus, and possibly large numbers of other Trojan objects in Jupiter's orbit, are likely composed of water ice, with a layer of dust, and the hypothesized large amounts of water ice on the closer, main-belt asteroid 1 Ceres, suggest that importing volatiles from this region via the Interplanetary Transport Network may be practical in the not-so-distant future. However, these possibilities are dependent on complicated and expensive resource utilization from the mid to outer solar system, which are not likely to become available to a Moon colony for a significant period of time.
- There is continuing uncertainty over whether the low (one-sixth *g*) gravity on the Moon is strong enough to prevent detrimental effects to human health in the long term. Exposure to weightlessness over month-long periods has been demonstrated to cause deterioration of physiological systems, such as loss of bone and muscle mass and a depressed immune system. Similar effects

could occur in a low-gravity environment, although virtually all research into the health effects of low gravity has been limited to zero gravity. Countermeasures such as an aggressive routine of daily exercise have proven at least partially effective in preventing the deleterious effects of low gravity.

- The lack of a substantial atmosphere for insulation results in temperature extremes and makes the Moon's surface conditions somewhat like a deep space vacuum. It also leaves the lunar surface exposed to half as much radiation as in interplanetary space (with the other half blocked by the moon itself underneath the colony). Although lunar materials would potentially be useful as a simple radiation shield for living quarters, shielding against solar flares during expeditions outside is more problematic.
- Also, the lack of an atmosphere increases the chances of the colonial site being hit by meteors, which would impact upon the surface directly, as they have done throughout the Moon's history. Even small pebbles and dust (micrometeoroids) have the potential to damage or destroy insufficiently protected structures.
- Moon dust is an extremely abrasive glassy substance formed by micrometeorites and unrounded due to the lack of weathering. It sticks to everything, can damage equipment, and it may be toxic.
- Growing crops on the moon faces many difficult challenges due to the long lunar night (nearly 15 earth days), extreme variation in surface temperature, exposure to solar flares, and lack of insects for pollination. (Due to the lack of any atmosphere on the Moon, plants would need to be grown in sealed chambers, though experiments have shown that plants can thrive at pressures much lower than those on Earth.) The use of electric lighting to compensate for the 28 day/night might be difficult: a single acre of plants on Earth enjoys a peak 4 megawatts of sunlight power at noon. Experiments conducted by the Soviet space programme in the 1970s suggest that it is possible to grow conventional crops with the 15 day light, 15 day dark cycle. A variety of concepts for lunar agriculture have been proposed, including the use of minimal artificial light to maintain plants during the night and the use of fast growing crops that might be started as seedlings with artificial light and be harvestable at the end of one lunar day. A farm at the lunar North Pole could provide eight hours of sunlight per day for rotating crops, a beneficial temperature, radiation protection, insects for pollination, and all other plant needs artificially during the local summer for a cost. One estimate suggested a 0.5 hectare space farm could feed 100 people.

Locations

Three criteria that a lunar outpost should meet are:

- good conditions for transport operations;

- a great number of different types of natural objects and features on the Moon of scientific interest; and
- natural resources, such as oxygen. The abundance of certain minerals, such as iron oxide, varies dramatically over the lunar surface.

While a colony might be located anywhere, potential locations for a lunar colony fall into three broad categories.

Polar Regions

There are two reasons why the lunar poles might be attractive as locations for a human colony. First, there is evidence that water may be present in some continuously shaded areas near the poles. Second, because the Moon's axis of rotation is almost perfectly perpendicular to the ecliptic plane, it may be possible to power polar colonies exclusively with solar energy. Power collection stations can be located so that at least one is in sunlight at all times. Some sites have nearly continuous sunlight. For example, Malapert mountain, located near the Shackleton crater at the lunar south pole, offers several advantages as a site:

- It is exposed to the sun most of the time; two closely spaced arrays of solar panels would receive nearly continuous power.
- Its proximity to Shackleton Crater (116 km, or 69.8 mi) means that it could provide power and communications to the crater. This crater is potentially valuable for astronomical observation. An infrared instrument would benefit from the very cold temperatures. A radio telescope would benefit from being shielded from Earth's broad spectrum radio interference.
- The nearby Shoemaker and other craters are in constant deep shadow, and might contain valuable concentrations of hydrogen and other volatiles.
- At around 5,000 metres (16,500 ft) elevation, it offers line of sight communications over a large area, as well as to Earth.
- The South Pole-Aitken basin is located at the south lunar pole. This is the second largest known impact basin in the solar system, and should provide geologists access to deeper layers of the Moon's crust.

NASA chose to use a south-polar site for the lunar outpost reference design in the Exploration Systems Architecture Study chapter on Lunar Architecture.

At the north pole, the rim of Peary crater has been proposed as a favourable location for a base. Examination of images from the Clementine mission appear to show that parts of the crater rim are permanently illuminated by sunlight (except during lunar eclipses). As a result, the temperature conditions are expected to remain very stable at this location, averaging –50 °C (–58 °F). This is comparable to winter conditions in Earth's the Poles of Cold in Siberia and Antarctica. The Peary crater interior may also harbour hydrogen deposits.

Although hydrogen appears to be concentrated at the poles, the presence of lunar ice has not yet been confirmed. A bistatic radar experiment performed during the Clementine mission suggested the presence of water ice around the south pole. The

Lunar Prospector spacecraft reported enhanced hydrogen abundances not only at the south pole, but also at the north pole—actually more so. On the other hand, results reported using the Arecibo radio telescope have been interpreted by some to indicate that the anomalous Clementine radar signatures are not indicative of ice, but surface roughness. This interpretation, however, is not universally agreed upon.

Equatorial Regions

The lunar equatorial regions are likely to have higher concentrations of helium-3 (rare on Earth but much sought after for use in nuclear fusion research) because the solar wind has a higher angle of incidence. They also enjoy an advantage in launching material from the Moon, but the advantage is slight due to the Moon's slow rotation.

Several probes have landed in the Oceanus Procellarum area. There are many areas and features that could be subject to long-term study, such as the Reiner Gamma anomaly and the dark-floored Grimaldi crater.

Far Side

The lunar far side lacks direct communication with Earth, though a communication satellite at the L_2 Lagrangian point, or a network of orbiting satellites, could enable communication between the far side of the Moon and Earth. The far side is also a good location for a large radio telescope because it is well shielded from the Earth. Due to the lack of atmosphere, the location is also suitable for an array of optical telescopes, similar to the Very Large Telescope in Chile. To date, there has been no ground exploration of the far side.

Scientists have estimated that the highest concentrations of helium-3 will be found in the maria on the far side, as well as near side areas containing concentrations of the titanium-based mineral ilmenite. On the near side the Earth and its magnetic field partially shields the surface from the solar wind during each orbit. But the far side is fully exposed, and thus should receive a somewhat greater proportion of the ion stream.

Structure

Habitat

There have been numerous proposals regarding habitat modules. The designs have evolved throughout the years as mankind's knowledge about the Moon has grown, and as the technological possibilities have changed. The proposed habitats range from the actual spacecraft landers or their used fuel tanks, to inflatable modules of various shapes. Early on, some hazards of the lunar environment such as sharp temperature shifts, lack of atmosphere or magnetic field (which means higher levels of radiation and micrometeoroids) and long nights, were recognized and taken into consideration.

Some suggest building the lunar colony underground, which would give protection from radiation and micrometeoroids. This is not the only advantage to this option. The average temperature on the moon is about –5 °C. The day period (two weeks) has an average temperature of about 107 °C (225 °F), although it can rise as high as 123 °C

(253 °F). The night period (also two weeks) has an average temperature of about –153 °C (–243 °F). Underground, both periods would be around 24 °C (75 °F), and humans could install ordinary air conditioners. The construction of such a base would probably be more complex; one of the first machines from Earth might be a remote controlled excavating machine to excavate living quarters. Once created, some sort of hardening would be necessary to avoid collapse, possibly a spray-on concrete-like substance made from available materials. A more porous insulating material also made *in situ* could then be applied. Inflatable self-sealing fabric habitats might then be put in place to retain air. As an alternative to excavating, it is possible that large underground extinct lava tubes might exist on the Moon.

A possibly easier solution would be to build the lunar base on the surface, and cover the modules with lunar soil. The lunar regolith is composed of a unique blend of silica and iron-containing compounds that may be fused into a glass-like solid using microwave energy. This may allow for the use of "lunar bricks" in structural designs, or the "glassing" of loose dirt to form a hard, ceramic crust. Others have put forward the idea that the lunar base could be built on the surface and protected by other means, such as improved radiation and micrometeoroid shielding. Artificial magnetic fields have been proposed as a means to provide radiation shielding for long range deep space manned missions, and it might be possible to use similar technology on a lunar colony. Some regions on the Moon possess strong local magnetic fields that might partially mitigate against exposure to charged solar and galactic particles.

Energy

A lunar base would need power for its operations—from fuel production and communications to life support systems and scientific research.

Nuclear Power

A nuclear fission reactor might fulfil most of the base's power requirements. Radioisotope thermoelectric generators could be used as backup and emergency power sources for solar powered colonies.

Solar Energy

Solar energy is a strong candidate. It could prove to be a relatively cheap source of power for a lunar base, especially since many of the raw materials needed for solar panel production can be extracted on site. However, the long lunar night (14 Earth days) is a drawback for solar power on the Moon's surface. This might be solved by building several power plants, so that at least one of them is always in daylight. Another possibility would be to build such a power plant where there is constant or near-constant sunlight, such as at the Malapert mountain near the lunar south pole, or on the rim of Peary crater near the north pole. A third possibility would be to leave the panels in orbit, and beam the power down as microwaves.

The solar energy converters need not be silicon solar panels. It may be more advantageous to use the larger temperature difference between sun and shade to run heat engine generators. Concentrated sunlight could also be relayed via mirrors and used in Stirling engines or solar trough generators, or it could be used directly for lighting, agriculture and process heat. The focused heat might also be employed in materials processing to extract various elements from lunar surface materials.

Energy Storage

In the early days, a combination of solar panels for 'day-time' operation and fuel cells for 'night-time' operation could be used.

Fuel cells on the Space Shuttle have operated reliably for up to 17 days at a time. On the Moon, they would only be needed for 13.7 days—the length of the lunar night. Fuel cells produce water directly as a waste product. Current fuel cell technology is more advanced than the Shuttle's cells—PEM (Proton Exchange Membrane) cells produce considerably less heat (though their waste heat would likely be useful during the lunar night) and are physically lighter, not to mention the reduced mass of the smaller heat-dissipating radiators. This makes PEMs more economical to launch from Earth than the shuttle's cells, but PEMs have not yet been proven in space.

Combining fuel cells with electrolysis would provide a 'perpetual' source of electricity—solar energy could be used to provide power during the Lunar 'day', and fuel cells at night. During the Lunar 'day', solar energy would also be used to electrolise the water created in the fuel cells—although there would be small losses of gases that would have to be replaced.

Transport

Earth to Moon

Conventional rockets have been used for most lunar exploration to date. The ESA's SMART-1 mission from 2003 to 2006 used Hall effect thrusters. NASA will use chemical rockets on its Ares V booster and Lunar Surface Access Module, being developed for a planned return to the Moon around 2019. The construction workers, location finders, and other astronauts vital to building, will be taken in NASA's Orion spacecraft.

On the Surface

Lunar colonists will want the ability to move over long distances, to transport cargo and people to and from modules and spacecraft, and to carry out scientific study of a larger area of the lunar surface for long periods of time. Proposed concepts include a variety of vehicle designs, from small open rovers to large pressurised modules with lab equipment, and also a few flying or hopping vehicles.

Rovers could be useful if the terrain is not too steep or hilly. The only rovers to have operated on the surface of the Moon (as of 2008) are the Apollo Lunar Roving

Vehicle (LRV), developed by Boeing, and the robotic Soviet Lunokhod. The LRV was an open rover for a crew of two, and a range of 92 km during one lunar day. One NASA study resulted in the Mobile Lunar Laboratory concept, a manned pressurised rover for a crew of two, with a range of 396 km. The Soviet Union developed different rover concepts in the Lunokhod series and the L5 for possible use on future manned missions to the Moon or Mars. These rover designs were all pressurised for longer sorties.

If multiple bases were established on the lunar surface, they could be linked together by permanent railway systems. Both conventional and magnetic levitation (Mag-Lev) systems have been proposed for the transport lines. Mag-Lev systems are particularly attractive as there is no atmosphere on the surface to slow down the train, so the vehicles could achieve velocities comparable to aircraft on the Earth. In addition achieving the extremely cold temperatures necessary for the superconducting magnets that levitate and drive the Mag-Lev trains would be much easier to achieve than on Earth due to the lack of an atmosphere. One significant difference with lunar trains, however, is that the cars would need to be individually sealed and possess their own life support systems. The trains would also need to be highly resistant to derailment, as a punctured car could lead to rapid loss of life.

For difficult areas, a flying vehicle may be more suitable. Bell Aerosystems proposed their design for the Lunar Flying Vehicle as part of a study for NASA. Bell also developed the Manned Flying System, a similar concept.

Surface to Space

Launch Technology

A lunar base will need efficient ways to transport people and goods of various kinds between the Earth and the Moon and, later, to and from various locations in interplanetary space. One advantage of the Moon is its relatively weak gravity field, making it easier to launch goods from the Moon than from the Earth. The lack of a lunar atmosphere is both an advantage and a disadvantage; while it is easier to launch from the Moon because there is no drag, aerobraking is not possible, which makes it necessary to bring extra fuel in order to land. An alternative, which may work for supplies, is to surround the payload with impact-absorbing materials, something that was tried in the Ranger Programme. This can be efficient if the impact protection is made of needed lighter elements that are absent from the Moon (Ranger used balsa wood).

One way to get materials and products from the Moon to an interplanetary waystation might be with a mass driver, a magnetically accelerated projectile launcher. Cargo would be picked up from orbit or an Earth-Moon Lagrangian point by a shuttle craft using ion propulsion, solar sails or other means and delivered to Earth orbit or other destinations such as near-Earth asteroids, Mars or other planets, perhaps using the Interplanetary Transport Network. If a lunar space elevator is ever built, it could transport people, raw materials and products to and from an orbital station at Lagrangian points L_1 or L_2.

Launch Costs

- Estimates of the cost per pound of launching cargo or people from the Moon vary and the cost impacts of future technological improvements are difficult to predict. An upper bound on the cost of launching material from the Moon might be about $40,000,000 per kilogram, based on dividing the Apollo programme costs by the amount of material returned. At the other extreme, the incremental cost of launching material from the moon using an electromagnetic accelerator could be quite low. The efficiency of launching material from the Moon with a proposed electric accelerator is suggested to be about 50 per cent. If the carriage of a mass driver weighs the same as the cargo, two kilograms must be accelerated to orbital velocity for each kilogram put into orbit. The overall system efficiency would then drop to 25 per cent. So 1.4 kilowatt-hours would be needed to launch an incremental kilogram of cargo to low orbit from the Moon. At $0.1/kilowatt-hour, a typical cost for electrical power on Earth, that amounts to $0.16 for the energy to launch a kilogram of cargo into orbit. For the actual cost of an operating system, energy loss for power conditioning, the cost of radiating waste heat, the cost of maintaining all systems, and the interest cost of the capital investment are considerations. David R. Criswell believes that there is a potential for the cost of electrical power on the Moon to become enough less than the cost on Earth for electrical power to be exported from the Moon to Earth by microwave.
- Passengers cannot be divided into the parcel size suggested for the cargo of a mass driver, nor subjected to hundreds of gravities acceleration. However, technical developments could also affect the cost of launching passengers to orbit from the Moon. Instead of bringing all fuel and oxidizer from Earth, liquid oxygen could be produced from lunar materials and hydrogen should be available from the lunar poles. The cost of producing these on the Moon is yet unknown, but they will be more expensive than on Earth. The situation of the local hydrogen is most open to speculation. As a rocket fuel, hydrogen could be extended by combining it chemically with silicon to form silane, which has yet to be demonstrated in an actual rocket engine. In the absence of more technical developments, the cost of transporting people from the Moon will be an impediment to colonization.

Surface to and from Cislunar Space

A cislunar transport system has been proposed using tethers to achieve momentum exchange. This system requires zero net energy input, and could not only retrieve payloads from the lunar surface and transport them to Earth, but could also soft land payloads on to the lunar surface.

Economic Development

For long-term sustainability, a space colony should be close to self-sufficient. On site mining and refining of the Moon's materials could provide an advantage over deliveries from Earth—for use both on the Moon and elsewhere in the solar system—as they can be launched into space at a much lower energy cost than from Earth. It is possible that vast sums of money will be spent in interplanetary exploration in the 21st century, and the cost of providing goods from the Moon might be attractive.

Space-based Materials Processing

In the long term, the Moon is likely to be very important in supplying space-based construction facilities with raw materials. Zero gravity allows materials to be processed in ways impossible or difficult on Earth, such as 'foaming' metals, where a gas is injected into a molten metal, and then the metal is annealed slowly. On Earth, the gas bubbles rise and burst, but in a zero gravity environment, that does not happen. Annealing is a process that requires large amounts of energy, as a material is kept very hot for an extended period of time. This allows the molecular structure to align in the strongest possible way. Materials which cannot be alloyed or mixed on Earth because of the gravity field effects on density differences could be combined in space, resulting in composites which could have exceptional qualities. No one knows, because no one has been able to experiment along these lines on any scale. However, it is possible that a material or process will be identified which will be highly valuable on Earth, but impossible to make here. This is the foundation of the free MoonBaseOne game made by a non-profit that teaches kids about space.

Exporting Material to Earth

Exporting material to Earth in trade from the Moon is more problematic due to the cost of transportation which will vary greatly if the Moon is industrially developed. One suggested candidate is Helium-3 from the solar wind, which has accumulated on the Moon's surface over billions of years, and which is rare on Earth. Helium is present in the lunar regolith in quantities of ten to a hundred (weight) parts per million, and 0.003 to 1 per cent of this amount (depending on soil). 2006 market price for He-3 was about $46,500 per troy ounce ($1500/gram, $1.5M/kg), more than 120 times the value per unit weight of Gold and over eight times the value of Rhodium.

In the long term future He-3 may prove to be a desirable fuel in thermonuclear fusion reactors.

Tourism

An economic possibility is the tourism industry. The low gravity may find health uses such as allowing the physically disabled to continue to enjoy an active lifestyle. Large, pressurized domes or caverns would permit human-powered flight, which may result in new sports activities. The film and TV industries may find the moon a good place for filming.

Research

The moon has advantages of low gravity and unparalleled quarantine, making it useful for research and processing of dangerous life forms, nanotechnology, and long-term storage of radioactive materials.

Technology Spinoff

Technology developed for a Lunar colony would likely have application to other potential space venues, including near-Earth asteroids and Mercury, which has many similarities to the Moon.

Solar Power Satellites

Gerard O'Neill, noting the problem of high launch costs in the early 1970s, came up with the idea of building Solar Power Satellites in orbit with materials from the Moon. Launch costs from the Moon will vary greatly if the Moon is industrially developed. This 1970s proposal was predicated on the then advertised future launch costs of NASA's space shuttle.

On 30 April 1979 the Final Report "Lunar Resources Utilization for Space Construction" by General Dynamics Convair Division under NASA contract NAS9-15560 concluded that use of lunar resources would be cheaper than terrestrial materials for a system comprising as few as thirty Solar Power Satellites of 10 GW capacity each.

In 1980, when it became obvious NASA's launch cost estimates for the space shuttle were grossly optimistic, O'Neill *et al.* published another route to manufacturing using lunar materials with much lower startup costs. This 1980s SPS concept relied less on human presence in space and more on partially self-replicating systems on the lunar surface under telepresence control of workers stationed on Earth.

COMMERCIALIZATION OF SPACE

Commercialization of space is the use of equipment sent into or through outer space to provide goods or services of commercial value, either by a corporation or state. Current examples of the commercial use of space include satellite navigation systems, satellite television and satellite radio.

Satellite Communication

The satellite communication industry is often broken into four sectors: transponder leasing, subscription satellite services, ground equipment manufacturing, and satellite manufacturing. Together these sectors produced 89 billion dollars in revenue as of 2002, and exhibited a 17 per cent annual growth rate between the years of 1996 and 2002.

Subscription Satellite Services

Subscription satellite service experienced the majority of the growth seen in the last decade. The reason for this growth can be attributed to the availability of Low Earth Orbit satellite constellations, which enhanced the services of direct-to-home (DTH) television service. In 1994, DirecTV debuted by introducing a dish only 18 inches in diameter. In 1996, Astro started in Malaysia with the launch of the MEASAT satellite. In November 1999, the Satellite Home Viewer Improvement Act became law, and local stations were then made available in satellite channel packages, fuelling the industry's growth in the years that followed. By the end of 2000, DTH subscriptions totalled over 67 million.

Transponder Leasing

Businesses that operate satellites often lease or sell access to their satellites to data relay and telecommunication firms. This service is often referred to as transponder leasing. Between 1996 and 2002, this industry experienced a 15 per cent annual growth. The United States accounts for about 32 per cent of the world's transponder market.

Ground Equipment Manufacturing

For satellites to operate, they need receivers and transmitters on the ground. The manufacturing of satellite uplink and downlink terminals (including VSATs), consumer mobile satellite telephone units, and direct-to-home television receivers and dishes make up the ground equipment manufacturing sector. This sector grew at a quick pace through the latter half of the 1990s as it manufactured equipment for the satellite services sector. Between the years of 1996 and 2002 this industry saw a 14 per cent annual increase.

Satellite Manufacturing

Commercial satellite manufacturing is defined by the United States government as satellites manufactured for civilian government or non-profit use. Not included are satellites constructed for military use, nor for activities associated with any human space flight programme. Between the years of 1996 and 2002, satellite manufacturing within the United States experienced an annual growth of 11 per cent. The rest of the world experienced higher growth levels of around 13 per cent. Less than 43 per cent of the satellites launched in 2002 for commercial use were manufactured in the United States. Fear of technology transfer to foreign governments prompted a 1999 law which allowed the US State Department to control export licensing of satellite technology. These heightened security measures have, some believe, stifled the commercial growth of satellite manufacturing within the US.

Satellite Imagery

Several operators of Earth observation satellites, such as GeoEye and Spot Image, provide images commercially.

Space Transportation

The commercial space transportation industry derives the bulk of its revenue from the launching of satellites into the Earth's orbit. Commercial launch providers typically place private and government satellites into Low Earth Orbit (LEO). In 2002, commercial space transportation generated 6.6 billion dollars, which made up 6 per cent of the total gross of commercial space activities.

The Federal Aviation Administration (FAA) has licensed four commercial spaceports in the United States: the Virginia Space Flight Center/Wallops Flight Facility, Kodiak Launch Complex, Spaceport Florida/Kennedy Space Center/Cape Canaveral Air Force Station, and the California Spaceport/Vandenberg AFB. Launch sites within Russia and China have added to the global commercial launch capacity. The Delta IV and Atlas V family of launch vehicles are made available for commercial ventures for the United States, while Russia promotes eight families of vehicles. The three largest Russian systems are the Proton, Soyuz, and Zenit.

Between 1996 and 2002, 245 launches were made for commercial ventures while government (non-classified) launches only total 167 for the same period. Commercial space flight has spurred investment into the development of an efficient reusable launch vehicle (RLV) which can place larger payloads into orbit. Several companies such as SpaceX are currently creating new RLV designs.

Space Tourism

Space tourism is the recent phenomenon of space travel by individuals for the purpose of personal pleasure. As of 2007, space tourism is only affordable to wealthy individuals and corporations, with the Russian space programme providing transport. It has become so popular that, even at $20 million a ticket, the Russian Space Agency is fully booked until 2009. Some are beginning to favour the term "personal spaceflight" instead, as in the case of the Personal Spaceflight Federation.

Among the primary attractions of space tourism are the uniqueness of the experience, the thrill and awe of looking at Earth from space (described by astronauts as extremely intense and mind-boggling), the experience's notion as an exclusive status symbol, and various advantages of weightlessness. The space tourism industry is being targeted by spaceports in numerous locations, including California, Oklahoma, New Mexico, Florida, Virginia, Alaska, Esrange in Sweden and Wisconsin, as well as Singapore and the United Arab Emirates.

Regulation

In the United States, Office of Commercial Space Transportation (generally referred to as FAA/AST or simply AST) is the branch of Federal Aviation Administration (FAA) that approves any commercial rocket launch operations—that is, any launches that are not classified as model, amateur, or "by and for the government."

QUASI UNIVERSAL INTERGALACTIC DENOMINATION

The **Quasi Universal Intergalactic Denomination** (QUID) was a proposed "space currency" created as a viral marketing campaign launched by Travelex with the London-based public relations and advertising firm, talkPR. The full name is a backronym from 'quid', a slang term for the British Pound. The campaign stated that Travelex was launching a new form of money for space tourists that had no sharp edges, was chemically inert, and had other advantages over paper money.

On October 5, 2007, a one-page press statement announcing the QUID was released and placed on the United Press International press release newswire. The campaign was launched in the midst of intense press coverage of the Virgin Galactic news. The story was picked up by major news agencies in the UK, and soon after, the US. Science magazines and technological blog writers weighed in on the topic, calling it "useless" and "nonsense", further spreading the story.

The QUID

After coming up with the idea of a space-money campaign, talkPR and Travelex contacted the National Space Centre, whose employees were presented with a number of mockups made by the campaign artists and were asked to select one.

The end result was a series of circular clear discs with colored centers, symbolizing the eight planets of the Solar System inside, and denominations ranging from 1 to 10. Each quid coin would have its own unique code number, similar to the serial number on paper currency, to allow tracking, and to prevent counterfeiting. Travelex stated that it planned to work with the Bank of England to begin registering the Quid as possible legal currency in the future.

Statements by members of the NSC and the University of Leicester (who started the NSC) were added to the campaign release. When the campaign concluded, NSC received the resulting coins and put them on display in their Space Now display.

3

Space Technology, Space Station and Spaceport: Select Case Studies

SPACE TECHNOLOGY

Space technology is technology that is related to entering space, maintaining and using systems during spaceflight and returning people and things from space.

"Every day" technologies such as weather forecasting, remote sensing, GPS systems, satellite television, and some long distance communications systems critically rely on space infrastructure. Of sciences astronomy and Earth sciences (via remote sensing) most notably benefit from space technology.

Computers and telemetry were once leading edge technologies that might have been considered "space technology" because of their criticality to boosters and spacecraft. They existed prior to the Space Race of the Cold War but their development was vastly accelerated to meet the needs of the two major superpowers' space programmes. While still used today in spacecraft and missiles, the more prosaic applications such as remote monitoring (via telemetry) of patients, water plants, highway conditions, etc. and the widespread use of computers far surpasses their space applications in quantity and variety of application.

Space is such an alien environment that attempting to work in it requires new techniques and knowledge. New technologies originating with or accelerated by space-related endeavours are often subsequently exploited in other economic activities. This has been widely pointed to as beneficial by space advocates and enthusiasts favouring the investment of public funds in space activities and programmes. Political opponents counter that it would be far cheaper to develop specific technologies directly if they are beneficial and scoff at this justification for public expenditures on space-related research.

Specific Space Technologies

- Ablative heat shield
- Aerobot (planetary probe suspended in atmosphere)
- Atmospheric braking
- Booster See also ICBM
- Centrifuge
- Gantry

- Human staffed missions
- Rocket sled
- Rover
  - Lunar Rover
  - Mars Rover
- Satellite
  - Communication satellite
  - Earth observation satellite
  - Navigation satellite
  - Space observatory
  - Satellite television
  - Telecommunications satellite
  - Weather satellite
- Spacecraft
- Spacecraft propulsion
- Space probe
  - Aerobot (planetary probe suspended in atmosphere)
- Space shuttle
- Space station
- Space suit
- Space capsule
- Splashdown
- Telemetryccc
- Thruster

Future Space Technologies

- Asteroid mining
- Single stage to orbit
- Solar power satellite
- Non-rocket spacelaunch
- Space manufacturing

SPACE STATION

A **space station** is an artificial structure designed for humans to live in outer space. To date, only low earth orbital (LEO) stations have been implemented, otherwise known as **orbital stations**. A space station is distinguished from other manned spacecraft by its lack of major propulsion or landing facilities—instead, other vehicles are used as transport to and from the station. Space stations are designed for medium-term living in orbit, for periods of weeks, months, or even years. The only space station currently in use is the International Space Station. Previous stations include the Almaz & Salyut series, Skylab and *Mir*.

Space stations are used to study the effects of long-term space flight on the human body as well as to provide platforms for greater number and length of scientific studies than available on other space vehicles. Since the ill-fated flight of Soyuz 11 to Salyut 1, all manned spaceflight duration records have been set aboard space stations. The duration record for a single spaceflight is 437.7 days, set by Valeriy Polyakov aboard *Mir* from 1994 to 1995. As of 2009, three astronauts have completed single missions of over a year, all aboard *Mir*.

Uses

Space stations have been used for both military and civilian purposes. The last military-use space station was Salyut 5, which was used by the Almaz programme of the Soviet Union in 1976 and 1977.

Types of Space Stations

Monolithic

Broadly speaking, the space stations so far launched have been of two types; the earlier stations, Salyut and Skylab, have been "monolithic", intended to be constructed and launched in one piece, and then manned by a crew later. As such, they generally contained all their supplies and experimental equipment when launched, and were considered "expended", and then abandoned, when these were used up.

Starting with Salyut 6 and Salyut 7, a change was seen; these were built with two docking ports, which allowed a second crew to visit, bringing a new spacecraft with them (for technical reasons, a Soyuz capsule cannot safely spend more than a few months in orbit, even powered down). This allowed for a crew to man the station continually. Skylab was also equipped with two docking ports, like second-generation stations, but the extra port was never utilized. The presence of a second port on the new stations allowed Progress supply vehicles to be docked to the station, meaning that fresh supplies could be brought to aid long-duration missions. This concept was expanded on Salyut 7, which "hard docked" with a TKS tug shortly before it was abandoned; this served as a proof-of-concept for the use of modular space stations. The later Salyuts may reasonably be seen as a transition between the two groups.

Modular

The second group, Mir and the ISS, have been modular; a core unit was launched, and additional modules, generally with a specific role, were later added to that. (On Mir they were usually launched independently, whereas on the ISS most are brought by the Shuttle). This method allows for greater flexibility in operation, as well as removing the need for a single immensely powerful launch vehicle. These stations are also designed from the outset to have their supplies provided by logistical support, which allows for a longer lifetime at the cost of requiring regular support launches.

Habitability Issues

These stations have various issues that limit their long-term habitability, such as very low recycling rates, relatively high radiation levels and a lack of gravity. Some of these problems cause discomfort and long-term health effects. In the case of solar flares, all current habitats are protected by the Earth's magnetic field, and are below the Van Allen belts.

Future space habitats may attempt to address these issues, and are intended for long-term occupation. Some designs might even accommodate large numbers of people, essentially "cities in space" where people would make their homes. No such design has yet been constructed, since even for a small station, the current (2009) launch costs are not economically or politically viable.

Possible ways to deal with these costs would be building a large amount of rockets (economies of scale), reusable rockets, *In Situ* Resource Utilisation or if space elevators are ever able to be constructed.

Architecture

A space station is a complex system with many interrelated subsystems:

1. Structure
2. Electrical power
3. Thermal control
4. Attitude determination and control
5. Orbital navigation and propulsion
6. Automation and robotics
7. Computing and communications
8. Environmental and life support
9. Crew facilities
10. Crew and cargo transportation

Past and Present Space Stations

- **Salyut** space stations (USSR, 1971-1986)
  - **Salyut 1** (1971, 1 crew and 1 failed docking)
  - **DOS-2** (1972, launch failure)
  - **Salyut 2/Almaz** (1973, failed shortly after launch)
  - **Cosmos 557** (1973, re-entered eleven days after launch)
  - **Salyut 3/Almaz** (1974, 1 crew and 1 failed docking)
  - **Salyut 4** (1975, 2 crews and 1 planned crew failed to achieve orbit)
  - **Salyut 5/Almaz** (1976-1977, 2 crews and 1 failed docking)
  - **Salyut 6** [1977-1981, 16 crews (5 long duration, 11 short duration) and 1 failed docking]
  - **Salyut 7** [1982-1986, 10 crews (6 long duration, 4 short duration) and 1 failed docking]

- **Skylab** (USA, 1973-1974, 3 crews)
- ***Mir*** (USSR/Russia, 1986-2000, 28 long duration crews)
- **International Space Station (ISS)** (USA, Russia, Japan, European Space Agency, Canada, Italy 2000-ongoing, 20 long duration crews to date)

Following the controlled deorbiting of Mir in 2001, the International Space Station is the only one of these currently in orbit; it has been continuously occupied since October 30, 2000.

List of Occupied Space Stations, with Statistics

Space station	*Launched*	*Reentered*	*Days in use*		*Total crew and visitors*	*Visits*		*Mass (kg)*
			In orbit	Occupied		Manned	Unmanned	
Salyut 1	19 April 1971 01:40:00 UTC	11 October 1971	175	24	3	2	0	18,425 kg (40,620 lb)
DOS-2	29 July 1972 Failed to enter earth orbit	29 July 1972	0	0	0	0	0	18,425 kg (40,620 lb)
Salyut 2	4 April 1973	28 May 1973	54	0	0	0	0	18,425 kg (40,620 lb)
Cosmos 557	11 May 1973	22 May 1973	11	0	0	0	0	18,425 kg (40,620 lb)
Skylab	14 May 1973 17:30:00 UTC	11 July 1979 16:37:00 UTC	2,249	171	9	3	0	77,088 kg (169,950 lb)
Salyut 3	25 June 1974 22:38:00 UTC	24 January 1975	213	15	2	1	0	18,500 kg (40,786 lb)
Salyut 4	26 December 1974 04:15:00 UTC	3 February 1977	770	92	4	2	1	18,500 kg (40,786 lb)
Salyut 5	22 June 1976 18:04:00 UTC	8 August 1977	412	67	4	2	0	19,000 kg (41,888 lb)
Salyut 6	29 September 1977 06:50:00 UTC	29 July 1982	1,764	683	33	16	14	19,000 kg (41,888 lb)
Salyut 7	19 April 1982 19:45:00 UTC	7 February 1991	3,216	816	26	12	15	19,000 kg (41,888 lb)
Mir	19 February 1986 21:28:23 UTC	23 March 2001 05:50:00 UTC	5,511	4,594	137	39	68	124,340 kg (274,123 lb)
ISS	20 November 1998	Currently in orbit	3,883	3,209	216	47	37	286,876 kg (632,453 lb)

Crew and visitors counting is non-distinct.

- ISS statistics as of 29 May 2009

Cancelled Space Stations

- A second Skylab unit (*Skylab B*) was manufactured, as a backup article; due to the high costs of providing launch vehicles, and a desire by NASA to cease Saturn and Apollo operations in time to prepare for the Space Shuttle coming into service, it was never flown. The hull can now be seen in the National Air and Space Museum, in Washington DC, where it is a popular tourist attraction.
- A number of additional *Salyuts* were produced, as backups or as flight articles that were later cancelled.
- The U.S. *Space Station Freedom* Programme, which—despite being under development for ten years—was never launched, evolved into the International Space Station
- The Soviet/Russian *Mir-2* station, which was never constructed, had some of its elements incorporated into the International Space Station.
- The *Industrial Space Facility* was a station proposed in the 1980s that was to be privately funded. The project was cancelled when the company created to build it, Space Industries Incorporated, was unable to secure funding from the United States government.
- United States Air Force *Manned Orbiting Laboratory* project, cancelled in 1969 about a year before the first planned test flight; this was unusual in being an explicitly military project, as opposed to the Soviet Almaz programme, which was heavily intertwined with—and concealed by—the contemporaneous Salyut Programme.
- The European *Columbus* project planned to create a small space station serviced by the Hermes shuttle. It evolved into the ISS Columbus module.

Future Developments

- Currently, Bigelow Aerospace is developing commercial inflatable habitat modules, derived from the earlier NASA Transhab concept, intended to be used for space station construction and for a space prize they are funding and operating, America's Space Prize. *Genesis I* and *Genesis II* are ⅓-scale unmanned prototype modules orbited to test the feasibility of inflatable structures and other systems in space. Future modules include the *Galaxy, Sundancer* and *BA 330*, each being progressively larger and more complicated, with the *BA 330* intended as the full-scale manned production model for Bigelow's expandable space habitation module programme.
- Project 921-2 is the working name given by the People's Republic of China for plans to create a manned space station by 2012.
- In April 2008, the Russian space agency has proposed the construction of an orbital construction yard for spacecraft too heavy to launch from Earth directly. It would not begin construction or be finished until after the decommission of the International Space Station.
- Galactic Suite is a space hotel planned to be operational by 2012.

INTERNATIONAL SPACE STATION

The **International Space Station (ISS)** is an internationally developed research facility currently being assembled in Low Earth Orbit. On-orbit construction of the station began in 1998 and is scheduled to be completed by 2011, with operations continuing until at least 2015. The ISS orbits at an altitude of approximately 350 kilometres (220 mi) above the surface of the Earth, travelling at an average speed of 27,724 kilometres (17,227 mi) per hour, completing 15.7 orbits per day. The station can be seen from the Earth with the naked eye, and, as of 2009, is the largest artificial satellite in Earth orbit, with a mass larger than that of any previous space station.

The ISS is a joint project among the space agencies of the United States (National Aeronautics and Space Administration—NASA), Russia (Russian Federal Space Agency—RKA), Japan (Japan Aerospace Exploration Agency—JAXA), Canada (Canadian Space Agency—CSA) and ten European nations (European Space Agency—ESA). The Brazilian Space Agency (AEB) participates through a separate contract with NASA. The Italian Space Agency (ASI) similarly has separate contracts for various activities not done within the framework of ESA's ISS projects (where Italy also fully participates). China has reportedly expressed interest in the project, especially if it would be able to work with the RKA, although as of 2009 it is not involved due to objections from the United States.

The ISS has been continuously staffed since the first resident crew, Expedition 1, entered the station on 2 November 2000. This has provided an uninterrupted human presence in space for the last 8 years, 284 days. Prior to May 2009, the station had the capacity for a crew of three. However, to fulfil an active research programme, since the arrival of Expedition 20, it has been staffed by a resident crew of six. The crew of Expedition 20 is currently aboard. Resident crews utilise the station as an orbital laboratory, carrying out research across a wide variety of fields, including biology, human biology, physics, astronomy and meteorology. The station also provides a safe testing location for efficient, reliable spacecraft systems that will be required for long-duration missions to the Moon and Mars.

The station consists of a number of pressurised modules and unpressurised components, which have been launched by Space Shuttle, Soyuz rocket or Proton rocket. The ISS is serviced by a wide variety of manned and unmanned spacecraft, including the Soyuz spacecraft, Progress spacecraft, Space Shuttle and Automated Transfer Vehicle, and has been visited by astronauts from 16 different nations. The various sections of the station are controlled by several mission control centres on the ground, including MCC-H, TsUP, Col-CC, ATV-CC, JEM-CC, HTV-CC and MSS-CC.

Purpose

The International Space Station serves primarily as a research laboratory and is the largest satellite ever launched into orbit. The station offers an advantage over spacecraft such as NASA's Space Shuttle because it is a long-term platform in the space environment, allowing long-duration studies to be performed, both on specific experiments and on the human crews that operate them. The presence of a permanent crew also means that the station offers benefits over other unmanned spacecraft as experiments can be monitored, replenished, repaired or replaced as required by the crew, as can various other components of the spacecraft itself. This means that scientists on the ground have swift access to their data and can modify experiments or fly new ones as and when required, benefits generally unavailable on specialised unmanned spacecraft.

Crews flying long-term expeditions, lasting several months, conduct science daily (approximately 160 man-hours a week) across a wide variety of fields, including human research, life sciences, physical sciences, and Earth observation, as well as education and technology demonstrations. As of June 2006, 90 science investigations had been conducted on the ISS over 64 months of continuous research. In addition, there have been nine research racks and more than 7,700 kg (17,000 lb) of research equipment and facilities launched to the station. Scientific findings, in fields ranging from basic science to exploration research, are being published every month.

The ISS also provides a testing location for efficient, reliable spacecraft systems that will be required for long-duration missions to the Moon and Mars, allowing for equipment to be evaluated in the relatively safe location of Low Earth Orbit. This provides experience in maintaining, repairing, and replacing systems on-orbit, which will be essential in operating spacecraft further from Earth. This aspect of ISS operations reduces mission risks, and advances the capabilities of interplanetary spacecraft.

Finally, in addition to the scientific and research aspects of the station, there are numerous opportunities for educational outreach and international cooperation. The crews of the ISS provide educational opportunities for students back home on Earth, including student-developed experiments, educational demonstrations, student participation in classroom versions of ISS experiments, NASA investigator experiments, and ISS engineering activities. The ISS programme itself, and the international cooperation that it represents, allows 14 nations to live and work together in space, providing important lessons that can be taken forward into future multi-national missions.

Scientific Research

One of the main goals of the ISS is to provide a place to conduct experiments that require one or more of the unusual conditions present on the station. The main fields of research include biology, physics, astronomy, and meteorology. The 2005 NASA Authorization Act designated the US segment of the International Space Station as a national laboratory with a goal to increase the use of the ISS by other Federal entities and the private sector.

One research goal is to improve the understanding of long-term space exposure on the human body. Subjects currently under study include muscle atrophy, bone loss, and fluid shift. The data will be used to determine whether space colonization and lengthy human spaceflight are feasible. As of 2009, data on bone loss and muscular atrophy suggest that there would be a significant risk of fractures and movement problems if astronauts landed on a planet following a lengthy space cruise.

The effect of near-weightlessness on non-human subjects is being considered as well. Researchers are investigating the relation of the near-weightless environment of outer space to evolution, development and growth, and the internal processes of plants and animals. In response to some of this data, NASA wants to investigate microgravity's effects on the growth of three-dimensional, human-like tissues, and the unusual protein crystals that can be formed in space.

Researchers are investigating the physics of fluids in microgravity, enabling them to better model the behaviour of fluids in the future. Due to the ability to almost completely combine fluids in microgravity, physicists are interested in investigating the combinations of fluids that will not normally mix well on Earth. In addition, by examining reactions that are slowed down by low gravity and temperatures, scientists hope to gain new insight regarding superconductivity.

Materials processing takes up a large part of the research time aboard the station, with the goal of reaping economic benefits by developing the science to improve techniques used on the ground. Experiments are intended to provide a better understanding of the relationship between processing, structure, and properties so the conditions required on Earth to achieve desired materials properties can be reliably predicted.

Other areas of interest include the effect of the low gravity environment on combustion, studying the efficiency of burning and control of emissions & pollutants. These findings may improve our understanding of energy production, and in turn have an economic and environmental impact. There are also plans to use the ISS to examine aerosols, ozone, water vapour, and oxides in Earth's atmosphere, as well as cosmic rays, cosmic dust, antimatter, and dark matter in the universe.

One component assisting in these various studies is the ExPRESS Logistics Carrier (ELC). Developed by NASA, four of these units are set to be launched to the ISS. As currently envisioned, the ELCs will be delivered on two separate Space Shuttle missions. They will allow experiments to be deployed and conducted in the vacuum of space, and will provide the necessary electricity and computing to process experimental data locally. Delivery is currently scheduled for STS-129 in November 2009 and STS-133 in May 2010.

The Alpha Magnetic Spectrometer (AMS), a particle physics experiment, is also scheduled to be added to the station. This device will be launched on STS-134 in 2010, and will be mounted externally on the Integrated Truss Structure. The AMS will search for various types of unusual matter by measuring cosmic rays. The experiments conducted will help researchers study the formation of the universe, and search for evidence of dark matter and antimatter.

Origins

Originating during the Cold War, the International Space Station represents a union of several space station projects from various nations. During the early 1980s, NASA had planned to launch a modular space station called *Freedom* as a counterpart to the Soviet *Salyut* and *Mir* space stations. In addition, the Soviets were planning a replacement for *Mir* to be constructed during the 1990s called *Mir*-2. Due to budget and design constraints, however, *Freedom* never progressed past mock-ups and minor component tests.

With the fall of the Soviet Union ending the Cold War and Space Race, *Freedom* was nearly cancelled by the United States House of Representatives. The post-Soviet economic chaos in Russia also led to the eventual cancellation of *Mir*-2, with only the base block of that station, DOS-8, having been constructed. Similar difficulties were being faced by the U.S. and other nations with plans for space stations. This prompted U.S. administration officials to start negotiations with partners in Europe, Russia, Japan, and Canada in the early 1990s to begin a collaborative, multi-national, space station project.

In June 1992, then U.S. president George H.W. Bush and Russian president Boris Yeltsin agreed to cooperate on space exploration by signing the Agreement between the United States of America and the Russian Federation Concerning Cooperation in the Exploration and Use of Outer Space for Peaceful Purposes. This agreement called for setting up a short, joint space programme, during which one U.S. astronaut would board the Russian space station *Mir* and two Russian cosmonauts would board a space shuttle.

In September 1993, U.S. vice-president Al Gore and Russian Prime Minister Viktor Chernomyrdin announced plans for a new space station, which eventually became the International Space Station. They also agreed, in preparation for this new project, that the US would be heavily involved in the *Mir* programme in the years ahead, as part of an agreement that later included Space Shuttle orbiters docking with *Mir*.

The ISS programme was planned to combine the proposed space stations of all participating space agencies, including *Freedom*, *Mir*-2 (with DOS-8 later becoming *Zvezda*), ESA's *Columbus*, and the Japanese *Kibō* laboratory. When the first module, *Zarya*, was launched in 1998, the station was expected to be completed by 2003. Due to delays, however, the estimated completion date has been put back to 2011.

Space Station

Assembly and Structure

The assembly of the International Space Station, a major aerospace engineering endeavour, began in November 1998. As of May 2009 the station is 82.8 per cent complete.

The first segment of the ISS, *Zarya*, was launched into orbit on November 20, 1998 on a Russian Proton rocket, followed two weeks later by the first of three node modules, *Unity*, launched aboard STS-88. This bare 2-module core of the ISS remained unmanned for the next one and a half years until the Russian module *Zvezda* was added in July 2000, allowing a maximum crew of three people to occupy the ISS continuously. The first resident crew, Expedition 1, was sent later that year in November. The year 2000 also saw the arrival of two segments of the station's Integrated Truss Structure, the Z1 and P6 trusses, providing the embryonic station with communications, guidance, electrical grounding (on Z1), and power via a pair of solar array wings, located on the P6 truss.

Over the next two years the station continued to expand with a Soyuz-U rocket delivering the *Pirs* docking compartment. Space Shuttles *Discovery, Atlantis,* and *Endeavour* delivered the *Destiny* laboratory and *Quest* airlock to orbit, in addition to the station's robot arm *Canadarm2,* and several more segments of the truss structure.

The expansion schedule was brought to an abrupt halt, however, following the destruction of the Space Shuttle *Columbia* on STS-107 in 2003. The resulting hiatus in the Space Shuttle programme halted station assembly until the launch of *Discovery* on STS-114 in 2005.

The official return to assembly was marked by the arrival of *Atlantis,* flying STS-115, delivering the station's second set of solar arrays. These were later followed by several more truss segments and a third set of arrays on STS-116, STS-117, and STS-118. This major expansion of the station's power generating capabilities meant that more pressurised modules could be accommodated, and as a result the *Harmony* node and *Columbus* European laboratory were added. These were followed shortly after by the first two components of *Kibō,* the Japanese Experiment Module. In March 2009, STS-119 marked the completion of the Integrated Truss Structure with the installation of the fourth and final set of solar arrays, whilst the final section of *Kibō* was delivered by *Endeavour* in July 2009 on STS-127.

As of July 2009, the station consisted of ten pressurised modules and the complete Integrated Truss Structure. Awaiting launch is the third and final American node, *Tranquility,* a Permanent Logistics Module, the European Robotic Arm, several Russian modules and the Alpha Magnetic Spectrometer (AMS). Assembly is expected to be completed by 2011, by which point the station will have a mass in excess of 400 metric tons (440 short tons).

Pressurised Modules

When completed, the ISS will consist of fourteen pressurised modules with a combined volume of around 1,000 m³. These modules include laboratories, docking compartments, airlocks, nodes and living quarters. Ten of these components are already in orbit, with the remaining four awaiting launch. Each module was or will be launched either by the Space Shuttle, Proton rocket or Soyuz rocket.

<table>
<tr><th>Module</th><th>Assembly mission</th><th>Launch date</th><th>Launch system</th><th>Nation</th></tr>
<tr><td rowspan="2">Zarya (FGB)</td><td>1A/R</td><td>November 20, 1998</td><td>Proton-K</td><td>Russia (Builder) US (Financier)</td></tr>
<tr><td colspan="4">The first component of the ISS to be launched, Zarya provided electrical power, storage, propulsion, and guidance during initial assembly. The module now serves as a storage compartment, both inside the pressurised section and in the externally mounted fuel tanks.</td></tr>
<tr><td rowspan="2">Unity (Node 1)</td><td>2A</td><td>December 4, 1998</td><td>Space Shuttle Endeavour, STS-88</td><td>US</td></tr>
<tr><td colspan="4">The first node module, connecting the American section of the station to the Russian section (via PMA-1), and providing berthing locations for the Z1 truss, Quest airlock, Destiny laboratory and Tranquility node.</td></tr>
</table>

Module	*Assembly mission*	*Launch date*	*Launch system*	*Nation*
Zvezda (Service Module)	1R	July 12, 2000	Proton-K	Russia
	The station's service module, which provides the main living quarters for resident crews, environmental systems and attitude and orbit control. The module also provides docking locations for Soyuz spacecraft, Progress spacecraft and the Automated Transfer Vehicle, and its addition rendered the ISS permanently habitable for the first time.			
Destiny (US Laboratory)	5A	February 7, 2001	Space Shuttle *Atlantis*, STS-98	US
	The primary research facility for US payloads aboard the ISS, *Destiny* is intended for general experiments. The module houses 24 International Standard Payload Racks, some of which are used for environmental systems and crew daily living equipment, and features a 51-centimetre (20 in) optically perfect window, the largest such window ever produced for use in space. *Destiny* also serves as the mounting point for most of the station's Integrated Truss Structure.			
Quest (Joint Airlock)	7A	July 12, 2001	Space Shuttle *Atlantis*, STS-104	US
	The primary airlock for the ISS, *Quest* hosts spacewalks with both US EMU and Russian Orlan spacesuits. *Quest* consists of two segments; the equipment lock, that stores spacesuits and equipment, and the crew lock, from which astronauts can exit into space.			
Pirs (Docking Compartment)	4R	September 14, 2001	Soyuz-U	Russia
	Pirs provides the ISS with additional docking ports for Soyuz and Progress spacecraft, and allows egress and ingress for spacewalks by cosmonauts using Russian Orlan spacesuits, in addition to providing storage space for these spacesuits.			
Harmony (Node 2)	10A	October 23, 2007	Space Shuttle *Discovery*, STS-120	Europe (Builder) US (Financier)
	The second of the station's node modules, *Harmony* is the utility hub of the ISS. The module contains four racks that provide electrical power, bus electronic data, and acts as a central connecting point for several other components via its six Common Berthing Mechanisms (CBMs). The European *Columbus* and Japanese *Kibō* laboratories are permanently berthed to the module, and US Space Shuttle Orbiters dock to the ISS via PMA-2, attached to *Harmony*'s forward port. In addition, the module serves as a berthing port for the Multi-Purpose Logistics Modules during shuttle logistics flights.			
Columbus (European Laboratory)	1E	February 7, 2008	Space Shuttle *Atlantis*, STS-122	Europe
	The primary research facility for European payloads aboard the ISS, *Columbus* provides a generic laboratory as well as facilities specifically designed for biology, biomedical research and fluid physics. Several mounting locations are affixed to the exterior of the module, which provide power and data to external experiments such as the European Technology Exposure Facility (EuTEF), Solar Monitoring Observatory, Materials International Space Station Experiment, and Atomic Clock Ensemble in Space. A number of expansions are planned for the module to study quantum physics and cosmology.			
Experiment Logistics Module (JEM—ELM)	1J/A	March 11, 2008	Space Shuttle *Endeavour*, STS-123	Japan
	Part of the *Kibō* Japanese Experiment Module laboratory, the ELM provides storage and transportation facilities to the laboratory, with a pressurised section to serve internal payloads and an unpressurised section to serve external payloads.			
Japanese Pressurised Module (JEM—PM)	1J	May 31, 2008	Space Shuttle *Discovery*, STS-124	Japan
	Part of the *Kibō* Japanese Experiment Module laboratory, the PM is the core module of *Kibō* to which the ELM and Exposed Facility are berthed. The laboratory is the largest single ISS module and contains a total of 23 racks, including 10 experiment racks. The module is used to carry out research in space medicine, biology, Earth observations, materials production, biotechnology, and communications research. The PM also serves as the mounting location for an external platform, the Exposed Facility (EF), that allows payloads to be directly exposed to the harsh space environment. The EF is serviced by the module's own robotic arm, the JEM—RMS, which is also mounted on the PM.			

<table>
<tr><th>Module</th><th>Assembly mission</th><th>Launch date</th><th>Launch system</th><th>Nation</th></tr>
<tr><td rowspan="2">Mini-Research Module 2</td><td>5R</td><td>November 10, 2009</td><td>Soyuz-FG</td><td>Russia</td></tr>
<tr><td colspan="4">One of the Russian ISS components, MRM2 will be used for docking of Soyuz and Progress ships, as an airlock for spacewalks and as an interface for scientific experiments.</td></tr>
<tr><td rowspan="2">Tranquility (Node 3)</td><td>20A</td><td>February 2010</td><td>Space Shuttle Endeavour, STS-130</td><td>Europe (Builder) US (Financier)</td></tr>
<tr><td colspan="4">The third and last of the station's US nodes, Tranquility will contain an advanced life support system to recycle waste water for crew use and generate oxygen for the crew to breathe. The node also provides four berthing locations for more attached pressurised modules or crew transportation vehicles, in addition to the permanent berthing location for the station's Cupola.</td></tr>
<tr><td rowspan="2">Cupola</td><td>20A</td><td>February 2010</td><td>Space Shuttle Endeavour, STS-130</td><td>Europe (Builder) US (Financier)</td></tr>
<tr><td colspan="4">The Cupola is an observatory module that will provide ISS crew members with a direct view of robotic operations and docked spacecraft, as well as an observation point for watching the Earth. The module will come equipped with robotic workstations for operating the SSRMS and shutters to prevent its windows from being damaged by micrometeorites.</td></tr>
<tr><td rowspan="2">Mini-Research Module 1</td><td>ULF4</td><td>May 2010</td><td>Space Shuttle Atlantis, STS-132</td><td>Russia</td></tr>
<tr><td colspan="4">MRM1 will be used for docking and cargo storage aboard the station.</td></tr>
<tr><td rowspan="2">Multipurpose Laboratory Module</td><td>3R</td><td>December 2011</td><td>Proton-M</td><td>Russia</td></tr>
<tr><td colspan="4">The MLM will be Russia's primary research module as part of the ISS and will be used for general microgravity experiments, docking, and cargo logistics. The module provides a crew work and rest area, and will be equipped with a backup attitude control system that can be used to control the station's attitude.</td></tr>
</table>

Cancelled Modules

Several planned pressurised modules have been cancelled, including the Centrifuge Accommodations Module, for producing varying levels of artificial gravity, the Habitation Module, which was to serve as the station's living quarters (sleep stations are now spread throughout the station), and several Russian modules, including two Russian Research Modules, planned to be used for general experimentation.

Power Supply

The source of electrical power for the ISS is the Sun. Light is converted into electricity through the use of solar arrays. Before assembly flight 4A (space shuttle mission STS-97, launched November 30, 2000) the only power sources were the Russian solar panels attached to the *Zarya* and *Zvezda* modules. The Russian segment of the station uses 28 volts DC, as does the space shuttle. In the remainder of the station, electricity is provided by the solar arrays attached to the truss at a voltage ranging from 130 to 180 volts DC. These arrays are arranged as four pairs of wings, and each pair is capable of generating nearly 32.8 kW of DC power.

Power is stabilised and distributed at 160 volts DC before being converted to the user-required 124 volts DC. This high-voltage distribution line allows for smaller power lines, thus reducing weight. Power can be shared between the two segments of the station using converters. This feature has become essential since the cancellation of the Russian Science Power Platform because the Russian segment now depends on the US-built solar arrays for power.

The solar arrays normally track the Sun to maximise the amount of solar power. Each array is about 375 m² (450 yd²) in area and 58 metres (190 ft) long. In the complete configuration, the solar arrays track the sun in each orbit by rotating the *alpha gimbal*, while the *beta gimbal* adjusts for the angle of the sun from the orbital plane. Until the main truss structure arrived, the arrays were in a temporary position perpendicular to the final orientation. In this configuration, as shown in the image to the right, the beta gimbal was used for the main solar tracking. Another tracking option, the Night Glider mode, can be used to reduce the effects of drag produced by the tenuous upper atmosphere, through which the station flies, by orienting the solar arrays edgewise to the velocity vector.

Attitude Control

The attitude (orientation) of the station is maintained by either of two mechanisms. Normally, a system using several control moment gyroscopes (CMGs) keeps the station oriented with *Destiny* forward of *Unity*, the P truss on the port side, and *Pirs* on the earth-facing (nadir) side. When the CMG system becomes saturated—a situation whereby a CMG exceeds its operational range or cannot track a series of rapid movements—it can lose its ability to control station attitude. In this event, the Russian attitude control system is designed to take over automatically, using thrusters to maintain station attitude, allowing the CMG system to desaturate. This scenario has only occurred once, during Expedition 10. When a space shuttle is docked to the station, it can also be used to maintain station attitude. This procedure was used during STS-117 as the S3/S4 truss was being installed.

Altitude Control

The ISS is maintained at an orbit from a minimum altitude of 278 km (173 mi) to a maximum of 460 km (286 mi). The normal maximum limit is 425 km (264 mi) to allow Soyuz rendezvous missions. As the ISS constantly loses altitude because of slight atmospheric drag, it needs to be boosted to a higher altitude several times each year. These effects vary from day to day, however, because of changes in the density of the outer atmosphere caused by changes in solar activity. This reboost can be performed by the station's two main engines on the *Zvezda* service module, a docked space shuttle, a Progress resupply vessel, or by ESA's ATV. It takes approximately two orbits (three hours) to be boosted several kilometres higher. In December 2008 NASA signed an agreement with the Ad Astra Rocket Company which may result in the testing on the ISS of a VASIMR plasma propulsion engine. This technology could, in the future, allow station-keeping to be done much more economically than at present.

Microgravity

At the station's orbital altitude, the gravity from the Earth is 88 per cent of that at sea level. The state of weightlessness is caused by the constant free fall of the ISS. Due to the equivalence principle, free fall is indiscernible from a state of zero gravity, however the environment on the station is instead often described as microgravity, as it is imperfect due to four effects:

- The drag resulting from the residual atmosphere.
- Vibratory acceleration caused by mechanical systems and the crew on board the ISS.
- Orbital corrections by the on-board gyroscopes (or thrusters).
- The spatial separation from the real centre of mass of the ISS—any part of the ISS not at the exact centre of mass will tend to follow its own orbit. However, as each point is physically part of the station, this is impossible, and so each component is subject to small accelerations from the forces which keep them attached to the station as it orbits. This is also called the tidal force.

Life Support

The ISS Environmental Control and Life Support System (ECLSS) provides or controls elements such as atmospheric pressure, fire detection and suppression, oxygen levels, and water supply. The highest priority for the ECLSS is the ISS atmosphere, but the system also collects, processes, and stores waste and water produced and used by the crew. This process includes recycling fluid from the sink, shower, toilet, and condensation from the air. The *Elektron* system aboard *Zvezda* and a similar oxygen generation system in *Destiny* generate oxygen aboard the station. If required, the crew has a backup option in the form of bottled oxygen and Solid Fuel Oxygen Generation (SFOG) canisters. Carbon dioxide is removed from the air by the *Vozdukh* system in *Zvezda*. Other by-products of human metabolism, such as methane from the intestines and ammonia from sweat, are removed by activated charcoal filters.

The atmosphere on board the ISS is maintained to have a composition similar to that of the Earth's atmosphere. Normal air pressure on the ISS is 101.3 kPa (14.7 psi), the same as at sea level on Earth. Whilst this type of atmosphere offers various benefits for crew comfort, an Earthlike atmosphere is also much safer than the alternative, a pure oxygen atmosphere, due to the increased risk of fire, responsible for the deaths of the Apollo 1 crew.

Sightings

Because of the size of the International Space Station (about that of an American football field) and the large reflective area offered by its solar panels, ground based observation of the station is possible with the naked eye if the observer is in the right location at the right time—in many cases, the station is one of the brightest naked-eye objects in the sky, although it is visible only for brief periods of time, ranging from two to five minutes.

In order to view the station, the following conditions need to be fulfilled, assuming the weather is clear: The station must be above the observer's horizon, and it must pass within about 2000 km of the observing site (the closer the better); it must be dark enough at the observer's location for stars to be visible; and the station must be in sunlight rather than in the Earth's shadow. It is common for the third condition to begin or end during what would otherwise be a good viewing opportunity. In the evening, this will cause the station to suddenly fade and disappear as it moves further from the dusk, going from west to east. In the reverse situation, it may suddenly appear in the sky as it approaches the dawn.

The station has now become bright enough to be seen during the day under certain conditions.

Politics and Financing

As a multinational project, the legal and financial aspects of the ISS are complex. Issues of concern include the ownership of modules, station utilisation by participating nations, and responsibilities for station resupply. The main legal document establishing obligations and rights between the ISS partners is the Space Station Intergovernmental Agreement (IGA). This international treaty was signed on January 28, 1998 by the primary nations involved in the Space Station project: the United States, Russia, Japan, Canada and ten Member States of the European Space Agency (Belgium, Denmark, France, Germany, Italy, The Netherlands, Norway, Spain, Sweden, Switzerland). This set the stage for a second layer of agreements, called Memoranda of Understanding (MOU), between NASA and ESA, CSA, RKA and JAXA. These agreements are then further split, such as for the contractual obligations between nations, and trading of partners' rights and obligations. Use of the Russian Orbital Segment is also negotiated at this level.

Hardware allocation within the other sections of the station has been assigned as follows:

- *Columbus*: 51 per cent for ESA, 46.7 per cent for NASA and 2.3 per cent for CSA.
- *Kibō*: 51 per cent for JAXA, 46.7 per cent for NASA and 2.3 per cent for CSA.
- *Destiny*: 97.7 per cent for NASA and 2.3 per cent for CSA.
- Crew time, electrical power and rights to purchase supporting services (such as data upload and download and communications) are divided 76.6 per cent for NASA, 12.8 per cent for JAXA, 8.3 per cent for ESA, and 2.3 per cent for CSA.

In addition to these main intergovernmental agreements, Brazil has a contract with NASA to supply hardware. In return, NASA will fly one Brazilian to the station during the ISS programme. Italy also has a separate contract with NASA to provide similar services, although Italy also takes part in the Programmeme directly via its membership in the ESA.

The most cited figure of an overall cost estimate for the ISS ranges from 35 billion to 100 billion USD. ESA, the only agency actually stating potential overall costs, estimates €100 billion for the entire station over a period of 30 years. Giving a precise cost estimate for the ISS is not straightforward, as it is difficult to determine which costs should actually be attributed to the ISS programme, or how the Russian contribution should be measured.

Criticism

The International Space Station has been the target of varied criticism over the years. Critics contend that the time and money spent on the ISS could be better spent on other projects—whether they be robotic spacecraft missions, space exploration, investigations of problems here on Earth, or just tax savings. Some critics, such as Robert L. Park, argue that very little scientific research was convincingly planned for the ISS in the first place, and that the primary feature of a space-based laboratory, its microgravity environment, can be studied less expensively with a "vomit comet".

The research capabilities of the ISS have been criticised, particularly following the cancellation of the ambitious Centrifuge Accommodations Module, which, alongside other equipment cancellations, means research done on the ISS is generally limited to experiments which do not require any specialized apparatus. For example, in the first half of 2007, ISS research dealt primarily with human biological responses to being in space, covering topics like kidney stones, circadian rhythm, and the effects of cosmic rays on the nervous system. Other criticisms hinge on the technical design of the ISS, including the necessity for a high level of maintenance to be carried out by the crew, particularly via risky EVAs, and the high inclination of the station's orbit, which leads to a higher cost for US-based launches to the station.

In response to some of these comments, advocates of manned space exploration say that criticism of the ISS project is short-sighted, and that manned space research and exploration have produced billions of dollars' worth of tangible benefits to people on Earth. It has been estimated that the indirect economic return from spin-offs of human space exploration has been many times the initial public investment. However, a review of the claims by the Federation of American Scientists argued that NASA's rate of return from spin-offs is actually very low, except for aeronautics work that has led to aircraft sales.

End of Mission/Deorbit Plans

A report in late May 2009 stated that RKK Energia has been asked to look at ways to remove the Russian modules from the station when the end of mission is reached sometime between 2015 and 2020, and use them as a basis for a new station, known as the Orbital Piloted Assembly and Experiment Complex. NASA has responsibility for de-orbit and is said to intend this around 2020. As the Russian modules have the motors that would be used for controlled de-orbit, this poses a potential issue if Russia takes that capability to a new, on-going station. Other options include using a European Automated Transfer Vehicle. One option stated for an ongoing station is for Russia to build a ball-shaped, six-port module to which existing modules could be attached. Later modules would also be launched to provide a Russian outpost for later missions to the Moon and Mars. The report quotes an unnamed Russian engineer stated that experience from *Mir* indicates that, except for micrometeorite damage, a thirty year life should be possible, given that the Russian modules have been built with on-orbit refurbishment in mind.

According to a Washington Post article published in July of 2009, NASA plans to de-orbit the space station in the first quarter of 2016 (presumably with the prior consent of the other ISS partners). However, the newly appointed NASA administrator, Charles Bolden Jr. has stated in a recent article that he plans to extend the lifetime of the International Space Station beyond 2016, the year in which the Bush administration proposed to abandon it.

Life on Board

Expeditions

Each permanent station crew is given a sequential Expedition number: *Expedition 1*, *Expedition 2*, and so on. Expeditions have an average duration of half a year, and they commence following the official handover of the station from one Expedition commander to another. Expeditions 1 through 6 consisted of three person crews, but the *Columbia* accident led to a reduction to two crew members from Expeditions 7 to 12. Expedition 13 saw the restoration of the station crew to three, and the station has been permanently staffed as such since. Whilst only three crew members are permanently on the station, however, several expeditions, such as Expedition 16, have consisted of up to six individual astronauts or cosmonauts, with individuals being flown up and down to the station on various individual flights.

On May 27, 2009, the current expedition to ISS Expedition 20 began. Expedition 20 is the first ISS crew of six. Before the expansion of the living volume and capabilities from STS-115 the station could only host a crew of three. Expedition 20's crew was lifted to the station in two separate Soyuz-TMA flights launched at two different times (each Soyuz-TMA can hold only three people): Soyuz TMA-14 on March 26, 2009 and Soyuz TMA-15 on May 27, 2009. However, the station will not be permanently occupied by six crew members during all 52 weeks of the year. For example, when the Expedition 20 crew (Roman Romanenko, Frank De Winne and Bob Thirsk) returns to Earth in November 2009, for a period of about two weeks only two crew members (Jeff Williams and Max Surayev) will be aboard. This will increase to five in early December, when another Soyuz, carrying Oleg Kotov, Timothy Creamer and Soichi Noguchi arrives. It will then decrease to three when Williams and Surayev depart in March 2010, returning to six in April 2010 with the launch of the next three-person Soyuz.

The International Space Station is the most-visited spacecraft in the history of space flight. As of 17 November 2008, it has had 213 non-distinct visitors comprising 167 individual people. *Mir* had 137 non-distinct visitors.

Crew Schedule

The time zone used on board the ISS is Coordinated Universal Time (UTC, sometimes informally called GMT). The windows are covered at night hours to give the impression of darkness because the station experiences 16 sunrises and sunsets a day. During visiting space shuttle missions, the ISS crew will mostly follow the shuttle's Mission Elapsed Time (MET), which is a flexible time zone based on the launch time of the shuttle mission. Because the sleeping periods between the UTC time zone and the MET usually differ, the ISS crew often has to adjust its sleeping pattern before the space shuttle arrives and after it leaves to shift from one time zone to the other in a practice known as sleep shifting.

A typical day for the crew begins with a wake-up at 06:00, followed by post-sleep activities and a morning inspection of the station. The crew then eats breakfast and takes part in a daily planning conference with Mission Control on the ground before starting work at around 08:10. The first scheduled exercise of the day follows, after which the crew continues work until 13:05. Following a one-hour lunch break, the afternoon consists of more exercise and work before the crew carries out its pre-sleep activities beginning at 19:30, including dinner and a crew conference. The scheduled sleep period begins at 21:30, when the daily schedule is complete. In general, the crew works 10 hours per day on a weekday, and 5 hours on Saturdays, with the rest of the time being their own for relaxation, games or work catch-up.

Station Operations

Mission Control Centres

As an international project, the various components of the ISS are operated and monitored by their respective space agencies at various control centres across the globe, including:

- NASA's Mission Control Center at Lyndon B. Johnson Space Center in Houston, Texas, serves as the primary control facility for the US segment of the ISS and also controls the various Space Shuttle missions that visit the station.
- NASA's Payload Operations and Integration Center at Marshall Space Flight Center in Huntsville, Alabama, serves as the centre that coordinates all payload operations in the US Segment.
- Roskosmos's TsUP at Korolyov, Moscow, controls the Russian Orbital Segment of the ISS, in addition to individual Soyuz and Progress missions.
- ESA's Columbus Control Centre at the German Aerospace Centre (DLR) in Oberpfaffenhofen, Germany, controls the European *Columbus* research laboratory.
- ESA's ATV Control Centre, at the Toulouse Space Centre (CST) in Toulouse, France, controls flights of the unmanned European Automated Transfer Vehicle.
- JAXA's JEM Control Centre and HTV Control Centre at Tsukuba Space Centre (TKSC) in Tsukuba, Japan, are responsible for operating the Japanese Experiment Module complex and all flights of the unmanned Japanese H-II Transfer Vehicle respectively.
- CSA's MSS Control at Saint-Hubert, Quebec, Canada, controls and monitors the Mobile Servicing System, or Canadarm2.

Visiting Spacecraft

Spacecraft from three different space agencies visit the International Space Station, serving a variety of purposes. The Automated Transfer Vehicle from the European Space Agency has provided resupply services to the station. Also serving the station in this capacity is the Russian Roskosmos Progress spacecraft. In addition, Russia also supplies a Soyuz spacecraft used for crew rotation and emergency evacuation which is replaced every six months. Finally, the United States services the ISS through its Space Shuttle Programme. Space shuttle missions provide resupply missions, assembly and logistics flights, and crew rotation. As of 10 June 2009, there have been 19 Soyuz, 33 Progress, 1 ATV and 28 Space Shuttle flights to the station. Expeditions require, on average, 2,722 kg of supplies, and as of 28 March 2009, crews had consumed a total of 19,000 meals. Soyuz crew rotation flights and Progress resupply flights visit the station on average twice three times annually respectively, with the ATV planned to visit annually from 2010 onwards.

As of 29 July 2009, there are three spacecraft docked with the ISS:

- Soyuz TMA-14 is at the *Pirs* Docking Compartment's nadir port. The spacecraft has brought two members of Expedition 19/20, Russian Commander Gennady Padalka and American Flight Engineer Michael R. Barrat' to the station, in addition to Spaceflight Participant Charles Simonyi.
- Soyuz TMA-15 is at *Zarya*'s nadir docking port. The spacecraft brought three members of Expedition 20, Commander Roman Romanenko and Flight Engineers Frank De Winne and Robert Thirsk, who became the first Canadian to fly aboard a Soyuz spacecraft.
- Progress M-67 is at the *Zvezda* Service Module's aft docking port.

Throughout the remainder of the station's operating life, a variety of spacecraft, operated by various ISS Programme members, are scheduled to service it. Currently under construction and planned for operation in 2009 is the Japanese H-II Transfer Vehicle (HTV), which is intended as a resupply vehicle for the JAXA *Kibō* modules. Still in initial funding stages is the Russian Kliper spacecraft, which, if it comes to fruition in 2012 as planned, is intended as a replacement of the Soyuz spacecraft. Being currently designed is the American Orion spacecraft, intended to serve as another resupply spacecraft and provide crew rotation. In hopes of bridging the gap between the Space Shuttle and Orion, NASA has started the Commercial Orbital Transportation Services Programme to develop commercial spacecraft services dedicated to the station.

Other Projects

- Japanese scientists and origami masters propose to launch a flotilla of paper planes from the ISS. Around 30 planes will make the descent, each gliding downward over what is expected to be the course of several months. If one of the planes survives to Earth, it will have made the longest flight ever by a paper plane, traversing some 400 km (250 mi), and will have demonstrated the feasibility of slow-speed, low-friction atmospheric reentry. A prototype of the origami aeroplane passed a durability test in a wind tunnel in March 2008, and Japan's space agency adopted it for feasibility studies.

- During an EVA during Expedition 14, a special golf ball equipped with a tracking device was hit from the station and sent into its own low Earth orbit. The stunt was paid for by Canadian golf equipment manufacturer Element 21.
- As of April 2009, six space tourists have visited the ISS, each paying around US$25 million. The tourists, or spaceflight participants, were launched and returned via Russian crew rotation missions on Soyuz spacecraft.
- The ISS was the location of the first space wedding, during which Russian cosmonaut Yuri Malenchenko, flying Expedition 7, married Ekaterina Dmitrieva, who was in Texas at the time.

SPACEPORT

A **spaceport**, **astrodrome** or **cosmodrome** is a site for launching (or receiving) spacecraft, by analogy with seaport for ships or airport for aircraft. The word *spaceport*, and even more so *cosmodrome*, has traditionally been used for sites capable of launching spacecraft into orbit around Earth or on interplanetary trajectories. However, rocket launch sites for purely sub-orbital flights are sometimes called spaceports. In recent years new and proposed sites for suborbital human flights have commonly been named spaceports. Space stations are sometimes called spaceports, in particular if intended as a base for further journeys.

The term **rocket launch site** is used for any facility from which rockets are launched. It may contain one or more launch pads or suitable sites to mount a transportable launch pad. It is surrounded with large safety area named **rocket range** or **missile range**. The range includes the area over which launched rockets are expected to fly, and within which some components of the rockets may land. Tracking stations, vessels, and aircraft are often located in the range to assess the progress of the launches.

Major spaceports often include more than one **launch complex**, which can be well-separated (for safety reasons) rocket launch sites adapted for different types of launch vehicles. For launch vehicles with liquid propellant, suitable storage facilities and, in some cases, production facilities are necessary. On-site processing facilities for solid propellants are also common.

A spaceport can also include runways for takeoff and landing of spacecraft equipped with wings.

History

The first rockets to reach space were V-2 rockets launched from Peenemünde in Germany during World War II. When launched vertically they could reach more than 200 km altitude. However, most V-2 rockets reached much lower altitudes on military sorties.

The world's first spaceport for orbital and human launches, the Baikonur Cosmodrome in Kazakhstan, started as a Soviet military rocket range in 1955. It achieved the first orbital flight (Sputnik 1) in October 1957. The exact location of the cosmodrome was intially held secret. Guesses to its location were misdirected by a name in common with a mining town 320 km away. The position became known outside the Soviet Union only after U-2 planes had identified the site by following railway lines in Kazakhstan.

The Baikonur Cosmodrome achieved the first launch of a human into space (Yuri Gagarin) in 1961. The launch complex used, Site 1, has reached a special symbolic significance and is commonly called Gagarin's Start. Baikonur was the primary Soviet cosmodrome, and is still widely used by Russia under a lease arrangement with Kazakhstan.

In response to the early Soviet successes, the United States built up a major spaceport complex at Cape Canaveral in Florida. A large number of unmanned flights, as well as the early human flights, were carried out at Cape Canaveral Air Force Station. For the Apollo programme, an adjacent spaceport, Kennedy Space Center, was constructed, and achieved the first manned mission to the lunar surface (Apollo 11) in July 1969. It has been the base for all Space Shuttle launches and most of their runway landings.

The Guiana Space Centre in Kourou, French Guiana, is the major European spaceport, with satellite launches that benefit from the location 4 degrees north of the equator.

In October 2003 the Jiuquan Satellite Launch Center achieved the first Chinese human spaceflight.

Breaking with tradition, in June 2004 on a runway at Mojave Spaceport, California, a human was for the first time launched to space in a privately funded, suborbital spaceflight, that was intended to pave the way for future commercial spaceflights. The spacecraft, SpaceShipOne, was launched by a carrier airplane taking off horizontally.

Placement Considerations

Rockets can most easily reach satellite orbits if launched near the equator in an easterly direction, as this maximizes use of the Earth's rotational speed (465 m/s). Such launches also give a good orientation for arriving at a geostationary orbit. For polar orbits and Molniya orbits this does not apply.

Altitude of the launch site is not a driving factor because most of the delta-v for a satellite launch is spent on achieving the required horizontal orbital speed. The small gains from a few kilometres of extra altitude at the start does not usually off-set the ground transport problems in mountainous terrain.

Many spaceports have been placed at existing military installations, such as intercontinental ballistic missile ranges, which is not always ideal for satellite launches.

A rocket launch site is built as far as possible away from major population centres in order to mitigate risk to bystanders should a rocket experience a catastrophic failure. In many cases a launch site is built close to major bodies of water to ensure that no components are shed over populated areas. Typically a spaceport site is large enough that, should a vehicle explode, it will not endanger human lives or adjacent launch pads.

Planned sites of spaceports for sub-orbital tourist spaceflight often make use of existing ground infrastructure, including runways. The nature of the local view from 100 km altitude is also a factor to consider.

Space Tourism

The space tourism industry is being targeted by spaceports in numerous locations worldwide. The establishment of spaceports for tourist trips raises legal issues, which are only beginning to be addressed. In particular, the transition between airspace legislation and spaceflight legislation need to be clear, and such that space tourism is not unduly disadvantaged.

Spaceports with Achieved Launches of Humans

The following is a table of spaceports and launch complexes with a documented achieved launch of humans to space (more than 100 km altitude). Spaceports that have only achieved human sub-orbital flights are listed at the end. Otherwise the sorting order is spaceport by spaceport according to the time of the first human launch.

Spaceport	*Launch complex*	*Launcher*	*Spacecraft*	*Flights*	*Years*
Baikonur Cosmodrome, Kazakhstan	Site 1	Vostok (rocket)	Vostok 1-6	6 Orbital	1961-63
	Site 1	Voskhod (rocket)	Voskhod 1-2	2 Orbital	1964-65
	Site 1, Site 31	Soyuz (rocket)	Soyuz 1-TMA15	100 Orbital	1967-
Cape Canaveral Air Force Station, USA	LC5	Redstone	Mercury 3-4	2 Sub-O	1961
	LC14	Atlas	Mercury 6-9	4 Orbital	1962-63
	LC19	Titan II	Gemini 3-12	10 Orbital	1965-66
	LC34	Saturn IB	Apollo 7	1 Orbital	1968
Kennedy Space Center, USA	LC39	Saturn V	Apollo 8-17	10 Lun/Or	1968-70
	LC39	Saturn IB	Skylab 2-4	3 Orbital	1973-74
	LC39	Saturn IB	Apollo-Soyuz	1 Orbital	1975
	LC39	STS 1-127	Space Shuttle	126 Orbital	1981-
Jiuquan Satellite Launch Center, China	SLS	Long March 2F	Shenzhou 5-7	3 Orbital	2003-
Edwards Air Force Base, USA	Runway	B52	X-15 90-91	2 Sub-O	1963
Mojave Spaceport, USA	Runway	White Knight	SpaceShipOne 15-17	3 Sub-O	2004

Spaceports with Achieved Satellite Launches

The following is a table of spaceports with a documented achieved launch to orbit. The table is sorted according to the time of the first launch that achieved satellite orbit insertion. The first column gives the geographical location. Operations from a different country are indicated in the last column. A launch is counted as one also in cases where the payload consists of multiple satellites.

Spaceport	*Years (orbital)*	*Launches to orbit or inter-planetary*	*Launch vehicles (operators)*
Baikonur Cosmodrome, Baikonur/ Tyuratam, Kazakhstan	1957-	>1000	R-7/Soyuz, Kosmos, Proton, Zenit, Energia
Cape Canaveral Air Force Station, Florida, USA	1958-	>400	Delta, Scout, Atlas, Titan, Saturn, Athena
Vandenberg Air Force Base, California, USA	1959-	>500	Delta, Scout, Atlas, Titan, Taurus, Athena
Kapustin Yar Cosmodrome, Astrakhan Oblast, Russia	1962-	>100	Kosmos
Hammaguira French Special Weapons Test Centre, Hammaguir, Algeria	1965-1967	4	Diamant A (France)
Plesetsk Cosmodrome, Arkhangelsk Oblast, Russia	1966-	>1000	Soyuz, Kosmos
San Marco platform, Broglio Space Centre, Malindi, Kenya	1967-1988	9	Scout (ASI and Sapienza, Italy)
Kennedy Space Center, Florida, USA	1967-	143	17 Saturn, 126 Space Shuttle
Uchinoura Space Center (Kagoshima), Japan	1970-2006	27	Mu
Guiana Space Centre, Kourou, French Guiana	1970-	>180	7 Diamant, Ariane (CNES, ESA)
Jiuquan Satellite Launch Center, China	1970-	>30	Long March
Woomera Launch Area 5, Woomera Prohibited Area, South Australia	1971	1	Black Arrow
Satish Dhawan Space Centre (Sriharikota), Andhra Pradesh, India	1980-	23	3 SLV, 2 ASLV, 14 PSLV, 4 GSLV
Xichang Satellite Launch Center, China	1984-	>40	Long March
Tanegashima Space Center, Japan	1986-	28	9 H-I, 5 H-II, 14 H-IIA
Palmachim Air Force Base, Israel	1988-	5	Shavit
Various airport runways	1990-	37	Pegasus (Orbital Sciences Corporation)
Svobodny Cosmodrome, Amur Oblast, Russia	1997	5	Start-1
Delta class submarine, Barents Sea	1998-	2	Shtil' (Russia)
Ocean Odyssey mobile platform, Pacific Ocean	1999-2009	28	Zenit-3SL (Sea Launch)
Kodiak Launch Complex, Alaska, USA	2001-	1	Athena
Yasny Cosmodrome (Dombarovsky), Orenburg Oblast, Russia	2006-	3	Dnepr-1
Mid-Atlantic Regional Spaceport (MARS), Virginia, USA	2006-	3	Minotaur I
Taiyuan Satellite Launch Center, China	2007-	4	Long March
Omelek, Marshall Islands	2008-	1	Falcon 1
Semnan, Iran	2009-	1	Safir

The U.S. White Sands Missile Range has had over 7,000 high altitude and sub-orbital flights since 1946 when it sent its first rocket into space. White Sands launches military and civilian flights and serves as an alternate landing site for the space shuttle.

MOJAVE AIR AND SPACEPORT

The **Mojave Air and Space Port** (IATA: **MHV**, ICAO: **KMHV**), also known as the **Civilian Aerospace Test Center**, is located in Mojave, California, at an elevation of 2,791 feet (851 m). It is the first facility to be licensed in the United States for horizontal launches of reusable spacecraft, being certified as a spaceport by the Federal Aviation Administration on June 17, 2004.

Activities

Besides being a general-use public airport, Mojave has three main areas of activity: flight testing, space industry development, and aircraft heavy maintenance and storage.

Flight Testing

Flight testing activities have been centered at Mojave since the early 1970s, due to the lack of populated areas surrounding the airport. It is also favoured for this purpose due to its proximity to the Edwards Air Force Base, where the airspace is restricted from ground level to an unlimited height, and where there is a supersonic corridor. Mojave is also the home of the National Test Pilot School.

Space Industry Development

Beginning with the Rotary Rocket programme, Mojave became a focus for small companies seeking a place to develop space access technologies. Mojave Spaceport has been a test site for several teams in the Ansari X Prize, most notably SpaceShipOne, which conducted the first privately funded human sub-orbital flight on June 21, 2004. Other groups based at the Mojave Spaceport include XCOR Aerospace, Masten Space Systems, Orbital Sciences Corporation, and Interorbital Systems.

On December 6, 2007, the *Antelope Valley Press* reported that Mojave Spaceport was in danger of losing the "spaceport" designation by the end of 2007. The Federal Aviation Administration (FAA) gave notice to spaceport officials of its intention to suspend or revoke the space launch site operator's license on December 31. The FAA's actions are a result of concerns of the Office of Commercial Space Transportation regarding the storage and handling of the related chemicals and explosives at the airport.

Aircraft Heavy Maintenance and Storage

The Mojave airport is also known as a storage location for commercial airliners. Numerous large Boeing, McDonnell Douglas, Lockheed, and Airbus aircraft owned by major airlines are stored at Mojave. Some aircraft reach the end of their useful lifetime and are scrapped at the Mojave aircraft boneyard, while others are refurbished and returned to active service.

History

The Mojave Airport was first opened in 1935 as a small, rural airfield serving the local gold and silver mining industry.

In July 1942, the U.S. Marine Corps took over the field and vastly expanded it as the Marine Corps Auxiliary Air Station (MCAAS) Mojave. Many of the Corps' World War II aces received their gunnery training at Mojave. With the end of World War II, MCAAS was disestablished in 1946, and became instead a U.S. Navy airfield. At the end of 1953, the USMC reopened MCAAS Mojave as an auxiliary field to MCAS El Toro.

In 1961, after the USMC transferred operations to MCAS El Centro, Kern County obtained title to the airport. In February 1972, the East Kern Airport District was formed to administer the airport; EKAD maintains the airport to this day. To a great extent EKAD was the brainchild of Dan Sabovich who heavily lobbied the state for the airport district's creation and ran EKAD until 2002.

First Flights and Significant Events

- July 1, 1942—Construction begins on Marine Corps Auxiliary Air Station at Mojave
- July 31, 1944—USMC Capt. Edward Shaw, a decorated World War II ace, was killed while test-flying an F4U Corsair
- February 7, 1946—MCAAS disestablished
- December 31, 1953—MCAAS Mojave reestablished
- May 21, 1975—First flight of the Rutan VariEze
- June 30, 1978—First flight of the Rutan Defiant
- June 12, 1979—First flight of the prototype of the Rutan Long-EZ
- April 3, 1980—First prototype Bombardier Challenger 600 crashed in the Mojave desert, killing one of the pilots; flight test programme was operating from Mojave at the time
- September 25, 1981—National Test Pilot School opens
- August 23, 1983—First flight of the Boeing Skyfox
- August 29, 1983—First flight of Beech/Scaled Composites Model 115 Starship
- January 7, 1986—Voyager homecoming, after round-the-world record flight
- July 12, 1988—First flight of the Scaled Composites Triumph
- February 19, 1990—First flight of the Scaled Composites ARES
- July 26, 1998—First flight of the Scaled Composites Proteus
- March 1, 1999—Rollout of the Rotary Rocket Roton ATV
- July 28, 1999—First flight of the Roton ATV
- October 12, 1999—Third, final and longest flight of Roton ATV
- October 8, 2000—First firing of an XCOR Aerospace LOX-powered rocket engine
- July 21, 2001—First flight of the XCOR EZ-Rocket, flown by Dick Rutan (single-engine configuration)

- October 6, 2001—First flight of a twin engine rocket plane, again the XCOR EZ-rocket
- May 31, 2002—First flight of the Toyota TAA-1, built by Scaled Composites
- July 24, 2002—First touch-and-go of a rocket powered aircraft, the XCOR EZ-Rocket (world record)
- August 1, 2002—First flight of Scaled Composites White Knight
- September 18, 2002—First flight of world's largest jet engine, GE90-115B on GE's Boeing 747 testbed aircraft
- May 20, 2003—First captive flight, unmanned, of SpaceShipOne
- July 29, 2003—First manned captive flight of SpaceShipOne
- August 7, 2003—First free-flight of SpaceShipOne
- December 17, 2003—First powered flight of SpaceShipOne, on 100th anniversary of powered flight by the Wright Brothers
- March 5, 2004—First flight of the Virgin Atlantic GlobalFlyer
- June 17, 2004—Mojave designated a Spaceport by the FAA
- June 21, 2004—SpaceShipOne flight 15P, the first spaceflight of SpaceShipOne
- September 29, 2004—First Ansari X Prize flight of SpaceShipOne
- October 4, 2004—X-Prize-winning flight of SpaceShipOne
- June 21, 2005—First captive flight of Boeing X-37 under Scaled Composites White Knight
- December 3, 2005—First departure of a rocket-powered aircraft on a point-to-point flight (XCOR EZ-Rocket, departed MHV for California City, flown by Dick Rutan)
- December 15, 2005—First arrival of a rocket-powered aircraft on a flight originating at another airport (XCOR EZ-Rocket return flight from California City, piloted by Rick Searfoss)
- April 7, 2006—First free flight of Boeing X-37 (take-off from Mojave, landing at Edwards)
- January 23, 2007—First flight of the Lockheed CATBird
- July 26, 2007—Explosion with at least three fatalities at Scaled Composites facility
- January, 2008—Arrival of Gimli Glider for retirement
- December 21, 2008 — First flight of Scaled Composites WhiteKnightTwo

Civilian Aerospace Test Center Test Programmes

- Boeing X-37
- Eclipse 500 (crosswind landing data)
- General Electric CF34
- General Electric GE90
- Lockheed CATBird (post modification and systems flight test)
- Lockheed Martin F-22 Raptor (crosswind landing data)
- Lockheed Martin VH-71 Kestrel
- McDonnell Douglas MD-90-30

- Air Tractor 401 modified with an Orenda Aerospace OE600 engine (certification flight test programme)
- Rotary Rocket
- Scaled Composites White Knight and SpaceShipOne
- Sino Swearingen SJ30-2 (envelope expansion, flutter, stability & control, crosswind takeoffs & landings)
- Virgin Atlantic GlobalFlyer
- Adaptive Compliant Wing developed by FlexSys Inc flight tested on White Knight

World Records Set

- FAI Class C-1, unlimited weight
  - Group 1, internal combustion engine
    - Speed over a straight 15/25 km course: P-51 Mustang N5410V piloted by Frank Taylor, 832.12 km/h, July 30, 1983
  - Group 3, turbojet
    - Speed over Recognised Course: Mojave to Gander, Newfoundland, Canadair Challenger CL601 N601TG piloted by Aziz Ojjeh, 816.48 km/h July 24, 1984
  - Group 4, rocket engine
    - Altitude Gain, Airplane Launched from a Carrier Aircraft: 85,743 metres, SpaceShipOne piloted by Mike Melvill, June 21, 2004
    - Distance: 16 km, XCOR EZRocket piloted by Dick Rutan, December 3, 2005
- FAI Class C-1a, Landplanes: take off weight 300 to 500 kg
  - Group 1, internal combustion engine
    - Distance, Rutan VariEze piloted by Frank Hertzler, Mojave to Martinsburg, West Virginia, 3,563.02 km, July 15, 1984
    - Speed over 3 km course with restricted altitude: DR90 *Nemesis* piloted by Jon Sharp, 466.83 km/h, November 15, 1998 (aircraft now on display at the National Air & Space Museum)
    - Speed over straight 15/25 km course: DR90 *Nemesis* piloted by Jon Sharp, 454.77 km/h, October 31, 1998
- FAI Class C-1b, Landplanes: take off weight 500 to 1000 kg
  - Group 1, internal combustion engine
    - Distance over a closed course: Rutan Long-EZ N79RA piloted by Dick Rutan, 7,725.3 km, December 15, 1979
    - Speed over a closed circuit of 2,000 km without payload. Rutan Catbird N187RA piloted by Dick Rutan, 401.46 km/h, January 29, 1994
  - Group 4, Rocket engine
    - Distance: 16 km, XCOR EZRocket piloted by Dick Rutan, December 3, 2005
- FAI Class C-1c, Landplanes: take off weight 1000 to 1750 kg

    - Group 1, internal combustion engine
        - o Speed over a closed circuit of 2,000 km without payload. Rutan Catbird N187RA piloted by Mike Melvill, 413.78 km/h, March 2, 1994
- FAI Class C-1d, Landplanes: take off weight 1750 to 3000 kg
    - Group 1, internal combustion engine
        - o Distance over a closed course, *Voyager* N269VA, piloted by Dick Rutan and Jeana Yeager, Vandenburg, California to Mojave, 18,658.16 km, July 15, 1986
    - Group 4, rocket engine
        - o Altitude Gain, Airplane Launched from a Carrier Aircraft: 85,743 metres, SpaceShipOne piloted by Mike Melvill, June 21, 2004
- FAI Class C-1e, Landplanes: take off weight 3,000 to 6,000 kg
    - Group 2, turbojet
        - o Altitude: Scaled Composites Proteus N281PR, piloted by Mike Melvill and Robert Waldmiller, 19,277 m, October 25, 2000
        - o Altitude in horizontal flight: Scaled Composites Proteus N281PR, piloted by Mike Melvill and Robert Waldmiller, 19,015 m, October 25, 2000
        - o Altitude with 1,000 kg payload: Scaled Composites Proteus N281PR, piloted by Mike Melvill and Robert Waldmiller, 17,067 m, October 27, 2000

Notable Pilots and Engineers

- Brian Binnie
- Fitzhugh L. Fulton
- Mike Melvill
- Burt Rutan
- Dick Rutan
- Richard A. Searfoss
- Doug Shane
- Peter Siebold

Movie/Television Location Credits

Due to the Mojave Spaceport's unique location and facilities, a number of movies, TV shows and commercials have been filmed on location here. The Airport Administration actively promotes the facility as a set. The airport has facilities dedicated for filming, a large supply of aircraft to use as props and two large film pads that can be flooded for water scenes. Action movies and car commercials make up the bulk of the filming at the airport.

Movie credits include:

- *Die Hard 2*
- *Dragnet*
- *Executive Decision*
- *Flags of Our Fathers*
- *Flightplan*
- *Hot Shots*
- *MacArthur*
- *Mojave Magic: A Turtle's Eye View of SpaceShipOne*
- *Moving Violations*
- *The Rookie*
- *Spartan*
- *Speed* (specifically, the exploding airliner)
- *S.W.A.T.*
- *Thirteen Days*
- *The Tuskegee Airmen*
- *Waterworld*

TV Show credits include:

- *Alias*
- *Amazing Stories*
- *Airwolf*
- *Boom*
- *Fear Factor*
- *JAG*
- *Man vs. Beast*
- *MythBusters*
- *The Rebel Billionaire*
- *S Club 7*
- *Smash Lab*
- *The Stand*
- *Stunt Junkies*
- *24*
- *The Othersiders*

Other credits:

- *The Automatic*—Steve McQueen music video.
- *Berlin*—"Take My Breath Away" music video from the soundtrack of Top Gun.
- *Dr. Dre*—"(Ring Ding Dong)" music video from the soundtrack of Friday.

SINGAPORE SPACEPORT

Space Adventures has proposed a US$115 million spaceport to be located in Singapore, near Singapore Changi Airport. If built, this spaceport will service the Space Adventures Explorer suborbital tourist rocketplane and provide astronaut training facilities and a public education and interactive visitor centre.

As of 2009, no site has been selected and the project appears to be on hold.

Site Selection

Sites in Australia, the Bahamas, Florida, Japan, Malaysia, Nevada, New Mexico, Oklahoma, Singapore and Dubai in the United Arab Emirates were considered. After a year-long selection process, the sites in Singapore and Dubai were chosen. One key difference between the two proposed spaceports is that while the Dubai spaceport will be mainly a launchpad for sub-orbital space flights, the Singapore spaceport will have many more facilities.

Planned Facilities

The planned attractions in the Singapore Spaceport are far more numerous. They include:

- **Sub-orbital Space Flights** that will blast passengers out of Earth's atmosphere to an altitude of 100 km so they can enjoy about five minutes of weightlessness. An entire flight will take about 90 minutes. There will be a four-day training programme before the flight. The entire experience is estimated to cost US$102,000.
- **Parabolic Flights.** These flights at an estimated US$10,000 produce the experience of weightlessness in an aircraft without going into space.
- **Flights in the Aero L-39 Albatros**, a high-performance jet trainer aircraft.
- A **four-day space camp** for children.
- For adults, a **full-day astronaut experience** that will include a spin in a centrifuge to simulate a high-gravity environment, astronaut meals and a stint in a hypobaric (low-pressure) chamber to simulate performing repairs on damaged spacecraft in orbit.
- An authentic VIP **astronaut training facility** for the public that will provide many of the training elements used by professional astronauts. These include simulated spacewalks in neutral buoyancy tanks on the ground. Courses will be taught by actual astronauts and other space, flight, and training experts.
- An **Interactive Visitor Centre**, where the public can enjoy flight simulators and interactive exhibit experiences, or learn about the history and technology of space travel.

The entire complex will be spread over 17,000 m^2 of floor area on a 1.8 ha site. It is expected to generate about $3 billion in economic benefits over 10 years. It hopes to attract more than half-a-million visitors a year from the region within two-and-a-half years of opening.

The estimated minimum cost of US$115 million will be partially funded by the private sector, undisclosed Singapore sources, as well Space Adventures' global spaceport development partner, His Highness Sheikh Saud Bin Saqr Al Qasimi, Crown Prince of Ras Al-Khaimah in the United Arab Emirates.

The consortium supporting Spaceport Singapore includes Octtane Pte, Batey Pte Ltd., Lyon Capital Inc., DP Architects, ST Medical and KPMG Corporate Finance.

Quotes

- *"Singapore is one of the best-connected countries in the world. It is home to one of the world's busiest air and sea ports. Singapore, with its superior geographical and economic infrastructure, is primed to be the hub of a new, revolutionary form of travel—in space."*

  —Eric Anderson, President and CEO of Space Adventures
- *"Countries around the world are only just realizing the enormous commercial possibilities of space tourism. The market potential for suborbital spaceflights alone is estimated at $1 billion (USD) annually. We are excited at the prospect of launching an integrated facility here in Singapore that will give the world a whole new perspective to space tourism."*

  —Eric Anderson
- *"Space Adventures and the consortium have given Singapore a big vote of confidence as a choice tourism investment location. Pending the finalization of funds that are expected in the near future, we are optimistic that Spaceport Singapore will quickly become a reality. With the proposed Spaceport Singapore, we now stand at the threshold of an unprecedented opportunity to launch into space practically from our own backyard. In addition, the Spaceport's integrated training, educational and entertainment facilities will open up many exciting experiences for both locals and tourists."*

  —Lim Neo Chian, deputy chairman and Chief Executive of the STB
- *"This world-class center will provide a mix of commercial, educational and tourist attractions, giving everyone a reason to visit. We identified Singapore as an ideal location for a spaceport as it has the right combination of foresight, entrepreneurialism and technological sophistication to support a project such as this."*

  —Michael Lyon, Managing Director of the Spaceport Singapore Project
- *"The commercial possibilities of space tourism are enormous. We are tremendously excited about working with Singapore on this innovative project that will bring space tourism to the public."*

  —Nick Marrett, founder of Octtane Pte, a member of the consortium

SPACEPORT AMERICA

Spaceport America (formerly named **Southwest Regional Spaceport**) is the "first purpose-built commercial spaceport" in the world, although it is not yet complete. As of May 2009, six suborbital missions have been launched from the port. Located near the White Sands Missile Range in state-owned desert 45 miles (72 km) north of Las Cruces and 30 miles (48 km) east of Truth Or Consequences, it is currently under active development and is expected to be completed in 2010.

History

The creation of Spaceport America was the result of a long-term effort by many individuals to bring orbital launch and recovery operations and infrastructure to southern New Mexico. The initial spaceport concept was suggested in 1990 by Dr. Burton Lee (Stanford University), who proposed the creation of a land recovery facility for commercial and government orbital re-entry capsules. Lee authored the initial business and strategic plans, secured seed funding in the amount of $1.4 million through a congressional earmark with the assistance of Sen. Pete Domenici, and worked closely with Bernie McCune and Len Sugerman of the NMSU Physical Science Laboratory (PSL) to develop local support for the spaceport concept. The non-profit group Southwest Regional Space Task Force was created in 1992 by Dr. Ave Tombes, VP for Research and Economic Development at NMSU, in response to these successful efforts to obtain congressional and local support for the initiative. The Taskforce coordinated local and statewide efforts to promote the Southwest Regional Spaceport (SRS), as it was originally designated, including ties with federal organizations such as White Sands Missile Range (WSMR).

The SRS was renamed Spaceport America in 2006 after Governor Bill Richardson and Secy. Rick Homans adopted the spaceport initiative as a formal state of New Mexico economic development programme, with Virgin Galactic slated to be the anchor tenant. Spaceport co-founders since 1990 include Lou Gomez, Bill Gutman, Rick Homans, Burton Lee, Bernie McCune, Gov. Bill Richardson, Hanson Scott, Len Sugerman, and Lonnie Sumpter, among others.

Spaceport America is the first built-from-scratch commercial spaceport in the world. The $225 million venture was announced in mid-December 2005 in Santa Fe. Richard Branson's Virgin Galactic plans to launch its first flight from the spaceport in 2011. Virgin has already collected its $200,000 per-person fee from the first 300 passengers. Once completed, Spaceport America is expected to be the venue for the annual X Prize Cup suborbital spaceflight competitions.

As of early 2007, the "fledgling spaceport" consisted of little more than "a 100-foot (30 m) by 25-foot (7.6 m) concrete slab," part of the launch facility for the spaceport's first launch tenant, UP Aerospace.

New Mexico Spaceport Authority received its launch license for vertical and horizontal launch in December 2008 from the Federal Aviation Administration's Associate Administrator for Commercial Space Transportation.

On December 31, 2008 Virgin Galactic signed a 20-year lease on terminal facilities at the spaceport. Under the deal Virgin Galactic will establish their world headquarters in New Mexico, and will pay $1 million per year for the first five years as well as payments on a tiered scale based on the number of launches the company makes. The agreement is one of several conditions that are required to release state funding for the spaceport.

Funding and Construction

Construction of a temporary launch facility at the spaceport site began on April 4, 2006. The early operations of the spaceport are thus dependent on temporary infrastructure, some of it borrowed from neighboring White Sands Missile Range.

On April 3, 2007 voters in neighboring Doña Ana County approved a spaceport tax referendum, which passed by only 270 out of nearly 18,000 votes cast. Although collection of the tax was set to begin in January 2008, in order for collection of the tax to begin, a spaceport district had to be created, which required that the tax be approved and collected in at least two counties. Since only voters in Doña Ana County had approved the tax as of January 2008, collection of the tax was placed on hold. In April 2008, voters in Sierra County, the actual home of the proposed spaceport, approved the collection of the Spaceport Tax in their county, thus finally enabling the creation of a spaceport tax district and freeing the disposition of over $40 million in funding. Voters in a third county, Otero, voted in the November 2008 general election to reject the spaceport tax.

The first images of what the new Virgin Galactic spaceport terminal will look like were released in early September 2007. Designed by Foster + Partners, with construction advice being given by the URS Corporation, construction of the permanent facilities began on June 19, 2009, and is expected to be completed in 2010.

Gerald Martin Construction Management from Albuquerque was chosen in December 2008 to oversee construction of the spaceport. The first of 13 bid packages for the spaceport is expected to be publicly released in late April 2009 and "all 13 bid packages should be released by June. ... The goal is to have it completed in 17 months, by December 2010."

A ground-breaking ceremony marking the beginning of construction was held on June 19, 2009. New Mexico Governor Bill Richardson presided over the ceremonies which included historical actors and model rocket launches as well as a keynote speech by Will Whitehorn, president of Virgin Galactic. A pre-groundbreaking ceremony and free community breakfast was held at Ralph Edwards Park, which is on the banks of the Rio Grande River in downtown Truth Or Consequences, New Mexico. Truth Or Consequences is the closest city to Spaceport America. A visitor center is planned in downtown Truth Or Consequences to provide shuttle bus services to the Spaceport.

Facility

The site area nets approximately 670,000 sq. ft., with the terminal and hangar facility grossing an area of 110,152 sq. ft.

The western zone of the Facility (25,597 sq. ft.) houses support and administrative facilities for Virgin Galactic and the New Mexico Spaceport Authority. The central zone contains the double-height hangar (47,000 sq. ft.) to store WhiteKnightTwo and SpaceShipTwo crafts. The eastern zone (29,419 sq. ft.) encompasses the principal operational training area, departure lounge, spacesuit dressing rooms, and celebration areas.

The onsite restaurant and mission control room have a direct east views across the apron, runway and landscape beyond.

The port is, also, designed with environmental sustainability in mind. It's designed to meet the requirements of the LEED Gold Certification. It's planned to incorporate "Earth Tubes" under the earth berm to cool the building, solar thermal panels, underfloor radiant cooling and heating, and natural ventilation during the mid seasons.

Launches

The port has operated several launches prior to its completion and start of full operations, 2010-2011.

Launch	*Date (UTC)*	*Vehicle*	*Payload*	*Launch pad*	*Launch contractor*	*Result*	*Remarks*
1	September 25, 2006	SpaceLoft XL	Various	Launch tower	UP Aerospace	Failure	The [unsuccessful] maiden launch of a SpaceLoft XL rocket by UP Aerospace. It veered off course and lost control shortly after lift-off
2	April 28, 2007	SpaceLoft XL	Celestis and other payloads	Launch tower	UP Aerospace	Success	The first successful launch, a second Spaceloft XL, primarily carried cremated human remains, including those of astronaut Gordon Cooper and *Star Trek* actor James Doohan
3	December 19, 2007	Proprietary test vehicle	Technology demonstration	Launch tower	UP Aerospace	Success	Low-altitude atmospheric launch
4	December 2007	Space plane prototype	None	Launch tower	UP Aerospace	Success	Proprietary technology launch for Lockheed Martin
5	August 12, 2008	Space plane prototype	None	Launch tower	UP Aerospace	Success (Spaceport America & UP Aerospace view) Anomalous (Lockeed-Martin view)	Proprietary technology launch for Lockheed Martin

(*Contd.*)

Launch	*Date (UTC)*	*Vehicle*	*Payload*	*Launch pad*	*Launch contractor*	*Result*	*Remarks*
6	May 2, 2009	SpaceLoft XL	New Mexico student payloads Celestis *Discovery*	UA launch tower	UP Aerospace	Anomalous	"Education opportunity for New Mexico students to design experiments that use the environment of suborbital space to answer scientific and engineering questions ". The craft failed to reach space.

4

Spaceflight: Typology, Elements, Dimensions and Records

SPACEFLIGHT

Spaceflight is the use of space technology to achieve the flight of spacecraft into and through outer space.

Spaceflight is used in space exploration, and also in commercial activities like space tourism and satellite telecommunications. Additional non-commercial uses of spaceflight include space observatories, reconnaissance satellites and other earth observation satellites.

A spaceflight typically begins with a rocket launch, which provides the initial thrust to overcome the force of gravity and propels the spacecraft from the surface of the Earth. Once in space, the motion of a spacecraft—both when unpropelled and when under propulsion—is covered by the area of study called astrodynamics. Some spacecraft remain in space indefinitely, some disintegrate during atmospheric reentry, and others reach a planetary or lunar surface for landing or impact.

History

The realistic proposal of space travel goes back to Konstantin Tsiolkovsky. His most famous work, (*The Exploration of Cosmic Space by Means of Reaction Devices*), was published in 1903, but this theoretical work was not widely influential outside of Russia.

Spaceflight became an engineering possibility with the work of Robert H. Goddard's publication in 1919 of his paper 'A Method of Reaching Extreme Altitudes', where his application of the de Laval nozzle to liquid fuel rockets gave sufficient power that interplanetary travel became possible. He also proved in the laboratory that rockets would work in the vacuum of space; not all scientists of that day believed they would. This paper was highly influential on Hermann Oberth and Wernher Von Braun, later key players in spaceflight.

The first rocket to reach space was the German V-2 Rocket, on a test flight in June, 1944, although sub-orbital flight is not considered a spaceflight in Russia. On October 4, 1957, the Soviet Union launched Sputnik 1, which became the first artificial satellite to orbit the Earth. The first human spaceflight was Vostok 1 on April 12, 1961, aboard which Soviet cosmonaut Yuri Gagarin made one orbit around the Earth. The lead architects behind the Soviet space programme's Vostok 1 mission were the rocket scientists Sergey Korolyov and Kerim Kerimov.

Rockets remain the only currently practical means of reaching space. Other non-rocket spacelaunch technologies such as scramjets still fall far short of orbital speed.

Earth-Launched Spaceflight

Reaching Space

The most commonly used definition of outer space is everything beyond the Kármán line, which is 100 kilometres (62 mi) above the Earth's surface. (The United States sometimes defines outer space as everything beyond 50 miles (80 km) in altitude.)

In order for a projectile to reach outer space from the surface, it needs a minimum delta-v. This velocity is much lower than escape velocity.

It is possible, indeed routine, for a spacecraft to leave a celestial body without reaching the surface escape velocity of a body by propelling itself after take-off. However, it is more fuel-efficient for a craft to burn its fuel as close to the ground as possible, keeping escape velocity a consideration.

Suborbital Spaceflight

On a suborbital spaceflight the spacecraft reaches space, but does not achieve orbit. Instead, its trajectory brings it back to the surface of the Earth. Suborbital flights can last many hours. Pioneer 1 was NASA's first space probe intended to reach the Moon. A partial failure caused it to instead follow a suborbital trajectory to an altitude of 113,854 kilometres (70,746 mi) before reentering the Earth's atmosphere 43 hours after launch.

On May 17, 2004, Civilian Space eXploration Team launched the GoFast Rocket on a suborbital flight, the first amateur spaceflight. On June 21, 2004, SpaceShipOne was used for the first privately-funded human spaceflight.

Orbital Spaceflight

A minimal orbital spaceflight requires much higher velocities than a minimal sub-orbital flight, and so it is technologically much more challenging to achieve. To achieve orbital spaceflight, the tangential velocity around the Earth is as important as altitude. In order to perform a stable and lasting flight in space, the spacecraft must reach the minimal orbital speed required for a closed orbit.

Leaving Orbit

Achieving a closed orbit is not essential to interplanetary voyages, for which spacecraft need to reach escape velocity. Early Russian space vehicles successfully achieved very high altitudes without going into orbit. In its early Apollo mission planning NASA considered using a direct ascent to the moon, but abandoned that idea later due to weight considerations. Many robotic space probes to the outer planets use direct ascent—they do not orbit the earth before departing.

It is possible, indeed routine, for a spacecraft to leave a celestial body without reaching the surface escape velocity of a body by propelling itself after take-off.

However, it is more fuel-efficient for a craft to burn its fuel as close to the ground as possible, keeping escape velocity a consideration.

Plans for future crewed interplanetary spaceflight missions often include final vehicle assembly in Earth orbit, such as NASA's Project Orion and Russia's Kliper/ Parom tandem.

Other Ways of Reaching Space

Many ways other than rockets to reach space have been proposed. Ideas such as the Space Elevator, while elegant are currently infeasible, whereas electromagnetic launchers such as launch loops have no known show stoppers. Other ideas include rocket assisted jet planes such as Reaction Engines Skylon or the trickier scramjets. Gun launch has been proposed for cargo, but this would incinerate the cargo due to air friction.

Spaceports

A spaceflight usually starts from a spaceport (cosmodrome), which may be equipped with launch complexes and launch pads for vertical rocket launches, and runways for takeoff and landing of carrier airplanes and winged spacecraft. Spaceports are situated well away from human habitation for noise and safety reasons.

A launch is often restricted to certain launch windows. These windows depend upon the position of celestial bodies and orbits relative to the launch site. The biggest influence is often the rotation of the Earth itself. Once launched, orbits are normally located within relatively constant flat planes at a fixed angle to the axis of the Earth, and the Earth rotates within this orbit.

Launch Pads, Takeoff

A launch pad is a fixed structure designed to dispatch airborne vehicles. It generally consists of a launch tower and flame trench. It is surrounded by equipment used to erect, fuel, and maintain launch vehicles.

Reentry and Landing/Splashdown

Reentry

Vehicles in orbit have large amounts of kinetic energy. This energy must be discarded if the vehicle is to land safely without vaporizing in the atmosphere. Typically this process requires special methods to protect against aerodynamic heating. The theory behind reentry is due to Harry Julian Allen. Based on this theory, reentry vehicles present blunt shapes to the atmosphere for reentry. Blunt shapes mean that less than 1 per cent of the kinetic energy ends up as heat that reaches the vehicle and the heat energy instead ends up in the atmosphere.

Landing

The Mercury, Gemini, and Apollo capsules all landed in the sea. These capsules were designed to land at relatively slow speeds. Russian capsules for Soyuz make use of braking rockets as were designed to touch down on land. The Space Shuttle glides into a touchdown at high speed.

Recovery

After a successful landing the spacecraft, its occupants and cargo can be recovered. In some cases, recovery has occurred before landing: while a spacecraft is still descending on its parachute, it can be snagged by a specially designed aircraft. This mid-air retrieval technique was used to recover the film canisters from the Corona spy satellites.

Expendable Launch Systems

All current spaceflight except NASA's Space Shuttle and the SpaceX Falcon 1 use multi-stage expendable launch systems to reach space.

Reusable Launch Systems

The first reusable spacecraft, the X-15, was air-launched on a suborbital trajectory on July 19, 1963. The first partially reusable orbital spacecraft, the Space Shuttle, was launched by the USA on the 20th anniversary of Yuri Gagarin's flight, on April 12, 1981. During the Shuttle era, six orbiters were built, all of which have flown in the atmosphere and five of which have flown in space. The *Enterprise* was used only for approach and landing tests, launching from the back of a Boeing 747 and gliding to deadstick landings at Edwards AFB, California. The first Space Shuttle to fly into space was the *Columbia,* followed by the *Challenger, Discovery, Atlantis,* and *Endeavour.* The *Endeavour* was built to replace the *Challenger* when it was lost in January 1986. The *Columbia* broke up during reentry in February 2003.

The first (and so far only) automatic partially reusable spacecraft was the Buran (Snowstorm), launched by the USSR on November 15, 1988, although it made only one flight. This spaceplane was designed for a crew and strongly resembled the U.S. Space Shuttle, although its drop-off boosters used liquid propellants and its main engines were located at the base of what would be the external tank in the American Shuttle. Lack of funding, complicated by the dissolution of the USSR, prevented any further flights of Buran.

Per the Vision for Space Exploration, the Space Shuttle is due to be retired in 2010 due mainly to its old age and high cost of the programme reaching over a billion dollars per flight. The Shuttle's human transport role is to be replaced by the partially reusable Crew Exploration Vehicle (CEV) no later than 2014. The Shuttle's heavy cargo transport role is to be replaced by expendable rockets such as the Evolved Expendable Launch Vehicle (EELV).

ORBITAL SPACEFLIGHT

An **orbital spaceflight** (or orbital flight) is a spaceflight in which a spacecraft is placed on a trajectory where it could remain in space for at least one orbit. To do this around the Earth, it must be on a free trajectory which has an altitude at perigee (altitude at closest approach) above 100 kilometres (62 mi) (this is, by at least one convention, the boundary of space). To remain in orbit at this altitude requires an orbital speed of ~7.8 km/s. Orbital speed is slower for higher orbits, but attaining them requires higher delta-v.

The expression "orbital spaceflight" is mostly used to distinguish from sub-orbital spaceflights, which are flights where apogee of a spacecraft reaches space but perigee is too low.

Orbital Launch

Orbital spaceflight from Earth has only been achieved by launch vehicles that use rocket engines for propulsion. To reach orbit, the rocket must impart to the payload a delta-v of about 9.3-10 km/s. This figure allows for atmospheric drag (approximately 300 m/s with the ballistic coefficient of a 20 m long dense fuelled vehicle), gravity losses (depending on burn time and details of the trajectory and launch vehicle), gaining altitude, and the horizontal acceleration needed to reach orbital speed.

The main proven technique involves launching nearly vertically for a few kilometres while performing a gravity turn, and then progressively flattening the trajectory out at an altitude of 170+ km and accelerating on a horizontal trajectory (with the rocket angled upwards to fight gravity and maintain altitude) for a 5-8 minute burn until orbital velocity is achieved. Currently, 2-4 stages are needed to achieve the required delta-v.

The Pegasus rocket for small satellites instead launches from an aircraft at an altitude of 12 km.

Other techniques, such as use of a launch loop, have been proposed for non-rocket spacelaunch. These techniques are theoretical: no attempts have been made to orbit a vehicle using any of them.

Stability

An object in orbit at an altitude of less than roughly 200 km is considered unstable due to atmospheric drag. For a satellite to be in a stable orbit (i.e. sustainable for more than a few months), 350 km is a more standard altitude for low Earth orbit. For example, on 1958-02-01 the Explorer 1 satellite was launched into an orbit with a perigee of 358 kilometres (222 mi). It remained in orbit for more than 12 years before its atmospheric reentry over the Pacific Ocean on 1970-03-31.

However, the exact behaviour of objects in orbit depends on altitude, their ballistic coefficient, and details of space weather which can affect the height of the upper atmosphere.

Orbits

There are three main 'bands' of orbit around the Earth: low Earth orbit (LEO), medium Earth orbit (MEO) and geostationary orbit (GEO).

Due to orbital mechanics orbits are in a particular, largely fixed plane around the Earth, which coincides with the centre of the Earth, and may be tilted with respect to the equator. The Earth rotates about its axis within this orbit, and the relative motion of the spacecraft and the movement of the Earth's surface determines the position that the spacecraft appears in the sky from the ground, and which parts of the Earth are visible from the spacecraft.

By dropping a vertical down to the Earth's surface it is possible to calculate a ground track which shows which part of the Earth a spacecraft is immediately above, and this is useful for helping to visualise the orbit.

NASA provides real-time tracking of over 500 artificial satellites maintained in orbit around Earth. For the position of these satellites see NASA satellite tracking.

Re-entry

Due to the high speeds of orbital spaceflight, atmospheric reentry is much more difficult compared to sub-orbital flights.

Even if the vehicle is a satellite that is ultimately expendable, most space authorities are pushing towards controlled re-entry techniques to avoid issues of space debris reaching the ground and causing a hazard to lives and property. In addition, this minimises the creation of orbital space junk.

Returning craft though (including all potentially manned craft), have to find a way of slowing down as much as possible while still in higher atmospheric layers and avoid hitting the ground (lithobraking) or burning up. The problem of deceleration from orbital speeds is solved through using atmospheric drag (aerobraking) to lose nearly all of the speed. On an orbital spaceflight initial deceleration is provided by the retrofiring of the craft's rocket engines, perturbing the orbit (by lowering perigee down into the atmosphere) onto a sub-orbital trajectory.

Aerobraking is achieved by orienting the returning spacecraft to fly so as to present the heat shields forwards towards the atmosphere so as to protect against the high temperatures generated by atmospheric compression and friction caused by passing through the atmosphere at hypersonic speeds. The thermal energy is dissipated mainly by compression heating the air in a shockwave ahead of the vehicle using a blunt heat shield shape, with the aim of minimising the heat entering the vehicle. Sub-orbital space flights, being at a much lower speed, do not generate anywhere near as much heat upon re-entry.

SUB-ORBITAL SPACEFLIGHT

A **sub-orbital spaceflight** is a spaceflight in which the spacecraft reaches space, but its trajectory intersects the atmosphere or surface of the gravitating body from which it was launched, so that it does not complete one orbital revolution.

For example, the path of an object launched from Earth that reaches 100 km (62 mi) above sea level, and then falls back to Earth, is considered a sub-orbital spaceflight. Some sub-orbital flights have been undertaken to test spacecraft and launch vehicles later intended for orbital spaceflight. Other vehicles are specifically designed only for sub-orbital flight; examples include manned vehicles such as the X-15 and SpaceShipOne, and unmanned ones such as ICBMs and sounding rockets.

Sub-orbital spaceflights are distinct from flights that attain orbit but use retro-rockets to deorbit after less than one full orbital period. Thus the flights of the Fractional Orbital Bombardment System would not be considered sub-orbital; instead these are simply considered flights to low Earth orbit.

Altitude Requirement

By one definition a sub-orbital spaceflight reaches an altitude higher than 100 km above sea level. This altitude, known as the Kármán line, was chosen by the Fédération Aéronautique Internationale because it is roughly the point where a vehicle flying fast enough to support itself with aerodynamic lift from the Earth's atmosphere would be flying faster than orbital speed. The US military and NASA award astronaut wings to those flying above 50 miles although the US State Department appears to not support a distinct boundary between atmospheric flight and spaceflight.

Orbit

During freefall the trajectory is part of an elliptic orbit as given by the orbital equation. The perigee distance is less than the radius of the Earth, hence the ellipse intersects the Earth, and hence the spacecraft will fail to complete an orbit. The major axis is vertical, the semi-major axis is more than one-half of the radius of the Earth, and almost always less than the radius.

Speed, Range, Altitude

To minimize the required delta-v (an astrodynamical measure which strongly determines the required fuel), the high-altitude part of the flight is made with the rockets off (this is technically called free-fall even for the upward part of the trajectory). The maximum speed in a flight is attained at the lowest altitude of this free-fall trajectory, both at the start and at the end of it.

If one's goal is simply to "reach space", for example in competing for the Ansari X Prize, horizontal motion is not needed. In this case the lowest required delta-v is about 1.4 km/s, for a sub-orbital flight with a maximum speed of about 1 km/s. Moving slower, with less free-fall, would require more delta-v.

Compare this with orbital spaceflights: a low Earth orbit (LEO), with an altitude of about 300 km), needs a speed around 7.7 km/s, requiring a delta-v of about 9.2 km/s.

For sub-orbital spaceflights covering a horizontal distance the maximum speed and required delta-v are in between those of a vertical flight and a LEO. The maximum speed at the lower ends of the trajectory is now composed of a horizontal and a vertical component. The higher the horizontal distance covered, the more are both speeds, and the more is the maximum altitude. For the V-2 rocket, just reaching space but with a range of about 330 km, the maximum speed was 1.6 km/s. Scaled Composites SpaceShipTwo which is under development will have a similar free-fall orbit but the announced maximum speed is 1.1 km/s (perhaps because of engine shut-off at a higher altitude).

For larger ranges, due to the elliptic orbit the maximum altitude can even be considerably more than for a LEO. On an intercontinental flight, such as that of an intercontinental ballistic missile or possible future commercial spaceflight, the maximum speed is about 7 km/s, and the maximum altitude about 1200 km. Note that an intercontinental flight at an altitude of 300 km would require a larger delta-v, that of a LEO. It should be noted that any spaceflight that returns to the surface, including sub-orbital ones, will undergo atmospheric reentry. The speed at the start of that is basically the maximum speed of the flight. The aerodynamic heating caused will vary accordingly: it is much less for a flight with a maximum speed of only 1 km/s than for one with a maximum speed of 7 or 8 km/s.

Flight Duration

In a vertical flight of not too high altitudes, the time of the free-fall is both for the upward and for the downward part the maximum speed divided by the acceleration of gravity, so with a maximum speed of 1 km/s together 3 minutes and 20 seconds. The duration of the flight phases before and after the free-fall can vary.

For an intercontinental flight the boost phase takes 3 to 5 minutes, the free-fall (midcourse phase) about 25 minutes. For an ICBM the atmospheric reentry phase takes about 2 minutes; this will be longer for any soft landing, such as for a possible future commercial flight.

Sub-orbital flights can last many hours. Pioneer 1 was NASA's first space probe, intended to reach the Moon. A partial failure caused it to instead follow a sub-orbital trajectory, reentering the Earth's atmosphere 43 hours after launch.

Flight Profiles

While there are a great many possible sub-orbital flight profiles, it is expected that some will be more common than others.

Ballistic Missiles

The first sub-orbital vehicles which reached space were ballistic missiles. The very first ballistic missile to reach space was the German V-2 on October 3, 1942 which reached an altitude of 60 miles. That in fact was the first man-made object of any kind to reach space. Then in the 1950s the USA and USSR concurrently developed much longer range Intercontinental Ballistic Missiles (ICBM). There are now many countries who possess ICBMs and even more with shorter range IRBMs (Intermediate Range Ballistic Missiles).

Tourist Flights

Sub-orbital tourist flights will initially focus on attaining the altitude required to qualify as reaching space. The flight path will probably be either vertical or very steep, with the spacecraft landing back at its take-off site.

The spacecraft will probably shut off its engines well before reaching maximum altitude, and then coast up to its highest point. During a few minutes, from the point when the engines are shut off to the point where the atmosphere begins to slow down the downward acceleration, the passengers will experience weightlessness.

In 2004, a number of companies worked on vehicles in this class as entrants to the Ansari X Prize competition. SpaceShipOne was officially declared by Rick Searfoss to have won the competition on October 4, 2004 after completing two flights within a two week period.

In 2005, Sir Richard Branson of the Virgin Group announced the creation of Virgin Galactic and his plans for a 9 seat capacity SpaceShipTwo named VSS *Enterprise.*

Scientific Experiments

A major use of suborbital vehicles today is as scientific sounding rockets. Scientific suborbital flights began in the 1920s when Robert H. Goddard launched the first liquid fuelled rockets, however they did not reach space altitude. Modern sounding rocket flights began in the late 1940s using vehicles derived from German V-2 ballistic missiles. Today there are dozens of different sounding rockets on the market, from a variety of suppliers in various countries. Typically, researchers wish to conduct experiments in microgravity or above the atmosphere. There have reportedly been several offers from researchers to launch experiments on SpaceShipOne, which have been turned down until the next version of the vehicle.

Intercontinental Flights

Another possibly lucrative market for sub-orbital spacecraft is intercontinental flight. Research, such as that done for the X-20 Dyna-Soar project suggests that a semi-ballistic sub-orbital flight could travel from Europe to North America in less than an hour.

The size of rocket, relative to the payload, necessary to achieve this, is similar to an ICBM. ICBMs have delta-v's somewhat less than orbital; and therefore would be somewhat cheaper than the costs for reaching orbit.

Thus due to the high cost, this is likely to be initially limited to high value, very high urgency cargo such as courier flights, or as the ultimate business jet; or possibly as an extreme sport, or for military fast response.

Reaching for Orbit

Commercial spacecraft operators may use sub-orbital flights to allow a constant progression towards full orbital flight. The test craft will reach higher and higher velocities until they reach low earth orbit. There is considerable debate about the validity of this approach, however, as the scale of the two problems (sub-orbital and orbital flight) are very different. Still, winged, single stage to orbit designs like Reaction Engines Skylon do exist, so it might not be a totally unreasonable approach.

Tether Launch Assist

There have been proposals to use tethers (commonly referred to as skyhooks) to put suborbital payloads into orbit. For example, an orbiting space station could extend a tether, and a suborbital vehicle rendezvous with the end of the tether and dock to it. If practical, this would be considerably less expensive than launching payloads directly into orbit on rockets on a per flight basis.

Notable Unmanned Sub-orbital Spaceflight

- The first sub-orbital spaceflight was in early 1944, when a V-2 test rocket launched from Peenemünde in Germany reached 189 kilometres altitude.
- 8 September 1944, the world's first successful ballistic missile (V-2, launched by Germany) hits its target for the first time, Chiswick in London, England. Three civilians were killed and seventeen injured, a massive crater was left. By September 1944, the V-2s routinely achieved Mach-4 during terminal descent.
- Bumper 5, a two-stage rocket launched from the White Sands Proving Grounds. On 24 February 1949 the upper stage reached an altitude of 248 miles (399 km) and a speed of 7,553 feet per second (2300 metres per second approx.)
- USSR—Energia, 1986, Polyus payload failed to reach orbit; this was the most massive object launched into sub-orbital spaceflight to date

Manned Sub-orbital Spaceflights

	Date (GMT)	*Mission*	*Crew*	*Country*	*Remarks*
1	1961-05-05	Mercury-Redstone 3	Alan Shepard	United States	First manned sub-orbital spaceflight, first American in space
2	1961-07-21	Mercury-Redstone 4	Virgil Grissom	United States	
3	1963-07-19	X-15 Flight 90	Joseph A. Walker	United States	First winged craft in space
4	1963-08-22	X-15 Flight 91	Joseph A. Walker	United States	First person and spacecraft to make two flights into space
5	1975-04-05	Soyuz 18a	Vasili Lazarev Oleg Makarov	Soviet Union	Failed orbital launch. Aborted after malfunction during stage separation
6	2004-06-24	SpaceShipOne flight 15P	Mike Melvill	United States	First commercial spaceflight
7	2004-09-29	SpaceShipOne flight 16P	Mike Melvill	United States	First of two flights to win Ansari X-Prize
8	2004-10-04	SpaceShipOne flight 17P	Brian Binnie	United States	

Future of Manned Sub-orbital Spaceflight

Private companies such as Rocketplane Limited and Blue Origin are taking an interest in sub-orbital spaceflight, due in part to ventures like the Ansari X Prize. NASA and others are experimenting with scramjet based hypersonic aircraft which may well be used with flight profiles that qualify as sub-orbital spaceflight.

INTERPLANETARY SPACEFLIGHT

Interplanetary spaceflight or **interplanetary travel** is travel between planets within a single planetary system. In practice, spaceflights of this type are confined to travel between the planets of the Solar System.

Current Achievements in Interplanetary Travel

Remotely guided space probes have flown by all of the planets of the Solar System from Mercury to Neptune. The four most distant spacecraft (Pioneer 10, Pioneer 11, Voyager 1 and Voyager 2) are on course to leave the Solar System.

Space probes have also been inserted into orbit around the planets Venus, Mars, Jupiter, and Saturn, and have returned data about these bodies and their natural satellites. Further probes are currently *en route* to orbit Mercury, the dwarf planets Ceres and Pluto as well as the large asteroid Vesta.

Remotely controlled landers such as Viking, Pathfinder and the two Mars Exploration Rovers have landed on the surface of Mars and several Venera and Vega spacecraft have landed on the surface of Venus. The NEAR Shoemaker orbiter successfully landed on the asteroid 433 Eros, even though it was not designed with this maneuver in mind. The Huygens probe successfully landed on Saturn's moon, Titan.

No manned missions have been sent to any other planet of the Solar System. NASA's Apollo programme, however, landed twelve people on the Moon and returned them to Earth. The American Vision for Space Exploration, originally introduced by President George W. Bush and put into practice through the Constellation programme, has as a long-term goal to eventually send human astronauts to Mars. An earlier project which received some significant planning by NASA included a manned flyby of Venus in the Manned Venus Flyby mission, but was cancelled when the Apollo Applications programme was terminated due to NASA budget cuts in the late 1960's.

Reasons for Interplanetary Travel

The costs and risk of interplanetary travel receive a lot of publicity—spectacular examples include the malfunctions or complete failures of unmanned probes such as Mars 96, Deep Space 2 and Beagle 2 (the article List of Solar System probes gives a full list).

Many astronomers, geologists and biologists believe that exploration of the Solar System provides knowledge that could not be gained by observations from Earth's surface or from orbit around Earth. But they disagree about whether manned missions make a useful scientific contribution—some think robotic probes are cheaper and safer, while others argue that either astronauts advised by Earth-based scientists, or spacefaring scientists advised by Earth-based astronauts, can respond more flexibly and intelligently to new or unexpected features of the region they are exploring.

Those who pay for such missions (primarily in the public sector) are more likely to be interested in benefits for themselves or for the human race as a whole. So far the only benefits of this type have been "spin-off" technologies which were developed for space missions and then were found to be at least as useful in other activities (NASA publicizes spin-offs from its activities).

Other practical motivations for interplanetary travel are more speculative, because our current technologies are not yet advanced enough to support test projects. But science fiction writers have a fairly good track record in predicting future technologies—for example geosynchronous communications satellites (Arthur C. Clarke) and many aspects of computer technology (Mack Reynolds).

Many science fiction stories (notably Ben Bova's Grand Tour stories) feature detailed descriptions of how people could extract minerals from asteroids and energy from sources including orbital solar panels (unhampered by clouds) and the very strong magnetic field of Jupiter. Some point out that such techniques may be the only way to provide rising standards of living without being stopped by pollution or by depletion of Earth's resources (for example peak oil).

Finally, colonizing other parts of the Solar System would prevent the whole human species from being exterminated by an asteroid impact like the one which may have resulted in the Cretaceous—Tertiary extinction event. Although various Spaceguard projects monitor the Solar System for objects that might come dangerously close to Earth, current asteroid deflection strategies are crude and untested. To make the task more difficult, carbonaceous chondrites are rather sooty and therefore very hard to detect. Although carbonaceous chondrites are thought to be rare, some are very large and the suspected "dinosaur-killer" may have been a carbonaceous chondrite.

Some scientists, including members of the Space Studies Institute, argue that the vast majority of mankind eventually will live in space and will benefit from doing this.

Economical Travel Techniques

Interplanetary travel has to solve two problems, other than escaping from the planet of origin:

- The planet from which the spaceship starts is moving round the Sun at a different speed than the planet to which the spaceship is travelling, because the two planets are at different distances from the Sun. So as it approaches its destination, the spaceship must decrease its speed if the destination is closer to the Sun, or increase its speed if the destination is further away (assuming a Hohmann transfer orbit).
- If the destination is farther away, the spaceship must lift itself "up" against the force of the Sun's gravity.

Doing this by brute force—accelerating in the shortest route to the destination and then, if it is farther from the Sun, decelerating to match the planet's speed—would require an extremely large amount of fuel. And the fuel required for deceleration and velocity-matching has to be launched along with the payload, and therefore even more fuel is needed in the acceleration phase.

The change in speed (delta-v) required to match velocity with another planet is surprisingly large. For example Venus orbits about 5.2 km/s faster than Earth and Mars orbits about 5.7 km/s slower. To put these figures in perspective, Earth's escape velocity is about 11.2 km/second (it varies slightly depending on the launch direction). So matching a space shuttle's velocity with that of Venus or Mars would require a significant percentage of the energy which is used to launch a shuttle from Earth's surface.

Hohmann Transfers

For many years economical interplanetary travel meant using the Hohmann transfer orbit. Hohmann demonstrated that the lowest energy route between any two orbits is an elliptical "orbit" which forms a tangent to the starting and destination orbits. Once the spacecraft arrives, a second application of thrust will re-circularize the orbit at the new location. In the case of planetary transfers this means directing the spacecraft, originally in an orbit almost identical to Earth's, so that the apogee of the transfer orbit is on the far side of the Sun near the orbit of the other planet. A spacecraft travelling from Earth to Mars via this method will arrive near Mars orbit in approximately 18 months, but because the orbital velocity is greater when closer to the centre of mass (i.e. the Sun) and slower when farther from the centre, the spacecraft will be travelling quite slowly and a small application of thrust is all that is needed to put it into a circular obit around Mars. If the manoeuver is timed properly, Mars will be "arriving" under the spacecraft when this happens.

The Hohmann transfer applies to any two orbits, not just those with planets involved. For instance it is the most common way to transfer satellites into geostationary orbit, after first being "parked" in low earth orbit. However the Hohmann transfer takes an amount of time similar to ½ of the orbital period of the outer orbit, so in the case of the outer planets this is many years—too long to wait. It is also based on the assumption that the points at both ends are massless, as in the case when transferring between two orbits around Earth for instance. With a planet at the destination end of the transfer, calculations become considerably more difficult.

Gravitational Slingshot

The gravitational slingshot technique uses the gravity of planets and moons to change the speed and direction of a spacecraft without using fuel. In typical example, a spacecraft is sent to a distant planet on a path that is much faster than what the Hohmann transfer would call for. This would typically mean that it would arrive at the planet's orbit and continue past it. However, if there is a planet between the departure point and the target, it can be used to bend the path toward the target, and in many cases the overall travel time is greatly reduced. A prime example of this are the two craft of the Voyager programme, which used slingshot effects to change trajectories several times in the outer Solar System. It is difficult to use this method for journeys in the inner part of the Solar System, although it is possible to use other nearby planets such as Venus or even the Moon as slingshots in journeys to the outer planets.

This manoeuvre can only change an object's velocity relative to a third, uninvolved object,—possibly the "centre of mass" or the Sun. There is no change in the velocities of the two objects involved in the manoeuvre relative to each other.

Fuzzy Orbits

Computers did not exist when Hohmann transfer orbits were first proposed (1925) and were slow, expensive and unreliable when gravitational slingshots were developed (1959). Recent advances in computing have made it possible to exploit many more features of the gravity fields of astronomical bodies and thus calculate even lower-cost trajectories. Paths have been calculated which link the Lagrange points of the various planets into the so-called Interplanetary Transport Network. Such "fuzzy orbits" use significantly less energy than Hohmann transfers but are often much slower. They may not offer much advantage for manned missions or for research missions, but may be useful for high-volume transport of low-value commodities if humanity develops a space-based economy.

Aerobraking

Aerobraking uses the atmosphere of the target planet to slow down. It was first used on the Apollo programme where the returning spacecraft did not enter Earth orbit but instead used a series of passes through Earth's atmosphere to reduce its speed until it was safe to land. Aerobraking does not require a thick atmosphere—for example most Mars landers use the technique, and Mars' atmosphere is only about 1 per cent as thick as Earth's.

Aerobraking converts the spacecraft's kinetic energy into heat, so it requires a heatshield to prevent the craft from burning up. As a result, aerobraking is only helpful in cases where the fuel needed to transport the heatshield to the planet is less than the fuel that would be required to brake an unshielded craft by firing its engines.

Improved Travel Technologies

Several technologies have been proposed which both save fuel and provide significantly faster travel than Hohmann transfers. Most are still just theoretical, but the DeepSpaceOne mission was a very successful test of an ion drive. These improved technologies focus on one or more of:

- Space propulsion systems with much better fuel economy. Such systems would make it possible to travel much faster while keeping the fuel cost within acceptable limits.

- Using solar energy and *In-Situ* Resource Utilization to avoid or minimize the expensive task of shipping components and fuel up from the Earth's surface, against the Earth's gravity.

Besides making travel faster, such improvements would allow greater design "safety margins" by reducing the imperative to make spacecraft lighter.

Electric Propulsion

Electric propulsion systems use an external source such as a nuclear reactor or solar cells to generate electricity, which is then used to accelerate a chemically inert propellant to speeds far higher than achieved in a chemical rocket. Such drives produce feeble thrust, and are therefore unsuitable for quick maneuvers or for launching from the surface of a planet. But they are so economical in their use of reaction mass that they can keep firing continuously for days or weeks, while chemical rockets use up reaction mass so quickly that they can only fire for seconds or minutes. Even a trip to the Moon is long enough for an electric propulsion system to outrun a chemical rocket—the Apollo missions took 3 days in each direction.

NASA's DeepSpaceOne was a very successful test of a prototype ion drive, which fired for a total of 678 days and enabled the probe to run down Comet Borrelly, a feat which would have been impossible for a chemical rocket. A more ambitious, nuclear-powered version was intended for an unmanned Jupiter mission, the Jupiter Icy Moons Orbiter, originally planned for launch sometime in the next decade. Due to a shift in priorities at NASA that favoured manned space missions, the project lost funding in 2005, effectively cancelling the JIMO mission.

Solar Sails

Solar sails rely on the fact that light reflected from a surface exerts pressure on the surface. The radiation pressure is small and decreases by the square of the distance from the Sun, but unlike rockets, solar sails require no fuel. Although the thrust is small, it continues as long as the Sun shines and the sail is deployed.

The original concept relied only on radiation from the Sun—for example in Arthur C. Clarke's 1965 story "Sunjammer". More recent light sail designs propose to boost the thrust by aiming ground-based lasers or masers at the sail. Ground-based lasers or masers can also help a light-sail spacecraft to *decelerate*: the sail splits into an outer and inner section, the outer section is pushed forward and its shape is changed mechanically to focus reflected radiation on the inner portion, and the radiation focused on the inner section acts as a brake.

Although most articles about light sails focus on interstellar travel, there have been several proposals for their use within the Solar System.

No spacecraft powered only or mainly by light sails have been built. But ordinary spacecraft and satellites sometimes use solar collectors, temperature-control panels and Sun shades as light sails, to make minor corrections to their attitude and orbit without using fuel. A few have even had small purpose-built solar sails for this use (for example Eurostar E3000 geostationary communications satellites built by EADS Astrium).

Nuclear Thermal and Solar Thermal Rockets

In a nuclear thermal rocket or solar thermal rocket a working fluid, usually hydrogen, is heated in a high temperature, and then expands through a rocket nozzle to create thrust. The energy replaces the chemical energy of the reactive chemicals in a traditional rocket engine. Due to the low molecular mass and hence high thermal velocity of hydrogen these engines are at least twice as fuel efficient as chemical engines, even after including the weight of the reactor.

The US Atomic Energy Commission and NASA tested a few designs from 1959 to 1968. The NASA designs were conceived as replacements for the upper stages of the Saturn V launch vehicle, but the tests revealed reliability problems, mainly caused by the vibration and heating involved in running the engines at such high thrust levels. Political and environmental considerations make it unlikely that such an engine will be used in the foreseeable future, since nuclear thermal rockets would be most useful at or near the Earth's surface and the consequences of a malfunction could be disastrous.

Cyclers

It is possible to put stations or spacecraft on orbits that cycle between different planets, for example a Mars cycler would synchronously cycle between Mars and Earth, with very little propellant usage to maintain the trajectory. Cyclers are conceptually a good idea, because massive radiation shields, life support and other equipment only need to be put onto the cycler trajectory once. A cycler could combine several roles: habitat (for example it could spin to produce an "artificial gravity" effect); mothership (providing life support for the crews of smaller spacecraft which hitch a ride on it). Cyclers' main limitation would be that they would be slow, because they would rely on gravitational techniques such as Hohmann transfer orbits and gravitational slingshots.

Space Elevator

A space elevator is a structure designed to transport material from a planet's surface into orbit. The fundamental idea is that, once the expensive job of building the elevator is complete, an indefinite number of loads can be transported into orbit at minimal cost. Even the simplest designs avoid the vicious circle of rocket launches from the surface, the difficulty that: the fuel needed to travel the last 10 per cent of the distance to orbit must be lifted all the way from the surface; that requires extra fuel; most of the extra fuel must be lifted most of the way before it is burned; that requires more extra fuel; and so on. More sophisticated space elevator designs reduce the energy cost per trip by using counterweights, and the most ambitious schemes aim to balance loads going up and down and thus make the energy cost close to zero. Space elevators have also sometimes been referred to as "beanstalks", "space bridges", "space lifts", "space ladders" or "orbital towers".

A terrestrial space elevator is beyond our current technology, although a lunar space elevator could theoretically be built using existing materials.

Using Non-terrestrial Resources

Current space vehicles attempt to launch with all their fuel (propellants and energy supplies) on-board that they will need for their entire journey, and current space structures are lifted from the Earth's surface. Non-terrestrial sources of energy and materials are mostly a lot further away, but most would not require lifting out of a strong gravity field and therefore should be much cheaper to use in space in the long term.

The most important non-terrestrial resource is energy, because it can be used to transform non-terrestrial materials into useful forms (some of which may also produce energy). At least two fundamental non-terrestrial energy sources have been proposed: solar-powered energy generation (unhampered by clouds), either directly by solar cells or indirectly by focusing solar radiation on boilers which produce steam to drive generators; and electrodynamic tethers which generate electricity from the powerful magnetic fields of some planets (Jupiter has a very powerful magnetic field).

Water ice would be very useful if it can be found on the moons of Jupiter or Saturn:

- The low gravity of these moons would make them a cheaper source of water for space stations and planetary bases than lifting it up from Earth's surface.
- Non-terrestrial power supplies could be used to electrolyse water ice into oxygen and hydrogen for use in bipropellant rocket engines.
- Nuclear thermal rockets or Solar thermal rockets could use it as reaction mass. Hydrogen has also been proposed for use in these engines and would provide much greater specific impulse (thrust per kilogram of reaction mass), but it has been claimed that water will beat hydrogen in cost/performance terms despite its much lower specific impulse by orders of magnitude.

Oxygen is a common constituent of the moon's crust, and is probably abundant in most other bodies in the Solar System. Non-terrestrial oxygen would be about as valuable as water ice, for example:

- In the life support systems of space ships, space stations and planetary bases.
- In rocket engines. Even if the other propellant has to be lifted from Earth, using non-terrestrial oxygen could reduce propellant launch costs by up to 2/3 for hydrocarbon fuel, or 85 per cent for hydrogen. The savings are so high because oxygen accounts for the majority of the mass in most rocket propellant combinations.

Scientists expect to find a vast range of organic compounds in some of the planets, moons and comets of the outer Solar System, and the range of possible uses is even wider. For example methane can be used as a fuel (burned with non-terrestrial oxygen), or as a feedstock for petrochemical processes such as making plastics. And ammonia could be a valuable feedstock for producing fertilizers to be used in the vegetable gardens of orbital and planetary bases, reducing the need to lift food to them from Earth.

Even unprocessed rock may be useful as rocket propellant if mass drivers are employed.

Exotic Propulsion

See the spacecraft propulsion article for a discussion of a number of other technologies that could, in the medium to longer term, be the basis of interplanetary missions. Unlike the situation with interstellar travel, the barriers to fast interplanetary travel involve engineering and economics rather than any basic physics.

Difficulties of Manned Interplanetary Travel

Life Support

Life support systems must be capable of supporting human life for weeks, months or even years. A breathable atmosphere of at least 35 kPa (5 psi) must be maintained, with adequate amounts of oxygen, nitrogen, and controlled levels of carbon dioxide, trace gases and water vapour.

In practice on the International Space Station the Elektron oxygen generator unit has been temperamental.

Radiation

Once a vehicle leaves low earth orbit and the protection of Earth's magnetosphere, it enters the Van Allen radiation belt, a region of high radiation. Once through there the radiation drops to lower levels, with a constant background of high energy cosmic rays. These are dangerous over periods of years to decades.

Scientists of Russian Academy of Sciences are searching for methods of reducing the risk of radiation-induced cancer in preparation for the mission to Mars. They consider as one of the options a life support system generating drinking water with low content of Deuterium (stabile isotope of hydrogen) to be consumed by the crew members. Preliminary investigations have shown that Deuterium-depleted water features certain anti-cancer effects. Hence, Deuterium-free drinking water is considered to have the potential of lowering the risk of cancer caused by extreme radiation exposure of the Martian crew.

In addition, Coronal mass ejections from the Sun are highly dangerous, and are fatal within a very short timescale to humans unless they are protected by massive shielding.

Reliability

Any major failure to a spacecraft *en route* is likely to be fatal, and even a minor one could have dangerous results if not repaired quickly, something difficult to accomplish in open space. The crew of the Apollo 13 mission survived despite an explosion caused by a faulty oxygen tank (1970); the crews of Soyuz 11 (1971), the Space Shuttles Challenger (1986) and Columbia (2003) were killed by malfunctions of their vessels' components.

Launch Windows

For astrodynamics reasons, cheap spacecraft travel to other planets is only practical within certain time windows. Outside these windows the planets are essentially inaccessible from Earth with current technology. This constrains flights and prevents rescue in an emergency.

Feasibility of Manned Interplanetary Travel

While manned interplanetary travel (with the arguable exception of the Apollo programme) has not yet been achieved, a manned mission to Mars is probably feasible, even with chemical rocket propulsion, and could probably be achieved within a decade (at most two) if the funds were made available. NASA's "Design Reference Mission" proposes a Mars exploration programme costing $50 billion, but others have made detailed proposals with projected costs much less.

HUMAN SPACEFLIGHT

A **human spaceflight** is a spaceflight with a human crew, and possibly passengers. This makes it unlike robotic space probes or remotely-controlled satellites. Human spaceflight is sometimes called **manned spaceflight**, a term now deprecated by major space agencies in favour of its gender-neutral alternative.

As of 2009, human spaceflights are being actively launched by the Soyuz programme conducted by the Russian Federal Space Agency, the Space Shuttle programme conducted by NASA, and the Shenzhou programme conducted by the China National Space Administration.

A number of non-governmental startup companies have sprung up in recent years, hoping to create a space tourism industry, for a list of such companies, and the spacecraft they are currently building.

History

Prehistory

The ancient Indian epics, *Mahabharata* and *Ramayana*, feature mythical Vimana flying machines that were able to fly within the Earth's atmosphere, and able to travel into space and travel submerged under water. At around 125 AD, a Syrian satirist named Lucian wrote a book on spaceflight called *True Histories*. The book was full of tall, unbelievable tales and travelogues on visits to the sun and the moon. Today, the book could easily be discarded as the fantasy of a people of a bygone era. But it was significant in the sense that it kindled the curiosities of the people of the day and stimulated interest in outer space and space travel.

During the Middle Ages, several stories within the *One Thousand and One Nights* (*Arabian Nights*) feature fantastic tales of human spaceflight. For example, "The Adventures of Bulukiya" features the protagonist Bulukiya journeying to the Garden of Eden and to Jahannam, and travelling across the cosmos to different worlds much larger than his own world, anticipating elements of galactic science fiction. "The Ebony Horse" features a robot in the form of a flying mechanical horse controlled using keys that could fly into outer space and towards the Sun. "The Ebony Horse" can be considered an early example of proto-science fiction.

The 10th century Japanese narrative, *The Tale of the Bamboo Cutter*, may also be considered proto-science fiction. The protagonist of the story, Kaguya-hime, is a princess from the Moon who is sent to Earth for safety during a celestial war, and is found and raised by a bamboo cutter in Japan. She is later taken back to the Moon by her real extraterrestrial family. A manuscript illustration depicts a round flying machine similar to a flying saucer.

American author Herbert S. Zim claimed in 1945 that there is a Chinese legend where a scientist named Wan Hu (d. 1500) in the early Ming Dynasty attempted to travel through space with the help of rockets. However, the account is unsourced, and no known Chinese account exists. In the story, Wan tied 47 rockets filled with explosives to the chair in which he was sitting and ignited them. There was a large explosion, but when the smoke cleared Wan Hu was gone and never seen again.

First Human Spaceflights

The first human spaceflight was undertaken on April 12, 1961, when cosmonaut Yuri Gagarin made one orbit around the Earth aboard the Vostok 1 spacecraft, launched by the Soviet space programme and designed by the rocket scientists Sergey Korolyov and Kerim Kerimov. Valentina Tereshkova became the first woman in space on board Vostok 6 on June 16, 1963. Both spacecraft were launched by Vostok 3KA launch vehicles. Alexei Leonov made the first spacewalk when he left the Voskhod 2 on March 8, 1965. Svetlana Savitskaya became the first woman to do so on July 25, 1984.

The United States became the second nation (and for four decades, one of only two) to achieve manned spaceflight, with the suborbital flight of astronaut Alan Shepard aboard *Freedom 7*, carried out as part of Project Mercury. The spacecraft was launched on May 5, 1961 on a Redstone rocket. The first U.S. orbital flight was that of John Glenn aboard *Friendship 7*, which was launched on February 20, 1962 on an Atlas rocket. Since April 12, 1981 the U.S. has conducted all its human spaceflight missions with reusable Space Shuttles. Sally Ride became the first American woman in space in 1983. Eileen Collins was the first female Shuttle pilot, and with Shuttle mission STS-93 in July 1999 she became the first woman to command a U.S. spacecraft.

The People's Republic of China became the third nation to achieve human spaceflight when Yang Liwei launched into space on a Chinese-made vehicle, the Shenzhou 5, on October 15, 2003. The flight made China the third nation capable of launching its own manned spacecraft using its own launcher. Previous European (Hermes) and Japanese (HOPE-X) domestic manned programmes were abandoned after years of development, as was the first Chinese attempt, the Shuguang spacecraft.

The furthest destination for a human spaceflight mission has been the Moon, and as of 2008 the only missions to the Moon have been those conducted by NASA as part of the Apollo programme. The first such mission, Apollo 8, orbited the Moon but did not land. The first Moon landing mission was Apollo 11, during which—on July 20, 1969—Neil Armstrong became the first person to set foot on the Moon. Six missions landed in total, numbered Apollo 11-17, excluding Apollo 13. Altogether twelve men reached the Moon's surface, the only humans to have been on an extraterrestrial body. The Soviet Union discontinued its programme for lunar orbiting and landing of human spaceflight missions on June 24, 1974 when Valentin Glushko became General Designer of NPO Energiya.

The longest single human spaceflight is that of Valeriy Polyakov, who left earth on January 8, 1994, and didn't return until March 22, 1995 (a total of 437 days 17 hr. 58 min. 16 sec. aboard). Sergei Krikalyov has spent the most time of anyone in space, 803 days, 9 hours, and 39 seconds altogether. The longest period of continuous human presence in space lasted as long as 3,644 days, eight days short of 10 years, spanning the launch of Soyuz TM-8 on September 5, 1989 to the landing of Soyuz TM-29 on August 28, 1999.

For many years beginning in 1961, only two countries, the USSR (later Russia) and United States, had their own astronauts. Later, cosmonauts and astronauts from other nations flew in space, beginning with the flight of Vladimir Remek, a Czech, on a Soviet spacecraft on March 2, 1978. As of 2007, citizens from 33 nations (including space tourists) have flown in space aboard Soviet, American, Russian, and Chinese spacecraft.

Space Programmes

As of 2009, human spaceflight missions have been conducted by the former Soviet Union/(Russia), the United States, the People's Republic of China and by the private spaceflight company Scaled Composites.

Several other countries and space agencies have announced and begun human spaceflight programmes by their own technology, including India (ISRO), Ecuador (EXA), Japan (JAXA), Iran (ISA), Malaysia (MNSA) and Turkey.

Currently the following spacecraft and spaceports are used for launching human spaceflights:

- Soyuz with Soyuz rocket—Baikonur Cosmodrome
- Space Shuttle—Kennedy Space Center
- International Space Station (ISS)—Assembled in orbit; crews transported by the previous two spacecraft
- Shenzhou spacecraft with Long March rocket—Jiuquan Satellite Launch Center

Historically, the following spacecraft and spaceports have also been used for human spaceflight launches:

- Vostok—Baikonur Cosmodrome
- Mercury—Kennedy Space Center
- Voskhod—Baikonur Cosmodrome
- X-15—Edwards Air Force Base (two internationally recognized suborbital flights in programme)
- Gemini—Kennedy Space Center
- Apollo—Kennedy Space Center
- Salyut space station—Baikonur Cosmodrome
- Almaz space station—Baikonur Cosmodrome
- Skylab space station—Kennedy Space Center
- Mir space station—Baikonur Cosmodrome
- SpaceShipOne with White Knight—Mojave Spaceport

Numerous private companies attempted human spaceflight programmes in an effort to win the $10 million Ansari X Prize. The first private human spaceflight took place on June 21, 2004, when SpaceShipOne conducted a suborbital flight. SpaceShipOne captured the prize on October 4, 2004, when it accomplished two consecutive flights within one week.

Most of the time, the only humans in space are those aboard the ISS, whose crew of six spends up to six months at a time in low Earth orbit.

NASA and ESA now use the term "human spaceflight" to refer to their programmes of launching people into space. Traditionally, these endeavours have been referred to as "manned space missions".

National Spacefaring Attempts

Successful manned programmes are in **bold**. Suborbital spaceflight in *italics*.

Nation Organization	*Space agency*	*First launched astronaut*	*Date*	*Spacecraft*	*Launcher*
Soviet Union	Soviet space programme (OKB-1 Design Bureau)	**Yuri Gagarin**	**April 12, 1961**	**Vostok 1**	**Vostok**
United States	*National Aeronautics and Space Administration (NASA)*	*Alan Shepard*	*May 5, 1961*	*Mercury-Redstone 3*	*Redstone*
China	China space programme	—	1973 (abandoned)	Shuguang 1	Long March 2A
China	China space programme	—	1981 (abandoned) January 7, 1979 (failed)	Piloted FSW	Long March 2

ESA	European Space Agency (ESA)	—	1999 (abandoned)	Hermes	Ariane V
Iraq	—	—	2001 (abandoned)	—	Tammouz 2 or 3
Japan	Japan Aerospace Exploration Agency (JAXA)	—	2003 (abandoned)	HOPE-X	H-II
China	**China National Space Administration (CNSA)**	**Yang Liwei**	**October 15, 2003**	**Shenzhou 5**	**Long March 2F**
India	Indian Space Research Organisation (ISRO)	—	2015 (approved)	Orbital Vehicle (OV)	GSLV Mk II
Iran	Iranian Space Agency (ISA)	—	2021 (planned)	ISA manned spacecraft	—
ESA	European Space Agency (ESA)	—	2025 (Project under evaluation)	ATV evolution	Ariane V
Japan	Japan Aerospace Exploration Agency (JAXA)	—	2025 (planned)	JAXA manned spacecraft	H-IIB
North Korea	Korean Committee of Space Technology (KCST)	—	TBA (planned)	—	—
Turkey	Scientific and Technological Research Council of Turkey (TÜBİTAK)	—	TBA (planned)	—	—
Malaysia	Malaysian National Space Agency (MNSA)	—	TBA (planned)	—	—
Ecuador	Ecuadorian Civilian Space Agency	—	TBA (planned)	EXA manned spacecraft	—

Safety Concerns

Planners of human spaceflight missions face a number of safety concerns.

Life Support

The immediate needs for breathable air and drinkable water are addressed by the life support system of the spacecraft.

Medical Issues

Effects of Microgravity

Medical data from astronauts in low earth orbits for long periods, dating back to the 1970s, show several adverse effects of a microgravity environment: loss of bone density, decreased muscle strength and endurance, postural instability, and reductions in aerobic capacity. Over time these deconditioning effects can impair astronauts' performance or increase their risk of injury.

In a weightless environment, astronauts put almost no weight on the back muscles or leg muscles used for standing up. Those muscles then start to weaken and eventually get smaller. If there is an emergency at landing, the loss of muscles, and consequently the loss of strength can be a serious problem. Sometimes, astronauts can lose up to 25 per cent of their muscle mass on long-term flights. When they get back to ground, they will be considerably weakened and will be out of action for a while.

Astronauts experiencing weightlessness will often lose their orientation, get motion sickness, and lose their sense of direction as their bodies try to get used to a weightless environment. When they get back to Earth, or any other mass with gravity, they have to readjust to the gravity and may have problems standing up, focusing their gaze, walking and turning. Importantly, those body motor disturbances after changing from different gravities only get worse the longer the exposure to little gravity. These changes will affect operational activities including approach and landing, docking, remote manipulation, and emergencies that happen by landing. This is a big problem for mission success.

Radiation

Without proper shielding the crews of missions beyond low Earth orbit might be at risk from high-energy protons emitted by solar flares. Lawrence Townsend of the University of Tennessee and others have studied the most powerful solar flare ever recorded. That flare was seen by the British astronomer Richard Carrington in September 1859. Radiation doses astronauts would receive from a Carrington-type flare could cause acute radiation sickness and possibly even death.

Radiation Damage to the Immune System

Another factor is that extended spaceflight might slow down the body's ability to protect itself against diseases. Some of the problems are a weakened immune system and the activation of dormant viruses in the body. Radiation can cause both short- and long-term consequences to the blood marrow stem cells which create the blood and immune systems. Because the interior of a spacecraft is so small, a weakened immune system and more active viruses in the body can lead to a fast spread of infection.

Isolation

During long missions, astronauts have to go through the isolation and confinement of a space environment. People isolated for a long period of time can go into depression. This can negatively influence the mission's success. Not only are astronauts subjected to near total isolation from the rest of the world, but they have very limited space to move around. These factors can lead to cabin fever and several other psychological problems.

When on long missions, astronauts will not be able to quickly return to Earth if a medical emergency occurs. For example, a scientist working in the south pole found a lump in her breast and had to wait two months before a helicopter could come in. In space, even that is not an option. When a medical emergency happens, the astronauts have to rely on the crew and the computers to solve the problem.

Fatality Risk

As of 2009, 18 crew members have died during actual spaceflight missions (see table). Over 100 others have died in accidents during activity directly related to spaceflight missions or testing.

Year	No. of deaths	Mission	Known or likely cause
1967	1	Soyuz 1	Trauma from Earth surface impact
1971	3	Soyuz 11	Asphyxia from cabin breach
1986	7	Space Shuttle Challenger	Trauma from Earth surface impact (mission never reached space)
2003	7	Space Shuttle Columbia	Asphyxia from cabin breach or trauma from object impact

PRIVATE SPACEFLIGHT

Private spaceflight is flight above 100 km (62 mi) Earth altitude conducted by and paid for by an entity other than a government. In the early decades of the Space Age, the government space agencies of the Soviet Union and United States pioneered space technology in collaboration with affiliated design bureaus and private enterprises. Later on, large defense contractors began to develop and operate space launch systems, derived from government rockets, and commercial satellites. Private spaceflight in Earth orbit includes communications satellites, satellite television, satellite radio and orbital space tourism. Recently, entrepreneurs have begun designing and deploying competitive space systems to the national-monopoly governmental systems of the early decades of the space age. Successes to date include flying suborbital spaceplanes and launching light weight orbital rockets. Planned private spaceflights beyond Earth orbit include solar sailing prototypes, deep space burial and personal spaceflights around the Moon. A private orbital habitat prototype is already in Earth orbit, with larger versions to follow.

History of Commercial Space Transportation

During the early years of spaceflight only nation states had the resources to develop and fly spacecraft. Both the U.S. space programme and Soviet space programme were operated using mainly military pilots as astronauts. During this period, no commercial space launches were available to private operators, and no private organization was able to offer space launches. Eventually, private organizations were able to both offer and purchase space launches, thus beginning the period of private spaceflight.

The first phase of private space operation was the launch of the first commercial communications satellites. The U.S. Communications Satellite Act of 1962 opened the way to commercial consortia owning and operating their own satellites, although these were still launched on state-owned launch vehicles.

European Sponsorship

On March 26, 1980, the European Space Agency created Arianespace, the world's first commercial space transportation company. Arianespace produces, operates and markets the Ariane launcher family. By 1995 Arianespace lofted its 100th satellite and by 1997 the Ariane rocket had its 100th launch. Arianespace's 23 shareholders represent scientific, technical, financial and political entities from 10 different European countries.

American Deregulation

From the beginning of the Shuttle programme until the Challenger disaster in 1986, it was the policy of the United States that NASA be the public-sector provider of U.S. launch capacity to the world market. Initially NASA subsidized satellite launches with the intention of eventually pricing Shuttle service for the commercial market at long-run marginal cost.

On October 30, 1984, United States President Ronald Reagan signed into law the Commercial Space Launch Act. This enabled an American industry of private operators of expendable launch systems. Prior to the signing of this law, all commercial satellite launches in the United States were limited to NASA's Space Shuttle.

On November 5, 1990, United States President George H.W. Bush signed into law the Launch Services Purchase Act. The Act, in a complete reversal of the earlier Space Shuttle monopoly, ordered NASA to purchase launch services for its primary payloads from commercial providers whenever such services are required in the course of its activities.

Commercial launches outnumbered government launches at the Eastern Test Range in 1997.

Russian Privatization

The Russian government sold part of its stake in RSC Energia to private investors in 1994. Energia together with Khrunichev constituted most of the Russian manned space programme. In 1997, the Russian government sold off enough of its share to lose the majority position.

American Subsidization

In 1996 the United States government selected Lockheed Martin and Boeing to each develop Evolved Expendable Launch Vehicles (EELV) to compete for launch contracts and provide assured access to space. The government's acquisition strategy relied on the strong commercial viability of both vehicles to lower unit costs. This anticipated market demand did not materialize, but both the Delta IV and Atlas V EELVs remain in active service.

Launch Alliances

Since 1995 Khrunichev's Proton rocket is marketed through International Launch Services while the Soyuz rocket is marketed via Starsem. Energia builds the Soyuz rocket and owns part of the Sea Launch project which flies the Ukrainian Zenit rocket.

In 2003 Arianespace joined with Boeing Launch Services and Mitsubishi Heavy Industries to create the Launch Services Alliance. In 2005, continued weak commercial demand for EELV launches drove Lockheed Martin and Boeing to propose a joint venture called the United Launch Alliance to service the United States government launch market.

Today many commercial space transportation companies offer launch services to satellite companies and government space organizations around the world. In 2005 there were 18 total commercial launches and 37 non-commercial launches. Russia flew 44 per cent of commercial orbital launches, while Europe had 28 per cent and the United States had 6 per cent.

Private Spaceflight Companies

Commercial Launchers

The space transport business serves primarily national government and large commercial customer segments. Launches of government payloads, including military, civilian and scientific satellites, is the largest market segment at nearly $100 billion a year. This segment is dominated by domestic favourites such as the United Launch Alliance for U.S. government payloads and Arianespace for European satellites. The commercial payload segment, valued at under $3 billion a year, is dominated by Arianespace, with over 50 per cent of the market segment, followed by Russian launchers.

Commercial Orbital Transportation Services

On January 18, 2006 NASA announced an opportunity for commercial providers to demonstrate orbital transportation services. NASA plans to spend $500 million through 2010 to finance development of private sector capability to transport payloads to the International Space Station (ISS). This is more challenging than extant commercial space transportation because it requires precision orbit insertion, rendezvous and possibly docking with another spacecraft. The commercial vendors will compete in specific service areas. NASA Administrator Michael D. Griffin has stated that without affordable commercial orbital transportation services (COTS), the agency will not have enough funds remaining to achieve the objectives of the Vision for Space Exploration.

In August 2006, NASA announced that two fledgling aerospace companies, SpaceX and Rocketplane Kistler, had been awarded $278m and $207, respectively, under the COTS programme. NASA anticipates that COTS services to ISS will be necessary through at least 2015. The NASA Administrator has suggested that space transportation services procurement may be expanded to orbital fuel depots and lunar surface deliveries should the first phase of COTS prove successful.

After it transpired that Rocketplane Kister was failing to meet its deadlines, the NASA terminated their contract in August 2008, after only $32m had been spent. Several months later, in December 2008, NASA announced that they have awarded the remaining $170m to the trusted Orbital Sciences Corporation to develop resupply services to the ISS.

Emerging Personal Spaceflight

Before 2004 no privately operated manned spaceflight had ever occurred. The only private individuals to journey to space went as space tourists in the Space Shuttle or on Russian Soyuz flights to Mir or the International Space Station.

All private individuals who flew to space before Dennis Tito's self-financed International Space Station visit in 2001 had been sponsored by their home governments. Those trips include US Congressman Bill Nelson's January 1986 flight on the Space Shuttle Columbia and Japanese television reporter Toyohiro Akiyama's 1990 flight to the Mir Space Station.

The Ansari X PRIZE was intended to stimulate private investment in the development of spaceflight technologies. The June 21, 2004 test flight of SpaceShipOne, a contender for the X PRIZE, was the first human spaceflight in a privately developed and operated vehicle.

On September 27, 2004, following the success of SpaceShipOne, Richard Branson, owner of Virgin and Burt Rutan, SpaceShipOne's designer, announced that Virgin Galactic had licensed the craft's technology, and were planning commercial space flights in 2.5 to 3 years. A fleet of five craft (SpaceShipTwo, launched from the WhiteKnightTwo carrier airplane) is to be constructed, and flights will be offered at around $200,000 each, although Branson has said that he plans to use this money to make flights more affordable in the long term.

XCOR Aerospace also plans to initiate a suborbital commercial spaceflight service with the Lynx rocketplane in 2012. First test flights are planned for 2010.

In December 2004, United States President George W. Bush signed in to law the Commercial Space Launch Amendments Act. The Act resolved the regulatory ambiguity surrounding private spaceflights and is designed to promote the development of the emerging U.S. commercial human spaceflight industry.

On July 12, 2006, Bigelow Aerospace launched the *Genesis I*, a subscale pathfinder of an orbital space station module. *Genesis II* was launched on June 28, 2007, and there are plans for additional prototypes to be launched in preparation for the production model *BA 330* spacecraft.

On September 28, 2006, Jim Benson, SpaceDev founder, announced that he was founding Benson Space Company with the intention of being first to market with the safest and lowest cost suborbital personal spaceflight launches, using the vertical takeoff and horizontal landing Dream Chaser vehicle based on the NASA HL-20 Personnel Launch System vehicle.

Failed Spaceflight Ventures

In the 1990s the projection of a significant demand for communications satellite launches attracted the development of a number of commercial space launch providers. The launch demand largely vanished when some of the largest satellite constellations, such as 288 satellite Teledesic network, were never built. The historic tendency of NASA to compete against the private sector and the Department of Defense's preference for the traditional military industrial complex has discouraged many new space launch ventures.

VentureStar

In 1996 NASA selected Lockheed Martin Skunk Works to build the X-33 VentureStar prototype for a single stage to orbit (SSTO) reusable launch vehicle. In 1999, the subscale X-33 prototype's composite liquid hydrogen fuel tank failed during testing. At project termination on March 31, 2001, NASA had funded $912 million of this wedge shaped spacecraft while Lockheed Martin financed $357 million of it. The VentureStar was to have been a full-scale commercial space transport operated by Lockheed Martin.

Beal Aerospace

In 1997 Beal Aerospace proposed the BA-2, a low-cost heavy-lift commercial launch vehicle. On March 4, 2000, the BA-2 project tested the largest liquid rocket engine built since the Saturn V. In October 2000, Beal Aerospace ceased operations citing a decision by NASA and the Department of Defense to commit themselves to the development of the competing government-financed EELV programme.

Rotary Rocket

In 1998 Rotary Rocket proposed the Roton, a Single Stage to Orbit (SSTO) piloted Vertical Take-off and Landing (VTOL) space transport. A full scale Roton Atmospheric Test Vehicle flew three times in 1999. After spending tens of millions of dollars in development the Roton failed to secure launch contracts and Rotary Rocket ceased operations in 2001.

Future Plans

Many have speculated on where private spaceflight may go in the near future. One possibility is for paid suborbital tourism on craft like SpaceShipOne. Additionally, suborbital spacecraft have applications for faster intercontinental package delivery and passenger flight.

Private Orbital Spaceflight, Space Stations

SpaceX's Falcon 9 rocket, scheduled to be first launched in mid 2009, is designed to be man-rated. This would be the first American orbital vehicle since the Space Shuttle to receive this designation, in principle allowing the vehicle to transport paying customers to orbit. Plans and a full-scale prototype for the SpaceX Dragon, a manned capsule carrying up to 7 passengers, were announced on March 6, 2006.

An early flight of the Falcon 9 is planned to carry Sundancer, the prototype expandable space complex module (based on the formerly NASA-owned Translab design) constructed by Bigelow Aerospace. Bigelow Aerospace expects such modules to be used for activities like microgravity research, space manufacturing, and space tourism (with modules serving as orbital hotels). To promote private manned launch efforts, Bigelow has offered the $50m America's Space Prize for the first US-based privately funded team to launch a manned reusable spacecraft to orbit on or before January 10, 2010.

Excalibur Almaz plans to launch a modernized Almaz space station, for tourism and other uses. It will feature the largest window ever on a spacecraft.

On-Orbit Propellant Depots

In a presentation given on November 15, 2005, to the 52nd Annual Conference of the American Astronautical Society, NASA Administrator Michael D. Griffin suggested that establishing an on-orbit propellant depot is, "Exactly the type of enterprise which should be left to industry and to the marketplace." At the Space Technology and Applications International Forum in 2007, Dallas Bienhoff of Boeing made a presentation detailing the benefits of propellant depots.

Asteroid Mining

Some have speculated on the profitability of mining metal from asteroids. According to some estimates, a one kilometre-diameter asteroid would contain 30 million tons of nickel, 1.5 million tons of metal cobalt and 7,500 tons of platinum; the platinum alone would have a value of more than $500 billion at current prices. While the potential rewards from asteroid mining are indeed huge, the technical challenges are equally large and it seems likely that the private sector will wait for the publicly funded space Programme to solve them (e.g. by establishing experimental mines on the Moon).

Energy from Space

Future energy development may use energy sources in space and on other planets. Examples include Helium-3 extraction from the Moon, and solar power satellite systems.

Space Elevators

A Space Elevator system is a possible launch system, currently under investigation by at least one private venture. There are concerns over cost, general feasibility and some political issues. On the plus side the potential to scale the system to accommodate traffic would (in theory) be greater than some other alternatives. Some factions contend that a space elevator—if successful—would not supplant existing launch solutions but complement them.

ASTRONAUT

An **astronaut** or **cosmonaut** is a person trained by a human spaceflight programme to command, pilot, or serve as a crew member of a spacecraft. While generally reserved for professional space travellers, the term is sometimes applied to anyone who travels into space, including scientists, politicians, journalists, and tourists.

Until 2003, astronauts were sponsored and trained exclusively by governments, either by the military, or by civilian space agencies. However, with the sub-orbital flight of the privately-funded SpaceShipOne in 2004, a new category of astronaut was created: the commercial astronaut.

Definition

The criteria for what constitutes human spaceflight vary. The Fédération Aéronautique Internationale (FAI) Sporting Code for astronautics recognizes only flights that exceed an altitude of 100 kilometres (62 mi). However, in the United States, professional, military, and commercial astronauts who travel above an altitude of 80 kilometres (50 mi) are awarded astronaut wings.

As of November 14, 2008, a total of 489 humans from 38 countries have reached 100 km or more in altitude, of which 486 reached Low Earth orbit or beyond. Of these, 24 people have travelled beyond Low Earth orbit, to either lunar or trans-lunar orbit or to the surface of the moon; three of the 24 did so twice (Lovell, Young and Cernan).

Under the U.S. definition, 496 people qualify as having reached space [above 50 miles (80 km) altitude]. Of eight X-15 pilots who reached 50 miles (80 km) or more in altitude, seven reached above 50 miles (80 km) but below 100 kilometres (about 62 miles). Space travellers have spent over 30,400 person-days (or a cumulative total of over 83 years) in space, including over 100 astronaut-days of spacewalks. As of 2008, the man with the longest time in space is Sergei K. Krikalev, who has spent 803 days, 9 hours and 39 minutes, or 2.2 years, in space. Peggy A. Whitson holds the record for most time in space by a woman, 377 days.

Terminology

In the United States, Canada, United Kingdom, and many other English-speaking nations, a professional space traveller is called an *astronaut*. The term derives from the Greek words *ástron*, meaning "star", and *nautes*, meaning "sailor". The first known use of the term "astronaut" in the modern sense was by Neil R. Jones in his short story *The Death's Head Meteor* in 1930. The word itself had been known earlier. For example, in Percy Greg's 1880 book *Across the Zodiac*, "astronaut" referred to a spacecraft. In *Les Navigateurs de l'Infini* (1925) of J.H. Rosny aîné, the word *astronautique* (astronautic) was used. The word may have been inspired by "aeronaut", an older term for an air traveller first applied (in 1784) to balloonists.

NASA applies the term astronaut to any crew member aboard NASA spacecraft bound for Earth orbit or beyond. NASA also uses the term as a title for those selected to join its Astronaut Corps. The European Space Agency similarly uses the term astronaut for members of its Astronaut Corps.

With the rise of space tourism, NASA and the Russian Federal Space Agency agreed to use the term "spaceflight participant" to distinguish those space travellers from astronauts on missions coordinated by those two agencies.

Russia

By convention, an astronaut employed by the Russian Federal Space Agency (or its Soviet predecessor) is called a *cosmonaut* in English texts. The word is an anglicisation of the Russian word *kosmonavt,* which in turn derives from the Greek words *kosmos,* meaning "universe", and *nautes,* meaning "sailor". For the most part, "cosmonaut" and "astronaut" are synonyms in all languages, and the usage of choice is often dictated by political reasons.

On March 14, 1995, Norman Thagard became the first American to ride to space on board a Russian launch vehicle, arguably becoming the first "American cosmonaut" in the process.

China

Official English-language texts issued by the government of the People's Republic of China use *astronaut* while texts in Russian use *kosmonavt*. In China, the terms "yuhángyuán", ("sailing personnel in universe") or "hángtiānyuán" ("sailing personnel in sky") have long been used for astronauts. The phrase "tàikōng rén", "Space man" is often used in Taiwan and Hong Kong.

The term *taikonaut* is used by some English-language news media organizations for professional space travellers from China. The word has featured in the Longman and Oxford English dictionaries, the latter of which describes it as "a hybrid of the Chinese term *taikong* (space) and the Greek *naut* (traveller), or astronaut"; the term became more common in 2003 when China sent its first astronaut Yang Liwei into space aboard the *Shenzhou 5* spacecraft. This is the term used by Xinhua in the English version of the Chinese People's Daily since the advent of the Chinese space programme. The origin of the term is unclear; as early as May 1998, Chiew Lee Yih from Malaysia, used it in newsgroups, while Chen Lan, almost simultaneously, announced it at his "Go Taikonauts!" GeoCities page.

Other Terms

While no nation other than Russia (formerly the Soviet Union), the United States, and China has launched a manned spacecraft, several other nations have sent people into space in cooperation with one of these countries. Inspired partly by these missions, other synonyms for astronaut have entered occasional English usage. For example, the term *spationaut* (French spelling: *spationaute*) is sometimes used to describe French space travellers, from the Latin word *spatium* or "space", and the Malay term *angkasawan* was used to describe participants in the Angkasawan programme.

Space Travel Milestones

The first human in space was Russian Yuri Gagarin, who was launched into space on April 12, 1961 aboard Vostok 1 and orbited around the Earth. There are allegations that Gagarin ejected from landing module after re-entering the atmosphere and parachuted back, due to safety concerns about the craft's landing systems. The first woman in space was Russian Valentina Tereshkova, launched in June 1963 aboard Vostok 6.

Alan Shepard became the first American and second person in space on May 5, 1961. The first American woman in space was Sally Ride, during Space Shuttle Challenger's mission STS-7, on June 18, 1983.

The first mission to orbit the moon was *Apollo 8*, which included William Anders who was born in Hong Kong, making him the first Asian-born astronaut in 1968. In April 1985, Taylor Wang became the first ethnic Chinese person in space. On 15 October 2003, Yang Liwei became China's first astronaut on the Shenzhou 5 spacecraft.

The Soviet Union, through its Intercosmos programme, allowed people from other "socialist" (i.e. Warsaw Pact and other Soviet-allied) countries to fly on its missions. An example is Vladimír Remek, a Czechoslovak, who became the first non-Soviet European in space in 1978 on a Russian Soyuz-U rocket. On July 23, 1980, Pham Tuan of Vietnam became the first Asian in space when he flew aboard Soyuz 37. Also in 1980, Cuban Arnaldo Tamayo Méndez became the first person of Hispanic and African descent to fly in space (the first person born in Africa to fly in space was Patrick Baudry, in 1985). In 1988, Abdul Ahad Mohmand became the first Afghan to reach space, spending nine days aboard the Mir space station.

With the larger number of seats available on the Space Shuttle, the U.S. began taking international astronauts. In 1983, Ulf Merbold of West Germany became the first non-US citizen to fly in a US spacecraft. In 1985, Rodolfo Neri Vela became the first Mexican-born person in space. In 1991, Helen Sharman became the first Briton to fly in space. In 2002, Mark Shuttleworth became the first citizen of an African country to fly in space, as a paying spaceflight participant. In 2003, Ilan Ramon became the first Israeli to fly in space, although he died during a landing accident.

Age Milestones

The youngest person to fly in space is Gherman Titov, who was 25 years old when he flew Vostok 2. (Titov was also the first person to suffer space sickness). The oldest person who has flown in space is John Glenn, who was 77 when he flew on STS-95. The longest stay in space was 438 days, by Russian Valeri Polyakov. As of 2006, the most spaceflights by an individual astronaut is seven, a record held by both Jerry L. Ross and Franklin Chang-Diaz. The furthest distance from Earth an astronaut has travelled was 401,056 km, during the Apollo 13 emergency.

Civilian and Non-Government Milestones

The first civilian in space was Neil Armstrong, who had retired from the United States Navy before his first spaceflight on Gemini 8. The first person in space who had never been a member of any country's armed forces was Harrison Schmitt, a geologist who first flew in space on Apollo 17. Both Armstrong and Schmitt were directly employed by NASA.

The first non-governmental space traveller was Byron K. Lichtenberg, a researcher from the Massachusetts Institute of Technology who flew on STS-9 in 1983. In December 1990, Toyohiro Akiyama became the first paying space traveller as a reporter for Tokyo Broadcasting System, a visit to Mir as part of an estimated $12 million (USD) deal with a Japanese TV station, although at the time, the term used to refer to Akiyama was "Research Cosmonaut". Akiyama suffered severe space-sickness during his mission, which affected his productivity.

The first self-funded space tourist was Dennis Tito onboard the Russian spacecraft Soyuz TM-3 on 28 April 2001.

Self-Funded Travellers

The first person to fly on an entirely privately-funded mission was Mike Melvill, piloting SpaceShipOne flight 15P on a sub-orbital journey, although he was a test pilot employed by Scaled Composites and not an actual paying space tourist. Six others have paid to fly into space:

1. Dennis Tito (American): April 28—May 6, 2001
2. Mark Shuttleworth (South African/British): April 25—May 5, 2002 (ISS)
3. Gregory Olsen (American): October 1—October 11, 2005 (ISS)
4. Anousheh Ansari (Iranian/American): September 18—September 29, 2006 (ISS)
5. Charles Simonyi (Hungarian/American): April 7—April 21, 2007 (ISS), March 26—April 8, 2009 (ISS)
6. Richard Garriott (American): October 12—October 24, 2008 (ISS)

Training

The first NASA astronauts were selected in 1959. Early in the space programme, military jet test piloting and engineering training were often cited as prerequisites for selection as an astronaut at NASA, although neither John Glenn nor Scott Carpenter (of the Mercury Seven) had any university degree, in engineering or any other discipline at the time of their selection. Selection was initially limited to military pilots. The earliest astronauts for both America and Russia tended to be jet fighter pilots, and were often test pilots.

Once selected, NASA astronauts go through 20 months of training in a variety of areas, including training for extra-vehicular activity in a facility such as NASA's Neutral Buoyancy Laboratory. Astronauts-in-training may also experience short periods of weightlessness in aircraft called the "vomit comet", the nickname given to a pair of modified KC-135s (retired in 2000 and 2004 respectively, and replaced in 2005 with a C-9) which perform parabolic flights. Astronauts are also required to accumulate a number of flight hours in high-performance jet aircraft. This is mostly done in T-38 jet aircraft out of Ellington Field, due to its proximity to the Johnson Space Center. Ellington Field is also where the Shuttle Training Aircraft is maintained and developed, although most flights of the aircraft are done out of Edwards Air Force Base.

NASA Candidacy Requirements

- Be citizens of the United States.
- Pass a strict physical examination, and have a near and distant visual acuity correctable to 20/20 (6/6). Blood pressure, while sitting, must be no greater than 140 over 90.

Commander and Pilot

- A bachelor's degree in engineering, biological science, physical science or mathematics is required.
- At least 1,000 hours flying time as pilot-in-command in jet aircraft. Experience as a test pilot is desirable.
- Height must be 5 ft 4 in to 6 ft 4 in (1.63 to 1.93 m).
- Distant visual acuity must be correctable to 20/20 in each eye.
- The refractive surgical procedures of the eye, PRK and LASIK, are now allowed, providing at least 1 year has passed since the date of the procedure with no permanent adverse after effects. For those applicants under final consideration, an operative report on the surgical procedure will be requested.

Mission Specialist

- A bachelor's degree in engineering, biological science, physical science or mathematics, as well as at least three years of related professional experience. An advanced degree can substitute for part or all of the experience requirement (master's degree = 1 year, doctoral degree = 3 years).
- Applicant's height must be 5 ft 2 in to 6 ft 4 in (1.57 to 1.93 m).

Mission Specialist Educator

- Bachelor's degree with teaching experience, including work at the kindergarten through 12th grade level. Advanced degree not required, but is desired.

Mission Specialist Educators, or "Educator Astronauts", were first selected in 2004, and as of 2007, there are three NASA Educator astronauts: Joseph M. Acaba, Richard R. Arnold, and Dorothy Metcalf-Lindenburger. Barbara Morgan, selected as back-up teacher to Christa McAuliffe in 1985, is considered to be the first Educator astronaut by the media, but she trained as a mission specialist. The Educator Astronaut Programme is a successor to the Teacher in Space Programme from the 1980s.

Insignia

At NASA, people who complete astronaut candidate training receive a silver lapel pin. Once they have flown in space, they receive a gold pin. U.S. astronauts who also have active-duty military status receive a special qualification badge, known as the Astronaut Badge, after participation on a spaceflight. The United States Air Force also presents an Astronaut Badge to its pilots who exceed 50 miles (80 km) in altitude.

Deaths

As of 2008, eighteen astronauts have lost their lives during spaceflight, on four missions. They include thirteen Americans, three Russians, one Ukrainian, and one Israeli.

The Space Mirror Memorial, which stands on the grounds of the John F. Kennedy Space Center Visitor Complex, commemorates the lives of the men and women who have died in the space programmes of the United States. In addition to twenty NASA career astronauts, the memorial includes the names of a U.S. Air Force X-15 test pilot, a U.S. Air Force officer who died while training for a then-classified military space programme, a civilian spaceflight participant who died in the Challenger disaster, and an international astronaut who was killed in the Columbia disaster.

COMMERCIAL ASTRONAUT

A commercial astronaut is a person trained to command, pilot, or serve as a crew member of a privately-funded spacecraft.

Criteria

The criteria for determining who has achieved human spaceflight vary. The FAI defines spaceflight as any flight over 100 kilometres (62 miles) of altitude. In the United States, professional, military, and commercial astronauts who travel above an altitude of 80 kilometres (50 miles) are eligible to purchase astronaut wings. Until 2003, professional space travellers were sponsored and trained exclusively by governments, either by the military or by civilian space agencies. However, with the first sub-orbital flight of the privately-funded Scaled Composites Tier One in 2004, the commercial astronaut category was created.

FAA Commercial Astronaut Rating

With the advent of private commercial spaceflight ventures in the U.S., the FAA has been faced with the task of developing a certification process for the pilots of commercial spacecraft. The Commercial Space Launch Act of 1984 established the FAA's Office of Commercial Space Transportation and required companies to obtain a launch license for vehicles, but at the time manned commercial flight—and the licensing of crewmembers—was not considered. The Commercial Space Launch Amendments Act has led to the issuance of draft guidelines by the FAA in February 2005 for the administration of vehicle and crew certifications. Currently, the FAA has not issued formal regulatory guidance for the issuance of a Commercial Astronaut Certificate, but as an interim measure, has established the practice of awarding "Commercial Astronaut Wings" to commercial pilots who have demonstrated the requisite proficiency.

Commercial Astronauts

Two awards have been made to SpaceShipOne pilots Mike Melvill and Brian Binnie.

SPACEFLIGHT PARTICIPANT

Spaceflight participant is the term used by National Aeronautics and Space Administration (NASA) and the Russian Federal Space Agency (RKA) for people who travel aboard space missions coordinated by those agencies who are not part of the crew. The term serves to distinguish tourists and other special travellers from the career astronauts.

While the term gained new prominence with the rise of space tourism, it has also been used for participants in NASA's Teacher in Space programme and for people who flew through inter-government agreements such as the Angkasawan programme and the Korean Astronaut programme.

Other terms used for space travellers who are not career astronauts include NASA's Payload Specialist and the RKA's Researcher-Cosmonaut.

Background

The Soviet Intercosmos programme included participants selected from Warsaw Pact members and later from allies of the USSR and non-aligned countries. Most of these people received full training for their missions and were treated as equals, but especially after the Mir programme began, were generally given shorter flights than Soviet cosmonauts. The European Space Agency took advantage of the programme as well.

The U.S. Space Shuttle programme included payload specialist positions which were usually filled by representatives of companies or institutions managing a specific payload on that mission. These payload specialists did not receive the same level of training as career NASA astronauts and were not employed by NASA, so they were essentially private astronauts.

In the early days of the Shuttle programme, NASA was also eager to prove its capability to Congressional sponsors, and Senator Jake Garn and (then Representative, now Senator) Bill Nelson were both given opportunities to fly on board a Shuttle mission.

As the Shuttle programme expanded, the Teacher in Space programme was developed as a way to expand publicity and educational opportunities for NASA. Christa McAuliffe would have been the first Teacher in Space, but she was killed in the Challenger disaster and the programme was cancelled. During the same period a Journalist in Space programme was frequently discussed, with individuals such as Walter Cronkite and Miles O'Brien considered front-runners, but no formal programme was ever developed.

With the realities of the post-Perestroika economy in Russia, its space industry was especially starved for cash. The Tokyo Broadcasting System (TBS) offered to pay for one of its reporters to fly on a mission. For $28 million, Toyohiro Akiyama was flown in 1990 to Mir with the eighth crew and returned a week later with the seventh crew. Akiyama gave a daily TV-broadcast from orbit and also performed scientific experiments for Russian and Japanese companies.

Since then, the Russian Federal Space Agency has also sold seats to a consortium of British companies for Project Juno, to six self-funded space tourists, to the Malaysian government as part of a contract to sell military planes, and to the South Korean government as part of the Korean Astronaut programme.

List of Spaceflight Participants

Name	*Nationality*	*Programme/Sponsor*	*Flight*	*Date*	*Comments*
Christa McAuliffe	United States	Teacher in Space Project	STS-51-L	28 January 1986	Killed alongside six fellow crew members in the Space Shuttle Challenger disaster. Back-up was Barbara Morgan, who was selected in 1998 to train as a Mission Specialist. Morgan finally flew to space aboard STS-118 in 2007, but as a "teacher-turned-astronaut", not a spaceflight participant.
Dennis Tito	United States	Self-funded space tourist	Soyuz TM-32/ Soyuz TM-31	April 28 - May 6, 2001	First space tourist
Mark Shuttleworth	South Africa	Self-funded space tourist	Soyuz TM-34/ Soyuz TM-33	April 25 - May 5, 2002	Shuttleworth was the first person with South African citizenship to fly in space.
Lance Bass	United States	Corporate-funded space tourist			Completed training but seat on Soyuz TMA-1 in 2002 was cancelled after funding fell through.
Gregory Olsen	United States	Self-funded space tourist	Soyuz TMA-7/ Soyuz TMA-6	October 1- October 11, 2005	
Daisuke Enomoto	Japan	Self-funded space tourist			Expected to fly on Soyuz TMA-9 in September 2006, but was grounded for medical reasons and seat was given to Ansari.
Anousheh Ansari	Iran/ United States	Self-funded space tourist	Soyuz TMA-9/ Soyuz TMA-8	September 18- September 29, 2006	Trained as back-up to Enomoto. Was the first person with Iranian citizenship to fly in space.
Charles Simonyi	Hungary/ United States	Self-funded space tourist	Soyuz TMA-10/ Soyuz TMA-9	April 7 - April 21, 2007	

Sheikh Muszaphar Shukor	Malaysia	Angkasawan programme	Soyuz TMA-11/ Soyuz TMA-10	10 October - 21 October 2007	Back-up was Faiz Khaleed.
Yi So-yeon	South Korea	Korean Astronaut programme	Soyuz TMA-12/ Soyuz TMA-11	8 April-19 April 2008	Back-up was Ko San.
Richard Garriott	United States	Self-funded space tourist	Soyuz TMA-13/ Soyuz TMA-12	12 October 2008 - 23 October 2008	Back-up was Nik Halik.
Charles Simonyi	Hungary/ United States	Self-funded space tourist	Soyuz TMA-14/ Soyuz TMA-13	26 March 2009- 8 April 2009	Backup was Esther Dyson. Simonyi was the first repeat space tourist.
Upcoming					
Vladimir Gruzdev	Russia	Political party-sponsored trip			Expected to fly in 2009. The United Russia political party may pay the estimated $25 million for the flight from the party funds.
Guy Laliberté	Canada	Self-funded space tourist	Soyuz TMA-16	NET September 30, 2009	Expected to fly in 2009. First Canadian space tourist. Backup is Barbara Barrett.

All seven space tourism trips went to and from the International Space Station on Soyuz spacecraft and were arranged through the space tourism company, Space Adventures.

Other Missions

While not labelled as "spaceflight participants", the following people participated in spaceflight missions under the auspices of special programmes outside of the professional astronaut corps.

Name	*Nationality*	*Programme/Sponsor*	*Flight*	*Date*	*Comments*
Jake Garn	United States	US Government	STS-51-D	12 April - 19 April 1985	To demonstrate the capabilities of the Space Shuttle, NASA offered a seat to Garn, a member of the Senate Appropriations Committee.
Bill Nelson	United States	US Government	STS-61-C	12 January - 18 January 1986	NASA also provided a seat to Nelson, a member of the U.S. House of Representatives. He was originally scheduled to be aboard STS-51-L.

Edward C. Aldridge, Jr.	United States	US Government	STS-62-A		NASA assigned a seat to Aldridge, the Secretary of the Air Force, on mission STS-62-A, the first Shuttle mission scheduled to launch from Vandenberg Air Force Base. After the Challenger disaster, the mission was cancelled and Aldridge never flew.
Toyohiro Akiyama	Japan	Tokyo Broadcasting System	Soyuz TM-11/ Soyuz TM-10	2 December - 10 December 1990	As an employee of TBS, Akiyama could be considered the first space business traveller.
Helen Sharman	United Kingdom	Project Juno	Soyuz TM-12/ Soyuz TM-11	18 May - 26 May 1991	Through Project Juno, a consortium of British companies partially funded a seat on a Soyuz flight to Mir (the Soviet Union covered the rest of the cost) in order to put the first Briton into space.

SPACEFLIGHT MANUAL: A MODEL CASE STUDY

Your Spaceflight Manual is a non-fiction book by David Ashford and Patrick Collins that investigates the possibility of a future space tourism industry. It was first published in 1990. The book contains analysis of the costs and benefits, the potential market and the safety factors of space tourism, and gives rough designs for the types of space vehicles and stations that would become necessary to support a full-fledged space tourism industry. This culminates with a description of a large space hotel (parts of which are spun to generate rotational artificial gravity) featuring attractions such as zero-gravity sports arenas and Earth-gazing observatories.

Predictions

The book gives a rough timeline of predictions for the future of space tourism, based on analogy with the history of commercial aviation.

- **2000-2005:** Pioneering—Using *Spacecab* a very low orbit two-stage reusable spaceplane to achieve a few hours of free fall. Cost per flight: 1,000,000 USD
- **2005-2020:** Exclusive—Again using Spacecab for a longer space trip, possibly visiting ISS. Cost per flight: 100,000 USD
- **2020-2050:** Mature—Transport now by second generation *Spacebus* with accommodation in a large space hotel. Cost per flight: 10,000 USD
- **2050-Onwards**—Mass use, Cost per flight: less than 10,000 USD

It predicts that the first space tourist would have flown around the year 2000. This proved accurate when the multimillionaire Dennis Tito paid for a seat on a Soyuz spacecraft in 2001. In 2005 the third space tourist, Gregory Olsen, paid an estimated 20 million USD for his trip to the International Space Station.

LIST OF SPACEFLIGHT RECORDS

This is a list of **spaceflight records**. Most of these records relate to human spaceflights, but some unmanned and canine records are included.

Longest Human Single Flight

- Valeri Polyakov, launched 8 January 1994 (Soyuz TM-18), stayed at Mir LD-4 for 437.7 days, during which he orbited the earth about 7,075 times and travelled 300,765,000 km (186,887,000 mi), returning 22 March 1995 (Soyuz TM-20). This record has stood for 14 years, 146 days.
- Sunita Williams holds the record for the longest single spaceflight by a woman at 195 days set on the International Space Station Expedition 15 in 2007. She landed with STS-117, 22 June 2007.

Longest Continuous Occupation of Space

- The Soviet Union and Russia, its successor, kept a continuous manned presence in space from the launch of Soyuz TM-8 on 5 September 1989 to the landing of Soyuz TM-29 on 28 August 1999, a span of about 3,644 days, or about eight days short of 10 years. The Soviet Union and Russia launched 22 manned Soyuz spacecraft during the time span, all of which docked with the orbiting Mir space station. The United States additionally docked the space shuttles Atlantis, Endeavour and Discovery with Mir nine times between 1995 and 1998, dropping off and/or picking up passengers eight times. This record has stood for 9 years, 353 days.
- The United States and Russia have jointly maintained a continuous manned presence in space since 31 October 2000 when Soyuz TM-31 was launched on a mission to dock with the International Space Station. The International Space Station has been in continuous use for 8 years, 288 days. Should the ISS occupation continue as planned, it will break the Mir record on 23 October 2010.

Longest Solo Flight

- Valery Bykovsky flew for 4 days and 23 hours solo in Vostok 5, 14-19 June 1963. The flight set a space endurance record which was broken in 1965 by the Gemini 7 crew, but the solo endurance record has stood for 46 years, 57 days.

Longest Canine Single Flight

- ***Veterok*** ("Little Wind") and ***Ugolyok*** ("Ember") were launched on 22 February 1966 on board Cosmos 110 and spent 22 days in orbit before landing on 16 March. This record has stood for 43 years, 152 days.

Longest Time on Lunar Surface

- Eugene Cernan and Harrison Schmitt of the Apollo 17 mission stayed for 74 hours 59 minutes 40 seconds on the lunar surface after they landed on 11 December 1972. This record has stood for 36 years, 247 days.

Farthest Humans from Earth

- Apollo 13 crew; Jim Lovell, Fred Haise, John Swigert while passing over the far side of the moon at an altitude of 254 km (158 mi) from the lunar surface, were 400,171 km (248,655 mi) from Earth. This record breaking distance was reached at 0:21 UTC on 15 April 1970. This record has stood for 39 years, 122 days.

Highest Altitude for Manned Non-Lunar Mission

- Gemini 11 crew Charles Conrad, Jr. and Richard F. Gordon, Jr. fired their Agena Target Vehicle rocket engine on 14 September 1966, at 40 hours 30 minutes after liftoff and achieved an apogee of 1,374.1 km (853.8 mi). This record has stood for 42 years, 335 days.

Fastest

- The Apollo 10 crew; Thomas Stafford, John W. Young and Eugene Cernan achieved the highest speed relative to Earth ever attained by humans; 39,896 km/h (11.1 km/s, 24,790 mph, approx 0.0037 per cent the speed of light). The record was set 26 May 1969 and has stood for 40 years, 81 days.

Oldest

- John Glenn at age 77 on 29 October 1998. This record has stood for 10 years, 290 days.

Youngest

- Gherman Titov, aged 25 years, on Vostok 2 on 6 August 1961. This record has stood for 48 years, 9 days.

Tallest

- James D. Wetherbee

Shortest

- Nancy Currie

Most Flights

- **7 Flights**
    - Franklin Chang-Diaz—Costa Rica/USA*
    - Jerry L. Ross—USA
    - John W. Young—USA (Flew 6 missions, with Apollo 16 having two distinct flights: launch from Earth landing on the Moon, and launch from the Moon landing on Earth.)
- **6 Flights**
    - Curtis Brown—USA
    - Michael Foale—Britain/USA+
    - Sergei Krikalev—Russia
    - Story Musgrave—USA
    - Gennady Strekalov—Russia
    - James Wetherbee—USA

Most Time in Space

- Sergei Krikalev has spent 803 days, 9 hours and 39 minutes, or 2.2 years in space over the span of six spaceflights on Soyuz, the Space Shuttle, Mir, and International Space Station.
- Peggy Whitson has spent 376 days, 17 hours and 22 minutes in space over the span of two spaceflights to the International Space Station.

Most Spacewalks

- Anatoly Solovyev, 16 spacewalks for total of 77 hours, 41 minutes (which is also the duration record).
- Peggy Whitson, 6 spacewalks for a total time of 39 hours and 46 minutes (the women's spacewalk and duration records).

Most Spacewalks during a Single Mission

- Michael Lopez-Alegria, five spacewalks during Expedition 14 on the ISS.

---

* Costa Rican-born and honorary citizen of Costa Rica
+ Dual citizen

Human Spaceflight Firsts

First	*Person(s)*	*Vehicle*	*Country*	*Date*
Spaceflight and Orbital flight	Yuri Gagarin	Vostok 1	USSR	12 April 1961
Person to land in a spacecraft	Alan Shepard	Freedom 7	USA	5 May 1961
Person in space for one day	Gherman Titov	Vostok 2	USSR	6 August 1961- 7 August 1961
Group flight Adjacent orbits Spacecraft-to-spacecraft communications	Andrian Nikolayev Pavel Popovich	Vostok 3 Vostok 4	USSR	12 August 1962- 15 August 1962
Woman in space Civilian in space	Valentina Tereshkova	Vostok 6	USSR	16 June 1963- 19 June 1963
Spaceflight by winged spacecraft	Joe Walker	X-15 Flight 90	USA	19 July 1963
Person to enter space twice (above 100 km)	Joe Walker	X-15 Flights 90 and 91	USA	22 August 1963
Three-person spacecraft	Vladimir Komarov Konstantin Feoktistov Boris Yegorov	Voskhod 1	USSR	12 October 1964- 13 October 1964
Two-person spacecraft	Pavel Belyayev Alexey Leonov	Voskhod 2	USSR	18 March 1965- 19 March 1965
Spacewalk	Alexey Leonov	Voskhod 2	USSR	18 March 1965
Orbital maneuvers (change orbit)	Gus Grissom, John W. Young	Gemini 3	USA	23 March 1965
Person to fly two orbital spaceflights	Gordon Cooper	Faith 7 Gemini 5	USA	15 May 1963- 16 May 1963; 21 August 1965- 29 August 1965
People to spend one week in space	Gordon Cooper Pete Conrad	Gemini 5	USA	21 August 1965- 29 August 1965
Space rendezvous (orbital maneuver and station keeping) Four people in space	Frank Borman, Jim Lovell Walter Schirra, Thomas Stafford	Gemini 7 Gemini 6A	USA	15 December 1965- 16 December 1965
Space docking	Neil Armstrong David Scott	Gemini 8 and Agena	USA	16 March 1966
Multiple rendezvous	John W. Young Michael Collins	Gemini 10 with Agena 10 and Agena 8	USA	19 July 1966; 20 July 1966
Lunar orbit	Frank Borman Jim Lovell Bill Anders	Apollo 8	USA	24 December 1968- 25 December 1968

Dual spacewalk; crew transfer	Aleksei Yeliseyev Yevgeny Khrunov	Soyuz 4 Soyuz 5	USSR	16 January 1969
Moon landing	Neil Armstrong Buzz Aldrin	Apollo 11	USA	20 July 1969
Time five people in space	Georgi Shonin, Valeri Kubasov Anatoli Filipchenko, Vladislav Volkov, Viktor Gorbatko	Soyuz 6 Soyuz 7	USSR	12 October 1969- 13 October 1969
Triple spaceflight Seven people in space	Shonin, Kubasov Filipchenko, Volkov, Gorbatko Vladimir Shatalov, Aleksei Yeliseyev	Soyuz 6 Soyuz 7 Soyuz 8	USSR	13 October 1969- 16 October 1969
Person to fly two lunar flights	James A. Lovell	Apollo 13	USA	11 April 1970- 17 April 1970
People to spend two weeks in space	Andrian Nikolayev Vitali Sevastyanov	Soyuz 9	USSR	1 June 1970- 19 June 1970
Manned space station	Georgi Dobrovolski Viktor Patsayev Vladislav Volkov	Soyuz 11 docked with Salyut 1	USSR	7 June 1971- 29 June 1971
People to EVA out of sight of their spacecraft	Alan Shepard Edgar Mitchell	Apollo 14	USA	6 February 1971
In-space fatalities	Georgi Dobrovolski Viktor Patsayev Vladislav Volkov	Soyuz 11	USSR	29 June 1971
People in orbit four weeks	Pete Conrad Joseph Kerwin Paul Weitz	Skylab 2	USA	25 May 1973- 22 June 1973
People in orbit eight weeks	Alan Bean Jack Lousma Owen Garriott	Skylab 3	USA	28 July 1973- 25 September 1973
People in orbit twelve weeks	Gerald Carr William Pogue Edward Gibson	Skylab 4	USA	16 November 1973- 8 February 1974
Crew to visit occupied space station	Vladimir Dzhanibekov, Oleg Makarov	Soyuz 27 visits Salyut 6 EO-1 crew	USSR	10 January 1978- 16 January 1978
People in orbit nineteen weeks (4 months)	Vladimir Kovalyonok, Aleksandr Ivanchenkov	Salyut 6 EO-2, Soyuz 29-Soyuz 31	USSR	15 June 1978- 2 November 1978
People in orbit twenty-six weeks (6 months)	Leonid Popov, Valery Ryumin	Salyut 6 EO-4, Soyuz 35-Soyuz 37	USSR	9 April 1980- 11 October 1980
Person to fly four different types of spacecraft	John Watts Young	STS-1	USA	12 April 1981
Four-person spaceflight, single spacecraft	Vance Brand, Robert F. Overmyer Joseph P. Allen, William B. Lenoir	STS-5	USA	11 November 1982- 16 November 1982
Five-person spaceflight, single spacecraft	Robert L. Crippen, Frederick H. Hauck John M. Fabian, Sally K. Ride, Norman E. Thagard	STS-7	USA	18 June 1983- 24 June 1983

Six-person spaceflight, single spacecraft	John W. Young, Brewster H. Shaw, Owen K. Garriott, Robert A. Parker, Byron K. Lichtenberg - *USA* Ulf Merbold - *Germany (European Space Agency)*	STS-9	USA West Germany	28 November 1983- 8 December 1983
Untethered spacewalk	Bruce McCandless II	STS-41-B	USA	7 February 1984
Time eight people in space, no docking	Oleg Atkov, Leonid Kizim, Vladimir Solovov - *USSR* Vance D. Brand, Robert L. Gibson, Bruce McCandless II, Ronald McNair,Robert L. Stewart - *USA*	Salyut 7 EO-3, Soyuz T-10, STS-41-B	USSR USA	8 February 1984- 11 February 1984
Time eleven people in space, no docking	Oleg Atkov, Leonid D. Kizim, Yuri Malyshev, Vladimir Solovov, Gennady Strekalov - *USSR* Robert L. Crippen, Terry J. Hart, George Nelson, Francis Scobee, James van Hoften - *USA* Rakesh Sharma - *India*	STS-41-C, Salyut 7 EO-3, Soyuz T-10-Soyuz T-11	USSR USA India	6 April 1984- 11 April 1984
People to complete four spacewalks during the same mission	Leonid Kizim, Vladimir Solovyov	Salyut 7	USSR	26 April 1984 - 18 May, 1984
Spacewalk by woman	Svetlana Savitskaya	Soyuz T-12	USSR	25 July 1984
People in orbit thirty-three weeks (7 months)	Leonid Kizim, Vladimir Solovyov, Oleg Atkov	Salyut 7 EO-3, Soyuz T-10-Soyuz T-11	USSR	8 February 1984- 2 October 1984
Seven person spaceflight, single spacecraft	Robert L. Crippen, Jon A. McBride, Kathryn D. Sullivan, Sally K. Ride, David C. Leestma, Paul D. Scully-Power - *USA* Marc Garneau-*Canada*	STS-41-G	USA Canada	5 October 1984- 13 October 1984
Partial crew exchange at a space station	Alexander Volkov, Vladimir Vasyutin replace Vladimir Dzhanibekov	Soyuz T-14, Salyut 7	USSR	17 September 1985- 26 September 1985

People in orbit fifty-two weeks (12 months)	Vladimir Titov, Musa Manarov	Mir EO-3, Soyuz TM-4-Soyuz TM-6	USSR	21 December 1987- 21 December 1988
Time twelve people in space; no docking	Shuttle: Vance Brand, Samuel Durrance, Guy S. Gardner, Jeffrey A. Hoffman, John M. Lounge, Ronald Parise, Robert A. Parker - *USA* Mir: Gennady Manakov, Gennady Strekalov – *Russia* Soyuz and Soyuz/Mir: Musa Manarov, Viktor Afanasyev - *Russia* Toyohiro Akiyama - *Japan*	STS-35, Mir EO-7, Soyuz TM-10-Soyuz TM-11	USSR USA Japan	2 December 1990- 10 December 1990
Three-person spacewalk	Pierre J. Thuot, Richard J. Hieb Thomas D. Akers	STS-49	USA	13 May 1992
Time thirteen people in space; no docking	Shuttle: Steve Oswald, William Gregory, John Grunsfeld, Wendy Lawrence, Tammy Jernigan, Sam Durrance, Ron Parise - *USA* Mir: Aleksandr Viktorenko, Yelena Kondakova, Valeriy Polyakov – *Russia* Soyuz/Mir: Vladimir Dezhurov, Gennady Strekalov - *Russia* Norman E. Thagard - *USA*	STS-67, Mir, Soyuz TM-20, Soyuz TM-21	USA Russia	14 March 1995- 18 March 1995
Time ten people in one spacecraft; docking	Robert L. Gibson, Charles J. Precourt, Ellen S. Baker, Bonnie J. Dunbar, Gregory J. Harbaugh Norman E. Thagard - *USA* Anatoly Solovyev, Nikolai Budarin, Vladimir Dezhurov, Gennady Strekalov - *Russia*	STS-71, Mir, Soyuz TM-21	USA Russia	29 June 1995- 4 July 1995
Person to complete seven trips to space	Jerry L. Ross	STS-110	USA	19 April 2002
Privately funded human space - flight	Mike Melvill	SpaceShipOne flight 15P	USA	21 June 2004
Time thirteen people in one spacecraft; docking	Michael Barratt, Mark L. Polansky, Douglas G. Hurley, Christopher J. Cassidy, Thomas H. Marshburn, David Wolf, Timothy Kopra - *USA* Gennady Padalka, Roman Romanenko - *Russia* Robert Thirsk, Julie Payette - *Canada* Frank De Winne - *Belgium (European Space Agency)* Koichi Wakata - *Japan*	ISS, Soyuz TMA-14, Soyuz TMA-15, STS-127	USA Russia Canada Belgium Japan	17 July 2009

Total Time in Space

Top 50 space travellers:

Rank	Person	Days	Country
1	Sergei Krikalev	804.371	Russia / Soviet Union
2	Sergei Avdeyev	747.593	Russia
3	Valeriy Polyakov	678.690	Russia / Soviet Union
4	Anatoly Solovyev	651.117	Russia / Soviet Union
5	Alexandr Kaleri	609.911	Russia
6	Viktor Afanasyev	555.772	Russia / Soviet Union
7	Yury Usachev	553.016	Russia
8	Musa Manarov	541.021	Russia / Soviet Union
9	Gennady Padalka**	528.822	Russia
10	Yuri Malenchenko	514.539	Russia
11	Alexander Viktorenko	489.066	Russia / Soviet Union
12	Nikolai Budarin	444.060	Russia
13	Yuri Romanenko	430.765	Soviet Union
14	Alexander Volkov	391.495	Russia / Soviet Union
15	Yuri I. Onufrienko	389.282	Russia
16	Vladimir G. Titov	387.036	Russia / Soviet Union
17	Vasili Tsibliyev	381.662	Russia
18	Valery G. Korzun	381.653	Russia
19	Pavel Vinogradov	380.678	Russia
20	Peggy A. Whitson	376.738	United States
21	Leonid Kizim	374.749	Soviet Union
22	Michael Foale	373.763	United States /United Kingdom*
23	Aleksandr Serebrov	372.954	Russia / Soviet Union
24	Michael Fincke	365.897	United States
25	Vladimir Solovyov	361.952	Soviet Union
26	Thomas Reiter	350.239	Germany
27	Mikhail Tyurin	344.213	Russia
28	Talgat Musabayev	339.409	Russia
29	Yuri P. Gidzenko	329.950	Russia
30	Gennadi Manakov	309.889	Russia / Soviet Union
31	Aleksandr P. Aleksandrov	309.758	Soviet Union
32	Valery Ryumin	297.924	Russia / Soviet Union
33	Gennady Strekalov	268.938	Russia / Soviet Union
34	Vladimir Lyakhov	259.563	Soviet Union
35	Michael Lopez-Alegria	257.944	United States
36	Viktor Savinykh	252.849	Soviet Union
37	Vladimir Dezhurov	244.229	Russia
38	Oleg Atkov	252.849	Soviet Union
39	Carl E. Walz	230.212	United States
40	Leroy Chiao	229.362	United States
41	Daniel W. Bursch	226.594	United States
42	William S. McArthur	224.930	United States

* **Michael Foale** holds dual U.S./British citizenship.

** Currently in space.

43	Shannon W. Lucid	223.161	United States
44	Valentin Lebedev	219.250	Soviet Union
45	Vladimir Kovalyonok	216.382	Soviet Union
46	Kenneth D. Bowersox	211.594	United States
47	Anatoli Berezovoy	211.378	Soviet Union
48	Susan J. Helms	211.048	United States
49	Jean-Pierre Haigneré	209.517	France
50	Fyodor Yurchikhin	207.218	Russia

As of 4 August 2009

Total Human Spaceflight Time by Country

Rank	*Nation*	*Total person-days*
1	USSR / Russia	over 17,000 days **
2	USA	over 10,000 days**
—	ESA	932.85 **
3	Germany	481.24
4	France	384.67
5	United Kingdom	381.65 *
6	Japan	253.53
7	Canada	161.76 **
8	Italy	87.11
9	Costa Rica	66.76 *
10	Switzerland	42.50
11	Hungary	34.448 *
12	Belgium	19.79 **
13	China	19.06
14	Spain	18.88
15	Netherlands	17.90
16	Israel	15.93
17	Ukraine	15.69
18	Sweden	12.83
19	Bulgaria	11.91
20	Malaysia	10.885
21	Iran	10.878 *
22	South Korea	10.875
23	South Africa	9.893
24	Brazil	9.888

* Dual citizens counted under both nationalities.
** and counting

25	Syria	8.9
26	Afghanistan	8.85
27	Czechoslovakia	7.93
28	Austria	7.928
29	Poland	7.919
30	Slovakia	7.914
31	India	7.903
32	Cuba	7.863
33	Mongolia	7.863
34	Vietnam	7.862
35	Romania	7.862
36	Saudi Arabia	7.069
37	Mexico	6.878

As of 6 November 2007

Notable Unmanned Spaceflights

Body	*Spacecraft*	*Event*	*Country*	*Date*
Earth	A-4(V-2)	First rocket to reach space	Germany	June 1944
Earth	Sputnik 1	First satellite in orbit	USSR	4 October 1957
Earth	Vanguard 1	Oldest satellite still in orbit—expected to stay in orbit 240 years. Ceased transmissions in May 1964	USA	17 March 1958
Moon	Luna 1	First flyby, dist. of 5,995 km	USSR	4 January 1959
Moon	Luna 2	First impact	USSR	14 September 1959
Moon	Luna 3	First image of lunar far-side	USSR	7 October 1959
Earth	Discoverer 13	First satellite recovered from orbit	USA	11 August 1960
Venus	Venera 1	First flyby, dist. of 100,000 km (lost communication contact before)	USSR	19 May 1961
Venus	Mariner 2	First planetary flyby, dist. of 34,762 km (with communication contact)	USA	14 December 1962
Mars	Mariner 4	First Mars flyby, first planetary imaging, dist. of 9,846 km	USA	14 July 1965
Moon	Luna 9	First soft landing, first lunar surface-level image	USSR	31 January 1966
Venus	Venera 3	First impact	USSR	1 March 1966
Moon	Luna 10	First orbiter	USSR	3 April 1966
Venus	Venera 7	First soft landing	USSR	1 August 1970
Moon	Luna 16	First automated sample return	USSR	24 September 1970

Moon	Luna 17	First automated roving vehicle - Lunokhod 1	USSR	17 November 1970
Mars	Mariner 9	First orbiter	USA	14 November 1971
Mars	Mars 2	First impact	USSR	27 November 1971
Mars	Mars 3	First soft landing, telemetry signal for 20 s before transmissions ceased	USSR	2 December 1971
Jupiter	Pioneer 10	First flyby, dist. of 130,000 km	USA	3 December 1973
Mercury	Mariner 10	First flyby, dist. of 703 km	USA	29 March 1974
Venus	Venera 9	First orbiter First surface-level imaging of another planet	USSR	22 October 1975
Sun	Helios 2	Highest velocity of a spacecraft relative to the sun, 247,510 km/h at. 29 AU perihelion	West Germany	17 April 1976
Mars	Viking 1	First surface-level imaging of Mars	USA	20 July 1976
Saturn	Pioneer 11	First flyby, dist. of 21,000 km	USA	1 September 1979
Venus	Venera 13	First sound record on another planet	USSR	1 March 1982
	Pioneer 10	First extra-solar spacecraft (disputed because only according to some definitions)	USA	13 June 1983
Venus	Vega 1	First helium balloon atmospheric probe	USSR	11 June 1985
Uranus	Voyager 2	First flyby, dist. of 81,500 km	USA	24 January 1986
Comet Halley	Vega 1	First comet flyby, dist. of 8,890 km	USSR	6 March 1986
Neptune	Voyager 2	First flyby, dist. of 40,000 km	USA	25 August 1989
951 Gaspra	Galileo probe	First asteroid flyby, dist. of 1,600 km	USA	29 October 1991
Jupiter	Galileo probe	First impact	USA	7 December 1995
Jupiter	Galileo probe	First orbiter	USA	7 December 1995
Mars	Mars Pathfinder	First automated roving vehicle-Sojourner	USA	4 July 1997
433 Eros	NEAR Shoemaker	First asteroid orbiter	USA	14 February 2000
433 Eros	NEAR Shoemaker	First asteroid soft landing	USA	12 February 2001
Saturn	Cassini orbiter	First orbiter	ESA USA	1 July 2004
Titan	Huygens probe	First soft landing	ESA USA	14 January 2005
Comet Tempel 1	Deep Impact	First comet impact	USA	4 July 2005
	Voyager 1	At greatest distance from Earth, 15 billion km	USA	As of 2006
	Pioneer 6	Longest operating space probe, brief contact was reestablished on 8 December 2000, after nearly 35 years in space.	USA	As of 2005

5

Private Spaceflight Companies Offering Services in Space and Space Tourism: An Exhaustive Listing

PRIVATE SPACEFLIGHT COMPANIES

Manufacturers of Space Vehicles

Crew and Cargo Capsules

Company name	*Craft name*	*Craft type*	*Launcher name*	*Launcher type*	*Maximum reach*	*Passenger capacity*	*Craft status*
ARCASPACE	Stabilo	capsule	Solar Montgolfier	balloon	sub-orbit	1	development
	Orizont	spaceplane	Solar Montgolfier	balloon	sub-orbit	2	cancelled
Bigelow Aerospace	Genesis I	space station	Dnepr-1	rocket	LEO	unmanned	currently in LEO
	Genesis II	space station	Dnepr-1	rocket	LEO	unmanned	currently in LEO
	Galaxy	space station	—	—	LEO	unmanned	cancelled
	Sundancer	space station	Falcon 9	rocket	LEO	3	development
	BA 330	space station	—	—	LEO	6	proposed
Blue Origin	New Shepard	rocket	*self-powered* (SSTSO)		sub-orbit	—	testing
EADS Astrium	*unnamed craft*	spaceplane	*self-powered* (SSTSO)		sub-orbit	4	development
Excalibur Almaz	*TKS derivative*	capsule	—	—	LEO	circa 3	development
	Almaz derivative	space station	—	—	LEO	—	development
da Vinci Project	Wild Fire	capsule	—	balloon	sub-orbit	3	cancelled
Galactic Suite Ltd.	Galactic Suite	space station	—	—	LEO	—	development

Interorbital Systems	Solaris X	capsule	*self-powered* (SSTSO)		sub-orbit	6	cancelled
	Crew Module	capsule	Neptune TSAAHTO	rocket	lunar orbit	6	development
Orbital Sciences Corp.	Cygnus	capsule	Taurus II	rocket	LEO	unmanned	development
PlanetSpace	Silver Dart	spaceplane	Canadian Arrow	rocket	LEO	3	development
Reaction Engines Ltd.	HOTOL	spaceplane	*self-powered* (SSTO)		LEO	—	cancelled
	Skylon	spaceplane	*self-powered* (SSTO)		LEO	5-20	development
Rocketplane Kistler	K-1	rocket	*self-powered* (TSTO)		LEO	—	cancelled
	Rocketplane XP	spaceplane	*self-powered* (SSTSO)		sub-orbit	6	development
Rotary Rocket	Roton	rocket	*self-powered* (SSTO)		LEO	2	cancelled
Scaled Composites and Virgin Galactic	SpaceShipOne	spaceplane	WhiteKnightOne	airplane	sub-orbit	2	retired (3/3)
	SpaceShipTwo	spaceplane	WhiteKnightTwo	airplane	sub-orbit	8	development
	SpaceShipThree	—	—	—	LEO	—	proposed
Space Adventures	Explorer	spaceplane	M-55X	airplane	sub-orbit	5	development
Space Transport Corp.	Rubicon I	rocket	*self-powered* (SSTSO)		sub-orbital	3	cancelled
SpaceDev	Dream Chaser	spaceplane	Atlas V	rocket	LEO	7	development
SpaceX	Dragon	capsule	Falcon 9	rocket	LEO	7	testing
t/Space	CXV	capsule	QuickReach	rocket	lunar orbit	6	development
Venturer Aerospace	S-550	capsule	Falcon 9	rocket	LEO	6	cancelled
XCOR	Xerus	spaceplane	*self-powered* (SSTSO)		sub-orbit	2	cancelled
	Lynx	spaceplane	*self-powered* (SSTSO)		sub-orbit	1	development

Launch Vehicles

Further information: List of orbital launch systems

Company name	*Launcher name*	*Launcher type*	*No. of stages*	*Maximum reach*	*Launcher status*
AirLaunch LLC	QuickReach	rocket	—	LEO	development
ARCASPACE	HAAS	light rocket	3	LEO	development
Armadillo Aerospace	*OTRAG derivative*	medium rocket	variable	LEO	cancelled
Beal Aerospace	BA-1	light rocket	—	LEO	cancelled
	BA-2	medium rocket	3	GTO	cancelled
Canadian Arrow	Canadian Arrow	rocket	2	LEO	testing

Interorbital Systems	Sea Star TSAAHTO	light rocket	2½	LEO	development
	Neptune 30	light rocket	multi	LEO	proposed
	Neptune 1000	medium rocket	multi	lunar orbit	proposed
	Neptune TSAAHTO	heavy rocket	2½	lunar orbit	proposed
Lockheed Martin	VentureStar	medium rocket	1	LEO	cancelled
Orbital Sciences Corp.	Taurus I	light rocket	4	LEO	operational (6/8)
	Taurus II	medium rocket	3	LEO	development
Orbital Transport & Raketen AG	OTRAG	medium rocket	variable	LEO	reached 50 km
Space Systems/Loral	Aquarius	light rocket	1	LEO	development
Space Transport Corp.	Spartan	light rocket	3	sub-orbit	reached 80 km
SpaceX	Falcon 1	light rocket	2	LEO	operational (2/5)
	Falcon 5	medium rocket	2	GTO	cancelled
	Falcon 9	medium rocket	2	GTO	testing
	Falcon 9 Heavy	heavy rocket	2+boosters	lunar orbit	development

Landers, Rovers and Probes

Further information: Google Lunar X Prize Competitors

Company name	*Craft name*	*Craft type*	*Craft status*
Armadillo Aerospace	*unnamed craft*	rocket module	testing
BlastOff! Corporation	Lunar 1	rover	cancelled
Odyssey Moon	MoonOne (M-1)	rover	development
Astrobotic Technology	Artemis Lander	lander	development
	Red Rover	rover	development
Team Italia		rover	development
Micro Space			development
Next Giant Leap			development
Team FREDNET			development
ARCASPACE	ELE	lunar orbiter	development
Lunatrex			development

Chandah			development
Advaeros			development
STELLAR			development
JURBAN			development
Omega Envoy			development
Independence-X			development
SYNERGY MOON			development
Euroluna	ROMIT		development
Team Selene	LuRcCa 1	rocket car	development
SCSG			cancelled
Quantum 3			cancelled

Research Craft and Tech Demonstrators

Company name	*Craft name*	*Craft purpose*	*Craft status*
Armadillo Aerospace	Quad	demonstrate VTOL	operational
Blue Origin	Goddard	demonstrate VTOL	operational
Interorbital Systems	Neutrino	systems testing	operational
	Tachyon	systems testing	operational
Lockheed Martin	X-33	demonstrate SSTO	cancelled
Masten Space Systems	XA-0.1	demonstrate VTOL	operational
	XA-0.2	systems testing	development
	XA-0.3	systems testing	proposed
McDonnell Douglas	DC-X	demonstrate VTOL	retired (11 test flights)
Rotary Rocket	Roton ATV	demonstrate VTOL	retired (3 test flights)
Swedish Space Corp.	Maxus	payload to 700 km	operational
	Maser	payload to 300 km	operational
UP Aerospace	SpaceLoft XL	payload to 140 km	operational

Propulsion Manufacturers

Company name	*Engine*	*Engine type*	*Applications*
American Rocket Company		hybrid rocket	intellectual property acquired by SpaceDev
Frontier Astronautics	VIPER	liquid oxygen	
	Asp	high test peroxide	
Orion Propulsion			Sundancer and Ares I
Ad Astra Rocket Company	VASIMR	magnetoplasma	may be used for future Mars missions
Reaction Engines Ltd.	SABRE	rocket/turbojet/ramjet	planned to be used in Skylon
SpaceDev		hybrid rocket	SpaceShipOne and SpaceShipTwo

Satellite Launchers

- Arianespace
- Antrix Corporation
- EADS Astrium Space Transportation
- Eurockot Launch Services
- International Launch Services
- ISC Kosmotras
- Orbital Sciences Corporation
- SpaceDev
- SpaceQuest, Ltd.
- SpaceX
- Sea Launch (and subsidiary Land Launch)
- Starsem

Spaceliner Companies

Company name	*Contracts for*	*Craft utilised*	*Status*
Benson Space Company	SpaceDev	Dream Chaser	waiting on hardware
Space Adventures	*none*	Soyuz and the ISS	active (6 tourists sent)
Virgin Galactic	Scaled Composites	SpaceShipTwo	waiting on hardware

Spacecraft Component Manufacturers

- Andrews Space
- EADS Astrium Satellites
- Rocketstar Robotics, Inc.
- Thortek Laboratories, Inc.
- Starsys (merged with SpaceDev)
- SpaceDev

ARCASPACE

Asociația Română pentru Cosmonautică și Aeronautică (ARCA) or **Romanian Cosmonautics and Aeronautics Association** is a non-governmental organization that promotes aerospace projects as well as other space-related activities. It is based in Râmnicu Vâlcea, Romania.

Beginnings

In Sibiu, Romania, in front of the Hermann Oberth memorial house, a group of students decided to intensify the low-level space activities in Romania. ARCA's members started to develop an ambitious high-performance rocket engine in 1998. ARCA was registered in 1999. Since then, ARCA became a united team and, despite a small budget in the first year, it succeeded in leading the field in rocket technology in Romania.

The first aerospace project started in 1998 was a high performance rocket engine designed to deliver 85,000 kgf. The engine used open cycle and 4 burning chambers were fed with liquid oxygen and kerosene at the combustion pressure of 70 bars.

The purpose of this project was to develop the abilities and skills needed for future activities by using local technology and materials. Another achievement was the creation of a united and specialized team of rocket engineers.

ELE and HAAS

HAAS is an innovative air-launched, 3 stages orbital rocket, preliminary designed in 2006 using the technology developed at ARCA during The Ansari X Prize Competition and The European Private Manned Space Programme. The rocket was named after Conrad Haas (1509-1579) Austrian-Romanian medieval rocket pioneer, the first creator of multiple stages rockets.

The European Lunar Explorer—ELE is a 3 stages space probe able to fly from the Earth's low orbit to the Moon surface and to send scientific data back to Earth. ELE will be placed into orbit by the HAAS launcher.

Flight Sequence

The Launch

The launch will be made from the sea with the help of a large marine platform designed by ARCA. The launch location will be established further, but it is preferred to launch as close as possible from the Earth Equator.

The rocket will be lifted from the sea using the world heaviest "0 pressure" balloon ever built. ARCA already has experience with solar Montgolfier balloons. Between 2006-2007 ARCA built and launched the world's largest solar Montgolfier balloon.

The main advantages of lifting the rocket from the sea is that no launch pad is required, and the launch point can be placed as close as possible to the Earth's Equator. Once the platform is in position, the rocket will be placed on the sea surface and the hydrogen peroxide oxidizer will be transferred into the fuel tanks. After the fuel tanks are filled, the team will start the balloon inflation procedure. This will take about 3 hours. When the balloon has reached the necessary lifting capability, the rocket will be lifted from the sea surface and placed into near vertical position beneath the balloon, attached with a cable. The distance between the balloon bottom and the rocket will be 200 m.

The balloon and rocket will fly to an altitude of 18,000 m for 1 hr 45 min.

Booster Flight

At 18,000 m the rocket will start its first stage rocket engine for 100 sec. After engine cut-off, the first stage will be detached. Soon after, the rocket's second stage will be ignited and it will burn for 110 sec. After the burn completion the second stage will be also detached.

The rocket's third and last stage will be ignited and will burn for another 168 sec, putting the ELE into an elliptical LEO to an altitude of 140 km. At this altitude the rocket's third stage will separate from the ELE probe.

Orbital Flight

After the HAAS's third stage burnout, the ELE spacecraft will be placed into orbit. ELE will start the Stage E1 main engine at first orbit's apogee for a V = 260m/s in order to circularize the orbit to an altitude of 250 km. After a short time spent in Earth orbit, ELE will ignite once again the E1 main engine that will increase vehicle's speed to 11.1 km/s. After Stage H1 fuel depletion it will be ejected on vehicle's way to the Moon.

From Earth to Moon

As the ELE will head to the Moon, the trajectory will be periodically corrected using the Stage E2 main brake engine. During the trip from the Earth to the Moon, ELE will deploy two 100 W solar panels that will allow to the vehicle to charge the internal batteries and to use the energy for the telemetry and video equipment. At a distance of around 38,000 km distance from the Moon, ELE will reach the Lagrange point where the force of gravity of the Earth and the force of gravity of the Moon will be almost equal. ELE will enter in this point with an excess speed of about 500m/s, which will allow it to be further attracted by Moon's force of gravity. Once this point passed, the ELE will be fast attracted by Moon's gravity. In this situation, ELE will start Stage E2 brake in an opposite direction faced to the speed vector. The team will try to reduce as much as possible the number of brake engine starts.

Lunar Landing

After Stage E2 fuel depletion, it will be ejected at an altitude of about 10 km from the lunar surface, the ELE Lunar Lander (ELL) will soft land on the Moon using the Stage E3 main engine and inertial guidance launch platform together with the onboard flight computer. The Stage E3 main engine is thrust adjustable, gimbaled, hydrogen peroxide (85 per cent concentration), monopropellant 14 kgf, rocket motor. The time from the Earth launch to the Moon surface will last for 116 hours (4 days, 2 hours).

The desired Moon landing point is the North region of the Carpathian Mountains. This spot was chosen because the Carpathian Mountains also pass through Romania from the North to the West.

Stabilo

STABILO is the latest suborbital manned system created by the European Team ARCA. ARCA hopes that its new spaceship, through its unique design and safety capabilities will capture the attention and will stimulate the imagination of the public.

ARCA's philosophy is that a manned suborbital ship for commercial applications must be designed taking into account the passengers and crew safety. For that purpose, the ship must have:

- a high reliability
- an excellent abort scenario and escape capabilities
- the stress for the pilot during flight reduced to minimum

In respect of these statements, ARCA team propose a new suborbital ship concept. The engine, placed at the top of the ship, offers an unconventional aspect for this spaceship. The tractor engine offers the possibility to place the crew cabin at the rear part of the ship, which offers extended abort capabilities. STABILO will be launched in a vertical position. In this situation the pilot activities are highly reduced.

The tractor engine generates reaction gases, close to the ship structure for a long period of time, without affecting the ship's integrity. This is possible due to the use of hydrogen peroxide as monopropellant which offers a low temperature for the reaction products. The purely space applications design of this ship makes it inappropriate for powered flights at low altitudes in dense atmosphere. Because of that the system is transported to an altitude of 22,000 m with a Solar Montgolfier.

The tractor engine solution isn't new. It was previously used in escape systems onboard Mercury, Apollo and Soyuz. The main difference is that an escape system has a low burning time. STABILO's engine will run for approximately one minute, a longer time.

The Flight Sequence

The Launch

STABILO was designed to be launched from an altitude of 22,000 m, in a two-stage manner. The first stage consists of a 1 h, 35 min ascension with a 350.000 mc Solar Montgolfier balloon to the altitude of 22,000 m (66,000 feet). The second stage commences by launching the actual suborbital vehicle vertically, through the very thin balloon envelope. At the bottom of the balloon, a composite materials ring of 2 m diameter allows the STABILO to enter into the balloon envelope.

Vertical Powered Flight

Immediately after the engine start, the vehicle will begin to accelerate on a vertical trajectory. The maximum speed will be 1,250 m/s and the maximum G load will be kept below 6.8 G.

Inertial Vertical Flight

After engine shut-down, the vehicle will continue the inertial climb. Immediately after engine shut-down the crew cabin will be separated from the rocket booster. The RCS system will command the cabin attitude. The maximum altitude is above 100 km.

The Reentry

After apogee the cabin and booster rocket will start the descent which, for almost half the distance, will be made in weightlessness. At low dynamic pressure, the RCS will keep the cabin with the base down. The aerodynamic stability system placed at the top of the capsule will keep the vehicle in a vertical position during the atmospheric phase of the reentry, without human intervention. The maximum deceleration during reentry will be –4.6 G.

The Recovery

The rocket booster's main parachute will be extracted from the nose-cone compartment at an altitude of 4,000 m and a speed of 400 km/h. The cabin's main parachute will be extracted at 4,000 m and a speed of about 350 km/h. The landing speed will be kept below 7 m/s.

The Monopropellant Rocket Engine

The main preoccupation for a spaceship designer is to ensure a high reliability. Since the appearance of rockets, until today, the main element that leads to a rocket vehicle failure is the engine. ARCA considers that the main issue that a designer has to deal with in order to create a reliable ship is the creation of a reliable rocket engine.

There are some alternatives, from the fuel point of view, regarding the type of a potential rocket engine that can equip such a vehicle: bipropellant liquid fuel, monopropellant liquid fuel, solid fuel and hybrid fuel.

Through 2000-2004, ARCA experimented a series of rocket engines with various types of fuels. After the tests in 2003 the team decided to go forward with a hydrogen peroxide monopropellant engine. This type of engine was tested intensively through 2003-2004. Demonstrator 2B rocket which was launched from Cape Midia Air Force Test Site on September 9, 2004 used this type of technology.

A monopropellant system used as a main engine for space propulsion is an unusual proposition mainly because of its low specific impulse. A vehicle launched from the ground, using this type of propulsion, in a suborbital mission, with a payload equivalent of about three passengers will be necessary to carry about 7 t of fuel, an unacceptable value. Furthermore, the final acceleration would be around 12G.

It is clear that a ship equipped with a hydrogen peroxide (85 per cent) monopropellant rocket engine, able to complete the above mentioned mission is not suitable for a ground launch. However a 24 per cent higher impulse can be obtained in the case of an air launch from an altitude of around 22,000 m, with an almost fully adapted nozzle.

STABILO is the first spaceship that uses a monopropellant tractor engine. This solution was chosen because it offers improved safety during the flight. Despite the presence of the four nozzles placed at an angle of 20°, STABILO has only one engine. The reaction gases from the reaction chamber are distributed through the four nozzles. The 20° angle leads to a 6 per cent thrust loss. Despite this, ARCA engineers considered that the advantages of having a safer flight resulting from a tractor engine are more important and the thrust loss could be compensated through a higher fuel quantity and a longer engine run.

The reaction is 100 per cent ecological since hydrogen peroxide decomposes in oxygen and hot water vapours. Function of the mission nature, and fuel concentration (65-85 per cent), the engine will be reusable or expandable. While the expandable engines raise no special problems, the reusable engines built from composite materials is a real challenge. Such engines were used before but with ablative cooling (inner layers vaporize in order to keep outer layers at a reasonable temperature). However, this process can be used on "hot" engines at high temperatures. At lower temperatures, the inner layers don't vaporize efficiently anymore. ARCA's engine accumulates the heat inside the inner and intermediate layers so that the outer layers don't change their mechanical characteristics even after a complete engine run. The heat is not released outside. This system is not very economical but is certainly very safe and reliable.

The Crew Cabin

The most important goal of the whole project is safety. Therefore, safety and backup systems for the pilot were designed for every stage of the flight. With the cabin placed at the bottom of the ship, the abort sequence has a simple procedure: the crew cabin can be gravitationally separated from the rocket booster and recovered with its parachute. The cabin offers protection for almost the entire flight sequence, even in unlikely events like complete equipment failure, structural damage, etc.

The cabin is pressurized at 0.8 atm and contains navigation, flight control and life support systems. It is designed for one pilot that sits on a chair, specially designed for flight accelerations. The access inside the cabin is assured by a lateral auto-pressurized hatch which can be opened both from inside and outside of the cabin. As an added safety, the pilot will use a pressurized suit, offered by another former X Prize competitor, which has a lot of experience with pressurized suits: DeLeon Company. DeLeon and ARCA are partners since 2005 and they are collaborating on various aspects regarding the manned spaceflight.

The pilot has a panoramic view through three portholes. The position of the portholes was chosen in order to offer the pilot a complete view without it being necessary to raise from his chair. The top engine with its four nozzles could offer a beautiful view for the passenger, since the exhaust, made of oxygen and water vapours will freeze immediately after ejection, in contact with the outside environment (–60 degrees C). The jet will form small ice particles on which the Sun will reflect. After engine stop and capsule release, the pilot could maneuver the cabin with the RCS to have a view of the Earth with the four engine traces of ice beneath the ship.

The Carrier Balloon

The carrier balloon used to raise the ship at the launch altitude is a zero pressure Solar Montgolfier type, made of 15 μm high density polyethylene. The balloon uses the Sun radiation to heat the inside air. This will lead to a temperature gradient between the interior and the exterior of the balloon. This gradient has a maximum value of around 30 degrees C, which makes the air from the inside to have a lower density comparing with the outside air. The balloon used for the Mission 5-8 flights has a capacity of 350.000 mc. It will be the biggest balloon of this type ever built.

The STABILO 1B System

This variant is different compared with the initial variant because of the rocket engine position. This allows a lower fuel consumption and the possibility to use a hot rocket engine. The crew cabin and the fuel tank are almost similar with the initial variant.

STABILO Flight Programme

Flight	*Category*	*Altitude*	*Ship configuration*	*Engine start*	*Status*
Mission1	Unmanned	22,000	Carrier balloon + Crew cabin	No	Completed
Mission2	Unmanned	22,000	Carrier balloon + Complete ship	No	Completed
Mission3	Manned	22,000	Carrier balloon + Crew cabin	No	
Mission4	Unmanned	100,000	Carrier balloon + Carrier rocket	Yes	
Mission5	Unmanned	100,000	Carrier balloon + Complete ship	Yes	
Mission6	Manned	30,000	Carrier balloon + Complete ship	Yes	
Mission7	Manned	60,000	Carrier balloon + Complete ship	Yes	
Mission8	Manned	100,000	Carrier balloon + Complete ship	Yes	

Orizont

The construction of ORIZONT began in mid-2004. At that time, ARCA was more concerned with the launch of Demonstrator 2B from Cape Midia and most of the members declined involvement in the ambitious ORIZONT project. However, a small group started the design and the construction of the new vehicle. The first element was the mold for the pressurized compartment of the spacecraft. The mold and the whole structure of the cabin were finished in February 2005.

The work itself was done in a very small workshop and it was obvious that the team needed a much larger space for the equipments and hardware.

At the beginning of June one of the major sponsors of ARCA offered an assembly facility of 1500m^2. Here, they began assembling the ORIZONT vehicle.

Launch

The air-launch solutions are flexible due to the variable geometry of the wings and the solutions that were selected for the propulsion system. The launch can be executed, depending on the carrier availability, from helicopter or airplane. In every situation the launch will be made with the wings at near 0 degree sweep angle because it is necessary that the wing generates the highest possible lift. In the case of helicopter launch, the ORIZONT vehicle will be lifted to an altitude of around 2,000-2,500 m. At this altitude, the vehicle will be released and will gravitationally accelerate to the required speed of about 210 km/h, necessary for the stable flight. In the case of the air launch, the ORIZONT vehicle will be transported to altitudes around 11,000 m, attached to the carrier at the top or at the bottom. Due to safety reasons, it is better to attach the vehicle at the bottom of the carrier. The launch from the helicopter is easier to implement from the logistical and technical point of view, but increases the stress of the pilot, because of the necessity to fly the ship in the atmosphere for a longer period of time.

Autonomous Atmospheric Flight

After the carrier release, the ORIZONT vehicle will start the air-breathing engine and will start to climb with the wings completely open to an altitude of around 17,000 m with a speed range of about 400-700 km/h. The maximum acceleration for this stage of the flight will be no higher than +4.6/–1.6 G

Rocket Engine

Immediately after the vehicle reaches the desired altitude, the air-breathing engine will be detached. This action is shortly followed by the modification of the wing sweep angle to a minimum value. The lift and drag will decrease significantly.

Rocket Engine Vertical Flight

The rocket engine will be started when ORIZONT will have 45 degrees angle of altitude which can be obtained from the stabilizers. Immediately after the start, the vehicle will begin to accelerate rapidly, the aerodynamic surfaces putting the vehicle to a near vertical trajectory. This trajectory will be kept for the entire time of the rocket engine run.

Inertial Vertical Flight and the Reentry Preparations

After the rocket engine shut-down, the ship will continue to climb inertly in a vertical position; in this time frame, the pilot will start the reconfiguration of the whole ship for re-entry mode: the wing sweep angle will be changed to a negative position and the stabilizers will change their position by 180°. The low atmospheric density at that altitude will not allow the pilot to control the altitude of the ship from the aerodynamic surfaces and the ship will be controlled with the reaction control system (RCS).

Flight

At the maximum altitude of 100 km, the ship will have the lowest speed in the entire flight sequence. The pilot will continue to control the ship with the RCS.

Re-entry

After reaching the 100 km altitude, the vehicle will start the descent. For less than half the distance, the pilot will experience the effects of weightlessness. The ship must be kept with the RCS in a vertical position with the nose up. This process does not require an intense effort from the pilot since, to some degree, even big altitude errors are allowed. When the ship encounters the first dense atmospheric layers the use of the RCS becomes unnecessary; the ship, due to the unique variable geometry system, will become auto-stabilized aerodynamically and inert. The maximum deceleration at reentry will reach –6.2 G for only 4 sec.

Recovery

Even though the variable geometry of the vehicle would allow a landing procedure on a runway, ARCA decided that the parachuted recovery system is safer from the following considerations:

- In the case of a trajectory error during the rocket engine powered flight, the vehicle could be deviated far away from the runway.
- The necessity of a runway presence limits the flight corridor definition possibilities.
- The stress for the pilot is lower because the necessity of a runway landing procedure is suppressed.
- It offers the possibility to abort the mission in almost every sequence of the flight and to bring the ship safely to the ground.

The deceleration parachute will be extracted at a height of about 6000 m and this operation is shortly followed by the main parachute extraction at 4000 m. The whole parachute system is placed in the front of the ship, at the bottom of the cabin. The landing in the sea will take place at a speed no higher than 7 m/s. The stress over the pilot, from the rocket engine shut-down to the landing moment, is reduced significantly.

Early Vehicles

Demonstrator

This technological demonstrator is at 1:2 scale of that of the X PRIZE vehicle, named Orizont and it is the first rocket designed by ARCA Team. It is an unguided but self-stabilized rocket. On this vehicle and on the sub-assembly systems many constructive solutions were tested, especially composite materials fuel tanks. Almost the entire structure is made of composite materials, but also from aluminium aloys. This rocket was created to simulate an almost complete (unmanned) X Prize mission. Demonstrator 1 was also used in public exhibitions in order to attract more funds for ARCA projects.

The old configuration used a liquid fuel rocket engine, designed to thrust 2,000 kgf during 60 sec. The fuel was: hydrogen peroxide 85 per cent + T1. In the new configuration will use a hybrid engine with hydrogen peroxide 85 per cent as an oxidizer, in combination with polyethylene as fuel.

Demonstrator 2

The technological demonstrator "2" is at 1:2.5 scale of that of the X PRIZE vehicle, named Orizont. ARCA started the work to this rocket in May 2003. The entire structure is made of composite materials. For this vehicle was created a whole launch complex, including the launch pad, the fuel transfer facility, etc. For this vehicle two propulsion configurations were proposed: monopropellant and hybrid.

Demonstrator 2 was the starting point for the development of the successful Demonstrator 2B rocket. The first public display of this vehicle took place in Drãgãșani, on September 27, 2003.

Demonstrator 2B

Demonstrator 2B is a modified version of Demonstrator 2, equipped with the world's first reusable rocket engine made of composite materials. The main objective of this rocket was to test in flight the engine and the vehicle-launch pad interaction in order to gather more data for the Orizont vehicle construction. For the Demonstrator 2B launch was used the Demonstrator 2 launch pad which was modified (the length was increased to 18.2 m) and also the command panel and fuel transfer facility previously developed at ARCA.

This rocket was the end of subscale system tests at ARCA and the beginning of the Orizont vehicle's final phase of construction.

The Demonstrator 2B rocket was successfully launched on September 9, 2004. The measurements indicated that the launch parameters were: 1,000 m altitude, 630 km/h, 2,100 m range.

Governmental Contracts

STRACAAT

In November 2005 ARCA succeeded to win a contract with the Research Ministry/ Romanian Space Agency for the development of a rocket system with military applications. The contract was awarded for a period of 12 months. ARCA's military application rocket was presented to the Bucharest International Fair on October 3, 2006. The rocket financed by the government through the Romanian Space Agency— "SECURITY" Programme, has a length of 4.1 m and is designed to fly with Mach 1.02 at sea level. The maximum flight altitude is 6.000 m. The main purpose of this project is to create a target able to simulate low altitude/high speed aggressor vehicles.

BASMATES

High Altitude Commercial Solar Balloon for Scientific Equipment—BASMATES project consists in designing, constructing, launching and recovering a high altitude solar balloon and pressurized capsule, built for transporting scientific and commercial payload. This programme started in 2007 and has a duration of 30 months.

VECSS

The project "Vehicle for commercial operation of suborbital space—VECSS" consists in designing, accomplishing, launching and recovering from suborbital flight, of a vehicle intended for transportation of scientific commercial payload, to 100 km altitude. This programme started in 2007 and has a duration of 36 months.

Lunar X-Prize Competition

The agency has committed itself as a competitor in the Google Lunar X-Prize. ARCA, the first European Union team to register for the competition, has a unique approach to completing their objective. The project is labelled "HAAS-ELE" and consists of a (high altitude) balloon-launch for a three-stage rocket.

BIGELOW AEROSPACE

Bigelow Aerospace is a North Las Vegas, Nevada space technology startup company that is pioneering work on expandable space station modules. It was founded in 1999 by hotelier Robert Bigelow.

An expandable module is a space structure that has a flexible outer shell, allowing conservation of diameter for launch and weight overall. Once in orbit, the module is inflated to allow for greater work, play and living area for astronauts. Expandable modules initially were proposed and designed by the United States National Aeronautics and Space Administration (NASA) under the Transhab programme. After cancellation of the Transhab programme, Bigelow Aerospace entered into three Space Act agreements whereby Bigelow Aerospace is the sole commercializer of several of NASA's key expandable module technologies.

Background

Bigelow Aerospace was founded by Robert Bigelow and is funded in large part by the fortune Bigelow gained through his ownership of the hotel chain Budget Suites of America. As of 2006, Bigelow had invested US$75 million in the company. Bigelow has stated that he is prepared to fund Bigelow Aerospace with about US$500 million through 2015.

Module Design and Business Plans

The company intends to develop a family of prototype and production space station modules, including: the Genesis I, a one-third scale prototype module launched on July 12, 2006 weighing approximately 3,000 pounds (1,360 kg), with approximate dimensions of 14.5 feet (4.4 metres) in length and 5.25 feet (1.6 metres) in diameter, expanding to nearly twice the diameter once in orbit; Genesis II, with the same dimensions as Genesis I but with additional systems to be tested and items being sent up by paying members of the public; the Galaxy, a 45 per cent scale prototype module designed to bridge the development gap between the Genesis modules and the eventual manned complex modules; the first manned test module Sundancer; and the BA 330, a full-scale production module weighing approximately 50,000 pounds (23,000 kg) when fully loaded, with dimensions of approximately 45 feet (13.7 metres) in length and 22 feet (6.7 metres) in diameter when expanded. The BA 330 was formerly referred to as the Nautilus.

Contrary to many expectations, Bigelow Aerospace anticipates that its inflatable modules will be more durable than rigid modules. This is partially due to the company's use of several layers of vectran, a material twice as strong as kevlar, and also because, in theory, flexible walls should be able to sustain micrometeorite impacts better than rigid walls.

Expected uses for Bigelow Aerospace's expandable modules include microgravity research and development and space manufacturing. Other potential uses include space tourism, such as modules for orbital hotels, and space transportation, such as components in spaceships for Moon or Mars manned missions. The company plans to sell BA 330 modules for US$100 million apiece. Bigelow also plans to launch by 2010 an orbital resort, tentatively called the CSS Skywalker. The company though is working for the launch much ahead of 2010.

On April 10, 2007, Bigelow Aerospace announced business plans to offer (by 2012) a four-week orbital stay for US$15 million, with another four weeks for an additional US$3 million. An entire orbital facility could also be leased for US$88 million a year, or half a facility for US$54 million a year.

Module Launch Timeline

On July 12, 2006 and June 28, 2007, Bigelow launched the Genesis I and II modules, respectively. In 2008, Bigelow Aerospace will complete the Galaxy module but will not launch it due to rising launch costs, testing it on the ground at its North Las Vegas facility instead.

Additionally, Bigelow has reserved a 2011 launch on the SpaceX Falcon 9 rocket. Bigelow has not yet announced the payload for the launch, but this timeframe roughly coincides with the launch of the Sundancer module. However, the Falcon 9 is also capable of launching the BA 330 module. Bigelow is also in talks with Lockheed Martin to contract launch services on its Atlas V - 401 vehicle.

Note: Dates of upcoming launches are proposed and are subject to change.

Module Type	*Module Name*	*Flight Date*	*Launch Vehicle*	*Mission Status*
Genesis Pathfinder	Genesis I	July 12, 2006 14:53 UTC	Dnepr	Launch successful, on orbit
Genesis Pathfinder	Genesis II	June 28, 2007 15:02 UTC	Dnepr	Launch successful, on orbit
Galaxy	Galaxy	Cancelled	none	Launch cancelled, tests on ground
Sundancer	unknown	2011 (SpaceX manifest)	SpaceX Falcon 9	Proposed
BA 330	unknown	2012-2014	unknown	Proposed

Genesis I Launch

On July 12, 2006, Genesis I launched on a Dnepr booster from Yasny Launch Base in Siberia. The launch was conducted by Bigelow and ISC Kosmotras. Despite ground-side difficulties during launch, the spacecraft performed as expected upon reaching orbit, inflating, deploying solar arrays and starting internal systems. The mission is planned to last for five years and include extensive observation of the craft's performance including testing, packing/deployment procedures and resistance to radiation and space debris, among other space hazards and conditions. Mike Gold, corporate counsel for Bigelow Aerospace, stated in relation to this mission and the next, "Our motto at Bigelow Aerospace is 'fly early and often'. Regardless of the results of Genesis I, we will launch a follow-up mission rapidly."

Genesis II Launch

On June 28, 2007, Genesis II launched on a converted SS-18 ICBM from Yasny Launch Base in Siberia. Launched at 8:02 a.m. PDT Genesis II was inserted into orbit at 8:16 a.m. PDT at an inclination of 64 degrees.

Although Genesis I and Genesis II are identical in size and similar in appearance there are several notable differences. Firstly, Genesis I contains 13 video cameras whereas Genesis II contains 22. Secondly, Genesis II includes a suite of additional sensors and avionics that are not present in Genesis I.

Atlas V as a Launch Vehicle

Bigelow is jointly funding studies with Lockheed Martin to investigate the usage of their Atlas V rocket as a vehicle for human transport to and from later Bigelow space stations. However, such usage remains uncertain as there is currently no existing crew capsule that could be used with the rocket.

Fly Your Stuff Programme

Bigelow Aerospace ran a Fly Your Stuff programme for the Genesis II launch. The cost to launch pictures or small items was around US$300. Bigelow now photographs each item with internal cameras as the items float inside the craft, displaying them on the company website.

The first image of the interior of Genesis II appeared on the company's website on June 29, 2007. Some of the pictures and other items placed aboard Genesis II as part of the Fly Your Stuff programme are clearly visible. Another interior image, apparently taken with more of the spacecraft's internal lights activated, was posted on July 2, 2007. Articles from the Fly Your Stuff programme are also visible in this image.

Test items, supplied by Bigelow Aerospace employees, were sent into orbit on Genesis I. No new images of items floating inside Genesis I have been released since shortly after the launch and initial activation of the spacecraft due to problems with a computer which controls several of the internal cameras.

Honours

Bigelow Aerospace has received several honours for its spaceflight efforts. On October 3, 2006, Bigelow Aerospace received the Innovator Award from the Arthur C. Clarke Foundation. The award recognizes "initiatives or new inventions that have had recent impact on or hold particular promise for satellite communications and society, and stand as distinguished examples of innovative thinking." Robert Bigelow was presented the award at the Arthur C. Clarke Awards in Washington D.C. alongside Walter Cronkite, who was honoured on the same night with the Arthur C. Clarke Lifetime Achievement Award.

On January 26, 2007, the Space Foundation announced that Bigelow Aerospace would be the recipient of its 2007 Space Achievement Award. Bigelow Aerospace joins a list of previous winners that include the Titan Launch Vehicle team; the Inertial Upper Stage team, the SpaceShipOne team; the Arianespace-CNES Ariane 4 launch team; the Evolved Expendable Launch Vehicle (EELV) team; the NASA/Industry Galileo space probe team; the Hubble Space Telescope team; Sea Launch; and the NASA/Boeing International Space Station team. The award was presented to Robert Bigelow on April 9, 2007 at the 23rd National Space Symposium in Colorado Springs, Colorado.

BLUE ORIGIN

Blue Origin is a privately-funded aerospace company set up by Amazon.com founder Jeff Bezos. Initially focused on sub-orbital spaceflight, the company has built and flown a testbed of its *New Shepard* spacecraft design at their Culberson County, Texas facility. According to company statements, it plans on placing the *New Shepard* in commercial suborbital tourist service in 2010 with flights about once a week. It is now confirmed that under the current timetable, Blue Origin will fly unmanned in 2011, and manned in 2012.

History

Since its founding the company has been notoriously tight-lipped about its plans. Although the company was formally incorporated in 2000, its existence only became public in 2003, when Bezos started buying land in Texas and interested parties followed up on the purchases. This was a topic of some interest in local politics, and his rapid aggregation of the lots under a variety of whimsically named shell companies was referred to as a "land grab".

In January 2005, Bezos told the editor of the *Van Horn Advocate* that Blue Origin is developing a sub-orbital space vehicle that will take off and land vertically and carry three or more astronauts to the edge of space. The spacecraft is based on technology like that used for the McDonnell Douglas DC-X and derivative DC-XA. Bezos told Reuters in November 2004 that his company hopes to progress to orbital spaceflight. As of January 2005, the company's website announced that it hopes to establish an "enduring human presence in space", but the 2007 version talks instead of aiming to "patiently and step-by-step, to lower the cost of spaceflight so that many people can afford to go and so that we humans can better continue exploring the solar system".

Employees of Blue Origin include Rob Meyerson (Programme manager) and science fiction author Neal Stephenson (part-time advisor).

Headquarters

The company is headquartered in a warehouse situated on 25 acres (100,000 m^2) of industrial land in the Seattle, Washington suburb of Kent, where its research and development is located. The spaceport facility was set up at the "Corn Ranch", a 165,000 acre (670 km^2) spread north of Van Horn and 15 miles (24 km) south of the Guadalupe Mountains, nearly 120 miles (190 km) east of El Paso.

New Shepard

During 2006 the company built a prototype of their *New Shepard* design. The *New Shepard* is controlled entirely by on-board computers, without ground control. The fuselage is roughly conical, with a rounded base, and roughly bullet-shaped overall. It is powered by a cluster of nine engines powered by high test peroxide (HTP) and RP-1 kerosene, arranged in a 3 by 3 grid on the bottom. Four landing legs containing shock absorbers also extend from the edges of the bottom.

The first example, christened the *Goddard,* first flew on November 13, 2006. The flight was a complete success, and pictures and movies from the launch form a major part of the company's spartan website. However, a second test flight filed for December 2nd never launched. Two successful flight tests have been recorded since then.

In an interview with Charlie Rose on November 19, 2007, Bezos reported that the construction of a second test vehicle was in progress and that a third development vehicle would be built after that before any commercial flights would begin.

Test Flights

- First Test Flight: 13 November 2006, 06:30, name of vehicle: Goddard
- Second Test Flight: 22 March 2007, name of vehicle: Goddard
- Third Test Flight : 19 April 2007, name of vehicle: Goddard

EADS ASTRIUM

EADS Astrium is an aerospace subsidiary of the European Aeronautic Defence and Space Company (EADS) and is dedicated to providing civil and defence space systems and services. In 2008, Astrium had a turnover of €4.3 billion and 15,000 employees in France, Germany, the United Kingdom, Spain and the Netherlands.

Business Layout

Its three main areas of activity are:

- EADS Astrium Satellites for spacecraft and ground segment
- EADS Astrium Space Transportation for launchers and orbital infrastructure
- EADS Astrium Services for the development and delivery of satellite services

Corporate History

In June 2006, EADS Astrium, EADS Space Transportation and EADS Space Services were merged into a single company: EADS SPACE. The next month, EADS announced that the newly merged company had been renamed "ASTRIUM - an EADS company". In December, the company's logo was unveiled, with the announcement from both CEOs that the space division would instead be called "EADS Astrium".

The new logo is a combination of the never released ASTRIUM logo and of the EADS logo, therefore a composite look.

Space Tourism

In June 2007, EADS Astrium announced that it would be entering the space tourism sector. On June 20, 2007 the company unveiled a model of the space jet, a one-stage sub-orbital hybrid craft, utilising both jet and rocket engines. Carrying four passengers, the space jet would take off from regular airports using conventional jet engines. Once flying to the needed altitude the rockets would then be fired. After reaching its final altitude of 100 km, passengers would experience weightlessness for three minutes. Tickets were expected to cost up to €200,000 with flights possibly beginning in 2012. EADS estimated that development cost will approach 1 billion Euros. On January 28, 2009 EADS Astrium confirmed that the Programme was on hold indefinitely.

EADS Astrium Space Tourism Project

The **EADS Astrium Space Tourism Project**, also called **EADS Astrium TBN** according to some sources, has been officially unveiled in Paris by EADS Astrium, the space subsidiary of the European consortium EADS, on June 13, 2007. The project is the first space tourism entry by a major aerospace contractor. A scale one mock-up of the cockpit has been exhibited at the 2007 Paris Air Show and is now on display in the Concorde hall of the Musée de l'Air et de l'Espace.

It is a rocket plane with a large wingspan, straight rearwards wing and a pair of canards. Propulsion is ensured by classical jet engines for the atmospheric phase and a methane-oxygen rocket engine for the space tourism phase. It can carry a pilot and four passengers. The dimensions and looks are somewhat similar to those of a business jet.

EADS Astrium hopes to start the development of this rocket plane by 2008, with the objective of a first flight in 2011. It has been announced that the Tunisian area of Tozeur could be used for the initial flights.

EADS Astrium plans to raise public and private money for its project.

Origin of the Project

The origin of the project is a proposal by a group of young French, German, British and Spanish engineers from EADS Astrium. It has been studied in great secrecy for two years and finally approved by the chairman of EADS Astrium, François Auque. The design is basically a copy of the Rocketplane XP concept. They looked at the main concepts under development and their studies showed that Rocketplane's jet and rocket combination made the most sense.

In the following months, a core team came up with a detailed concept and assembled the required expertise from different areas of Astrium and other EADS subsidiaries.

The **European Aeronautic Defence and Space Company N.V. (EADS)** is a large European aerospace corporation, formed by the merger on 10 July 2000 of DaimlerChrysler Aerospace AG (DASA) of Germany, Aérospatiale-Matra of France, and Construcciones Aeronáuticas SA (CASA) of Spain. The company develops and markets civil and military aircraft, as well as communications systems, missiles, space rockets, satellites, and related systems. The company is headquartered in the Netherlands in Schiphol-Rijk and operates under Dutch law.

History

The 1997 merger of American corporations Boeing and McDonnell Douglas, which followed the forming of Lockheed Martin, the world's largest defense contractor in 1995, increased the pressure on European defense companies to consolidate. In June 1997 British Aerospace Defence Managing Director John Weston commented "Europe... is supporting three times the number of contractors on less than half the budget of the U.S." European governments wished to see the merger of their defence manufacturers into a single entity, a European Aerospace and Defense Company.

As early as 1995 the German aerospace and defence company DaimlerChrysler Aerospace (DASA) and its British counterpart British Aerospace were said to be keen to create a transnational aerospace and defense company. The two companies envisaged including Aérospatiale, the other major European aerospace company, but only after its privatisation. The first stage of this integration was seen as the transformation of Airbus from a consortium of British Aerospace, DASA, Aérospatiale and Construcciones Aeronáuticas SA into an integrated company; in this aim BAe and DASA were united against the various objections of Aérospatiale. As well as Airbus, British Aerospace and DASA were partners in the Panavia Tornado and Eurofighter Typhoon aircraft projects. Merger discussions began between British Aerospace and DASA in July 1998, just as French participation became more likely with the announcement that Aérospatiale was to merge with Matra and emerge with a diluted French government shareholding. A merger was agreed between British Aerospace Chairman Richard Evans and DASA CEO Jürgen Schrempp in December 1998. However when the British General Electric Company put its defense electronics business Marconi Electronic Systems up for sale on 22 December 1998, British Aerospace abandoned the DASA merger in favour of purchasing its British rival. The merger of British Aerospace and MES to form BAE Systems was announced on 19 January 1999 and completed on 30 November. Evans stated that in 2004 that his fear was that an American defense contractor would acquire MES and challenge both British Aerospace and DASA.

Formation

DASA and the Spanish aircraft company Construcciones Aeronáuticas SA agreed to merge with the signature of a memorandum of understanding on 11 June 1999. On 14 October 1999 DASA agreed to merge with Aérospatiale-Matra to create the

European Aeronautic Defence and Space Company. 10 July 2000 was "Day One" for the new company which became the world's second largest aerospace company after Boeing and the second largest European arms manufacturer after BAE Systems.

In January 2001 Airbus Industrie was transformed from an inherently inefficient consortium structure to a formal joint stock company, with legal and tax procedures being finalised on 11 July. Both EADS and BAE transferred ownership of their Airbus factories to the new Airbus SAS in return for 80 per cent and 20 per cent shares in the new company respectively. In April 2001 EADS agreed to merge its missile businesses with those of BAE Systems and Alenia Marconi Systems (BAE/Finmeccanica) to form MBDA. EADS took a 37.5 per cent share of the new company which was formally established in December 2001 and which thus became the world's second largest missile manufacturer.

On 16 June 2003 EADS acquired BAE's 25 per cent share in Astrium, the satellite and space system manufacturer, to become the sole owner. EADS paid £84 million, however due to the lossmaking status of the company BAE invested an equal amount for "restructuring". It was subsequently renamed EADS Astrium. In November 2003, EADS announced that it was considering working with Japanese companies, and the Japanese METI, to develop a hypersonic airliner intended to be a larger, faster, and quieter, replacement for the Concorde, which was retired in October the same year.

Despite repeated suggestions as early as 2000 that BAE Systems wished to sell its 20 per cent share of Airbus, the possibility was consistently denied by the company. However on 6 April 2006 BBC News reported that it was indeed to sell its stake, then "conservatively valued" at £2.4 billion. Due to the slow pace of informal negotiations, BAE exercised its option which saw investment bank Rothschild appointed to give an independent valuation. Six days after this process began, Airbus announced delays to the A380 with significant effects on the value of Airbus shares. On 2 June 2006 Rothschild valued BAE's share at £1.87 billion, well below BAE's analysts and even EADS' expectations. The BAE board recommended that the company proceed with the sale and on 4 October 2006 shareholders voted in favour; the sale was completed on 13 October making EADS the sole shareholder of Airbus.

In March 2007 EADS Defence and Security Systems division was awarded an eight year, £200 m contract to provide the IT infrastructure for the FiReControl project in the UK.

Recent Activities

On 29 February 2008, the United States Air Force awarded a $35 billion contract for aerial refueling tankers (the KC-45) to Northrop Grumman, with EADS as a major subcontractor. The contract, one of the largest created by the Department of Defense, is initially valued at $35 billion but has the potential to grow to $100 billion. It is also a sign of the growing influence of foreign suppliers within the Pentagon and breaks a relationship that has lasted decades with Boeing, which had built the bulk of the existing tanker fleet and had fought hard to land the new contract.

Merged companies	*Resulting company*	*Merged companies*	*Resulting company*	*Merged companies*	*Resulting company*	*Merged companies*	*Resulting company*	*Merged companies*	*Resulting company*
Potez CAMS Romano Lioré et Olivier SPCA	Société nationale des constructions aéronautiques du sud-est (1937)								
Blériot Aéronautique Société des Avions Marcel Bloch SASO UCA SAB	Société nationale des constructions aéronautiques du sud-ouest (1936)	Sud-Est Sud-Ouest	Sud Aviation (1957)	Sud Aviation Nord Aviation SEREB	SNIAS (SNI Aérospatiale) (1970)	Aérospatiale Matra	Aérospatiale-Matra (1999)	Aérospatiale-Matra Construcciones Aeronáuticas CASA (Spain) DaimlerChrysler Aerospace DASA (Germany)	EADS
Focke-Wulf Focke-Achgelis Weserflug	Vereinigte Flugtechnische Werke (1964)	Messerschmitt Bölkow Hamburger Flugzeugbau Vereinigte Flugtechnische Werke	Messerschmitt-Bölkow-Blohm (MBB) (1969)	Daimler-Benz Messerschmitt-Bölkow-Blohm	Daimler-Benz Aerospace (1989)	Daimler-Benz Aerospace MTU Aero Engines Dornier 2 divisions of AEG	DaimlerChrysler Aerospace (1989)		

Under the contract, Northrop Grumman and EADS would build a fleet of 179 planes, based on the existing Airbus 330, to provide in-air refueling to military aircraft, from fighter jets to cargo planes. While final assembly of the craft would take place at an Airbus plant near Mobile, Alabama, parts would come from suppliers across the globe.

However, the award was protested by Boeing, the other bidder on the project, which was upheld by the GAO. The Air Force announced a partial reopening of the bid, focusing on the eight (of nearly 110) areas where Boeing's protests were upheld, with a final decision due by the end of 2008.

Both the giants, Airbus and Boeing shall again compete for the $40 billion contract from the U.S. Air Force to supply aerial refueling planes to which WSJ describes as a restart of competition for the order.

Organization

- Airbus
  - EADS Sogerma
- Military Transport Aircraft Division
- Eurocopter
- EADS Astrium
  - EADS Astrium Satellites
  - EADS Astrium Space Transportation
  - EADS Astrium Space Services
- EADS Defence & Security
  - Defence Electronics
  - EADS Military Air Systems, including products such as the Mako/HEAT, and stakes in the following companies:
    - Dassault Aviation (45.76 per cent)—manufacturer fighters like the Dassault Rafale or the Dassault Mirage 2000.
    - Eurofighter GmbH (46 per cent)—manufacturer of Eurofighter Typhoon.
    - EADS 3 Sigma—a Hellenic company focused in the design, development, production and services provision of airborne and surface target drone systems.
  - Defence and Communication Systems
  - MBDA (37.5 per cent)—missile manufacturer

Other Units

- EADS North America—the U.S. holding company for the North American activities of EADS.
  - American Eurocopter
  - PlantCML
- ATR (50 per cent)—regional aircraft manufacturer
- EADS Socata

- EADS CASA
- EADS EFW
- Arianespace (30 per cent)
- Dornier Consulting

Corporate Governance

EADS' Executive Committee is headed by Louis Gallois, the EADS CEO. Other members are François Auque (Astrium), Lutz Bertling (Eurocopter), Jean Botti (Chief Technical Officer), Fabrice Brégier (EADS Operational Performance), Ralph Crosby (EADS North America), (Airbus), Jussi Itävuori (Human Resources), Marwan Lahoud (Chief Marketing and Strategy Officer), Hans Peter Ring (Chief Financial Officer, EADS and Airbus), Carlos Suárez (Military Transport Aircraft Division) and Stefan Zoller (Defence and Security).

The Executive Committee is appointed by the board of directors, itself appointed by Daimler AG and SOGEADE. Both appoint four directors plus one independent director. As of July 2003 SEPI no longer nominates a board member, but a Spanish director is retained as the 11th member. The board also appoints the company's chairmen, one from the Daimler nominated directors and from the SOGEADE nominated directors. As of September 2007 the Chairmen are Rüdiger Grube and Arnaud Lagardère. The other board members are Louis Gallois, Thomas Enders, Hans Peter Ring, Juan Manuel Eguiagaray, Michel Pébereau, Bodo Uebber, François David and Michael Rogowski.

In late 2004 Noël Forgeard (then Airbus CEO) was nominated by Lagardère as the next French CEO of EADS. Forgeard had suggested that this system should be abolished in favour of a single CEO in a move that DaimlerChrysler saw as an attempt to engineer a French dominated management team. Following protracted arguments, which caused embarrassment to EADS at the Paris Air Show, the appointment was confirmed by the EADS Board of Directors on 25 June 2005. At the same meeting the Board, in consultation with partner BAE Systems, named Gustav Humbert as President and CEO of Airbus.

Financial Information

As of 3 July 2007 41.63 per cent of EADS stock is publicly traded on six European stock exchanges, while the remaining 58.37 per cent is owned by a "Contractural Partnership". The latter is owned by SOGEADE (27.38%), Daimler AG (22.41%), SEPI (5.46%) and Dubai Holding (3.12%). SOGEADE is owned by the French State and Lagardère, while SEPI is a Spanish state holding company. France also owns 0.06 per cent of publicly traded stock.

In October 2005 the British Ministry of Defence warned European politicians to stop, as it sees it, interfering in the corporate governance of EADS. The UK Defence Procurement Minister Lord Drayson has hinted that the UK government, a major customer for EADS, may withhold future contracts. "As a key customer, we see it as important for EADS to move in a direction that is free from political interference."

On 4 April 2006, DaimlerChrysler announced its intention to reduce its shareholding from 30 per cent to 22.5 per cent. The company places a value of the stake at "approximately €2.0 billion." Lagardère will reduce its holding by an identical amount. However, Caisse des Dépôts et Consignations, a unit of the French government, acquired 2.25 per cent of EADS. At issue as a result is the fact that the German and French shareholdings are now in imbalance.

On 30 August 2006, shortly after the stock price decline caused by the A380 delivery delays, more than 5 per cent of EADS stock has been reportedly purchased by the Russian state-owned Vneshtorgbank. Now its share is nearly 6 per cent. In December 2007, Vneshtorgbank sold EADS shares to another state-controlled bank Vneshekonombank. EADS sharers are to be delivered by Vneshekonombank to the charter capital of JSC "United Aircraft Corporation" in 2008.

On 3 October 2006, shortly after EADS admitted further delays in the Airbus 380 programme would cost the company 4.8 billion euros in lost earnings in 2010, EADS shares, traded on the Paris arm of Euronext, were suspended after they surpassed the 10 per cent loss limit. Trading resumed later in the day with the one day loss holding at 7 per cent.

Criticisms

Cluster Bomb Allegation

In 2005 the Norwegian Government Pension Fund recommended the exclusion of several companies producing cluster bombs or components. EADS and its sister company EADS Finance BV were among them, arguing that EADS manufactures "key components for cluster bombs." The criticism was centered around TDA, a joint venture between EADS and Thales S.A. TDA produced the mortar ammunition PR Cargo, which can be considered cluster ammunition, however this definition has since been successfully battled by EADS. EADS and its subsidiaries are now regarded as fulfilling all the conditions of the Ottawa Treaty. According to the new point of view, no product of EADS or its subsidiaries falls into the category of antipersonnel mines as defined by the Ottawa Treaty ("landmines under the Ottawa Treaty"). In April 2006, the fund declared that the basis for excluding EADS from investments related to production of cluster munitions is no longer valid, however its shareholding of MBDA means the fund still excludes EADS due to its indirect involvement in nuclear weapons production.

Bribery

In 2003 Tony Yengeni, former chief whip of South Africa's ANC, was convicted of fraud relating to an arms deal with South Africa, in which EADS were major players, worth around $5bn. The BBC reported that EADS had admitted that it had "rendered assistance" to some 30 senior officials to obtain luxury vehicles, including defence force chief General Siphiwe Nyanda.

Insider Trading Investigation

On 2 June 2006 co-CEO Noël Forgeard and Airbus CEO Gustav Humbert resigned following the controversy caused by the June 2006 announcement that deliveries of the A380 would be delayed by a further six months. Forgeard was one of a number of executives who exercised stock options in November 2005 and March 2006. He and 21 other executives are under investigation as to whether they knew about the delays in the Airbus A380 project which caused a 26 per cent fall in EADS shares when publicised.

The French government's actions are also under investigation. The state-owned bank Caisse des Dépots et Consignations (CDC) bought part of Lagardère's 7.5 per cent stake in EADS in April 2006, allowing that latter to partially escape the June 2006 losses.

In June 2008, law firm Coughlin Stoia Geller Rudman and Robbins announced that a class action has been commenced on behalf of an institutional investor in the United States District Court for the Southern District of New York on behalf of U.S. citizens who purchased the publicly traded stock of EADS.

EXCALIBUR ALMAZ

Excalibur Almaz is a private spaceflight company which plans to orbit manned spacecraft, by using modernized *TKS* space capsules and *Almaz* space stations, derived from the formerly secret Soviet space programme. Missions will support orbital space tourism, and provide test beds for experiments in a microgravity environment.

Spacecraft

The *TKS*-derived space capsules, which vaguely resemble a cross between the American *Gemini* and *Apollo* capsules, are unique by Russian/Soviet standards. They are equipped to carry three passengers or operate autonomously, but unlike the American capsules the Almaz capsules are reusable from 50 to 100 times. They can launch atop any of several rockets of various spacefaring countries, and they possess a Launch Escape System to ensure the safety of their passengers. They use parachutes and retrorockets to return to Earth, and have soft landing engines which fire just prior to touching down on land. Water-landings are also possible.

The *Almaz*-derived space stations are closely related to modules used on the International Space Station, and on the Soviet and Russian *Salyut* and *Mir* space stations. This is because the design of the original Almaz (Salyut 2, 3, and 5) stations was used as a basis for capsules on Mir and ISS. Excalibur Almaz's space stations will feature the largest windows ever on spacecraft.

Company

Excalibur Almaz is based in Douglas, Isle of Man, with offices in Houston and Moscow. The company owns its spacecraft but contracts expert services, including refurbishment, launch, control, and recovery.

Company founders include CEO and space law expert Arthur M. Dula and space commercialization veteran Buckner Hightower. Chief of spacecraft operations is Leroy Chiao, formerly a NASA astronaut and Commander of the International Space Station.

Advisory Board members include: former Johnson Space Center Director, George Abbey; former Kennedy Space Center Director and former President of Lockheed Martin Space Operations, Jay Honeycutt; former space shuttle astronaut and VASIMR plasma rocket engine inventor, Franklin Chang-Diaz; former French astronaut Jean-Loup Chrétien, and former Russian cosmonauts, Vladimir Titov and Yuri Glazkov.

DA VINCI PROJECT

The **da Vinci Project** was a privately funded, volunteer-staffed attempt to launch a reusable manned suborbital spacecraft. It was formed in 1996 specifically to be a contender for the Ansari X PRIZE for the first non-governmental reusable manned spacecraft. The project was based in Toronto, Ontario, Canada and led by Brian Feeney.

The original da Vinci Project is no longer operating. A documentary was filmed throughout much of the project's life from 2000 through post-X PRIZE roundup footage in 2008. The documentary accumulated some 1000 hours or so of footage. It was a private undertaking by Michel Jones of Riverstone Productions, Toronto, and as of early 2009 was still in a preliminary stage of editing and completion.

The project participated in the X PRIZE Cup 2005, displaying a mock-up of its Wild Fire MK Vl spacecraft. In early 2006 it was decided to reorganize the manned spaceflight effort as well as develop a new winged spacecraft design. A new brand and commercial venture was developed—DreamSpace Group—built on the foundations of the da Vinci Project.

At X PRIZE Cup 2006 a new preliminary manned suborbital space tourism craft design, designated the XF1, was unveiled. Design and engineering work has continued since, with a stated intention to unveil the first full scale XF1 flight demonstrator sometime in 2010.

The Team

The da Vinci Project was staffed by a revolving group of volunteers, more than 600 in all by project's end in 2006. At its most active, the team maintained a normal strength of 20-30. Brian Feeney established the project in 1996 to compete for the international X PRIZE competition. The core of the team was located in Toronto, Canada with Engineering and Ground Operation Teams located across Canada and around the world.

Spacecraft Design

The project's design was a rocket-powered spacecraft to be air-launched from a helium balloon at an altitude of about 21 km (65,000 ft). The project scope included design and construction of both the spacecraft and the launching balloon. The chosen design can be described as a manned rockoon.

The spacecraft design, Wild Fire, was predominantly cylindrical, with a diameter of 2.00 m and overall length of 8.00 m. It had a crew capsule at one end, rocket motor at the other, and propellant tanks between.

The crew capsule was spherical, with a diameter of 1.98 m. It was intended to accommodate three humans in a pressurised atmosphere, but the crew would also wear pressure suits. The capsule would separate from the remainder of the craft in the course of a normal reentry, and if necessary could also separate during some emergency scenarios. It was designed to carry 2 small high-speed parachutes and 2 primary recovery parachutes made by Ballistic Recovery Systems. There were six large windows covering the front half of the capsule.

The spacecraft was designed to use a hybrid rocket engine, with solid paraffin fuel and liquid nitrous oxide oxidiser.

There was also a cold gas reaction control system, using cold gas nitrogen propellant.

The craft used an INS (Inertial Navigation System) autopilot and could also be flown manually through activation of the RCS system.

In the original design, during reentry, the vehicle deployed a ballute, an inflated conical balloon intended to make the vehicle aerodynamically stable, provide drag, and act as a heat shield. The ballute would remain inflated until landing, where it would cushion the impact. Between 7 km and 3 km altitude the vehicle would also deploy a parafoil, which would be used both to slow descent and to steer toward the landing zone. There would also be a backup parachute for the spacecraft, in addition to a separate parachute for the separable crew capsule.

By 2003, the design had been revised to a simpler pattern: the ballute concept was abandoned, and the crew capsule and propulsion stage would separate and independently descend with parachutes.

Vehicle Specifications

- Name: Wild Fire MKVI;
- Dimensions: 8 m (26 ft) long, 1.98 m (78 in) in diameter;
- Gross take-off weight: 4,090 kg (9,000 lbm);
- Dry weight: 1,660 kg (3,650 lbm);
- Crew capsule: 1.98 m (78 in) diameter sphere;
- Crew environment: Pressurized to 1 atm (100 kPa) with pressure suits;
- Payload capacity: 410 kg (900 lbm);
- Propulsion system: Single, pressure-fed, hybrid engine;
- Propellants: Nitrous oxide and proprietary solid paraffin fuel;
- Total thrust: 80,000 N (18,000).

INTERORBITAL SYSTEMS

Interorbital Systems Corporation (IOS) is an American aerospace company based in Mojave, California. It was founded in 1996 by Roderick and Randa Milliron, who also co-founded Trans Lunar Research.

Interorbital Systems is currently working on a line of launch vehicles aimed at winning both the Google Lunar X Prize and America's Space Prize. The company was also a competitor in the Ansari X Prize.

Current Research and Development

Interorbital Systems is currently pursuing two separate lines of research. The first is Sea Star TSAAHTO, a small rocket capable of delivering small satellite payloads into orbit, and so generate capital for pursuing the companies flagship programme: the Neptune, a line of launch vehicles designed to put humans into orbit.

Human Spaceflight Programme

Neptune is a line of heavy launch vehicles, consisting of the Neptune 30, the Neptune 1000, and the Neptune TSAAHTO.

- The Neptune 30, the smallest, is to be used to deliver 30 kilo payloads into low Earth orbit. It is composed of four "common propulsion modules" (essentially long tubes of rocket fuel).
- The Neptune 1000 is designed to launch a one tonne payload into low-earth orbit or a 190 kg payload to Earth escape velocity. The rocket is composed of 33 common propulsion modules, and makes up the Interorbital Systems's contribution to SYNERGY MOON a three-company attempt to win the Google Lunar X Prize.
- The Neptune TSAAHTO, the largest of the three, can be fitted to carry either cargo or human passengers. To do so, the Crew Module has been designed. This space capsule is to be capable of housing five crew members and a pilot, and sits atop the Neptune TSAAHTO during launch. The rocket itself is composed of eight large common propulsion modules and eight small common propulsion modules and can place a 7,000-pound payload into a 250 mile 51° orbit.

Sounding Rockets

Interorbital Systems has successfully tested a number of rocket engines in the 500-5,000 lbf (2 to 22 kN) thrust range and conducted flight tests of its small testbed, Neutrino. Neutrino is a sounding rocket designed for low-altitude suborbital flight, for the purpose of testing systems of its larger follow-on rockets.

IOS holds an active Office of Commercial Space Transportation Launch License for Tachyon, a sounding rocket designed for 120 mile apogee suborbital flight.

Retired Designs

SolarX was a suborbital rocket design that was IOS' attempt to win the Ansari X Prize. It didn't get off the ground in time and was beaten by Scaled Composites' SpaceShipOne.

Launch Sites

Interorbital Systems' prototypes are all designed to be amphibious (capable of launch from land or sea). Although IOS currently tests its spacecraft at the Mojave Airport & Spaceport and conducts testbed launches from the Mojave Desert, it plans to develop and implement a method for launching directly from the water without a launch platform. The vehicle is towed into position by a 33 m (100 ft) crew boat, then a ballast is suspended from the submerged tail-section to provide proper orientation and stability during launch. According to IOS, sea launches are inherently less dangerous than land launches because they reduce the chance of damage to people or property in the event of a failed launch. As a result it is easier and less expensive to obtain a license for sea operations.

MOJAVE AEROSPACE VENTURES

Mojave Aerospace Ventures (MAV) is a company founded by Paul Allen and Burt Rutan to handle the commercial spinoffs from the Tier One project. It owns the intellectual property arising from Tier One, and it is in turn owned by Paul Allen (the majority shareholder) and Burt Rutan. It has signed a deal with Virgin Galactic to develop the Virgin SpaceShip, a suborbital spacecraft, for space tourism. Virgin Group and Scaled have subsequently formed a joint venture, The Spaceship Company to manufacture the spacecraft.

Company

The structure of Mojave Aerospace Ventures appears to be the basis of the deal between Allen and Rutan for the funding of Tier One. The company owns all the intellectual property of the Tier One project, such as patents, and so controls commercial exploitation. Allen, the sole source of funding for Tier One, is the majority owner. Rutan, having developed the technology, owns a minority stake. This stands in contrast to the company more usually associated with Tier One, Scaled Composites, which is owned by Northrop Grumman. MAV serves to separate Tier One spinoffs from Scaled Composites.

When the Tier One programme was announced, Scaled Composites initially expressed a hope that by about 2013 it would be possible for members of the public to experience a suborbital flight for about the price of a luxury cruise.

Virgin Galactic

On September 25, 2004 MAV agreed on a joint venture with Richard Branson's newly-formed company Virgin Galactic, to develop a suborbital spacecraft for the space tourism market. The initial plan is to build five Virgin SpaceShips, based on scaling up the SpaceShipOne design. These could start revenue flights in 2007-2008, with tickets initially costing around US$190,000 each, including three days of flight training. It is anticipated that the price would drop substantially as more companies break into the space tourism market 10-15 years down the road. This deal could see the company profit by up to US$21million in the next few years, depending on how many spacecraft Virgin Galactic decides to build.

The spacecraft would be manufactured by The Spaceship Company.

The designs for the Tier 1b customer suborbital spaceflight vehicles are referred to as SpaceShipTwo and its first stage White Knight Two.

ORBITAL SCIENCES CORPORATION

Orbital Sciences Corporation (**OSC**, though commonly referred to as **Orbital**) is a Dulles, Virginia company which specializes in satellite launch and manufacture. Its Launch Systems Group is heavily involved with missile defense launch systems. Orbital formerly owned ORBIMAGE (now GeoEye) and the Magellan line of GPS receivers, though they are now divested (the latter to Thales). Orbital's NYSE ticker symbol is **ORB**. This company should not be confused with the Australian Orbital.

History

Orbital was founded in 1982 by David Thompson, Bruce Ferguson and Scott Webster. In 1990, the company successfully carried out eight space missions, highlighted by the initial launch of the Pegasus rocket. In 2006 Orbital conducted its 500th mission since the company's founding.

In 1997 it spun off its space imaging division Orbital Space Imaging or ORBIMAGE (with Thompson then as chairman). It is now GeoEye.

Business Groups

- **Space Systems Group (SSG):** Orbital is one of the world's leading providers of small- to medium-class satellites. Since the company's founding in 1982, Orbital has delivered over 110 spacecraft to commercial, military and civil customers worldwide. To date, these spacecraft have amassed in nearly 630 years of on-orbit operations.
- **Launch Systems Group (LSG):** Orbital's space launch vehicles are the industry standard for boosting small payloads to orbit. The Pegasus rocket is launched from the company's "Stargazer" L-1011 carrier aircraft and has proven to be the industry's small space launch workhorse, having conducted 40 missions from six different launch sites worldwide since 1990. The Taurus and Minotaur ground-launched rockets combine Pegasus upper stages with either government-supplied or commercially available first-stage rocket motors to boost larger payloads to orbit. Minotaur IV is the newest addition to Orbital's line of space boosters and combines decommissioned Peacekeeper rocket motors with proven Orbital avionics and fairings to provide increased lifting capacity for government-sponsored payloads. Orbital is also an industry-leading provider of suborbital launch vehicles for the nation's missile defense systems. In the last 10 years it has conducted nearly 50 major launches

for the U.S. Missile Defense Agency (MDA), the Air Force, the Army and Navy to develop, test and enhance U.S. missile defense systems.

- **Advanced Programmes Group (APG):** Orbital's extensive experience in developing innovative and reliable small launch and space systems is currently being applied to new technologies for human spaceflight, commercial transportation, aeronautical research and space transportation.
- **Technical Services Division (TSD):** Orbital provides cost-effective engineering, production and technical management expertise primarily for space-related science and defense programmes. Typically, it supplies specialized personnel—engineers, scientists, technicians and other professionals—with specific knowledge in the areas that the customer is pursuing. The Orbital employees often work side-by-side with the customers' technical staff at their facilities. They perform a wide range of functions, from system-level efforts such as special payload equipment and training support for NASA's Hubble Space Telescope servicing missions to component-level tasks including development of high-energy microwave transmitters for the National Radio Astronomy Observatory.

Primary Facility Locations

- Dulles, Virginia
- Chandler, Arizona
- Orange County, California
- Greenbelt, Maryland
- Vandenberg Air Force Base, California
- Wallops Flight Facility, Virginia (under construction)

Orbital Products

International Space Station Resupply

The Taurus rocket lifts off successfully from Vandenberg Air Force Base

- Commercial Orbital Transportation Services (COTS) Demonstration resupply mission to ISS: debut of Cygnus spacecraft and Taurus II launch vehicle
- Commercial Resupply Services (CRS) $1.9 billion NASA contract for 8 Cygnus/Taurus II resupply missions to the ISS

NASA Constellation Programme

- Launch Abort System (LAS) for Orion Capsule

Satellite Launch Vehicles

- Minotaur solid fuel satellite launcher rocket
- Pegasus winged space booster component of an expandable launch system
- Taurus four stage, solid fuel launch vehicle
- OSP-2 Minotaur IV, a satellite launching version of the LG-118A Peacekeeper

- Minotaur V Five stage satellite launching version of the LG-118A Peacekeeper
- Taurus II Three stage kerosene/oxygen—solid—hypergolic rocket (in development)

Experimental Vehicles

- X-34 reusable launch vehicle demonstrator
- DART Rendezvous Vehicle
- Hyper-X
- Orbital Space Plane

Missile Defense Systems and Ballistic Target Vehicles

- Ground-Based Midcourse Defense (GMD) Orbital Boost Vehicle (OBV) for the United States Missile Defense Agency (MDA)
- Kinetic Energy Interceptor (KEI)
- GQM-163A Coyote
- Target Test Vehicle (TTV)
- Minotaur II
- Minotaur III

GEO Satellites

- **STAR 2 platform:** At its Dulles, Virginia plant Orbital builds medium-sized spacecraft based on the company's STAR 2 platform. Both payloads of a September 2007 Ariane 5 launch—Optus D2 and Intelsat 11 were built on the STAR 2 platform.
    - IndoStar-1
    - BSAT-2a
    - BSAT-2b
    - BSAT-2c
    - N-Star c
    - Galaxy 12
    - Galaxy 14
    - Galaxy 15
    - TELKOM-2
    - Optus D1
    - Optus D2
    - Optus D3
    - Intelsat 11
    - Horizons-2
    - Thor 5
    - AMC-21
    - MEASAT-3a
    - NSS-9
    - Intelsat-15 (in production)
    - Intelsat-16 (in production)
    - Intelsat-18 (in production)
    - Koreasat-6 (in production)
    - AMC-5R (in production)
    - FM-1 (in production)
    - FM-2 (in production)

LEO Satellites

- GALEX
- SORCE
- DART
- AIM
- OCO
- GLORY (in production)
- ORBCOMM Fleet
- FORMOSAT-3/COSMIC
- NuSTAR (in development)
- OrbView-3
- Space Technology 8 (ST8) (in development)

Planetary Probes

- Dawn
- IBEX

Client Countries

- Australia
- France
- Indonesia
- Japan
- South Korea
- Malaysia
- Netherlands
- Norway
- Pakistan
- Philippines
- Taiwan
- United States

Launch Sites

Orbital's launch vehicles have been staged from many sites worldwide. These include:

- Vandenberg Air Force Base (VAFB) in California
- Cape Canaveral Air Force Station (CCAS) in Florida
- Wallops Flight Facility (WFF) in Virginia
- Kodiak Launch Complex in Alaska
- Edwards Air Force Base in California
- Kwajalein Atoll in the Marshall Islands
- Canary Islands in Spain
- Pacific Missile Range Facility (PMRF) in Hawaii

Notable Partnerships

- Lockheed Martin
- Alliant Techsystems (ATK)
- Aerojet
- Yuzhnoye Design Bureau
- Yuzhmash
- Thales Alenia Space
- Mid-Atlantic Regional Spaceport

PLANETSPACE

PlanetSpace is a privately funded Chicago-based rocket and space travel project founded by Geoff Sheerin, CEO of the Canadian Arrow Corporation and Dr. Chirinjeev Kathuria in 2005.

In February, 2007, NASA announced plans to provide PlanetSpace with requirements and specifications to provide crew and cargo flights to the International Space Station under the terms of the National Aeronautics and Space Act. Initially

PlanetSpace planned to utilize the Silver Dart for this purpose, but on 2007-11-21 PlanetSpace announced that its COTS proposal would utilize a spacecraft provided by Lockheed Martin. This proposal does not include use of the Silver Dart.

Background

The mission of PlanetSpace is to make space travel accessible to the general public. The company has focused its main efforts on two major projects: the Canadian Arrow, which is in development, and the Silver Dart, which is a proposed orbital spaceplane.

Geoff Sheerin, President of Canadian Arrow and Dr. Chirinjeev Kathuria, two entrepreneurs with a love of space, joined forces to create PLANETSPACE in the spring of 2005. At a press conference in May 2005 in London Ontario Canada, Sheerin told the United Press International that Canadian Arrow was nearing completion and that it was missing only one important component in its plan to develop its space tourism business: money. Geoff Sheerin proudly announced, "We have found our Paul Allen". Presenting the newly formed company PlanetSpace and his new partner Dr. Chirinjeev Kathuria.

Dr. Kathuria was a founding director of MirCorp, the company that made history on April 4, 2000 when it launched the world's first privately funded manned space programme and signed up Dennis Tito to space as Earth's first space tourist or citizen explorer. MirCorp was a joint venture with RSC Energia. RSC Energia launched the first satellite (Sputnik), sent the first man to orbit the Earth (Yuri Gagarin), built the Mir Space Station, and is a major partner in the International Space Station.

Canadian Arrow

The Canadian Arrow is a 16.5 m tall two-stage rocket, where the second stage is a three-person space capsule. In a somewhat conservative approach, the design of the rocket engine and aerodynamics are based on the well proven V-2 design from WWII. The vehicle will launch vertically from the ground, on a sub-orbital trajectory, and will return to Earth via parachutes and make a water landing, similar to the splashdowns of the Mercury, Gemini and Apollo spacecraft.

Silver Dart

Based on the U.S. Air Force's Flight Dynamics Laboratory-7 (FDL-7) programme, the Silver Dart is a lifting body designed to glide from hypersonic speeds of Mach 22 down to landing. The goal is to develop an orbital space craft/hypersonic glider capable of carrying around eight passengers. The spacecraft is expected to launch vertically atop a two-stage-plus-boosters rocket, propelled at takeoff by 28 Canadian Arrow rocket engines (slightly updated replicas of the German V-2 engine) and land horizontally on an aircraft runway, in an arrangement reminiscent of the Dynasoar project by NASA.

NASA based its X-24B test aircraft on the FDL-7 lifting body and valued the added range and stability the sleek, sharp-nosed design. FDL-7's lifting body design would also give the Silver Dart about twice the lift coefficient of NASA's space shuttles at subsonic speeds. The design is expected to have extremely higher glide range and cross range than the Shuttle Orbiter, thus relaxing requirements on reentry windows and thermal shielding.

ROCKETPLANE XP

The **Rocketplane XP** is a suborbital spaceplane under development by Rocketplane Limited, Inc. The vehicle is powered by two jet engines and a rocket engine, enabling it to reach suborbital space. The XP is designed to operate from existing spaceports in a manner consistent with established commercial aviation practices.

Flight Trajectory

The Rocketplane XP, carrying a pilot and five spaceflight participants (passengers), has a flight profile that will take off from a runway using a jet engine just like regular aircraft and ascend to about 12 km (40,000 feet). At this point, a reusable rocket engine powers the XP until it shuts off and the XP continues in free-fall to altitudes of over 100 km (62 miles). The XP will then reenter Earth's atmosphere and land at the same spaceport under conventional jet power.

The XP will operate from the Clinton-Sherman Industrial Airpark near Burns Flat, Oklahoma.

Loan of Flight Test Engine

On January 24, 2006 Rocketplane Limited announced a Space Act agreement with NASA Johnson Space Center for the loan of a Rocketdyne RS-88 rocket engine for three years, for use in flight tests of the XP vehicle.

New Configuration

Rocketplane CEO George French Sr. told NASA SpaceFlight that the company is working on a new Rocketplane XP configuration. He said the new configuration would be announced at the X Prize Cup.

Other Rocketplane Limited Spaceplanes

In addition to the XP, Rocketplane Limited is trying to develop multiple generations of spaceplanes to serve the civilian and military markets based on successful United States Department of Defense (DOD) and NASA awards as well as continued growth in the space tourism market. However, the energy and technology gap between a suborbital spaceplane and an orbital one is huge. Even if the suborbital Rocketplane XP is successful, Rocketplane will need a lot of resources and technology breakthroughs to build an orbital craft.

ROTARY ROCKET

Rotary Rocket, Inc. was a rocketry company headquartered in a 45,000-square-foot (4,200 m^2) facility at Mojave Airport that developed the **Roton** concept in the late

1990s as a fully reusable Single Stage to Orbit (SSTO) manned spacecraft. Roton was intended to reduce costs of launching payloads into low earth orbit by a factor of ten. Gary Hudson championed the design and formed the company. A full-scale test vehicle made three hover flights in 1999, but the company ran out of funds and closed its doors in early 2001.

Rotary Rocket Design Evolution

Helicopter to Orbit

Gary Hudson's and Bevin McKinney's initial concept was to merge a rocket with a helicopter: spinning blades, powered by tip jets, would lift the vehicle in the earliest stage of launch. Once the air thinned to the point that helicopter flight was impractical, the vehicle would continue on pure rocket power, with the rotor acting as a giant turbopump.

VIRGIN GALACTIC

Virgin Galactic is a company within Sir Richard Branson's Virgin Group which plans to provide sub-orbital spaceflights to the paying public. Further in the future Virgin Galactic plans to offer orbital spaceflights as well.

Spacecraft

Overview of the Spacecraft Flights

It is planned that the spacecraft are to be robust and affordable enough to take paying passengers. The craft is projected to be a six passenger, two pilot craft. Its planned trajectory will overlap the Earth's atmosphere at 70,000 feet (21,000 m), which will make it a sub-orbital journey with a short period of weightlessness. At around 16 kilometres or 52,000 ft (16,000 m), the rocket will separate when the plane reaches its maximum height. The time from liftoff of the White Knight II booster carrying SpaceShipTwo until the touchdown of SpaceShipTwo after the suborbital flight will be about 2.5 hours. The suborbital flight itself will only be a small fraction of that time. The weightlessness will last approximately 6 minutes. Passengers will be able to release themselves from their seats during these 6 minutes and float around the cabin.

SpaceShipTwo's Performance

SpaceShipTwo will fly a little higher than SpaceShipOne, to a height of 110 km in order to go beyond the defined boundary of space (100 km) and lengthen the experience of weightlessness. The spacecraft will reach around Mach 3 (1000 m/s), which is slightly faster than current fighter jets are capable of attaining; however, the spacecraft will not be able to sustain that speed for long periods of time. To re-enter the atmosphere SpaceShipTwo folds its wings up, and then returns them to their original position for a smooth and gentle glide back onto the runway. The craft has a very limited cross-range capability and therefore has to land in the area where it started.

TSC Aerospace

TSC is a new aerospace production company, founded by Sir Richard Branson's Virgin Group and Scaled Composites, which is building a fleet of commercial spaceships and launch aircraft with the intention of making widespread space travel a reality. TSC's launch customer is Virgin Galactic. To meet Virgin Galactic's requirements, TSC has contracted Scaled Composites to develop and build prototypes of WK2 and SS2, which TSC is now taking into full-scale production.

Competition

There are numerous other companies actively working on commercial passenger suborbital spaceflight. Virgin Galactic's most likely competitors include Rocketplane Limited, Space Adventures, SpaceX, Blue Origin and Armadillo Aerospace.

Fleet

Virgin Galactic is planning to have a fleet of two White Knight Two motherships and five or more SpaceShipTwo tourist suborbital spacecraft.

WhiteKnightTwo carrier aircraft: Virgin MotherShips

1. VMS Eve
2. VMS Spirit of Steve Fossett

SpaceShipTwo suborbital spacecraft: Virgin SpaceShips

1. VSS Enterprise
2. VSS Voyager
3. unnamed
4. unnamed
5. unnamed

Base

Test launches are planned to take place from the Mojave Spaceport, where Scaled Composites is constructing the spacecraft. Virgin Galactic expects that initial passenger flights will take place there as well.

An international architectural competition was held for the design of Virgin Galactic's operating base, Spaceport America in New Mexico. The contract was awarded to URS and Foster + Partners architects. Upon the completion of the spaceport, flight operations will transfer from the California desert to the new bases.

Virgin Galactic also announced on April 3, 2008 that in the future they will operate in Europe out of Spaceport Sweden.

Will Whitehorn stated in an interview with Space.co.uk on 29 April 2008 that the company was considering flying from a UK base: RAF Lossiemouth in Scotland, during the summer months only. There are also rumours that the base could be located in

RAF Machrihanish (Campbeltown, Scotland) or an unnamed location in south-west England.

Commencement of Space Flights

Will Whitehorn, president of Virgin Galactic, has stated that the company would "not put a definite timeline on when the commercial flights would begin" but that "all was on track with its development plans" and that "If all goes to plan", the inaugural sub-orbital flight should happen "within two years [of June 2009]".

Collaboration with NASA

In February 2007, officials from Virgin and NASA signed a memorandum of understanding to explore the potential for collaboration.

Virgin Group

Virgin Group Ltd. is a branded venture capital organisation founded by British business tycoon Sir Richard Branson. The core business areas are travel, entertainment and lifestyle, among others. Virgin Group's date of incorporation is listed as 1989 by Companies House, who class it as a holding company; however Virgin's business and trading activities date to the 1970s. The net worth of Virgin Group Ltd. as of September 2008 is £5,010,000,000.

Virgin Group operates its headquarters at The School House, 50 Brook Green in the London Borough of Hammersmith and Fulham.

Although Branson retains complete ownership and control of the Virgin Brand, the commercial set-up of companies using it is varied and complex. Each of the companies operating under the Virgin brand is a separate entity, with Branson completely owning some and holding minority or majority stakes in others. Occasionally, he simply licenses the brand to a company that has purchased a division from him, such as Virgin Mobile USA, Virgin Mobile Australia, Virgin Radio (now part of TIML Radio Limited) and Virgin Music (now part of EMI).

The brand name "Virgin" arose when Branson and a partner were starting their first business, a record shop. They considered themselves virgins in business. The Virgin logo was originally sketched on a paper napkin and remains largely unchanged from the original style used.

Virgin Brands

Further information: List of Richard Branson's business ventures

- AirAsia X—long-haul budget airline operating from Malaysia (20% owned by Virgin Group)
- Oüi FM—rock radio station in France and Asia
- V Festival—two-day music festival held in two separate locations in the United Kingdom

  - V Festival (Australia)—an Australian version of the V Festival
  - Virgin Festival—a North American version of the V Festival
- Virgin Active—a health club chain in Australia, South Africa, Spain, Portugal, Italy and the UK
- Virgin America—a United States budget airline based at San Francisco International Airport (25% owned by Virgin Group)
- Virgin Atlantic Airways—an international carrier based at Heathrow Airport, London
- Virgin Balloon Flights—a hot air balloon operator
- Virgin Blue Holdings Limited
  - Virgin Blue— an Australian-based airline operating in the South Pacific
  - Blue Holidays—The holiday programme of Virgin Blue, now a joint venture between Virgin Blue and Zuji
  - Pacific Blue—a Virgin Blue subsidiary based in New Zealand
  - Polynesian Blue—a Virgin Blue subsidiary based in Samoa
  - V Australia—a Virgin Blue international subsidiary offering flights between Australia and the USA
- Virgin Books—publisher, retailer and distributor of books
- Virgin Brides—bridal wear shop in Manchester, UK
- Virgin Cars—internet automobile retailer
- Virgin Charter—a private jet online marketplace
- Virgin Comics—comic book producer
- Virgin Drinks—drink manufacturer
  - Virgin Cola—carbonated cola soft drink
  - Virgin Vodka—alcoholic beverage
  - v-Mix—spirit mixers
- Virgin Energy—a former UK energy supplier
- Virgin Experience Days—corporate and consumer experience events
- Virgin Flowers—Internet florist
- Virgin Galactic—a venture to market and operate commercial spaceflights, using spacecraft designed by Scaled Composites
- **Virgin Games**—online games and gambling
- Virgin Green Fund (originally known as Virgin Fuels)—venture capital firm for investing in petroleum alternatives
- Virgin Health Bank—a business enabling parents to store their baby's stem cells
- Virgin Healthcare provides a selection of healthcare services tailored to local demand
- Virgin HealthMiles
- Virgin Holidays—UK travel agency and tour operator for worldwide destinations served by Virgin Atlantic and its partner companies
  - Virgin Holidays Cruises—UK cruise holiday agent

    - Travel City Direct—UK Online Travel Agent for holidays to Florida. Acquired from the now defunct XL Leisure Group after it went into administration.
        - Travel City Direct Cruises - UK cruise holiday operator for holidays to Florida and the Caribbean
- Virgin Limited Edition—exclusive hotel operator
    - Kasbah Tamadot—exclusive Moroccan holiday destination
    - Lady B—luxurious Catamaran available for Caribbean charters
    - The Lodge—ski lodge
    - Natirar—private spa located in Somerset County, New Jersey
    - Necker Island—exclusive island in British Virgin Islands for private hire
    - The Roof Gardens and Babylon—1.5 acres (6,100 m^2) open air gardens, venue, nightclub and restaurant in Kensington, London
    - Ulusaba—exclusive game reserve in South Africa
- Virgin Limobike—passenger bike service in London
- Virgin Limousines—chauffeured limousine service in San Francisco and Northern California
- Virgin Media—provider or home telephone, cable television, broadband and mobile services to the United Kingdom
- Virgin Media Television—a British television network, made up of Virgin 1, Trouble, Bravo, Living TV and 50 per cent stake in UKTV
    - Virgin 1—a general entertainment channel on Freeview, Virgin Media and Sky Digital
- Virgin Megastores—CD, DVD and games retailer chain with high—street and online stores
    - Virgin XS—Factory Outlet—orientated format of Virgin Megastores
- Virgin Mobile—brand used by several companies providing mobile phone service around the world
    - Virgin Mobile UK—provides mobile phone service in the United Kingdom, now part of Virgin Media
    - Virgin Mobile Australia—provider of mobile phone service in Australia
    - Virgin Mobile Canada—provider of mobile phone service in Canada
    - Virgin Mobile South Africa—provider of mobile phone service in South Africa
    - Virgin Mobile USA—provider of mobile phone service in the United States
    - Virgin Mobile France—provider of mobile phone service in France
    - Virgin Mobile India—provider of mobile phone service in India
- Virgin Money—providers of financial services
    - Virgin Credit Card
- Virgin Nigeria—international, regional and domestic Nigerian airline
- Virgin Play—a Spanish publisher of video games, once part of the now defunct Virgin Interactive

- Virgin Radio—Virgin branded radio stations around the world
  - Virgin Radio Asia—collection of station operating in India and Thailand including Virgin Soft, Hitz, Easy FM and Oui
  - Virgin 99.9FM—a Canadian radio station, broadcasting a hot adult contemporary format at 99.9 on the FM dial in Toronto, Ontario. The station is owned by Astral Media. Formerly branded as 99.9 Mix FM, it adopted its current brand on 2008-08-25, pursuant to a licence from the Virgin Group.
  - Virgin 95.9FM—a Canadian radio station, broadcasting a hot adult contemporary format at 95.9 on the FM dial in Montreal, Quebec. This 41,200 watts station is owned by Astral Media. Station serves Montreal and adjacent eastern Ontario and Northern New York and Vermont.
  - Virgin Radio (France)—(Lagardère Active) a rebranding of the "Europe 2" radio station
  - Virgin Radio Groove—(TIML Radio Limited) soul, motown and disco music station broadcast on DAB, internet and Satellite TV
  - Virgin Radio Italia—(Gruppo Finelco) An Italian radio station
- Virgin Records—record label now owned by EMI
- Virgin Spa—shop chain retailing Virgin Cosmetics product
- Virgin Trains—a railway operator in the United Kingdom
- Virgin Unite—charitable foundation
- Virgin Vacations—U.S. travel agency
- Virgin Vie At Home—retailer of body care, cosmetics, homeware and jewellery products through the Internet, direct selling and Virgin Vie stores
- Virgin Wines—A Californian-based company, created in 2005 and producer of Red and White wines
- Virgin Voucher—gift voucher scheme, also functions as a staff reward scheme
- Virgin Ware—clothes brand and retailer
- Virgin Wines—Internet based wine retailer

Virgin Balloon Flights

Virgin Balloon Flights began flying hot air balloons in 1987 and its passengers are still flown in red and white balloons with the Virgin Group logo emblazoned on the side of the balloon.

Virgin Balloon Flights also own and operate the largest passenger carrying balloon in the United Kingdom as well as the largest balloon fleet in the UK.

The company has 102 launch sites throughout the United Kingdom (including Crowborough, Shrewsbury and Castle Fraser), employs 16 pilots that perform the balloon flights and is affiliated to the following organizations:

- Civil Aviation Authority (CAA)
- British Balloon & Airship Club (BBAC)
- British Association of Balloon Operators (BABO)

Rather than operating chartered flights, the company uses a Ticket system, of which there are 6 types as listed below:

- Weekday Morning (allowing for morning flights Monday to Friday)
- Weekday Anytime (allowing for morning and evening flights Monday to Friday)
- 7 Day Anytime (allowing for morning and evening flights Monday to Sunday)
- 7 Day Anytime Plus (allowing for morning and evening flights Monday to Sunday, and has a refundability option)
- Adventure Package (allowing for morning and evening flights Monday to Sunday, and has a refundability option)
- Celebration Package (allowing for morning and evening flights Monday to Sunday, and has a refundability option)

The Adventure Package includes a set of binoculars, pen, cap, flight bag, keyring, limited edition **BLOC** sunglasses and DVD.

The Celebration Package includes a set of binoculars, pen, cap, flight bag, keyring, a bottle of **Heidsieck & Co.** Champagne (20cl) and DVD.

SPACE ADVENTURES

Space Adventures Ltd. is a space tourism company that provides human space missions to the world marketplace. It is the only company that is sending private space explorers.

Background

Eric C. Anderson is the president and CEO of Space Adventures. He co-founded Space Adventures in 1998 with several other entrepreneurs from the aerospace, adventure travel and entertainment industries and has managed the company over the past several years, selling more than $170m in space tourist flights.

The company's advisory board includes Apollo 11 moonwalker Buzz Aldrin, shuttle astronauts Sam Durrance, Thomas David Jones, Byron Lichtenberg, Norm Thagard, Kathy Thornton, Pierre Thuot, Charles Walker, Skylab/Shuttle astronaut Owen Garriott and Russian cosmonaut Yuri Usachev.

Space Adventures offers a variety of programmes such as the availability today for spaceflight missions to the International Space Station and around the moon, Zero-Gravity flights, cosmonaut training, spaceflight qualification programmes and reservations on future suborbital spacecrafts. In May 2001, it sent American businessman Dennis Tito to the International Space Station (ISS) aboard a Soyuz spacecraft for a reported $20 million payment, making him the first space tourist in history. South African businessman Mark Shuttleworth did the same in April 2002, becoming the 'First African in Space'. Gregory Olsen became the third private citizen to travel to the ISS in October 2005, followed by the first female space tourist, Anousheh Ansari, who completed her 10-day orbital mission in September 2006. Charles Simonyi, an ex-executive at Microsoft who managed the Office product group became the world's fifth space tourist in April 2007. In 2008, Richard Garriott, the first second-generation U.S. astronaut and pre-eminent game developer, became Space Adventures sixth orbital space client to travel to the ISS.

In 2009, Charles Simonyi became Space Adventures first repeat client to launch to the ISS. Additionally, Space Adventures will launch its first private mission in 2011.

Space Adventures acquired Zero Gravity Corporation [1] in March 2008.

World's First Space Explorers

Dennis Tito

Space Adventures' first orbital spaceflight client and the world's first private space explorer launched to the ISS in 2001. American businessman Dennis Tito received comprehensive training at the Yuri Gagarin Cosmonaut Training Center in Star City, Russia. His participation in Space Adventures' other programmes, including a Zero-Gravity flight, centrifuge training and the supersonic jet flight to the Edge of Space, is what ultimately inspired him to take the final step. "When I reached 2.5 times the speed of sound and saw the curvature of the Earth below and the dark sky above, I knew I wanted to keep on going," said Tito after completing his flight in a MiG-25, the world's fastest and highest flying operational aircraft.

Mark Shuttleworth

'First African in Space' Mark Shuttleworth and his two crewmates, Russian commander Yuri Gidzenko and Italian astronaut Roberto Vittori spent 10 days in space. They took off on a Russian Soyuz rocket from the Baikonur Cosmodrome, Kazakhstan on April 25, 2002. Prior to his flight, Mr. Shuttleworth completed Space Adventures' Orbital Pre-Qualification programme and underwent almost eight months of training and medical exams, including a one-week orientation programme at NASA's Johnson Space Center in Houston. A Zero-Gravity flight, centrifuge training, and spacecraft communication, guidance and control system lessons of the Russian Soyuz spacecraft and ISS were also required. "Space Adventures has been invaluable in supporting me on this long journey towards the realization of my dream of spaceflight. This flight is a personal challenge and adventure, and it's an opportunity to encourage students in South Africa to embrace mathematics, science and technology," said Mr. Shuttleworth.

Later Explorers

- Greg Olsen
- Anousheh Ansari
- Charles Simonyi
- Richard Garriott

Lunar Mission

This new mission offers the chance to travel to and orbit the moon for a cost of $100 million.

Orbital Mission Explorers Circle

This programme allows individuals to reserve seats on future orbital spaceflights. They have the option to fly to orbit as their schedule allows with preferential access to mission seats or they can opt to sell their seat to another private astronaut. Sergey Brin, co-founder and president of technology for Google Inc., has become the founding member of the 'Founding Explorer' group by placing a $5 million deposit on a future orbital spaceflight.

Space Adventures has established the Orbital Mission Explorers Circle to build a definitive consortium of future private space explorers who share a lifetime goal of orbital spaceflight or the investment therein. Space Adventures has initially created six 'Founding Explorer' positions in the Orbital Mission Explorers Circle, each of whom will have priority access to participate in future orbital space missions.

Explorer Suborbital Vehicle

The company, along with Prodea and FSA, is currently developing a suborbital space transportation system, called Explorer. The vehicle has been designed by Myasishchev Design Bureau, a Russian aerospace organization which has developed a wide-array of aircraft and space systems.

The Explorer aerospace system will consist of a flight-operational carrier aircraft, the M-55X, and a rocket spacecraft. It will have the capacity to transport up to five people to space.

Spaceports

Space Adventures is involved in the development of two commercial spaceports, one in the United Arab Emirates and the other in Singapore. The UAE spaceport is to be located in Ras al-Khaimah, located less than an hour drive from Dubai. In addition to suborbital spaceflights, Spaceport Singapore will operate astronaut training facilities and a public education and interactive visitor center. Spaceport Singapore visitors will be able to experience Zero-Gravity flights, G-force training in a centrifuge, and simulated space walks in a neutral buoyancy tank. However, the company has found it difficult to attract funding and partners for the Singapore project.

Spacewalk

On July 21, 2006 the company announced that it would begin offering a spacewalk option to its clients travelling to the ISS. The addition of the spacewalk, which would allow participants to spend up to 1.5 hours outside of the space station, would cost about $15 million and would lengthen the orbital mission approximately six to eight days. The spacewalk would be completed in the Russian designed Orlan space suit. The training for the spacewalk would require an extra month of training on top of the six months already required.

Lawsuit

Japanese businessman Daisuke Enomoto is suing Space Adventures as his trip was cancelled by them for medical reasons after he paid $21,000,000 and no refund was given.

Space Adventures Claims Two Soyuz Tickets Sold

The Reuters news agency reported that the space tourist company Space Adventures has selected two unnamed tourists for Soyuz flights in 2004 and 2005 to the International Space Station.

Both tourists were reported to be Americans including a 38-year-old male Manhattan real estate developer. But no other details were available.

The Soyuz taxi flights to the International Space Station have reportedly cost up to $20 million per person for a 10-day flight.

Previously tourists have flown twice to the $100 billion orbiting "science" facility. First up was former NASA engineer Dennis Tito who left the space agency decades ago to start a highly successful investment company and was eventually able to pay his own way into space.

The last flight was in 2002 when South African IT entrepreneur Mark Shuttleworth was able to secure a more friendly welcome from NASA which had belatedly realized the value in having paying customers on board the Station.

According to the Reuters report, Space Adventures has two additional seats available on flights in 2006 and 2007.

The names of the two new space tourists will be announced in January.

With the US Space Shuttle fleet grounded for another year, Russia's Soyuz spacecraft and associated expendable launcher is currently the only working transport system keeping the Station crewed and supplied.

Citizens in Space, Yes. Publicly-Funded Space Tourism, No

The embattled Shuttle/ISS complex is hearing some faint support recently from an unexpected direction: certain space tourism advocates. This is not good. For one thing, nobody really knows if the first two visitors fully paid their way. Accounting in space programmes is a black art—even now, nobody knows for sure how much the Apollo missions really cost writes Michael Turner.

Space Exploration and Tourism Need Shuttle to Fly Again

Future space exploration and tourism need shuttle to fly again, says Professor Book for great Earth views, the Moon and Mars but leave the stars to your dreams.

Space Adventures Announces Global Spaceport Development Project in Ras Al Khaimah, UAE

Space Adventures Ltd., the world's leading space experienced company, announced today its plans to develop a commercial spaceport in Ras Al-Khaimah (the UAE), with plans to expand globally. Other potential spaceport locations include Asia, specifically Singapore, and North America. The total estimated cost of the global spaceport development project is at least $265 million (USD) and will be funded by various parties, along with shared investments by Space Adventures and the government of Ras Al-Khaimah.

SPACE TRANSPORT CORPORATION

Space Transport Corporation, or STC, was a company based in Forks, Washington whose goal is to commercialize space. The company was founded in 2002 by Eric Meier and Philip Storm. The company plans to provide small payload launch and space tourism services. The company liquidated its assets in February 2005 and was completely defunct by late 2006.

STC Vehicles

Spartan

The Spartan Three Stage Rocket is a vehicle intended to carry payloads of 1 to 5 kg into suborbit. The rocket has been tested to 80 km, and commercial launches are planned for 2005.

Nano-Satellite Orbital Launch Vehicle

The Nano-Satellite Orbital Launch Vehicle, or N-SOLV, is a vehicle designed to carry a 10 kg payload to orbit. The corporation plans to sell the launch service for under a million United States dollars. The vehicle's intended payload is nano-satellites.

Rubicon I

Rubicon I was a test vehicle designed to carry 270 kg (or three people) to 100 km for under $200,000. The vehicle was destroyed in August 2004 during a launch test due to a propellant formulation error. Rubicon I, launched by Space Transport Corporation of Forks, Washington, was the only other Ansari X Prize entrant to launch during the entire duration of the prize with the exception of Paul Allen and Burt Rutan's winning SpaceShipOne. ABC Nightline featured both the Rubicon I developers and SpaceShipOne's winning team in its 2004 presentation of the Ansari X Prize.

Rubicon II

The Rubicon II is the replacement to Rubicon I. The design is identical to the Rubicon I, except for a few error fixes. As of November 22, 2004, work on the Rubicon II has ceased in favour of the Spartan.

SPACE ENVIRONMENT

Space environment is a branch of astronautics, aerospace engineering and space physics that seeks to understand and address conditions existing in space that affect the operation of spacecraft. A related subject—space weather—deals with dynamic processes in the solar-terrestrial system that can give rise to effects on spacecraft, but that can also affect the atmosphere, ionosphere and geomagnetic field, giving rise to several other kinds of effects on human technologies.

Problems for spacecraft can arise from radiation, space debris, upper atmospheric drag and spacecraft electrostatic charging.

Radiation in space usually comes from three main sources: (*i*) the Van Allen radiation belts; (*ii*) solar proton events and solar energetic particles; and (*iii*) galactic cosmic rays. For long duration missions, the high doses of radiation can damage electronic components and solar cells. A major concern is also radiation-induced "single-event effects" such as single event upset. Manned missions usually avoid the radiation belts and the international space station is at an altitude well below the most severe regions of the radiation belts. During solar energetic events (solar flares and coronal mass ejections) particles can be accelerated to very high energies and can reach the Earth in times as short as 30 minutes (but usually take some hours). These particles are mainly protons and heavier ions that can cause radiation damage, distruption to logic circuits and even hazards to astronauts. Manned missions to return to the Moon or to travel to Mars will have to deal with the major problems presented by solar particle events to radiation safety, in addition to the important contribution to doses from the low-level background cosmic rays. In near-Earth orbits, the Earth's geomagnetic field screens spacecraft from a large part of these hazards—a process called geomagnetic shielding.

Spacecraft electrostatic charging is caused by the hot plasma environment around the Earth. The plasma encountered in the region of the geostationary orbit becomes heated during geomagnetic "sub-storms" caused by disturbances in the solar wind. "Hot" electrons (with energies in the kilo-electron volt range) collect on surfaces of spacecraft and can establish electrostatic potentials of the order of kilovolts. As a result, discharges can occur and are known to be the source of many spacecraft anomalies.

Solutions devised by scientists and engineers include, but are not limited to, spacecraft shielding, special "hardening" of electronic systems, various collision detection systems. Evaluation of effects during spacecraft design includes application of various "models" of the environment, including radiation belt models, spacecraft-plasma interaction models and atmospheric models to predict drag effects encountered in lower orbits and during reentery.

The field often overlaps with the disciplines of astrophysics, atmospheric science, space physics, and geophysics, albeit usually with an emphasis on application.

The United States government maintains a Space Weather Prediction Center at Boulder, Colorado. The Space Weather Prediction Center (SWPC) is part of the National Oceanic and Atmospheric Administration (NOAA). SWPC is one of the National Weather Services (NWS) National Centers for Environmental Prediction (NCEP).

Space weather effects on Earth can include ionospheric storms, temporary decreases in ozone densities, disruption to radio communication, to GPS signals and submarine positioning. Some scientists also theorize links between sunspot activity and ice ages.

SPACEDEV

SpaceDev, a part of the "Space Systems Business" of Sierra Nevada Corporation, is prominent for its spaceflight and microsatellite work. It designed and built the hybrid rocket motors for Paul Allen's Tier One suborbital SpaceShipOne space programme operated by Scaled Composites. It is also developing micro- and nano-satellites, a small expendable launch vehicle, the SpaceDev Streaker, and has designed a piloted suborbital and orbital spaceship of its own, the SpaceDev Dream Chaser, in collaboration with NASA.

SpaceDev is based near San Diego in Poway, California. Its objective is to make routine commercial spaceflight possible and to help open space for all of humanity.

Previously a publicly traded company (OTCBB:SPDV), on 20 October 2008 SpaceDev officials announced that the company would be acquired by Sierra Nevada Corporation, a privately-owned company. The announced acquisition price was 38 million dollars. The role of SpaceDev will be melded into another of Sierra Nevada's subsidiary companies, MicroSat, to create a more complete space technology unit. On December 16, 2008 SpaceDev announced that its acquisition by Sierra Nevada Corporation had been completed.

History

SpaceDev was founded in 1997 by Jim Benson, who acquired Integrated Space Systems of Southern California and merged it with a defunct publicly traded corporate shell to create the publicly traded SpaceDev. For a while, SpaceDev also owned UK-based Space Innovations Limited. In August 1998 SpaceDev acquired all patents, intellectual property, test results, and documents that had been produced by the out of business American Rocket Company (AMROC).

On August 6, 1998 the United States Securities and Exchange Commission filed an administrative proceeding alleging securities fraud against SpaceDev Inc. According to the SEC, SpaceDev promotes itself extensively on the Internet. The SEC alleged that the company made false and misleading statements over the Internet and via other media in violation of U.S. securities laws in an attempt to increase its stock value. The SEC was seeking cease and desist orders against SpaceDev and its chairman, James W. Benson. A settlement was reached between the SEC, SpaceDev and James W. Benson. The settlement states that the SEC was founded in its allegations and SpaceDev cease and desist from committing or causing violations or future violations of Section 17(a) of the Securities Act and Section 10(b) of the Exchange Act and Rule 10b-5 thereunder; and Mr. Benson cease and desist from committing or causing violations or future violations of Section 17(a) of the Securities Act and Section 10(b) of the Exchange Act and Rule 10b-5 thereunder.

The company's first big project was to be the Near Earth Asteroid Prospector, or NEAP, an innovative commercial small spacecraft mission that would have rendezvoused with and landed on a Near Earth Asteroid (NEO), conducted scientific experiments, and claimed the asteroid as private property. As it turned out, however, the company's first big break would come a little closer to home, in the form of CHIPSat, the Cosmic Hot Interstellar Plasma Spectrometer microsatellite. SpaceDev built and operated the Low Earth Orbit (LEO) microsat, the first to use only the Internet for its communications, for Berkeley under NASA's University Explorer Programme (UNEX). This was followed one year later by supplying the rocket motors that propelled SpaceShipOne into the history books by creating the world's first civilian astronauts and helping Paul Allen win the $10 million Ansari X Prize.

On October 26, 2005 SpaceDev announced that Starsys Research Corporation of Boulder, Colorado would merge with SpaceDev, which would provide SpaceDev with additional expertise and experience with microsatellite technologies. The acquisition of Starsys on January 31, 2006 put the number of SpaceDev employees over 200, located in three states. The Starsys division is being groomed to become a center of space robotics for SpaceDev. Over 18 years Starsys developed and delivered 2,000 space mechanisms that have flown on over 200 missions, all successfully. SpaceDev has most or all of the moving parts on Mars at this time, had mechanisms on Deep Impact, is supplying the separation system and docking mechanism for the soon to be launched Orbital Express, and has mechanisms on the way to Pluto.

On September 28, 2006, SpaceDev announced that founder and CEO Jim Benson was stepping down to start a new space tourism venture, Benson Space Company (BSC). BSC expects to be one of SpaceDev's largest customers, purchasing multiple Dream Chaser spaceships and safe hybrid rocket motors for use in personal spaceflight. Benson died on 10 October 2008, victim of a brain tumour.

Dream Chaser

On November 16, 2005 SpaceDev announced its Dream Chaser concept for a four passenger sub-orbital and a six passenger orbital vehicle, both based on NASA's HL-20 "Personnel Launch System" or "Space Taxi". SpaceDev's suborbital Dream Chaser will use internal hybrid rocket motors similar to those SpaceDev developed for Paul Allen's SpaceShipOne, while the orbital version will use the internal motors plus larger external hybrid motors. SpaceDev's hybrid rocket technology was pioneered by the American Rocket Company, or AmRoc.

On May 5, 2006, SpaceDev announced that it was selected as a finalist in NASA's $500 million Commercial Orbital Transportation Services (COTS) demonstration programme. SpaceDev has been working with NASA Ames to design a modern version of the NASA HL-20 Personnel Launch System, called the SpaceDev Dream Chaser. However, on August 18, 2006 it was revealed that SpaceDev did not win the contract.

On December 18, 2006, SpaceDev announced that it has been awarded a $330,000 Phase I study contract from Benson Space Company to further the SpaceDev Dream Chaser spaceship programme. The study will contribute to the on-going development of the spaceship and will result in space vehicle and rocket motor designs ready for Phase II vehicle fabrication and testing. The SpaceDev Dream Chaser spaceship is based on NASA's design of the ten passenger orbital HL-20 Personnel Launch System, and will launch vertically and land horizontally in direct sight of viewers.

On April 10, 2007, SpaceDev announced that it had finalized a Memorandum of Understanding with United Launch Alliance on exploring the potential of launching the SpaceDev Dream Chaser spaceship using a Atlas V 431 configuration. Destinations could include the International Space Station (ISS) and other commercial orbital destinations as well as for commercial orbital space tourism flights.

Trailblazer

SpaceDev manufactured the Trailblazer satellite selected by the Operationally Responsive Space Office for its Jumpstart mission. Trailblazer was a microsatellite developed under a Missile Defense Agency contract. After being launched Trailblazer would have collected image data and communicated with a ground station.

Trailblazer was the primary payload for the third attempted flight of a Falcon 1 launch vehicle. The launch was attempted on 2008-08-03 and ended in failure, with loss of both vehicle and payload.

Trailblazer was researched, designed, assembled, tested and packed for shipping almost entirely at the Poway SpaceDev location. With a team of about 25 employees working around the clock, the satellite was assembled and ready for launch in just under 4 months, thus meeting their advanced deadline, winning their opportunity for launch and as far as anyone else is able to substantiate, now holds the record for assembly of a launched spacecraft.

SpaceDev Dream Chaser

The **SpaceDev Dream Chaser** is a planned crewed suborbital and orbital spacecraft being developed by SpaceDev. Dream Chaser will be able to carry six to eight people to and from space. The vehicle launches vertically and lands horizontally on conventional runways.

History

The Dream Chaser was publicly announced on September 20, 2004 as candidate for NASA's Vision for Space Exploration and later Commercial Orbital Transportation Services Programme.

When the Dream Chaser was not selected under Phase 1 of the COTS programme, SpaceDev founder Jim Benson stepped down as Chairman of SpaceDev and started Benson Space Company to pursue the development of the Dream Chaser.

In April 2007, SpaceDev announced that it had partnered with the United Launch Alliance to pursue the possibility of utilizing the Atlas V booster rocket as the Dream Chaser's launch vehicle.

Specifications

The original design concept calls for a spaceplane with a single hybrid rocket engine, launching vertically from the ground. Current plans are to launch it from an Atlas V.

It will carry one to six humans and/or cargo to orbital destinations such as the International Space Station. The vehicle will be able to return from space by gliding and landing at almost any aircraft runway in the world.

The Dream Chaser was originally based on the X-34 for the COTS programme. The design has since been revised and is now based on NASA's HL-20 lifting body design. It is intended to be an orbital spacecraft, with a proposed man-rated United Launch Alliance Atlas V 431 launch vehicle as the main booster.

The Benson Space Company was expected to be one of SpaceDev's largest customers, purchasing up to 3 initial spaceships and safe hybrid rocket motors for use in personal spaceflight. However, the Benson Space Company have since decided to pursue its own sub-orbital design.

LYNX ROCKETPLANE

The **Lynx rocketplane** is a rocket-powered aircraft being developed by the California-based company XCOR to compete in the future suborbital spaceflight market. The Lynx is projected to carry one pilot and a ticketed passenger above 60 km altitude. The ticket will cost $95,000.

Description

The Lynx will have four liquid rocket engines at the rear of the fuselage burning a mixture of LOX-Kerosene and each of them will give between 2500-2900 lbf (11120-12900 N) of thrust.

Operations

According to XCOR, the Lynx will operate several times a day, and will also have the capacity to deliver payloads into space. The Lynx is currently scheduled to have its first flight in 2010. XCOR currently plans to have the Lynx's initial flights from the Mojave Air and Spaceport in Mojave, California. Because it lacks any propulsion system other than its rocket engines, the Lynx will have to be towed to the end of the runway. Once positioned on the runway, the pilot will ignite the four rocket engines and begin a steep climb. The engines will be shut off at approximately 138,000 feet and Mach 2. The spaceplane will then continue to climb, unpowered until it reaches an apogee of approximately 200,000 feet or 61 km. The spacecraft will experience a little over four minutes of weightlessness before re-entering the Earth's atmosphere. The occupants of the Lynx may experience up to four times normal gravity during re-entry. Once it has completed re-entry, the Lynx will then glide down and perform an unpowered landing. The total flight time is projected to last about 30 minutes.

A successor aircraft, known as the Mark 2, is expected to have an apogee of 110 km.

XERUS (SPACEPLANE)

Xerus (pronunciation: zEr'us), was a suborbital spaceplane proposed by XCOR Aerospace. It would be capable of transporting one pilot and one passenger as well as some science experiments and it would even be capable of carrying an upper stage which launches near apogee and therefore would be able to carry satellites into LEO.

Xerus would depart the runway under rocket power and glide back for a runway landing, even retaining some fuel for approach and touchdown maneuvers. In comparison to other orbital gliders like the Space Shuttle or SpaceShipOne, this would make it much more controllable during the landing phase. Its engine, dubbed XR-4K5, is a restartable liquid oxygen/kerosene rocket engine developed by XCOR Aerospace itself.

On April 11, 2007, XCOR announced that it has been awarded a nearly $100,000 research contract and that, after eight years in the space business, the hardware and funding are finally coming together to enable the development of the Xerus spaceplane.

On March 26, 2008, XCOR announced a new design that would supersede Xerus called Lynx.

SPACEX

Space Exploration Technologies Corporation (**SpaceX**) is an American space transport company founded by PayPal co-founder Elon Musk. It has developed the Falcon 1 and is developing the Falcon 9, both of which are partially reusable launch vehicles. SpaceX is also developing the Dragon series of spacecraft to be orbited by Falcon 9 launchers. SpaceX designs, tests and fabricates the majority of their components in-house, including the Merlin, Kestrel, and Draco rocket engines.

Originally based in El Segundo, SpaceX now operates out of Hawthorne, California.

Background

SpaceX was founded in June 2002 by PayPal founder Elon Musk who has invested $100 million of his own money as of March 2006. On 4 August 2008, SpaceX accepted a further US$20 million investment from the Founders Fund.

SpaceX grew from 160 employees in November 2005 to more than 500 by July 2008. The launch crew in the Marshall Islands has 25 people with 6 in mission control. This small number, compared to similar space launch companies is part of Musk's design to reduce costs. Musk believes that the high prices of other space-launch services are driven in part by unnecessary bureaucracy. He has stated that one of his goals is to improve the cost and reliability of access to space, ultimately by a factor of ten.

In January 2005, SpaceX bought a 10 per cent stake in Surrey Satellite Technology Ltd.

On 18 August 2006, SpaceX announced that it has won a NASA Commercial Orbital Transportation Services (COTS) contract to demonstrate cargo delivery to the International Space Station with a possible option for crew transport.

On 23 December 2008, SpaceX announced that it had won a Commercial Resupply Services (CRS) contract, which guarantees NASA missions worth US$1.6 billion for resupplying the International Space Station, after the Space Shuttle retires in 2010.

Space Vehicles

SpaceX is manufacturing two main space launch vehicles: the Falcon 1 which made its first successful flight on September 28, 2008, and the large EELV class Falcon 9 which is scheduled to have its first launch in 2009. A Falcon 5 launcher was also planned, but its development was stopped in favour of the Falcon 9. SpaceX is also designing the SpaceX Dragon, a human-rated orbital vehicle that will be launched on top of a Falcon 9 rocket.

On May 2, 2005, SpaceX announced that it had been awarded an Indefinite Delivery/Indefinite Quantity (IDIQ) contract for Responsive Small Spacelift (RSS) launch services by the United States Air Force, which could allow the Air Force to purchase up to $100,000,000 worth of launches from the company. On April 22, 2008, NASA announced that it had awarded an IDIQ Launch Services contract to SpaceX for Falcon 1 and Falcon 9 launches. The contract will be worth between $20,000 and $1 billion, depending on the number of missions awarded. The contract covers launch services ordered by June 30, 2010, for launches through December 2012.

Elon Musk stated in the same April 22 announcement that SpaceX has sold 14 contracts for flights on the various Falcon vehicles.

On June 16, 2009, SpaceX announced the opening of its Astronaut Safety and Mission Assurance Department. It hired former NASA astronaut Ken Bowersox to oversee the department as a vice president of the company.

Falcon 1

The Falcon 1 is a small, partially reusable rocket capable of placing several hundred kilograms into low earth orbit. It also functions as a testbed for developing concepts and components for the larger Falcon 9.

The Falcon 1 succeeded in reaching orbit at its fourth attempt on September 28, 2008, becoming the first privately funded, liquid-fuelled rocket to do so.

The Falcon 1 carried its first successful commercial payload into orbit on July 13, 2009. This was the fifth launch of the Falcon 1.

Falcon 9

On 8 September 2005, SpaceX announced the development of the Falcon 9 rocket, which was to have nine Merlin engines in its first stage. The design is an EELV-class vehicle, intended to compete with the Delta IV and the Atlas V rockets. Both stages were to be designed to be reusable. A similarly designed Falcon 5 rocket was also envisioned to fit between the Falcon 1 and Falcon 9, but development was dropped to concentrate on the Falcon 9.

The company purchased the McGregor, Texas testing facilities of defunct Beal Aerospace, where it refit the largest test stand at the facilities for Falcon 9 testing. On 22 November 2008, the stand tested the nine Merlin 1C engines of the Falcon 9, which deliver 350-metric-tons-force (3.4-meganewtons) of thrust, well under the stand's capacity of 1,500 metric-tons-force (15 meganewtons).

Company plans in 2004 called for "development of a heavy lift product and even a super-heavy, if there is customer demand" with each size increase resulting in a significant decrease in cost per pound to orbit. Projected dollar cost per pound to orbit could drop from $4,000 to $1,300 ($8,800/kg to $2,900/kg) between Falcon 1 and the five-engine concept vehicle, Falcon 5. CEO Elon Musk said: "I believe $500 per pound ($1,100/kg) or less is very achievable."

The Falcon 9 vehicle was integrated at Cape Canaveral on 30 December 2008. NASA was planning for a flight to take place in January 2010.

SpaceX revealed in a June 2009 AIAA presentation another future plan, the Raptor project to create a higher performance LOX/liquid hydrogen second stage.

Dragon

SpaceX announced plans to pursue a manned commercial space programme through the end of the decade.

On Friday 18 August 2006, NASA announced that the company was one of two selected to provide crew and cargo resupply demonstration contracts to the International Space Station (ISS) under the Commercial Orbital Transportation Services (COTS) programme. SpaceX will demonstrate crew and cargo resupply using the SpaceX Dragon, a conventional blunt-cone ballistic capsule, which is capable of carrying 7 persons or a mixture of personnel and cargo to and from low Earth orbit. It will be launched atop a Falcon 9 vehicle. The nose cone of the vehicle has a hinged cap, which opens to reveal a standard ISS Common Berthing Mechanism, which allows the Dragon to dock to the U.S. segment of the ISS. NASA's plan calls for SpaceX demonstration flights between 2008 and 2010. SpaceX may receive up to $278 million if it meets all NASA milestones.

First flight of Dragon is planned for 2009 from Cape Canaveral.

Launcher Versions

Launcher Versions	*Falcon 1*	*Falcon 1e*	*Falcon 9*	*Falcon 9 Heavy*
Stage 1	1 × Merlin 1A (2006-2007); 1 x Merlin 1C (2008 ff)	1 x Merlin 1C	9 × Merlin 1C	3 boosters with 9 × Merlin 1C each
Stage 2	1 × Kestrel	1 x Kestrel	1 × Merlin 1C	1 × Merlin 1C
Height (max; m)	21.3	26.83	50 or 54	54
Diameter (m)	1.7	1.7	3.6	3.6
Initial thrust (kN)	318	454	3,400	12,258
Takeoff weight (tonnes)	27.2	38.56	325	885
Fairing diameter (Inner; m)	1.5	1.71	3.6 or 5.2	5.2
Payload (LEO; kg)	570	1010 (430 to SSO)	9,900	27,500
Payload (GTO; kg)	—	—	4,900	12,000

Price (Mil. USD)	6.7	9.1	35 to LEO or GEO	90 to LEO or between 55 and 90 (according to Satellite Mass) to GEO
minimal **price/kg** (LEO; USD)	11,754	9,010 (21,163 to SSO)	3,535	3,273
minimal **price/kg** (GTO; USD)	—	—	7,143	7,826
Success ratio (successful/total)	2/5	—	—	—

Cancelled Launcher Designs

- Falcon 5

Launch Sites

- Ronald Reagan Ballistic Missile Defense Test Site, Omelek Island
- Cape Canaveral Air Force Station, Space Launch Complex 40
- Vandenberg Air Force Base, Space Launch Complex 3

All Falcon 1 launches have taken place at Omelek Island. All Falcon 9 launches on the SpaceX manifest are planned for Cape Canaveral SLC-40.

6

Successful Spacecrafts, Spaceplanes and Spacetourists: Model Case Studies

SPACECRAFT

A **spacecraft** is a craft or machine designed for spaceflight. On a sub-orbital spaceflight, a spacecraft enters space, then returns to the Earth. For an orbital spaceflight, a spacecraft enters a closed orbit around the planetary body. Spacecraft used for human spaceflight carry people on board as crew or passengers. Spacecraft used for robotic space missions operate either autonomously or telerobotically. Robotic spacecraft that leave the vicinity of the planetary body are space probes. Robotic spacecraft that remain in orbit around the planetary body are artificial satellites. Starships, which are built for interstellar travel, are so far a theoretical concept only (aside from a handful of interstellar probes such as Pioneer 10 and 11, Voyager, and New Horizons).

Spacecraft are used for a variety of purposes, including communications, earth observation, meteorology, navigation, planetary exploration and space tourism. Spacecraft and space travel are common themes in works of science fiction.

SPACEPLANE

A **spaceplane** is an aircraft designed to pass the edge of space. It combines some of the features of an aircraft and some of a spacecraft. Typically, it takes the form of a spacecraft equipped with wings, and may be airbreathing or be purely rocket based.

To date, only pure rocket spaceplanes have succeeded in reaching space, although several have been carried up to an altitude of several tens of thousands of feet by conventional aircraft before release.

Description

An aerospace plane features some differences from rocket launch systems.

Aerodynamic Lift

All aircraft utilize aerodynamic surfaces in order to generate lift. Typically the force of lift generated by these surfaces is many times that of the drag that they induce. The ratio of these forces (the Lift-to-drag ratio or L/D) varies between different aircraft designs but can be as high as 60 in high performance gliders but is closer to 7 or less for the aircraft configurations more typical of supersonic aircraft including aerospace planes.

In practice a lift to drag ratio of 7 means that a thrust force equal to 1/7th of the weight of the aircraft is sufficient to support it in flight. This low thrust requirement significantly reduces the amount of fuel required to carry the weight of an aerospace plane in comparison to rocket launch systems which must provide thrust greater than the weight of the vehicle.

A partially off-setting difference between these systems is that the aerospace plane would typically experience powered flight for much longer periods of time than a rocket. In addition winged vehicles need extra dry mass for the wings, and this penalises vehicles towards the end of the flight. Rockets are also able to use their high thrust at an angle which gives reasonable lifting efficiency when burning for orbit.

Propulsion

Rocket Engines

All spaceplanes to date have used rocket engines. Rockets are the only kind of engines that work in space.

Air Breathing Engines

A difference between rocket based and air breathing aerospace plane launch systems is that aerospace plane designs typically include minimal oxidizer storage for its propulsion. The air breathing aerospace plane designs include engine inlets so its propulsion system uses atmospheric oxygen during combustion. Since the mass of the oxidizer is, at takeoff, the single largest mass of most rocket designs (the Space Shuttle's liquid oxygen tank weighs 1,387,457 lb—more than one of its solid rocket boosters), this provides a huge potential weight savings benefit. However, air breathing engines are usually very much heavier than rocket engines and the empty weight of the oxidiser tank, and since, unlike oxidiser, this extra weight must be carried into space it greatly offsets the overall system performance.

Types of air breathing engines proposed for spaceplanes include scramjet, liquid air cycle engines, precooled jet engines, pulse detonation engine and ramjets.

Complexity

Because air breathing aerospace planes must operate in harsh environments, utilize a number of different propulsion systems, and require more control systems (e.g. aerodynamic as well as thrust vectoring), they are typically far more complicated in design than equivalent rocket systems.

In fact, just a comparison of a typical jet engine to that of a rocket engine gives some indicator of the difference in complexity of the engine components. Additionally most aerospace vehicles also include rocket engines in addition to their 1 or more jet engine types.

Harsh Flight Environment

The flight trajectory required of air breathing aerospace vehicles fly what is known as a 'depressed trajectory' which places the aerospace plane in the high-altitude hypersonic flight regime of the atmosphere. This environment induces high dynamic pressure, high temperature, and high heat flow loads particularly upon the leading edge surfaces of the aerospace plane. These loads typically require special advanced materials, active cooling, or both for the structures to survive the environment.

Center of Mass Issues

A wingless launch vehicle has lower aerodynamic forces affecting the vehicle, and attitude control can be active perhaps with some fins to aid stability. For a winged vehicle the centre of lift moves during the atmospheric flight as well as the centre of mass; and the vehicle spends longer in the atmosphere as well. Historically, the X-33 and HOTOL spaceplanes were rear engined and had relatively heavy engines. This puts a heavy mass at the rear of the aircraft with wings that had to hold up the vehicle. As the wet mass reduces, the centre of mass tends to move rearward behind the centre of lift, which tends to be around the centre of the wings. This can cause severe instability that is usually solved by extra fins which add weight and decrease performance.

Overall Weight

A vertically-launched rocket forms the shape of a cylinder stood on end. This structure can be made very light and strong. A horizontally-launched spaceplane approximates a cylinder on its side. This structure experiences greater bending forces, so must be strengthened. This makes it heavier, requiring advanced materials and design techniques to reduce weight. For example Burt Rutan of Scaled Composites recently patented a method of gluing the fuel tank directly to the vehicle skin, saving the weight of fasteners while also stiffening both parts.

Flown Spaceplanes

Orbital Spaceplanes

The *orbital* spaceplanes successfully flown to date, the United States Space Shuttle and the Soviet Buran, have used their wings to provide aerobraking to return from orbit and to provide lift to allow them to land on a runway like conventional aircraft. Both these vehicles are still designed to ascend to orbit vertically under rocket power like conventional expendable launch vehicles. Each of these vehicles has a much smaller payload fraction than a ballistic design with the same takeoff weight. This is primarily due to the weight of the wings—around 9-12 per cent of the weight of the atmospheric flight weight of the vehicle. This significantly reduces the payload size, but the reusability is intended to offset this disadvantage.

Suborbital Spaceplanes

Other (suborbital) spaceplane designs use the vehicle's wings to provide lift for the *ascent to* space as well, in addition to the rocket. As of June 21, 2004, the only such craft to reach space have been the X-15 and SpaceShipOne. Neither of these craft was capable of entering orbit, and both began independent flight only after being lifted to high altitude by a carrier aircraft.

Atmospheric Reentry

Because spaceplanes designed for sub-orbital trajectories do not reach orbital speed, they do not need the kinds of thermal protection orbital spacecraft require during the hypersonic phase of atmospheric reentry. The Space Shuttle thermal protection system, for example, protects the orbiter from surface temperatures that could otherwise reach as high as 3,000 °F (1,650 °C), well above the melting point of steel.

Single Stage to Orbit

Future orbital spaceplanes may take off, ascend, descend, and land like conventional aircraft, providing true single stage to orbit or SSO capability.

Proponents of scramjet technology often cite such a vehicle as being a possible application of that type of engine, however pure rocket and turbojet designs have also been proposed and may be easier to design and build.

The problems of overall weight described above are at their worst for SSO operation.

Other Designs

Various types of spaceplanes have been suggested since the early twentieth century. Notable early designs include Friedrich Zander's spaceplane equipped with wings made of combustible alloys that it would burn during its ascent, and Eugen Sänger's Silbervogel bomber design. Winged versions of the V2 rocket were considered during and after World War II, and when public interest in space exploration was high in the 1950s and 60s, winged rocket designs by Wernher von Braun and Willy Ley served to inspire science fiction artists and filmmakers.

The USAF invested some effort in a paper study of a variety of spaceplane projects under their aerospaceplane efforts of the late 1950s, but later ended these when they decided to use a modified version of Sänger's design. The result, X-20 Dyna-Soar was to have been the first orbital spaceplane, but was cancelled in the early 1960s in lieu of NASA's Project Gemini and the U.S. Air Force's Manned Orbiting Laboratory programme.

The Rockwell X-30 National Aero-Space Plane (NASP), begun in the 1980s, was an attempt to build a scramjet vehicle capable of operating like an aircraft and achieving orbit like the shuttle. It was cancelled due to increasing technical challenges, growing budgets, and the loss of public interest.

The Multi-Unit Space Transport and Recovery Device (MUSTARD) was a concept explored by the British Aircraft Corporation (BAC) around 1964-1965 for launching payloads weighing as much as 5,000 lb. into orbit. It was never constructed.

The British Government began a project known as HOTOL whose ultimate goal would have been a spaceplane, but the project was cancelled due to technical and financial issues. The lead engineer from the HOTOL project has since set up a private company dedicated to creating a similar plane called Skylon with a different combined cycle rocket/turbine precooled jet engine called SABRE. This vehicle is intended to be capable of a single stage to orbit launch and if successful would be far in advance of anything currently in operation.

In 1994 Mitchell Burnside Clapp proposed a single stage to orbit peroxide/kerosene spaceplane called "Black Horse". This was notable in that it took off almost empty and underwent mid-air refuelling before burning for orbit.

The X-33 was a prototype made as part of an attempt by NASA to build a SSTO hydrogen fuelled space plane that failed when the hydrogen tank design proved to be unconstructable in the planned way.

The Roton was an unusual attempt to build a spaceplane. Several configurations were evaluated ranging from a helicopter ascent to a pure rocket ascent; all landings were to use a helicopter landing system. It failed due to funding issues.

Germany

After the Sänger-Bredt RaBo and Silbervogel of the 1930s and 1940s, Sänger worked for time on various spaceplane projects, coming up with several designs for Messerschmitt Bölkow Blohm such as the MBB Raumtransporter-8. In the 1980s, West Germany funded design work on the MBB Sänger II with the Hypersonic Technology programme. Development continued on MBB/Deutsche Aerospace Sänger II/HORUS until the early 1990s, when it was cancelled in favour of the Ariane rocket, despite predicted cost savings of up to 30 per cent. Also in the 1980s, Germany funded its own Space Shuttle mission known as Spacelab D-1 using the U.S. Space Shuttle. Although superficially similar to other U.S. flights, it was actually funded by West Germany with German controlled mission science. *Deutschland 1* (D-1), with corresponding NASA designation STS-61-A, marked the first German astronauts in space not in a guest programme, the first manned German space mission, and the only non-U.S. funded manned space mission. A D-2 mission was planned for 1988, but delayed until 1993; *Deutschland 2* marked the first manned German space mission after German reunification (NASA designation STS-55). The Daimler-Chrysler Aerospace RLV was a much later small reusable space shuttle design.

Unconfirmed Reports

The March 5, 2006 edition of Aviation Week & Space Technology published a story purporting to be "outing" a highly classified US military two-stage-to-orbit spaceplane system with the code name Blackstar, SR-3/XOV among other nicknames. The alleged system, using an XB-70-like first-stage mothership, capable of Mach 3, is said to launch an upper-stage wave-rider spaceplane capable of carrying small payloads and crews near to or into orbit or on skip-diving flights, ostensibly for reconnaissance and other missions, achieving surprise that cannot be attained by satellite. There has been considerable controversy over this story and its claims.

The Soviet Union supposedly developed the spaceplane Uragan in the 1980s. Intended as a follow-on to Spiral and a smaller sibling to Buran, the project was cancelled in 1987, a year before the first Buran flight. The project has never been confirmed by Soviet or Russian authorities, however.

SUBORBITAL SPACEPLANE

A **suborbital spaceplane** is a spaceplane designed specifically for suborbital spaceflight. From late 2007, it is expected that this type of spacecraft will play a key role in early space tourism.

History

The first ever true suborbital spaceplane was the North American X-15, which first flew above the Kármán line in 1963.

The first privately built and privately funded suborbital spaceplane was Scaled Composites SpaceShipOne, which first flew above the Kármán line in 2004.

List

- EADS Astrium Space Tourism Project
- Rocketplane XP
- Scaled Composites SpaceShipOne —retired
- Scaled Composites SpaceShipTwo
- Space Adventures C-21
- SpaceDev Dream Chaser
- Lynx rocketplane (supersedes Xerus)
- Some successful spacecrafts and spaceplanes

GENESIS I

Genesis I is an experimental space habitat designed and built by the private American firm Bigelow Aerospace and launched in 2006. It was the first module to be sent into orbit by the company, and is testing various systems, materials and techniques related to determining the viability of long-term inflatable space structures. Such structures, including this module and others built by Bigelow Aerospace, are based on the NASA Transhab design, which provides increased interior volume at a reduced launch diameter and potentially reduced mass compared to traditional rigid structures.

Spacecraft History

Genesis I was launched on July 12, 2006 at 14:53:30 UTC aboard an ISC Kosmotras Dnepr rocket, launched from Dombarovskiy missile base near Yasniy, Russia. Spacecraft control was transferred to Bigelow Aerospace at 15:08 UTC after a successful orbital insertion. Designed as a one-third scale model of the full size *BA 330*, when in orbit the main body of the craft measures 4.4 m (14.4 ft) long and 2.54 m (8.3 ft) in diameter, with an interior habitable volume of 11.5 cubic metres (406.1 cubic feet). As part of the expandable design, however, the module launched with a diameter of only 1.6 m (5.25 ft), inflating to its full size after entering orbit. The expansion process took approximately ten minutes.

Genesis I suffered a major radiation event in December 2006 as a result of a solar storm. Mission controllers were able to restart the system in time, though the situation was described as being "one fault away from the spacecraft being dead." Despite this, no lasting damage appears to have occurred and the spacecraft was operating in "excellent shape" as of March 2007.

The spacecraft completed its 10,000th orbit on May 8, 2008, some 660 days after launch. Since that launch, "*Genesis 1* has travelled the equivalent of more than 270 million miles, which would take it to the Moon and back 1,154 times," and has taken more than 14,000 images, including images of all seven continents. Its electrical equipment has been continuously powered since it first became operational.

Systems

Genesis I is outfitted with eight GaAs solar panel arrays, four on each end, which produce one kilowatt total power and maintain a 26 volt battery charge. The craft carries thirteen cameras, seven external to monitor the physical condition of the spacecraft, such as the outer shell and solar arrays, and six internal to photograph the various objects and experiments. Internal systems established an atmospheric pressure of 7.5 psi (51.7 kPa) and use passive thermal control to keep temperatures at an average of 26 degrees Celsius (79 degrees Fahrenheit), with observed limits of approximately 4.5 °C (40 °F) and 32 °C (90 °F). *Genesis I* uses a single gas tank for its inflation system, and guidance/stabilization control is performed using a network of torque rods, sun sensors, GPS and a magnetometer.

Payload

Aside from the various systems and monitoring equipment, *Genesis I* is orbiting with a wide variety of cargo. Bigelow employees contributed numerous photographs, toys, cards and other items, which can be seen in still images floating around the cabin. Bigelow also placed a life-sciences experiment on board, which contains Madagascar hissing cockroaches (*Gromphadorhina portentosa*) and so-called Mexican jumping beans, which are seeds containing the live larva of the moth *Cydia deshaisiana*. In addition, the company allowed NASA to include a prototype for the GeneSat series of nanosatellites. This device, called GeneBox, tested the systems and procedures that will be used on future GeneSat missions. While GeneBox carries no living organisms, future flights will use sensors and optics to measure how weightlessness affects genes and the genetic activity of cells and microscopic life.

GENESIS II

Genesis II is the second experimental space habitat designed and built by the private American firm Bigelow Aerospace, and was launched in 2007. As the second module sent into orbit by the company, this spacecraft builds on the data and experience gleaned from its previously orbited sister-ship *Genesis I* to continue testing the viability of long-term inflatable space structures. Like its sister-ship and other modules being designed by Bigelow Aerospace, this spacecraft is based on the NASA Transhab design, which provides increased interior volume and reduced launch diameter along with potentially reduced mass compared to traditional rigid structures.

Spacecraft History

Genesis II was launched on June 28, 2007 at 15:02 UTC. As with *Genesis I*, it was launched aboard an ISC Kosmotras Dnepr rocket from Dombarovskiy missile base near Yasniy, Russia. It successfully reached orbit after separation from the rocket at 15:16 UTC. Due to the mechanics of its orbit, first contact with the craft was established once it passed over SpaceQuest, Ltd.'s Fairfax, Virginia receiving station at 22:20 UTC, confirming that it was alive and functioning nominally with power and air pressure at expected levels. Externally, *Genesis II* is identical in size to *Genesis I*; as such, it is a one-third scale of the full-size *BA 330* model, with on-orbit measurements of 4.4 metres (14.4 ft) in length and 2.54 m (8 ft 4 in) in diameter, with an interior habitable volume of 11.5 cubic metres (406.1 cu ft). As part of its inflatable design, *Genesis II* launched with a diameter of 1.6 m (5 ft 2.99 in), expanding to its full size after entering orbit. Within two days of launch, attitude control systems had damped all rotation and oriented antennae toward Earth.

Similar to the process endured by Bigelow for *Genesis I*, transporting *Genesis II* to Russia for launch was the end result of nearly a year of regulatory processes due to restrictions imposted by International Traffic in Arms Regulations (ITAR) and other procedures, both in the United States and abroad. After leaving North Las Vegas, Nevada in the United States, the spacecraft made a stopover in Luxembourg before being flown on an Antonov An-124 to Orsk, Russia, and transported over ground to the Dombarovskiy base. *Genesis II* made its final move into the Assembly, Integration and Test Building on March 29, 2007.

Originally slated for an August 6, 2006 launch, ISC Kosmotras delayed the launch to January 30, 2007 due to the failure of a Dnepr rocket in July 2006. The launch was delayed an additional four times (April 1, April 19, April 26 and May 23) due to technical and scheduling concerns before its eventual launch on June 28.

On December 12, 2007, Bigelow Aerospace provided an update indicating that *Genesis II* was in good health. All cameras have been tested and more than 4,000 photographs have been captured. The craft is in a nearly circular orbit with an eccentricity of 0.028, and having lost only 5 kilometres (3 mi) since launch, current predictions indicate that it will remain in orbit for more than 12 years. Attitude control systems and all eight solar arrays are operational, and no damage to the outer surface of the craft has been observed. Internal pressure was noted as holding between 69.6 and 72.4 kilopascals (10.1 and 10.5 psi), with the variation caused by *Genesis II* moving in and out of sunlight during its orbit.

Systems

Genesis II features a number of improvements over the first pathfinder that was launched. In addition to the standard guidance control systems used on *Genesis I*, it has reaction wheel assemblies and a precision measurement system, which are used to affect the spacecraft's rotation rate and angular momentum without expending fuel. It carries 22 cameras—nine more than on *Genesis I*—for photographing and filming cargo and ship conditions both inside and out. Some of these are on articulated platforms, and one wireless camera will be capable of additional exterior shots. Instead of the single-tank inflation system used on the first craft, *Genesis II* employs multiple tanks for added reliability and to allow for more finely-tuned gas control. Additional layers have been added to the outer shield for increased protection and thermal management. Finally, the on-board sensor suite has been enhanced with additional sensors for pressure, temperature, attitude control and radiation detection, which will help determine the impact of the orbital environment on shipboard systems integrity.

Payload

On both the interior and exterior, *Genesis II* carries several non-critical systems for scientific, commercial and entertainment purposes.

For the science aspect, *Genesis II* carries an upgraded version of the original life-sciences module and is colloquially termed "Life in a Box". This module includes habitats for three organisms: the Madagascar hissing cockroach, previously carried aboard *Genesis I*; the South African flat rock scorpion, *Hadogenes troglodytes*; and a colony of seed-harvester ants, *Pogonomyrmex californicus*, along with the queen ant for long-term colonization possibilities. This biobox system includes automated food and water delivery systems, and fans keep fresh air available by circulating internal air with that inside the rest of the spacecraft. Sensors and cameras will monitor the health and activities of the biobox inhabitants, and images of the interior are intended for display on Bigelow's website.

There are two commercial payloads included on *Genesis II*. The first is the "Fly Your Stuff" programme, which allowed individuals and customers to send photographs and other small items into orbit for a fee. Several dozen of these objects were launched, and were later photographed and filmed by cameras in the spacecraft and posted on the Bigelow website for the customers to view. By December 2007, all objects launched as part of this programme had been photographed and distributed to customers. This included the first lychee in space. Guy Pignolet de Pluton, a professor at Université de la Réunion in Sainte-Rose, Réunion, provided the lychee which has been imaged on Bigelow Aerospace's website.

A secondary payload is the external image projection system that tested the capability for flashing images and messages on the spacecraft's hull. Two projectors and associated cameras are positioned on the tips of solar arrays, and the company has eventual plans for allowing the public to send images and video to be displayed. As of August 2007, there were no firm plans on how this would be handled due to current limits of uplink bandwidth, and was considered an experimental "fun" project.

For entertainment, *Genesis II* carries a "Space Bingo" game intended to foster public interest in the programme. The game will be started several months into the mission and will be free to play, though no actual gambling is involved. The game module contains a full set of Bingo balls which are randomly manipulated one at a time by a system of fans and levers, resetting after forty balls have entered play. During play, images will be broadcast to those who are playing along.

SCALED COMPOSITES SPACESHIPONE

SpaceShipOne is a spaceplane that completed the first privately funded human spaceflight on June 21, 2004. It was developed by Scaled Composites.

SpaceShipOne was developed by Mojave Aerospace Ventures (A joint venture between Paul Allen and Scaled Composites, Burt Rutan's aviation company, in their Tier One programme), without government funding. On June 21, 2004, it made the first privately funded human spaceflight, and on October 4, it won the $10 million Ansari X PRIZE, by reaching 100 kilometres in altitude twice in a two-week period with the equivalent of three people on board, with no more than ten per cent of the non-fuel weight of the spacecraft replaced between flights. Development costs were estimated to be $25 million, funded completely by Paul Allen.

During its testing regimen, SpaceShipOne set a number of important "firsts", including first privately funded aircraft to exceed Mach 2 and Mach 3, first privately funded manned spacecraft to exceed 100 km altitude, and first privately funded reusable manned spacecraft.

SpaceShipOne is an experimental air-launched suborbital spaceplane that uses a hybrid rocket motor. The design features a unique "feathering" atmospheric reentry system where the rear half of the wing and the twin tail booms folded upward along a hinge running the length of the wing; this increased drag while remaining stable. The achievements of SpaceShipOne are more comparable to the X-15 than orbiting spacecraft like the Space Shuttle. Accelerating a spacecraft to orbital speed requires more than 60 times as much energy as lifting it to 100 km.

Prior unmanned privately funded space flights were successfully achieved by the Orbital Sciences Pegasus since 1990 and the Civilian Space eXploration Team 5 weeks earlier in May 2004.

History

SpaceShipOne is registered with the FAA as **N328KF**. *N* is the prefix for US-registered aircraft; *328KF* was chosen by Scaled Composites to stand for 328 kilo feet (about 100 kilometres), the officially designated edge of space. The original choice of registry number, **N100KM**, was already taken. N328KF is registered as a glider, reflecting the fact that most of its independent flight is unpowered.

SpaceShipOne's first flight, 01C, was an unmanned captive carry flight test on May 20, 2003. Glide tests followed, starting with flight 03G on August 7, 2003. Its first powered flight, flight 11P, was made on December 17, 2003, the 100th anniversary of the first powered flight.

On April 1, 2004, Scaled Composites received the first license for sub-orbital rocket flights to be issued by the US Office of Commercial Space Transportation. This license permitted the company to conduct powered test flights over the course of one year. On June 17, 2004, Mojave Airport reclassified itself (part-time) as the Mojave Spaceport.

Flight 15P on June 21, 2004, was SpaceShipOne's first spaceflight, and the first privately funded human spaceflight. Ansari X PRIZE flights followed, with flight 17P on October 4, 2004, winning the prize.

The SpaceShipOne Team was awarded the Space Achievement Award by the Space Foundation in 2005.

Retirement

SpaceShipOne's spaceflights were watched by large crowds at Mojave Spaceport. A fourth suborbital flight, Flight 18P, was originally scheduled for October 13, 2004. However, Burt Rutan decided not to risk damage to the historic craft, and cancelled it and all future flights.

On July 25, 2005 SpaceShipOne was taken to the Oshkosh Airshow in Oshkosh, Wisconsin. After the airshow, Mike Melvill and crew flew the White Knight, carrying SpaceShipOne, to Wright-Patterson Air Force Base in Dayton, Ohio, where Mike spoke to a group of about 300 military and civilian personnel. Later in the evening, Mike gave a presentation at the Dayton Engineers Club, entitled "Some Experiments in Space Flight", in honour of Wilbur Wright's now famous presentation to the American Society of Mechanical Engineers in 1901 entitled "Some Experiments in Flight." The White Knight then transported SpaceShipOne to the Smithsonian Institution's National Air and Space Museum to be put on display. It was unveiled on Wednesday October 5, 2005 in the Milestones of Flight gallery and is now on display to the public in the main atrium between the Spirit of St. Louis and the Bell X-1.

SpaceShipOne became a popular model rocket in 2004. Estes Industries currently offers several flying model rockets of SpaceShipOne. A piece of SpaceShipOne's carbon fiber material was launched aboard the New Horizons mission to Pluto in 2006.

Replica

A year after its appearance in the Oshkosh Airventure airshow, the Experimental Aircraft Association featured a full-scale replica of the spacecraft in a wing of its museum which housed other creations of Burt Rutan. Using the same fiberglass molds as the original, it was so exact in its replication—despite not having any doors or interior—that it was dubbed "Serial 2 Scaled" by Scaled Composites. Each and every painstaking detail in its appearance was matched, down to the N328KF registration number on its fuselage. It is so precise that, during a video presentation held every hour in the museum, it can display the two different modes of its 'feathering' ability, albeit through the aid of pulleys and wires (there is no machinery in the replica).

Future Efforts

The development of a larger, more powerful space plane capable of reaching 120 km was announced in 2004. It will be named Scaled Composites SpaceShipTwo, and is currently under development by The Spaceship Company, a joint venture between Scaled Composites and Sir Richard Branson's Virgin Group, as part of the Tier 1b programme. The Virgin Galactic spaceliner plans to operate a fleet of five of these craft in passenger-carrying private spaceflight service starting no earlier than 2011.

The vehicle itself was unveiled to the public at the Experimental Aircraft Association's Air Venture in Oshkosh, Wisconsin on July 28, 2009. Following a series of 50-100 test flights, the first paying customers are expected to fly aboard the craft in 2011. In August 2005, Virgin Galactic stated that if the upcoming suborbital service with SpaceShipTwo is successful, the follow-up SpaceShipThree will be an orbital craft.

Flights

All of the flights of SpaceShipOne were from the Mojave Airport Civilian Flight Test Center. Flights were numbered, starting with flight 01 on May 20, 2003. One or two letters are appended to the number to indicate the type of mission. An appended **C** indicates that the flight was a captive carry, **G** indicates an unpowered glide, and **P** indicates a powered flight. If the actual flight differs in category from the intended flight, two letters are appended: the first indicating the intended mission and the second the mission actually performed.

In the table below, the "top speed" reported is the Mach number at burn-out (the end of the rocket burn). This is not an absolute speed.

SpaceShipOne flights					
Flight	*Date*	*Top speed*	*Altitude*	*Duration*	*Pilot*
01C	May 20, 2003			1 h 48 min	unmanned
02C	July 29, 2003			2 h 06 min	Mike Melvill
03G	August 7, 2003			0 h 19 min	Mike Melvill
04GC	August 27, 2003			1 h 06 min	Mike Melvill
05G	August 27, 2003			10 min 30 s	Mike Melvill
06G	September 23, 2003			12 min 15 s	Mike Melvill
07G	October 17, 2003			17 min 49 s	Mike Melvill
08G	November 14, 2003			19 min 55 s	Peter Siebold
09G	November 19, 2003			12 min 25 s	Mike Melvill
10G	December 4, 2003			13 min 14 s	Brian Binnie
11P	December 17, 2003	Mach 1.2	20.7 km	18 min 10 s	Brian Binnie
12G	March 11, 2004			18 min 30 s	Peter Siebold
13P	April 8, 2004	Mach 1.6	32.0 km	16 min 27 s	Peter Siebold
14P	May 13, 2004	Mach 2.5	64.3 km	20 min 44 s	Mike Melvill
15P	June 21, 2004	Mach 2.9	100.1 km	24 min 05 s	Mike Melvill
16P	September 29, 2004	Mach 2.92	102.9 km	24 min 11 s	Mike Melvill
17P	October 4, 2004	Mach 3.09	112.0 km	23 min 56 s	Brian Binnie

The flights were accompanied by two chase planes: an Extra 300 owned and flown by Chuck Coleman, and a Beechcraft Starship.

Astronauts

The SpaceShipOne pilots came from a variety of aerospace backgrounds. Mike Melvill is a test pilot, Brian Binnie was [illegible], and Doug Shane and Peter Siebold are engineers at Scaled Composites [illegible] qualified to fly SpaceShipOne by training on the Tier One flight simulator [illegible] White Knight and other Scaled Composites aircraft.

Specifications

General Characteristics

- **Crew:** one, pilot
- **Capacity:** 2 passengers
- **Length:** 16 ft 5 in (5 m)
- **Wingspan:** 16 ft 5 in (5 m)
- **Height**
- **Wing area:** 161.4 ft² (15 m²)
- **Empty weight:** 2,640 lb (1,200 kg)
- **Loaded weight:** 7,920 lb (3,600 kg)
- **Powerplant:** 1× N2O/HTPB SpaceDev Hybrid rocket motor, 7,500 kgf (74 kN)
- **I_{sp}:** 250 s (2450 Ns/kg)
- **Burn time:** 87 seconds
- **Aspect ratio:** 1.6

Performance

- **Maximum speed:** Mach 3.09 (2,170 mph, 3,518 km/h)
- **Range:** 35 nm (40 mi, 65 km)
- **Service ceiling:** 367,360 ft (112,000 m)
- **Rate of climb:** 82,000 ft/min (416.6 m/s)
- **Wing loading:** 49.07 lb/ft² (240 kg/m²)
- **Thrust/weight:** 20

SCALED COMPOSITES SPACESHIPTWO

Scaled Composites' **Model 339 SpaceShipTwo** (SS2) is a suborbital spaceplane for carrying space tourists, under development by The Spaceship Company, a joint venture between Scaled Composites and Sir Richard Branson's Virgin Group, as part of the Tier 1b programme. Branson stated at the Oshkosh Airshow of July 2009 that the spaceship would be unveiled in December, 2009, after which test flights are to begin. The Virgin Galactic spaceline plans to operate a fleet of five of these craft in passenger-carrying private spaceflight service starting no earlier than 2011.

Design and Development

The SpaceShipTwo project is based in part on technology developed for SpaceShipOne as part of the Scaled Composites Tier One programme, funded by Paul Allen. The

Spaceship Company licenses this technology from Paul Allen's Mojave Aerospace Ventures.

SpaceShipTwo will carry passengers to space; the capacity will be eight people: six passengers and two pilots. The apogee of the new craft will be approximately 110 km (68 miles) and in the thermosphere, 10 km (6 miles) higher than both the SpaceShipOne target (though the last flight of the SpaceShipOne reached 112 km), and the Kármán line. SpaceShipTwo will reach 4,200 km/h (2,600 mph), using a single hybrid rocket motor. It will launch at 15,200 m (50,000 ft) from its mothership, WhiteKnightTwo. SpaceShipTwo's crew cabin is 3.66 m (12 ft) long and 2.28 m (7.5 ft) in diameter. The wing span is 8.23 m (27 ft), the length is 18.29 m (60 ft) and the tail height is 4.57 m (15 ft).

SpaceShipTwo uses a feathered reentry system, feasible due to the low speed of re-entry—by contrast, space shuttles and other orbital spacecraft re-enter at orbital speeds, closer to 25,000 km/h (16,000 mph), using heat shields. It is designed to reenter the atmosphere at any angle. "This vehicle is designed to go into the atmosphere in the worst case straight in or upside down and it'll correct", says Burt Rutan. As for safety, he states "This is designed to be at least as safe as the early airliners in the 1920s...Don't believe anyone that tells you that the safety will be the same as a modern airliner, which has been around for 70 years."

SpaceShipTwo and its new carrier aircraft, WhiteKnightTwo, are roughly twice the size of the first generation spacecraft SpaceShipOne and mothership White Knight that won the Ansari X Prize. SpaceShipTwo will have 43 cm and 33 cm (17 and 13 in) diameter windows for the passengers' viewing pleasure, and all seats will recline back during landing to decrease the discomfort of G-forces. Reportedly, the craft can land safely even if "catastrophic damage" occurs during the flight.

Explosion

On 26 July, 2007 a fatal explosion occurred at the Mojave airport during a fuel flow test that included filling the oxidizer tank with 4,500 kg (10,000 pounds) of nitrous oxide followed by a 15 second cold flow injector test. The explosion was around 14:30 (2:30 PM). Though the tests did not ignite the gas, three employees were killed and three injured, two critically and one seriously, from shrapnel wounds.

Commercial Introduction

In August 2005, the president of space tourism company Virgin Galactic stated that if the suborbital service with SpaceShipTwo is successful, the follow-up SpaceShipThree will be an orbital craft.

On September 28, 2006, Sir Richard Branson unveiled a mock-up of the SpaceShipTwo passenger cabin at the NextFest exposition, in the Javits Convention Center, New York.

The design of the vehicle was revealed to the press in January 2008, with the statement that the vehicle itself was around 60 per cent complete. The launch customer of SpaceShipTwo is Virgin Galactic, which will have the first five units, and exclusive craft rights for the first few years.

Following 50-100 test flights, the first paying customers are expected to fly aboard the craft in 2011.

Spacecraft

Seven vehicles have been ordered by Virgin Galactic. As of October 2007, only the first two have been named, the VSS (Virgin Space Ship) *Enterprise*, and the VSS *Voyager*. Both are in development.

1. VSS *Enterprise* (2009)
2. VSS *Voyager*
3. Not yet named
4. Not yet named
5. Not yet named

Flight

More than 65,000 would-be space tourists have applied for the first batch of 100 tickets. The price will initially be $200,000. However, after the first 100 tickets are sold, the deposit would be dropped to around $100,000. Then deposits after the first year will drop to around $20,000. The deposit for the near future is expected to remain at $20,000 per person per flight. The duration of the flights will be approximately 2.5 hours, though only a few minutes of that will be in space. Weekly launches are planned.

In December 2007 Virgin Galactic had 200 paid-up applicants on its books for the early flights, and 95 per cent were passing the 6-8 g centrifuge tests.

Launch Site

The SpaceShipTwo craft will take off from the Mojave Spaceport in California during testing. Spaceport America (formerly Southwest Regional Spaceport), a $200 million spaceport in New Mexico partly funded by the state government, will become the permanent launch site when commercial launches begin. The company is also exploring building spaceports in Saudi Arabia and Scotland.

MARK SHUTTLEWORTH

Mark Richard Shuttleworth (born 18 September 1973) is a South African entrepreneur who was the second self-funded space tourist. Shuttleworth founded Canonical Ltd. and as of 2009, provides leadership for the Ubuntu operating system.

He currently lives in London and holds dual citizenship of South Africa and the United Kingdom.

Early Life

Shuttleworth was born in Welkom, Orange Free State, South Africa as a son of a surgeon and a kindergarten teacher. After attending school at Rondebosch Boys' High School and Diocesan College, Shuttleworth obtained a Business Science degree in Finance and Information Systems at the University of Cape Town. He lived in Smuts Hall, where he was involved in the installation of the first residential Internet connections at the university.

Work

Shuttleworth founded Thawte in 1995, which specialised in digital certificates and Internet security and then sold it to VeriSign in December 1999, earning Rs. 3.5 billion (about US$ 575 million at the time).

In September 2000, Shuttleworth formed HBD Venture Capital, a business incubator and venture capital provider.

In March 2004 he formed Canonical Ltd., for the promotion and commercial support of free software projects.

Linux

In the 1990s, Shuttleworth participated as one of the developers of the Debian operating system.

In 2001 he formed the Shuttleworth Foundation, a non-profit organization dedicated to social innovation which also funds educational, free, and open source software projects in South Africa, such as the Freedom Toaster.

In 2004 he returned to the free software world by funding the development of Ubuntu, a Linux distribution based on Debian, through his company Canonical Ltd.

In 2005 he founded the Ubuntu Foundation and made an initial investment of 10 million dollars. In the Ubuntu project, Shuttleworth is often referred to with the tongue-in-cheek title *Self-Appointed Benevolent Dictator for Life,* abbreviated *SABDFL.* To come up with a list of names of people to hire for the project, Mr. Shuttleworth took six months of Debian mailing list archives with him whilst travelling to the Antarctic aboard the icebreaker Kapitan Khlebnikov in early 2004. In September 2005, he purchased a 65 per cent stake of Impi Linux.

On 15 October 2006 it was announced that Mark Shuttleworth became the first patron of KDE, the highest level of sponsorship available.

Spaceflight

Shuttleworth gained worldwide fame on 25 April 2002 as the second self-funded spaceflight participant. Working with Space Adventures, he launched aboard the Russian Soyuz TM-34 mission, paying approximately US$ 20 million for the voyage. Two days later, the Soyuz spacecraft arrived at the International Space Station, where he spent eight days participating in experiments related to AIDS and genome research. On 5 May 2002, he returned to Earth. In order to participate on the flight, Shuttleworth had to undergo one year of training and preparation, including seven months spent in Star City, Russia.

While in space he had a radio conversation with Nelson Mandela and a 14 year old South African girl, Michelle Foster, who asked him to marry her. He politely dodged the question, stating that he was "very honoured at the question" before changing the subject. The terminally ill Miss Foster was provided the opportunity to have a conversation with Mark Shuttleworth and Nelson Mandela by the Reach for a Dream foundation.

Transport

He has a private jet, a Bombardier Global Express, which is often referred to as *Canonical One* but is in fact owned through his *HBD Venture Capital* company. The dragon depicted on the side of the plane is "Norman", the HBD Venture Capital mascot.

CHARLES SIMONYI

Charles Simonyi (Hungarian: *Simonyi Károly*; born September 10, 1948) is a Hungarian-American computer software executive who, as head of Microsoft's application software group, oversaw the creation of Microsoft's flagship office applications. He now heads his own company, *Intentional Software*, with the aim of developing and marketing his concept of intentional programming. In April 2007, aboard Soyuz TMA-10, he became the fifth space tourist and the second Hungarian in space. In March 2009, aboard Soyuz TMA-14, he made a second trip to the International Space Station. His estimated net worth is US$1 billion.

Biography

Early Life in Hungary

Simonyi was born in Budapest, Hungary, the son of Károly Simonyi, a professor of electrical engineering at Technical University of Budapest. While in high school he worked part-time as a night watchman at a computer laboratory, overseeing a large Soviet Ural II mainframe. He took interest in computing and learned to programme from one of the laboratory's engineers. By the time he left school, he had learned to develop compilers and sold one of these to a government department. He presented a demonstration of his compiler to the members of a Danish computer trade delegation.

Denmark, USA

He was hired by Denmark's A/S Regnecentralen in 1966 and moved to the United States in 1968 to attend the University of California, Berkeley, where he earned his B.S. in Engineering Mathematics & Statistics in 1972.

Simonyi then went to Stanford University for graduate studies and was hired by Xerox PARC during its most productive period, working alongside luminaries such as Alan Kay, Butler Lampson and Robert Metcalfe on the development of the *Xerox*

Alto, the first personal computer. He and Lampson developed *Bravo*, the first WYSIWYG document preparation programme, which became operational in 1974. He received his Ph.D. in computer science from Stanford in 1977 with a dissertation on a software project management technique called "meta programming". This approach sought to defeat Brooks' law by requiring all programmers to communicate through the manager rather than directly. Simonyi remained at PARC until 1981.

Microsoft

In 1981, at Metcalfe's suggestion, he applied directly to Bill Gates for a job at Microsoft. At the firm, Simonyi oversaw the development of what became its most profitable products, Word and Excel, as well as Excel's predecessor Multiplan. With Multiplan, Simonyi pursued a strategy called the "revenue bomb", whereby the product ran on a virtual machine that was ported to each platform. The resulting application was highly portable, although Simonyi did not foresee the rapid adoption of MS-DOS that made such efforts less important. Simonyi introduced the techniques of object-oriented programming that he had learned at Xerox to Microsoft. He developed the Hungarian notation convention for naming variables. Originally these standards were part of his doctoral thesis. The Hungarian notation has been widely used inside Microsoft.

Own Company

Simonyi remained at Microsoft during its rapid rise in the software industry, becoming one of its highest-ranking developers. He left abruptly in 2002 to co-found, with business partner Gregor Kiczales, a company called Intentional Software. This company markets the intentional programming concepts Simonyi developed at Microsoft Research. In this approach to software, a programmer first builds a toolbox specific to a given problem domain (such as life insurance). Domain experts, aided by the programmer, then describe the programme's intended behaviour in a What You See Is What You Get (WYSIWYG)-like manner. An automated system uses the programme description and the toolbox to generate the final programme. Successive changes are only done at the WYSIWYG level.

In 2004, Simonyi received the Wharton Infosys Business Transformation Award for the industry-wide impact of his innovative work in information technology.

Philanthropy

Simonyi has been an active philanthropist. In 1995 he established an endowed chair, the Simonyi Professorship of the Public Understanding of Science at Oxford University, first held by the now retired Richard Dawkins. He also established a Charles Simonyi Professor for Innovation in Teaching endowed chair at Stanford University. In January 2004, Simonyi created the $50 million Charles Simonyi Fund for Arts and Sciences, through which Simonyi plans to support Seattle-area arts, science, and educational programmes. Initial grant recipients include the Seattle Symphony ($10 million), and the Seattle Public Library ($3 million). In 2005, the Fund donated $25 million to the Institute for Advanced Study in Princeton, New Jersey. In January, 2008 the Simonyi

Fund and Bill Gates pledged $20 million and $10 million respectively to the Large Synoptic Survey Telescope.

Personal Life

As of February 2008, Simonyi had been dating Martha Stewart for 15 years. In 2008, however, the two separated. On August 8, 2008, Simonyi became engaged to a Swedish millionaire's daughter, Lisa Persdotter, who is 32 years his junior. On November 22, 2008, the couple married in a private ceremony in Gothenburg, Sweden attended by their closest friends, among them Bill Gates.

Simonyi spends six months a year on his custom-built 233 ft (71 m) long super yacht named *Skat*.

Simonyi's residence in Medina, Washington, "Villa Simonyi", is a modern house designed by architect Wendell Lovett, where Simonyi displays his collection of paintings by Roy Lichtenstein and Victor Vasarely.

Space Tourist

In early 2006, Simonyi expressed interest in becoming a space tourist and signed agreements with the space tourism company, Space Adventures Ltd., for a ten-day mission to the International Space Station (ISS).

In August 2006, he passed a pre-qualification medical exam by the Russian Federal Space Agency, called the State Medical Commission (GMK). He started training at Star City in September 2006.

He launched on April 7, 2007 (GMT), on board Soyuz TMA-10. He shared a ride with two Russian cosmonauts to the International Space Station, and returned aboard Soyuz TMA-9, scheduled to depart from the ISS on April 20, 2007.

Upon arrival to the ISS on April 9, 2007 Simonyi said, "It is amazing how it appears from the blackness of the sky. It was very, very dramatic. It was like a big stage set, a fantastic production of some incredible opera or modern play. That's what I was referring to when I said I was blown away."

Simonyi's expected return on April 20 was delayed by one day due to 'boggy ground'. He returned to Earth on April 21 along with an American astronaut and a Russian cosmonaut.

In October 2008, he booked for a second trip to the ISS through Space Adventures on board Soyuz TMA-14. On March 26, 2009 he returned to space aboard Soyuz TMA-14. His return flight was aboard Soyuz TMA-13. He and two other crewmembers landed in Kazakhstan on April 8, 2009.

Radio Communication while Aboard ISS

Charles Simonyi is a licensed amateur radio operator with the call sign KE7KDP, and planned to contact a number of schools while on his flight on the International Space Station utilizing amateur radio for the communication with those schools. On April 11, 2007 the American Radio Relay League reported that Simonyi was already making ham radio contacts from space.

One of the schools Simonyi contacted was Cedar Point Elementary in Bristow, Virginia. A telebridge conversation was held on Tuesday, April 17, 2007. Onboard with him were Oleg Kotov and Fyodor Yurchikhin. On March 30, 2009 he held a phone conversation with students at the Girls' Middle School in Mountain View, CA, USA in which he said that one of the most surprising things about travelling to space was that upon returning to earth the air feels very thick, very heavy, like "breathing Pepto-Bismol." He also stated that talking with the students from the school "made his day."

Simonyi used his Hungarian call sign HA5SIK when he contacted 25 radio amateurs from Hungary in a record attempt on April 12. He contacted former and current students of Tivadar Puskás Polytechnic, Budapest on April 13.

GREGORY OLSEN

Gregory Hammond "Greg" Olsen (born April 20, 1945) is an American entrepreneur and scientist who, in October 2005, became the third private citizen to make a self-funded trip into space with Space Adventures.

Olsen was the co-founder and chairman of Sensors Unlimited Inc., a company developing optoelectronic devices such as sensitive near-infrared (NIR) and shortwave-infrared (SWIR) cameras. One of Sensors Unlimited's major customers is NASA. Currently, Olsen is President of GHO Ventures, LLC, in Princeton, New Jersey, where he manages his angel investments, South African winery, Montana ranch, and performs numerous speaking engagements to encourage children—especially minority and female children—to consider careers in science or engineering. He also is a professor at Rider University where he teaches a physics class.

Early Life and Education

Olsen, born in Brooklyn, New York, was the son of an IBEW Local 3 electrician. He graduated from Ridgefield Park High School, Ridgefield Park, New Jersey in 1962. After being written off as a failure by teachers due to poor grades in high school, Olsen planned to join the United States Army until he was counselled to try college for several months. Through an IBEW Local 3 scholarship, Olsen attempted college, kept his grades high, and graduated *magna cum laude* with multiple degrees from Fairleigh Dickinson University. He later graduated with a PhD from the University of Virginia.

Olsen admits to little business training and believes that for companies making less than 100 million (the smaller companies as he calls them) that success is based more on "intuition, instinct and hard work." He does credit his success to his graduate science training. "Two of my start-up companies are from the fields I trained in. For instance, my first company EPITAXX (a supplier of optical detectors and receivers for fiber optic telecommunications and cable television networks) relied on my knowledge of physics and material science." Olsen likes to put his money into high-risk start-ups.

Spaceflight Details

Flown to the International Space Station (ISS) with Soyuz TMA-7 (launched October 1, 2005, docked October 3) and landed with Soyuz TMA-6 (October 10), Olsen is the third self-funded space tourist to visit the ISS, following Dennis Tito (2001) and Mark Shuttleworth (2002) (all three space tourists flew through Space Adventures, Ltd.). Gregory Olsen has made some comments indicating that he is unhappy with the "space tourist" designation. The following is from National Geography's coverage "Space Launch—Along for the Ride (2007)": "Greg: The term space tourist implies that you'll write a check and you go for a joyride. And believe me that is not the case at all. Narrator: Greg worked hard to get this far, training for two years with the Russian Space Agency."

He conducted several experiments in remote sensing and astronomy while aboard the space station. Dr. Olsen is a licensed Amateur Radio operator holding FCC callsign KC2ONX and spoke to students via ham radio from space through the ARISS project. In an informal presentation at a New Jersey high school, Dr. Olsen estimated the price of his space excursion at US$20 million.

ANOUSHEH ANSARI

Anousheh Ansari (born September 12, 1966 in Mashhad, Iran) is an engineer and the Iranian-American co-founder and chairman of Prodea Systems, Inc and a spaceflight participant with the Russian space programme. Her previous business accomplishments include serving as co-founder and CEO of Telecom Technologies, Inc. (TTI). The Ansari family is also the title sponsor of the Ansari X PRIZE. On September 18, 2006, a few days after her 40th birthday, she became the first Muslim female in space. Ansari is the fourth overall self-funded space tourist, and the first self-funded woman to fly to the International Space Station.

Early Life

Anousheh Ansari born in Mashhad, Iran. Anousheh and her parents moved to Tehran shortly afterward. Anousheh witnessed the Iranian Revolution in 1979. She emigrated to the United States in 1984 as a teenager. Apart from her native Persian, she is fluent in English and French, and acquired a working knowledge of Russian for her spaceflight experience.

She received her Bachelor of Science degree in electrical engineering and computer science at George Mason University and her master's degree at George Washington University.

After graduation, Anousheh began work at MCI, where she met her future husband, Hamid Ansari. They married in 1991. Mrs. Ansari is proud of being an Iranian Muslim and proud of her Persian roots.

Business Career

In 1993, she persuaded her husband, Hamid Ansari, and her brother-in-law, Amir Ansari, to co-found Telecom Technologies, Inc., using their savings and corporate retirement accounts, as a wave of deregulation hit the telecommunications industry. The company was acquired by Sonus Networks, Inc. in 2000 for $550 million in stock.

Since the sale, Sonus' stock has fallen from $40 a share to under $5. Ansari and eight other individuals are defendants in a shareholder suit that, among other things, accuses her of insider trading.

Spaceflight

Ansari has expressed that she does not consider herself a "space tourist", and prefers the title of "spaceflight participant". Ansari is a member of the X PRIZE Foundation's Vision Circle, as well as its Board of Trustees. Along with her brother-in-law, Amir Ansari, she made a multi-million dollar contribution to the X PRIZE foundation on May 5, 2004, the 43rd anniversary of Alan Shepard's sub-orbital spaceflight. The X PRIZE was officially renamed the *Ansari X PRIZE* in honour of their donation.

The Ansari family investment firm, also named Prodea, has announced a partnership with Space Adventures Ltd. and the Federal Space Agency of the Russian Federation (FSA) to create a fleet of suborbital spaceflight vehicles (the Space Adventures Explorer) for global commercial use.

Ansari trained as a backup for Daisuke Enomoto for a Soyuz flight to the International Space Station, through Space Adventures Ltd. On August 21, 2006, Enomoto was medically disqualified from flying the Soyuz TMA-9 mission that was due to launch the following month. The next day Ansari was elevated to the prime crew.

Asked what she hoped to achieve on her spaceflight, Ansari said, "I hope to inspire everyone—especially young people, women, and young girls all over the world, and in Middle Eastern countries that do not provide women with the same opportunities as men—to not give up their dreams and to pursue them...It may seem impossible to them at times. But I believe that they can realize their dreams if they keep it in their hearts, nurture it, and look for opportunities and make those opportunities happen." The day before her departure, she was interviewed on Iran national television for the astronomy show *Night's Sky*. The hosts wished her success and thanked her on behalf of Iranians. Ansari, in return, thanked them.

Ansari lifted off on the Soyuz TMA-9 mission with commander Mikhail Tyurin (RSA) and flight engineer Michael Lopez-Alegria (NASA) at 04:59 (UTC) on Monday September 18, 2006 from Baikonur, Kazakhstan. Ansari became the fourth (and first female) space tourist. Her contract did not allow for disclosure of the amount paid, but previous space tourists have paid in excess of US $20 million. The spacecraft docked with the International Space Station (ISS) on Wednesday September 20, 2006, at 05:21 (UTC). Ansari landed safely aboard Soyuz TMA-8 on September 29, 2006 at 01:13 UTC on the steppes of Kazakhstan (90 kilometres north of Arkalyk) with U.S. astronaut Jeffrey Williams and Russian cosmonaut Pavel Vinogradov. She was given red roses from an unidentified official, and a surprise kiss from her husband, Hamid. Rescuers moved them to Kustanai for welcome ceremony with helicopters.

During her eight day stay on board the International Space Station, Ansari agreed to perform a series of experiments on behalf of the European Space Agency. She conducted four experiments, including:

- Researching the mechanisms behind anaemia.
- How changes in muscles influence lower back pain.
- Consequences of space radiation on ISS crew members and different species of microbes that have made a home for themselves on the space station.

She also became the first person to publish a weblog from space.

Iranian Flag Controversy

Ansari intended to wear the U.S. flag on her spacesuit alongside with a politically-neutral version of the Iranian flag, i.e. the simple 3-color flag with no government-specific emblem, to honour the two countries that have contributed to her life. A few U.S.-based media wrongly speculated that she was intending to wear the version of the Iranian flag that predated the 1979 Islamic revolution in Iran.

At the insistence of the NASA and Russian officials, she did not wear the Iranian flag officially, but wore the Iranian flag colors instead and kept the Iranian flag on her official flight patch. She and her husband said that no political message was intended, despite the increasing tensions with United States and Iran relations, which had dominated world headlines in the weeks leading up to her launch. She noted that she had "plans to devote her mission to expanding a global consciousness she expected would be seeded with her first look at Earth from space."

Reactions to Ansari's Flight

Crewmates

Michael Lopez-Alegria, the Spanish-born NASA astronaut who flew on the Russian Soyuz spacecraft on the return flight with Ansari, expressed his doubts to reporters before the flight: "I'm not a big fan personally of having those guys go visit the space station because I think the space station is still a place that is under construction, and not quite operational. I don't think it's ideal."

Lopez-Alegria later stated that he was skeptical of private tourists a few years ago, but now believes it is essential to the survival of the Russian space programme which is important to the U.S. space programme: "If that's the correct solution... then not only is it good from the standpoint of supporting the Russian space programme, but it's good for us as well," he said. Ansari's presence in space "is a great dream and a great hope not just for our country but for countries all around the world."

The same Associated Press story also quoted Mikhail Tyurin describing Ansari as "very professional" and said he felt like they had worked together for a decade.

Reactions in Iran

Reactions to the flight in Ansari's native Iran were generally mixed. It was given significant coverage by state television. IRIB aired a live 1 hour interview with Anousheh in Aseman-e-Shab (Night Sky) live show. Anousheh was praised by newspapers such as *Hambastegi* and *Jam-e-Jam Daily*, which published daily columns detailing the journey. The astronomy magazine *NOJUM* also published an exclusive interview of Pouria

Nazemi with Anousheh before her trip, in which she discussed her vision for commercial spaceflight. *NOJUM* also organized and held gatherings when the ISS passed over Iran's cities. Shahram Yazdanpanah, made a special part about Anousheh's trip to space at Persian "Space Science" website and covered all the news of trip.

Interviews

On September 22, 2006, she told reporters that she has no regrets and said "I am having a wonderful time here. It's been more than what I expected, and I am enjoying every single second of it. The entire experience has been wonderful up here."

Honours and Awards

Ansari has received multiple honours, including the George Mason University Entrepreneurial Excellence Award, the George Washington University Distinguished Alumni Achievement Award, and the Ernst & Young Entrepreneur of the Year Award for the Southwest Region. While under her leadership, Telecom Technologies, Inc. earned recognition as one of Inc. magazine's 500 fastest-growing companies and one of Deloitte & Touche's Fast 500 technology companies. She was listed in Fortune magazine's "40 under 40" list in 2001 and honoured by Working Woman magazine as the winner of the 2000 National Entrepreneurial Excellence award.

The Ansari family was recently honoured with an Orbit Award by the National Space Society and Space Tourism Society for underwriting the Ansari X PRIZE.

DENNIS TITO

Dennis Anthony Tito (born August 8, 1940 in Queens, New York) is a United States engineer, multimillionaire, and most widely known as the first space tourist to pay for his own ticket. In mid-2001 he spent nearly eight days in orbit on Soyuz TM-32, the International Space Station, and Soyuz TM-31.

Career

Tito has a Bachelor of Science in Astronautics and Aeronautics from New York University, 1962 and a Master of Science in Engineering Science from Rensselaer Polytechnic Institute satellite campus in Hartford, Connecticut. He is a member of Psi Upsilon and received an honorary doctorate of engineering from Rensselaer Polytechnic Institute on 18 May 2002 and is a former scientist of the NASA Jet Propulsion Laboratory. In 1972, he founded Wilshire Associates, a leading provider of investment management, consulting and technology services in Santa Monica, California. Tito serves an international clientèle representing assets of $12.5 trillion. Wilshire relies on the field of quantitative analytics, which uses mathematical tools to analyze market risks—a methodology Tito is credited with helping to develop by applying the same techniques he used to determine a spacecraft's path at JPL. Despite a career change from aerospace engineering to investment management, Tito remained interested in space exploration.

Tito was appointed to the Los Angeles Department of Water and Power Board of Commissioners in the 1990s and led the board to support the landmark 1994 state ruling protecting Mono Lake from excessive water diversions by the city.

In 1964 Tito had a short spell playing in goal for Hartlepool United, but soon left.

Spaceflight

In a project first arranged by MirCorp, Tito was accepted by the Russian Federal Space Agency as a candidate. Tito met criticism from NASA before the launch, primarily from Daniel Goldin, at that time the Administrator of NASA, who considered him "un-American" for using the Russian Soyuz as his ticket to space. When Tito arrived at the Johnson Space Center for additional training on the American sections of the ISS, Robert Cabana, NASA manager, sent Tito and his two fellow cosmonauts home, stating "...We will not be able to begin training, because we are not willing to train with Dennis Tito."

Later, through an arrangement with space tourism company Space Adventures Ltd., Tito joined Soyuz TM-32 on April 28, 2001, spending 7 days, 22 hours, 4 minutes in space and orbiting Earth 128 times. Tito performed several scientific experiments in orbit that he said would be useful for his company and business. Tito paid a reported $20 million for his trip, although close friends suggest it was much less, as low as $12 million.

Since returning from space, he has testified at the Senate Committee on Commerce, Science & Transportation, Subcommittee on Science, Technology, and Space and the House Committee on Science, Subcommittee on Space & Aeronautics Joint Hearing on "Commercial Human Spaceflight" on July 24, 2003.

RICHARD GARRIOTT

Richard Allen Garriott (born July 4, 1961), also known as **Lord British** in *Ultima* and **General British** in *Tabula Rasa,* is a significant figure in the video game industry. He was originally a game designer and programmer, but now engages in various aspects of computer game development. On October 12, 2008, Garriott launched aboard Soyuz TMA-13 to the International Space Station as a self-funded tourist, returning 12 days later aboard Soyuz TMA-12.

Biography

Early Life

Garriott was born in Cambridge, England, and raised in Nassau Bay, Texas. He is the son of scientist Owen K. Garriott, who became an astronaut and flew with Skylab 3 and Space Shuttle mission STS-9. At Clear Creek High School, he took interest in computers and began self-directed courses in programming in which he created fantasy computer games. In the summer of 1977, Richard's parents sent him to the University of Oklahoma for a seven-week computer camp. Shortly after he arrived, some of the other boys attending the camp introduced themselves. When Garriott replied to their greeting of "Hi" with "Hello" they decided he sounded like he was from Britain, and gave him the nickname "British". Garriott uses the name to this day for his various gaming characters, including Ultima character Lord British and Tabula Rasa character General British, despite the fact that Garriott's parents moved to Texas when he was a baby and—despite his nickname and birthplace — his accent is American rather than British.

Programming Career

Richard continued programming many games, often offering them to friends for free. He produced his first published game, *Akalabeth (DND28b)*, in the summer of 1980 while working at a ComputerLand retail store. Garriott earned more than enough money from *Akalabeth* to pay to continue his education. In the fall, he entered the University of Texas at Austin, joined the school's fencing team and later joined the Society for Creative Anachronism.

In the early 1980s, Garriott developed the *Ultima* computer game series (sequels after the first were numbered, such as *Ultima II*, *Ultima III* and so on). Originally programmed for the Apple II, the first was published by California Pacific Computers, and sold in Ziploc plastic bags to interested parties. The second part was published by Sierra On-Line. By the time he developed his third installment, the games had such a large following that Garriott (along with his brother, Robert, and father and others) established Origin Systems, their own video game publisher, to handle the publishing and distribution of his title, now available on several platforms. Origin went on to become one of the most influential game developers in the history of video games.

Garriott sold Origin to Electronic Arts in September 1992. In 1999 and 2000, EA cancelled all of Origin's new development projects, including *Privateer Online*, and *Harry Potter Online*. In the midst of these events, Garriott resigned from the company and returned to the industry by forming Destination Games in April 2000 with his brother and Starr Long (the producer of *Ultima Online*). Once Garriott's non-compete agreement with EA expired a year later, Destination partnered with NCSoft where he acted as a producer and designer of MMORPGs. After it, he became the current CEO of NCSoft Austin, also known as NC Interactive.

In an open letter on the *Tabula Rasa* website posted November 11, 2008, Garriott announced his plans to leave NCSoft to pursue new interests sparked by his spaceflight experiences. Later, however, Garriott claimed the letter was forged as a means of forcing him out of his position and had no intention of leaving. On the 24th of November NCSoft announced that they planned to end the live service of *Tabula Rasa*. The servers shut down on February 28, 2009, after a period of free play from January 10th onward for existing account holders.

Spaceflight

On September 28, 2007, Space Adventures announced that Garriott would fly to the International Space Station in October 2008 as the sixth spacetourist, reportedly paying US $30 million. On October 12, 2008, Garriott became the second second-generation space traveller and the first offspring of an American astronaut to go into space, and the second person to wear the British Union flag in space. The Soyuz docked with the station on October 14, and Garriott returned to Earth on October 24 aboard the Soyuz TMA-12 with two members of Expedition 17, cosmonauts Oleg Kononenko and Sergei Volkov. Volkov is the first second-generation space traveller.

During his spaceflight, Garriott took part in several education outreach efforts. He is an Amateur Radio Operator (callsign W5KWQ), and during his stay on the International Space Station (ISS), communicated with students and other Amateur Radio operators using Amateur Radio. Garriott also transmitted photographs using the ARISS SSTV amateur radio system. Garriott also worked with the Windows on Earth project, which provides an interactive, virtual view of Earth as seen from the ISS. Garriott used Windows on Earth software to assist in the selection of locations on Earth to photograph, and the public were able to use the same online tool to track the ISS and see the view Richard was experiencing out an ISS window. Richard's photographs, along with images taken by his astronaut father Owen Garriott in 1973, will be available to the public through Windows on Earth, adding a personal element to studies of Earth and how Earth has changed over time.

Also, Tracy Hickman wrote a screenplay for Garriott, for the first science-fiction film shot in space, *Apogee of Fear*.

On October 24, Russian cosmonauts, ISS Crew 17 Sergei Volkov and Oleg Kononenko, space tourist Richard Garriott, aboard Soyuz TMA-12 capsule, landed safely ("ideal") at 9:37 a.m. (0336GMT, 07:36 Moscow time), 55 miles north of Arkalyk, Kazakhstan. They were lifted to the Kazakhstan Baikonur space center by helicopter, and then flew to Zvezdny Gorodok (Star City), Moscow Region.

On June 3, 2009, the New York Daily News announced that Garriott would officiate at the first wedding to be held in zero gravity. The wedding took place in a specially modified Boeing 727-200 aircraft, G-Force One, operated by Zero Gravity Corp, or ZERO-G, a company offering weightless flight experiences, of which he is the co-founder.

Other Accomplishments and Interests

Garriott acted as corner man for professional boxer and friend Jesús Chávez in his first title defense against Erik Morales in 2004.

He is also an avid magician and magic collector, and appeared on the cover of the January 2008 *MUM*, the magazine of the Society of American Magicians.

Garriott built a "haunted house"/museum at his residence called Britannia Manor in Austin, Texas. He also promotes private spaceflight as vice-chairman of the board of directors for Space Adventures and as a trustee of the XPrize.

Ham radio callsign: W5KWQ

When aboard the International Space Station in October 2008 he delighted many amateur radio operators and school children with contacts.

Awards

Garriott became the ninth inductee into the Academy of Interactive Arts and Sciences' Hall of Fame in 2006.

Video Game Works

Game Name	First Released	System Name(s)	Garriott's Role(s)
Akalabeth: World of Doom	1980	Apple II & DOS	Game Designer & Programmer
Ultima I: The First Age of Darkness	1980	Apple II, Atari 8 bit systems, Commodore 64, DOS, FM Towns & MSX	Original Conceptor, Programmer & Graphic Artist
Ultima II: The Revenge of the Enchantress	1982	Apple II, Atari 8 bit systems, Commodore 64, DOS & FM Towns	Programmer
Ultima III: Exodus	1983	Apple II, Amiga, Atari 8 bit systems, Commodore 64, DOS, FM Towns, Mac OS & NES	Project Director
Ultima IV: Quest of the Avatar	1985	Apple II, Amiga, Atari 8 bit systems, Atari ST, Commodore 64, DOS, FM Towns, MSX, NES, Sega Master System	Project Director
Autoduel	1985	Apple II, Amiga, Atari 8 bit systems, Atari ST, Commodore 64 & DOS	Programmer & Designer
Ultima V: Warriors of Destiny	1988	Apple II, Amiga, Atari ST, Commodore 64, DOS, FM Towns & NES	Designer, Writer & Programmer
Omega	1989	Apple II, Amiga, Atari ST, Commodore 64 & DOS	Designer
Ultima VI: The False Prophet	1990	DOS, Amiga, Atari ST, Commodore 64, FM Towns, SNES	Designer, Producer, Sound Effect Worker, Writer & Voice Actor
Worlds of Ultima: The Savage Empire	1990	DOS & SNES	Executive Producer
Ultima: Worlds of Adventure 2: Martian Dreams	1991	DOS	Creative Director
Ultima: Runes of Virtue	1991	Game Boy	Creative Director
Ultima Underworld: The Stygian Abyss	1992	DOS, FM Towns & PlayStation	Director & Voice Actor
Ultima VII: The Black Gate	1992	DOS & SNES	Director & Producer
Ultima VII: The Forge of Virtue	1993	DOS	Creative Assistance & Producer

Ultima VII Part Two: Serpent Isle	1993	DOS	Creative Director & Audio Team Member
Ultima VII Part Two: The Silver Seed	1993	DOS	Director & Voice Actor
Ultima Underworld II: Labyrinth of Worlds	1993	DOS, FM Towns & NEC PC-9801	Director & Voice Actor
Ultima VIII: Pagan	1994	DOS	Producer
Ultima: Runes of Virtue II	1994	Game Boy	Creative Director & Additional Design
Ultima VIII: The Lost Vale Expansion Pack	Cancelled	DOS	Producer
Bioforge	1995	DOS	Executive Producer
Ultima Online	1997	Windows	Producer
Ultima Online: The Second Age	1998	Windows	Executive Designer
Lineage	1998	Windows & Mac OS X	Executive Producer
Ultima IX: Ascension	1999	Windows	Director
Lineage II: The Chaotic Chronicle	2003	Windows	Executive Producer
City of Heroes	2004	Windows	Executive Producer
City of Villains	2005	Windows	Executive Management
Tabula Rasa	Nov. 2 2007	Windows	Executive Producer

JAMES BENSON

James William Benson (1945—October 10, 2008), also known as **Jim Benson**, was the founder of SpaceDev, a commercial satellite and satellite component development company, and **Benson Space Company**, a civilian spaceflight venture focused on commercial space tourism.

Biography

Benson spent thirty years associated with the computer field, spanning the era from the introduction of modern mainframe computers, to the dominance of the computer industry by microcomputers. Benson invented modern full text computer indexing and searching in 1984, and exploited the new field through companies he founded: Compusearch and ImageFast of McLean, Virginia.

Benson was a founding member of the Personal Spaceflight Federation. Benson was recently appointed to the Board of Directors of the California Space Authority, was named one of the "50 People to Watch in 2005" by San Diego magazine, and was named "Alumnus of the Year" by the University of Missouri at Kansas City. He founded the non-profit Space Development Institute, and introduced the Benson Prize for Amateur Discovery of Near Earth Objects. He was Vice-Chairman and private sector representative on NASA's national Space Grant Review Panel. Benson received a Bachelor of Science degree in Geology from the University of Missouri at Kansas City, in his hometown.

SpaceDev

After a successful career as a computer industry entrepreneur, Benson decided to take on the challenge of starting a space commercialization venture. It combined his lifelong interests in science, technology and astronomy with his successful business experience.

Benson started the trend of successful high tech entrepreneurs moving into the space development arena, by incorporating SpaceDev, Inc. as a publicly owned space exploration and development company in 1997.

Benson and SpaceDev worked to develop the world's first private sector enterprise to profitably explore and develop space beyond earth orbit. SpaceDev's mission is to help "make space happen" for all of humanity, through the development of a comprehensive private space programme, by delivering affordable and practical space technologies, products and solutions to SpaceDev's government and commercial customers, while creating value for SpaceDev stockholders.

SpaceDev acquired the former Integrated Space Systems, a space systems engineering firm, in 1998.

SpaceDev acquired the intellectual property of American Rocket Company in 1999 after AMROC's 1996 bankruptcy. The AMROC-derived hybrid rocket motors were used in several SpaceDev projects that followed.

SpaceDev started developing the science mission CHIPSat for the University of California, Berkeley in 1999. In 2003, SpaceDev launched the United States' smallest, low-cost, high performance satellite named CHIPSat for NASA. CHIPSat is a suitcase-size science microsatellite that is also the first U.S. mission to use only TCP/IP Internet communications for end-to-end satellite operations control, becoming the first satellite whose mission control and operations center is any laptop computer located anywhere in the world. Although the nominal mission duration was one year, the satellite operated successfully for almost five years when mission was terminated in April 2008.

In 2004, SpaceDev's hybrid rocket motors were used by Burt Rutan's SpaceShipOne to win the $10 million Ansari X Prize.

During his 10 years with the company, Benson served as founder, chairman, chief executive officer and chief technology officer of SpaceDev. He stepped down on September 28, 2006 to announce that he was starting a new venture called Benson Space Company.

Benson Space Company

Jim Benson announced on September 28, 2006 that he had launched an ambitious new venture focused on commercial space tourism, Benson Space Company.

Benson Space intends to be first to market in the emerging multi-billion dollar space tourism or personal spaceflight industry, with the safest and lowest cost astronaut-making suborbital missions.

"I am dedicated to opening space for all of humanity and, with SpaceDev well-managed and growing, I plan to spend the next several years creating the possibility that anyone who wants to go to space will be able to, safely and affordably," said Benson. SpaceDev owns many of the patents and intellectual property rights associated with hybrid rocket motors used for safe human spaceflight. Under Benson's guidance, SpaceDev developed critical hybrid rocket motor technology and furnished all of the rocket motors for Paul Allen's SpaceShipOne, the craft that earned the $10 million Ansari X Prize in 2004.

Benson Space has completed its first round of financing and submitted a request for proposal to SpaceDev for the design and development of its SpaceDev Dream Chaser spaceships. BSC expects to be one of SpaceDev's largest customers, purchasing multiple spaceships and safe hybrid rocket motors for use in personal spaceflight.

Death

SpaceDev announced on October 10, 2008, that James Benson had died earlier that day. He had been diagnosed with Glioblastoma multiforme, a type of brain tumour, in 2007.

TIMELINE OF SPACE TRAVEL BY NATIONALITY

Since the first human spaceflight by the Soviet Union, citizens of 38 countries have flown in space. For each nationality, the launch date of the first mission is listed. The list is based on the nationality of the person at the time of the spaceflight. Only three of the thirty-eight "first flyers" have been women (Sharman in 1991, Ansari in 2006, Yi in 2008).

Note: All dates given are UTC. Suborbital flights are *Cursive.*

	Country	Name	Flight	Date (UTC)
1960s				
1	Soviet Union[1, 2]	Yuri Gagarin	Vostok 1	12 April 1961
2	United States[3]	Alan Shepard	MR-3	5 May 1961
1970s				
3	Czechoslovakia[4]	Vladimír Remek	Soyuz 28	2 March 1978
4	Poland	Mirosław Hermaszewski	Soyuz 30	27 June 1978
5	East Germany[5]	Sigmund Jähn	Soyuz 31	26 August 1978

6	Bulgaria	Georgi Ivanov	Soyuz 33	10 April 1979
1980s				
7	Hungary	Bertalan Farkas	Soyuz 36	26 May 1980
8	Vietnam	Ph?m Tuân	Soyuz 37	23 July 1980
9	Cuba	Arnaldo Tamayo Méndez	Soyuz 38	18 September 1980
10	Mongolia	Jügderdemidiin Gürragchaa	Soyuz 39	22 March 1981
11	Romania	Dumitru Prunariu	Soyuz 40	14 May 1981
12	France	Jean-Loup Chrétien	Soyuz T-6	24 June 1982
13	West Germany[5]	Ulf Merbold	STS-9	28 November 1983
14	India	Rakesh Sharma	Soyuz T-11	3 April 1984
15	Canada	Marc Garneau	STS-41-G	5 October 1984
16	Saudi Arabia	Salman al-Saud	STS-51-G	17 June 1985
17	Netherlands	Wubbo Ockels	STS-61-A	30 October 1985
18	Mexico	Rodolfo Neri Vela	STS-61-B	26 November 1985
19	Syria	Muhammed Faris	Soyuz TM-3	22 July 1987
20	Afghanistan	Abdul Ahad Mohmand	Soyuz TM-6	29 August 1988
1990s				
21	Japan	Toyohiro Akiyama	Soyuz TM-11	2 December 1990
22	United Kingdom	Helen Sharman	Soyuz TM-12	18 May 1991
23	Austria	Franz Viehböck	Soyuz TM-13	2 October 1991
24	Russia[1]	Alexandr Kaleri, Alexandr Viktorenko	Soyuz TM-14	17 March 1992
25	Belgium	Dirk Frimout	STS-45	24 March 1992
26	Italy	Franco Malerba	STS-46	31 July 1992
27	Switzerland	Claude Nicollier	STS-46	31 July 1992
28	Ukraine	Leonid Kadenyuk	STS-87	19 November 1997
29	Spain	Pedro Duque	STS-95	29 October 1998
30	Slovakia[4]	Ivan Bella	Soyuz TM-29	20 February 1999

2000s				
31	South Africa	Mark Shuttleworth	Soyuz TM-34	25 April 2002
32	Israel[6]	Ilan Ramon	STS-107	16 January 2003
33	People's Republic of China	Yang Liwei	Shenzhou 5	15 October 2003
34	Brazil	Marcos Pontes	Soyuz TMA-8	30 March 2006
35	Iran[7]	Anousheh Ansari	Soyuz TMA-9	18 September 2006
36	Sweden	Christer Fuglesang	STS-116	10 December 2006
37	Malaysia	Sheikh Muszaphar Shukor	Soyuz TMA-11	10 October 2007
38	South Korea	Yi So-yeon	Soyuz TMA-12	8 April 2008

Notes

1. This person flew as a commercial non-governmental space tourist.
2. The first cosmonaut Yuri Gagarin had citizenship of both the USSR and the Russian SFSR according the Constitution of the USSR. In 1991, the Soviet Union broke up into Armenia, Azerbaijan, Belarus, Estonia, Georgia, Kazakhstan, Kyrgyzstan, Latvia, Lithuania, Moldova, Russia, Tajikistan, Turkmenistan, Ukraine, and Uzbekistan. At the time of the breakup, Sergei Krikalev and Alexander Volkov were orbiting Earth on Mir, having gone into orbit as Soviet citizens. They returned to Earth as Russian citizens. Kaleri and Viktorenko were the first Russians to go into orbit after the Soviet breakup.
3. Under Fédération Aéronautique Internationale rules, the Vostok missions are not true spaceflights, as cosmonauts did not land with the spacecraft but ejected and landed separately. The first Soviet mission that did fulfil this requirement was Voskhod 1. (Reference: "FAI Astronautic Records Commission—Sporting Code Section 8" (PDF). *Fédération Aéronautique Internationale.* http://www.fai.org/sporting_code/sc08.pdf. Retrieved 2006-04-09.) However, despite this issue, the FAI does recognize Yuri Gagarin as the first person to complete a spaceflight. (Reference: "FAI Award: The Yuri A. Gagarin Gold Medal". *Fédération Aéronautique Internationale.* http://www.fai.org/awards/award.asp?id=9. Retrieved 2007-10-10.)
4. Shepard's spaceflight was suborbital. The first American to go into orbit was John Glenn, on 20 February 1962.
5. In 1993, Czechoslovakia broke up into the Czech Republic and Slovakia.
6. In 1978, both Jähn himself and the socialist authorities of the GDR (a.k.a. East Germany) pronounced him the "first German in space", rather than the first "GDR citizen", as usual. In 1990, the states of the GDR acceded to Federal Republic of Germany (previously a.k.a. West Germany). On 22 January 1992,

Ulf Merbold again travelled into space, now representing the enlarged Germany. Jähn is nevertheless still considered the first German in space in united Germany today.

7. Ilan Ramon was the first Israeli to go into space but he died during reentry. This was not a complete spaceflight under FAI rules.
8. Although recognized as an Iranian citizen by Iranian law, Ansari is also an American citizen and was prohibited from wearing Iranian state symbols by both the United States and Russian governments.

Other Claims

The above list uses the nationality at the time of launch. Lists with differing criteria might include the following people:

- **Pavel Popovich,** first launched 12 August 1962, was the first Ukrainian-born man in space. At the time, Ukraine was a part of the Union of Soviet Socialist Republics.
- **Vladimir Shatalov,** first launched 14 January 1969, was the first Kazakh-born man in space. At the time, Kazakhstan was a part of the Union of Soviet Socialist Republics.
- **Bill Pogue,** first launched 16 November 1973, as an inductee to the 5 Civilized Tribes Hall of Fame can lay claim to being the first Native American in space.
- **Pyotr Klimuk,** first launched 18 December 1973, was the first Belorussian-born man in space. At the time, Belarus was a part of the Union of Soviet Socialist Republics.
- **Vladimir Dzhanibekov,** first launched 16 March 1978, was the first Uzbek-born man in space. At the time, Uzbekistan was a part of the Union of Soviet Socialist Republics.
- **Paul D. Scully-Power,** first launched 5 October 1984, was born in Australia, but was an American citizen when he went into space.
- **Taylor Gun-Jin Wang,** first launched 29 April 1985, was born in China to Chinese parents, but was an American citizen when he went into space.
- **Lodewijk van den Berg,** first launched 29 April 1985, was born in The Netherlands, but was an American citizen when he went into space.
- **Patrick Baudry,** first launched 17 June 1985, was born in French Cameroun (now part of Cameroon), but was a French citizen when he went into space.
- **Shannon Lucid,** first launched 17 June 1985, was born in China to American parents of European descent, and was an American citizen when she went into space.
- **Franklin Chang-Diaz,** first launched 12 January 1986, was born in Costa Rica, but was an American citizen when he went into space.
- **Musa Manarov,** first launched 21 December 1987, was the first Azerbaijan-born man in space. At the time, Azerbaijan was a part of the Union of Soviet Socialist Republics.

- **Anatoly Solovyev,** first launched 7 June 1988, was the first Latvian-born man in space. At the time, Latvia was a part of the Union of Soviet Socialist Republics.
- **Toktar Aubakirov,** first launched 2 October 1991, was the first ethnic Kazakh to go into space.
- **Andy Thomas,** first launched 19 May 1996, was born in Australia, but was an American citizen when he went into space.
- **Carlos I. Noriega,** first launched 15 May 1997, was born in Peru, but was an American citizen when he went into space.
- **Bjarni Tryggvason,** first launched 7 August 1997, was born in Iceland, but was a Canadian citizen when he went into space.
- **Salizhan Sharipov,** first launched 22 January 1998, was born in Kyrgyzstan (then the Kirghiz SSR), but was a Russian citizen when he went into space. Sharipov is of Uzbek ancestry.
- **Philippe Perrin,** first launched 5 June 2002, was born in Morocco, but was a French citizen when he went into space.
- **John Herrington,** an American citizen first launched 24 November 2002, is the first *tribal registered* Native American in space (Chickasaw).
- **Fyodor Yurchikhin,** first launched 7 October 2002, was born in Georgia (then the Georgian SSR). He was a Russian citizen at the time he went into space and is of Pontian Greek descent.

7

Select Global Projects Related to Low-Cost Access to Space for Promoting Space Tourism

TIER ONE

Tier One is Scaled Composites' programme of suborbital human spaceflight using the reusable spacecraft SpaceShipOne and its launcher White Knight. The craft are designed by Burt Rutan, and the project is funded 20 million US Dollars by Paul Allen. In 2004 it made the first privately funded human spaceflight and won the 10 million US Dollars Ansari X Prize for the first non-governmental reusable manned spacecraft.

The objective of the project is to develop technology for low-cost routine access to space. Tier One is not itself intended to carry paying passengers, but it is envisioned that there will be commercial spinoffs, initially in space tourism. The company Mojave Aerospace Ventures was formed to manage commercial exploitation of the technology. A deal with Virgin Galactic could see routine space tourism, using a spacecraft based on Tier One technology, starting as soon as 2009.

Design

The design concept is to air launch a three-person piloted spacecraft which climbs to slightly above 100 km (62 mi) altitude using a hybrid rocket motor and then glides to the ground and lands horizontally. Scaled Composites lists the following components of the programme:

- launch aircraft (White Knight)
- three-seater human-rated spacecraft (SpaceShipOne)
- hybrid rocket propulsion system
- mobile propulsion test facility
- flight simulator
- inertial-nav flight director
- mobile mission control center
- spacecraft systems
- pilot training programme
- flight test programme

Spacecraft

Tier One's spacecraft, Scaled Composites model **316**, known as **SpaceShipOne**, is a spaceplane designed to:

- carry three humans (one of them a pilot) in a sea-level pressurized cabin
- be propelled by rocket from an altitude of 15 km (9.3 mi) in excess of 100 km (62 mi)
- reenter atmosphere and shed kinetic energy in an aerodynamically stable configuration
- glide transonically and subsonically
- land horizontally on a standard runway

The fuselage is cigar-shaped, with an overall diameter of about 1.5 km (0.93 mi). The main structure is of a graphite/epoxy composite material. From front to back, it contains the crew cabin, oxidizer tank, fuel casing, and rocket nozzle. The craft has short, wide wings, with a span of 5 km (3.1 mi) and a chord of 3 km (1.9 mi). There are large vertical tailbooms mounted on the end of each wing, with horizontal stabilisers protruding from the tailbooms. It has gear for horizontal landings.

The overall mass of the fully-fuelled craft is 3,600 kg (7,900 lb), of which approximately 270 kg (600 lb) is fuel and 1,400 kg (3,100 lb) is oxidizer. Thus the dry mass is 2000 kg.

Originally the nozzle protruded from the back, but this turned out to be aerodynamically disadvantageous. In June 2004, between flights 14P and 15P, a fairing was added, smoothly extending the fuselage shape to meet the flared end of the nozzle. On flight 15P the new fairing overheated, due to being black on the inside and facing a hot, black nozzle. The fairing softened, and the lower part crumpled inwards during boost. Following that flight the interior of the fairing was painted white, and some small stiffening ribs were added.

The craft has a single unsteerable and unthrottleable hybrid rocket motor, a cold gas reaction control system, and aerodynamic control surfaces. All can be controlled manually.

The reaction control system is the only way to control spacecraft attitude outside the atmosphere. It consists of three sets of thrusters: there are thrusters at each wingtip to control roll, at the top and bottom of the nose to control pitch, and at the sides of the fuselage to control yaw. All thrusters have redundant backups, so there are twelve thrusters in all.

The aerodynamic control surfaces are designed to operate in two distinct flight regimes, subsonic and supersonic. The supersonic flight regime is of primary interest during the boost phase of a flight, and the subsonic mode when gliding. There are separate upper and lower rudders, and elevons. These are controlled using aviation-style stick and pedals. In supersonic mode the trim tabs are controlled electrically, whereas the subsonic mode uses mechanical cable-and-rod linkage.

The wings can be pneumatically tilted forwards into an aerodynamically-stable high-drag "feathered" shape. This removes most of the need to actively control attitude during the early part of reentry: Scaled Composites refer to this as "care-free reentry". One of the early test flights actually performed re-entry inverted, demonstrating the flexibility and inherent stability of Burt Rutan's "shuttlecock" design.

This feathered reentry mode is inherently far safer than the behaviour at similar speeds of the only comparable craft previously built, the Space Shuttle. The Shuttle undergoes enormous aerodynamic stresses and must be precisely steered in order to remain in a stable glide. (Although this is an interesting comparison of behaviour, it is not an entirely fair comparison of design concepts: the Shuttle starts reentry at much higher speed than SpaceShipOne and so has some very different requirements.)

An early design called for a permanently shuttlecock-like shape, with a ring of feather-like stabilising fins. This would have made the spacecraft incapable of landing independently, requiring mid-air retrieval. This was deemed too risky, and the hybrid final design manages to incorporate the feathering capability into a craft that can land in a conventional manner. The tiltable rear sections of the wings and the tailbooms are collectively referred to as "the feather".

The landing gear consists of two widely-separated main wheels and a nose skid. These are deployed using springs, assisted by gravity. Once deployed, they cannot be retracted inflight.

The spacecraft is incapable of independent takeoff from the ground. It requires a launch aircraft to carry it to launch altitude for an air launch.

The parts of the craft that experience the greatest heating, such as the leading edges of the wings, have about 6.5 kg (14 lb) of ablative thermal protection material applied. The main ingredient of this material was accidentally leaked to *Air and Space.* If it flew with no thermal protection, the spacecraft would survive reentry but would be damaged.

There is an acknowledged "known deficiency" with the spacecraft's aerodynamic design that makes it susceptible to roll excursions. This has been seen on SpaceShipOne flight 15P where wind shear caused a large roll immediately after ignition, and SpaceShipOne flight 16P where circumstances not yet fully understood caused multiple rapid rolls. This flaw is not considered dangerous, but in both of these flights led to the achievement of a much lower altitude than expected. The details of the flaw are not public.

Navigation

The core of the spacecraft avionics is the **System Navigation Unit** (**SNU**). Together with the **Flight Director Display** (**FDD**), it comprises the **Flight Navigation Unit**. The unit was developed jointly by Fundamental Technology Systems and Scaled Composites.

The SNU is a GPS-based inertial navigation system, which processes spacecraft sensor data and subsystem health data. It downlinks telemetry data by radio to mission control.

The FDD display data from the SNU on a colour LCD. It has several distinct display modes for different phases of flight, including the boost phase, coast, reentry, and gliding. The FDD is particularly important to the pilot during the boost and coast phase in order to "turn the corner" and null rates caused by asymmetric thrust. A mix of commercial and bespoke software is used in the FDD.

Cabin

The spacecraft cabin, designed to hold three humans, is shaped as a short cylinder, diameter 1.5 km (0.93 mi), with a pointed forward end. The pilot sits towards the front, and two passengers can be seated behind.

The cabin is pressurized, maintaining a sea level breathable atmosphere. Oxygen is introduced to the cabin from a bottle, and carbon dioxide and water vapour are removed by absorbers. The occupants do not wear spacesuits or breathing masks, because the cabin has been designed to maintain pressure in the face of faults: all windows and seals are doubled.

The cabin has sixteen round double-pane windows, positioned to provide a view of the horizon at all stages of flight. The windows are small compared to the gaps between them, but there are sufficiently many for human occupants to patch together a moderately good view.

The nose section can be removed, and there is also a hatch below the rear windows on the left side. Crew ingress and egress is possible by either route.

Launch Aircraft

Tier One's launch aircraft, Scaled Composites model **318**, known as **White Knight**, is designed to take off and land horizontally and attain an altitude of about 15 km, all while carrying the Tier One spacecraft in a parasite aircraft configuration. Its propulsion is by twin turbojets: afterburning J-85-GE-5 engines, rated at 15.6 kN thrust each.

It has the same cabin, avionics, and trim system as SpaceShipOne. This means that it can flight-qualify almost all components of SpaceShipOne. It also has a high thrust-to-weight ratio and large speed brakes. These features combined allow it to be used as a high-fidelity moving platform flight simulator for SpaceShipOne. White Knight is also equipped with a trim system which (when activated) causes it to have the same glide profile as SpaceShipOne; this allows the pilots to practice for landing SpaceShipOne. The same pilots fly White Knight as fly SpaceShipOne.

The aircraft's distinctive shape features long, thin wings, in a flattened "W" shape, with a wingspan of 25 km (16 mi), dual tailplanes, and four wheels (front and rear at each side). The rear wheels retract, but the front ones, which are steerable, are permanently deployed, with small fairings, referred to as "spats", in front. Another way to look at the overall shape is as two conventional planes, with very thin fuselages, side-by-side and joined together at their wingtips, with the cockpit and engines mounted at the point of joining.

Although White Knight was developed for certain roles in the Tier One programme, it is a very capable aircraft in its own right. Scaled Composites describe it as a "high-altitude research aircraft".

Hybrid Rocket Motor

Tier One uses a hybrid rocket motor supplied by SpaceDev, with solid hydroxyl-terminated polybutadiene (HTPB, or rubber) fuel and liquid nitrous oxide oxidiser. It generates 88 kN thrust, and can burn for about 87 s.

The physical layout of the engine is novel. The oxidiser tank is a primary structural component, and is the only part of the engine that is structurally connected to the spacecraft: the tank is in fact an integral part of the spacecraft fuselage. The tank is a short cylinder of diameter approximately 1.5 km (0.93 mi), with domed ends, and is the forwardmost part of the engine. The fuel casing is a narrow cylinder cantilevered to the tank, pointing backwards. The cantilevered design means that a variety of motor sizes can be accommodated without changing the interface or other components. The nozzle is a simple extension of the fuel casing; the casing and nozzle are actually a single component, referred to as the **CTN** (**c**ase, **t**hroat, and **n**ozzle). Burt Rutan has applied for a patent on this engine configuration.

There is considerable use of composite materials in the engine design. The oxidiser tank consists of a composite liner with graphite/epoxy over-wrap and titanium interface flanges. The CTN uses a high-temperature composite insulator with a graphite/epoxy structure. Incorporating the solid fuel (and hence the main part of the engine) and the ablative nozzle into this single bonded component minimizes the possible leak paths.

The oxidiser tank and CTN are bolted together at the main valve bulkhead, which is integrated into the tank. There are O-rings at the interface to prevent leakage; this is the main potential leak path in the engine. The ignition system, main control valve, and injector are mounted on the valve bulkhead, inside the tank. Slosh baffles are also mounted on this bulkhead. Because the oxidiser is stored under pressure, no pump is required.

The tank liner and the fuel casing are built in-house by Scaled Composites. The tank over-wrap is supplied by Thiokol. The ablative nozzle is supplied by AAE Aerospace. The oxidiser fill, vent, and dump system is supplied by Environmental Aeroscience Corporation. The remaining components—the ignition system, main control valve, injector, tank bulkheads, electronic controls, and solid fuel casting—are supplied by SpaceDev.

The CTN must be replaced between firings. This is the only part of the craft, other than the fuel and oxidiser themselves, that must be replaced.

The solid fuel is cast with four holes. This has the disadvantage that it is possible for chunks of fuel between the holes to become detached during a burn and obstruct the flow of oxidiser and exhaust. Such situations tend to rapidly self-correct.

The oxidiser tank is filled and vented through its forward bulkhead, on the opposite side of the tank from the fuel and the rest of the engine. This improves safety. It is filled to a pressure of 4.8 MPa at room temperature.

The nozzle has an expansion ratio of 25:1, which is optimised for the upper part of the atmosphere. A different nozzle, with an expansion ratio of 10:1, is used for test firing on the ground. The nozzles are black on the outside, but for aerodynamic testing, red dummy nozzles are used instead.

The rocket is not throttleable. Once lit, the burn can be aborted, but the power output cannot otherwise be controlled. The thrust in fact varies for two reasons. Firstly, as the pressure in the oxidiser tank decreases, the flow rate reduces, reducing thrust. Secondly, in the late stages of a burn the oxidiser tank contains a mixture of liquid and gaseous oxidiser, and the power output of the engine varies greatly depending on whether it's using liquid or gaseous oxidiser at a particular moment. (The liquid, being far denser, allows a greater burn rate.)

Both the fuel and oxidiser can be stored without special precautions, and they do not burn when brought together without a significant source of heat. This makes the rocket far safer than conventional liquid or solid rockets. It is also relatively nonpolluting: the combustion products are water vapour, carbon dioxide, hydrogen, nitrogen, and some carbon monoxide.

The engine was upgraded in September 2004, between flights 15P and 16P. The upgrade increased the oxidiser tank size, to provide greater thrust in the early part of the burn, allow a longer burn, and delay the onset of the variable thrust phase at the end of the burn. Prior to the upgrade the engine generated 76 kN thrust and could burn for 76 s. After the upgrade it was capable of 88 kN thrust and an 87 s burn.

Flight Profile

SpaceShipOne takes off from the ground, attached to White Knight in a parasite configuration, and under White Knight's power. The combination of SpaceShipOne and White Knight can take off, land, and fly under jet power to high altitude. A captive carry flight is one where the two craft land together without launching SpaceShipOne; this is one of the main abort modes available.

For launch, the combined craft flies to an altitude of around 14 km, which takes about an hour. SpaceShipOne is then drop-released, and briefly glides unpowered. Rocket ignition may take place immediately, or may be delayed. If the rocket is never lit then SpaceShipOne can glide down to the ground. This is another major abort mode, in addition to being flown deliberately in glide tests.

The rocket engine is ignited while the spacecraft is gliding. Once under power, it is raised into a 65° climb, which is further steepened in the higher part of the trajectory. The maximum possible burn duration is about 80 s. The maximum possible acceleration is about 4 g.

By the end of the burn the craft is flying upwards at some multiple of the speed of sound, up to about 900 m/s and Mach 3.5, and it continues to coast upwards unpowered (i.e. ballistically). If the burn was long enough then it will exceed an altitude of 100 km, at which height the atmosphere presents no appreciable resistance, and the craft experiences free fall for a few minutes.

While at apogee the wings are reconfigured into high-drag mode. As the craft falls back it achieves high speeds comparable to those achieved on the way up; when it subsequently reenters the atmosphere it decelerates violently, up to about 5 g. At some altitude between 10 km and 20 km it reconfigures into low-drag glider mode, and glides down to a landing in about 20 minutes.

White Knight takes longer to descend, and typically lands a few minutes after SpaceShipOne.

Mission Control

In addition to an office-based mission control, Tier One has a mobile mission control center. This is relatively small, built into a large road-going truck. It bears the Scaled Composites logo, but no other overt indication of its link to Tier One. The vehicle performs a combination of support functions:

- telemetry monitoring and recording

- telecommunications
- auxiliary environment control for White Knight and SpaceShipOne

This control center is used to support both rocket motor ground tests and all flight tests of White Knight and SpaceShipOne. Its primary function is to monitor and record test data, and to this end it is equipped with computers and radio communication gear. SpaceShipOne's avionics displays are duplicated in mission control. Telemetry data is received on a **Data Reduction System** (**DRS**), which automatically directs radio antennas to point at the craft being monitored. The telemetry system has a range of about 280 km.

The control center is equipped to communicate with Scaled Composites' offices, as well as the aircraft and spacecraft.

The control center maintains a temperature-controlled atmosphere for its staff, and can be hooked up to provide temperature control for the White Knight and SpaceShipOne cabins. The physical structure of mission control also provides easier access to the White Knight cabin.

Nitrous Oxide Delivery

Unlike the solid fuel, the nitrous oxide oxidiser is handled as a bulk commodity and pumped into the spacecraft's oxidiser tank in the field. Tier One therefore has a mobile delivery system for nitrous oxide, which they call **MONODS** (**mo**bile **n**itrous **o**xide **d**elivery **s**ystem).

MONODS is built on an open trailer, which can be carried by road in conventional manner. It consists principally of a 6.5 cubic metre tank, a temperature control unit, and a generator to power the temperature control unit. The nitrous oxide is stored at room temperature, at a pressure of 4.8 MPa.

MONODS is refilled from a commercial supplier, which uses 50 cubic metre tankers and delivers the nitrous oxide at about –17°C (0°F) and 2.0 MPa. MONODS heats the nitrous oxide to room temperature, increasing its pressure.

Propulsion Testing

Tier One has a mobile thrust test stand, known as the **Test Stand Trailer** (**TST**). The advantage of making it mobile is that all the mounting and instrumentation work can be done in the hangar, so that at the test site all that needs to be done is to fill the oxidiser tank (from MONODS) and conduct the firing.

The test stand replicates the essential structural components of the spacecraft. It has an oxidiser tank and associated fittings identical to the one used in flight. This means that the motor test also automatically performs appropriate vibration, stress, and heat tests of the spacecraft structure. The crew cabin, however, is not replicated.

For ground-based thrust tests, a rocket nozzle with an expansion ratio of 10:1 is used, differing from the 25:1 nozzle used at altitude during actual flight.

The test stand is instrumented to record not only thrust but also side force and temperature and strain experienced by components. Data is recorded on a computer in a bunker at the test site. The data acquisition computer is remotely controlled from mission control.

Flight Simulator

The SpaceShipOne flight simulator consists of a simulator programme and a cockpit.

The flight simulator programme aims to accurately simulate SpaceShipOne's behaviour under any circumstances and in all phases of flight. Rather than having a model of SpaceShipOne's overall flight behaviour, it uses computational fluid dynamics to model the air around the craft. It calculates the aerodynamic and other forces operating on the craft, taking into account the positions of its control surfaces. This simulation is based on the computer modelling that was used during the design process and refined using data from flight tests. This yields a highly accurate image of craft behaviour, even in unanticipated modes of flight. (This is one of the first modern aircraft to be designed without wind tunnel testing.)

The cockpit replica is on a static base, and so cannot accurately reproduce the equilibrioceptive and accelerative aspects of flight. However, White Knight is equipped to operate as a high-fidelity moving-base simulator; see White Knight's section above. The simulator cockpit is an accurate copy of the SpaceShipOne cabin, including its avionics. It is the system of pilot plus avionics, not just the pilot, that is being simulated to. The flight simulator programme drives the sensor inputs that are used by the avionics, and also drives twelve display computers which use commercial graphics software to generate high-resolution images of the outside view for the pilot. These views appear on eleven monitors and one projector screen. Stick force feedback is not simulated in real time.

Ground-based flight simulation is not only used for pilot training. It is also used to train ground crew, develop procedures, and test the avionics software and hardware.

History and Status

According to Scaled Composites, the concept for the programme originated in April 1996, preliminary development began in 1999, and full development began in April 2001. It was initially kept secret, even after White Knight first flew on August 1, 2002. The programme was announced to the public on April 18, 2003, when the programme was ready to flight-test SpaceShipOne. Its first flight test, SpaceShipOne flight 01C, took place on May 20, 2003.

After months of glide tests, the first powered flight, SpaceShipOne flight 11P, was made on December 17, 2003. Further powered tests followed, reaching increasing altitudes, culminating on June 21, 2004 with the first privately funded human spaceflight, SpaceShipOne flight 15P. Ansari X Prize competitive flights followed. SpaceShipOne flight 16P on September 29, 2004 and SpaceShipOne flight 17P on October 4, 2004 were successful competitive flights, winning the X Prize.

The programme will continue making test flights, to develop the technology further, in support of the development of successor spacecraft such as the Virgin SpaceShip. The programme has ruled out carrying scientific payloads, despite several requests.

Specifications (SpaceShipOne)

General Characteristics

- **Crew:** one pilot
- **Length:** 5 km (3.1 mi)
- **Wingspan:** 5 km (3.1 mi)
- **Core diameter:** 1.52 km (0.94 mi)
- **Wing area:** 15 m^2 (49.2 ft^2)
- **Empty:** 1,200 kg (2,600 lb)
- **Loaded:** 3,600 kg (7,900 lb)
- **Powerplant:** 1x N2O/HTPB SpaceDev Hybrid Solid rocket engine 7,500 kgf (73.5 kN) thrust. Isp: 250 s (2.45 kN·s/kg) burn time: 87 seconds

Performance

- **Maximum speed:** Mach 3.09 (3,518 km/h) (2,352 mph)
- **Range:** 65 km (40.4 mi)
- **Service ceiling:** 112,000 m (367,454 ft)
- **Rate of climb:** 25,000 m/min (82, 021 ft/min)
- **Wing loading:** 240 kg/m^2
- **Thrust-to-Weight:** 20 N/kg

Funding

The costs of development, construction, and operation of Tier One, although not publicly released, are estimated to be in the range of 20 million to 30 million US dollars, roughly two to three times the value of the Ansari X Prize award. The sole sponsor, initially secret, was revealed to be Paul Allen, a co-founder of Microsoft and the fifth richest person in the world. The revelation, on December 17, 2003, the same day as the programme's first powered flight test, followed speculation that Allen was involved.

Some commentators have drawn comparisons between the relative inexpense of the Tier One programme and the high cost of the Space Shuttle programme, though the technological difficulties of the two programmes are completely different. SpaceShipOne, because it flies suborbitally, does not need to reach the high speeds of the Space Shuttle (Mach 3 vs. Mach 25), nor the same altitude (100 km suborbital vs. 400 km orbit). SpaceShipOne also does not carry the same crew (3 members vs. 7) or payload (negligible vs. 25 tons), and makes much shorter flights (a few minutes vs. several days). The SpaceShipOne programme is a technical achievement more on a par with the X-15 than the Shuttle.

Inflation adjusted comparisons of the SpaceShipOne programme with that of the X-15 budget, indicate that the Tier One programme cost 1/100th that of the X-15 programme, although the three X-15 aircraft made almost 200 test flights in their entire test programme, typically exploring hypersonic flight between Mach 4-7. Only a few dozen X-15 flights specificially sought to reach peak altitudes rather than achieve top speeds, though only two flights ever reached altitudes near those achieved by SpaceShipOne. On the other hand, the Tier One project also paid for construction of the White Knight mothership within its budget, while NASA had nearly free use of a pre-existing USAF B-52 bomber modified to perform drop tests of experimental aircraft of many kinds (currently in use for PegasusXL launches).

Publicity

Tier One was initially developed secretly, as is Scaled Composites' policy with new programmes. On April 18, 2003 the programme was publicly announced, and SpaceShipOne and White Knight were demonstrated to the media at a rollout attended by between 550 and 600 people. Media interest was so intense that what had been intended as a Family and Friends Day on April 24, 2003 was turned into a second media day.

Scaled Composites again courted publicity by announcing in advance the final test flight, SpaceShipOne flight 15P, intended to be the programme's first spaceflight. About 11,000 people went to Mojave Spaceport to watch the flight, which was also televised. The flight was run as an airshow, with both the principal craft and the chase planes making takeoffs and landings in front of the crowd, and celebratory flybys when the test succeeded. The flight was not only a technical success but also an unqualified popular success, triggering intense public interest in spaceflight.

Scaled Composites unsurprisingly remains very media-friendly with respect to Tier One, and more public spectacles are to be expected.

Future

The programme name "Tier One" raises the question of what Tier Two will be.

In *The Space Review* on June 21, 2004 (the day of Tier One's first spaceflight), Rutan was quoted as stating "The spaceship is model number 316 and the White Knight is model number 318. I will be making a presentation very quick of a model number 346." Whether this refers to a prototype orbital craft, a suborbital tour bus, or some other concept remains to be seen.

In 2004 Rutan suggested that a ten-passenger suborbital spacecraft would make a profitable tour bus. On September 27, 2004, entrepreneur Sir Richard Branson announced a deal with Mojave Aerospace Ventures to carry paying passengers on suborbital tourist flights, using a scaled-up version of SpaceShipOne, possibly beginning service in 2008. That same year, Burt Rutan also said "we're heading for orbit sooner than you think".

During an interview in the documentary *Black Sky: The Race for Space*, Rutan stated that Tier One will cover suborbital flights, Tier Two will cover orbital flights, and Tier Three will cover flights beyond Earth's orbit (including flights to the moon and other planets). In the same documentary he displayed designs for an orbital craft based on SpaceShipOne, which had a rocket roughly twice SpaceShipOne's length mounted to the ship's rear.

Commercial Aspects

The stated objective of the Tier One programme is to demonstrate suborbital human spaceflight operations at low cost. Before Burt Rutan began considering this project, there were three major barriers to the goal of affordable suborbital spaceflight:

1. the dangers and costs of liquid propulsion fuels (they explode);
2. the uncontrollable nature of solid fuel rocket motors (you can't turn them off);
3. the difficulties in getting back without burning up in the atmosphere.

Rutan's design appears to provide a cost-effective solution to all three issues.

Tier One itself is not intended to carry paying passengers, and US Government permits would be required if it did intend to do so. It is a technology testbed, and it is expressly intended that the technology developed in the programme will later be used in commercial spaceflights. To that end, Paul Allen and Burt Rutan created a company, Mojave Aerospace Ventures, which owns the project's intellectual property and will manage all commercial exploitation of it.

Scaled Composites initially expressed a hope that by about 2013 it would be possible for members of the public to experience a suborbital flight for about the price of a luxury cruise. On September 25, 2004 a deal was struck with Virgin Galactic to develop the Virgin SpaceShip based on a scaled-up version of SpaceShipOne. These spacecraft will be built by The Spaceship Company.

TIER 1B

Tier 1b is Burt Rutan's nickname for the suborbital tourist human spaceflight platform in development at Scaled Composites with Mojave Aerospace Ventures by The Spaceship Company for Virgin Galactic. It is an evolutionary development of Tier One, the Ansari X-Prize winning entry in the demonstration suborbital space tourism contest held by the X-Prize Foundation.

White Knight Two will be an aircraft capable of attaining an altitude of at least 50,000 ft (15,000 m) or 15 km and be aerobatic, offering several seconds of weightlessness. This will allow space tourists to train before their flight. White Knight Two will have a twin-boom design, with SpaceShipTwo nestled between the two hulls. One hull will contain tourists on zero-g flights, the other hull will contain astronauts in training, and be identical to SpaceShipTwo's cabin. White Knight Two is a development upon the White Knight (or *White Knight One*) design.

SpaceShipTwo will have a cockpit similar to SpaceShipOne, and a large cabin to allow tourists to float weightlessly. It is anticipated that the flight profile will allow for 4 minutes of weightlessness and 40 seconds transition from weightless to one g. SpaceShipTwo is a development upon the SpaceShipOne design.

White Knight Two will carry SpaceShipTwo up to launch altitude, where it will be air launched, and will rocket through suborbital trajectory.

The launch customer of Tier 1b is Virgin Galactic, which will have the first two WK2 units, first five SS2 units, and exclusive rights to the craft for the first few years.

The first WK2 was rolled out on July 28, 2008 and named VMS Eve. Its first test flight was on December 21, 2008.

TIER TWO

Tier Two is Scaled Composites and Virgin Galactic's orbital human spaceflight programme. The programme's spacecraft will be based on SpaceShip Two if that is successful. Initial plans call for the spacecraft to be named SpaceShip Three.

RUTAN VOYAGER

The **Model 76 Voyager** was the first aircraft to fly around the world without stopping or refuelling. It was piloted by Dick Rutan and Jeana Yeager (no relation to Chuck Yeager). The flight took off from Edwards Air Force Base's 15,000 foot (4,600 m) runway in the Mojave Desert on December 14, 1986, and ended successfully 9 days, 3 minutes and 44 seconds later, on December 23. The aircraft flew westerly 26,366 statute miles (42,432 km; the FAI accredited distance is 40,212 km) at an average altitude of 11,000 feet (3.4 km). This definitively broke a previous record set by a United States Air Force crew piloting a Boeing B-52 that flew 12,532 miles (20,168 km) in 1962.

Record Flight

Voyager's takeoff took place at 8:01 AM local time. As the plane accelerated, the tips of the wings, which were heavily loaded with fuel, were damaged as they scraped against the runway, ultimately causing pieces (winglets) to break off at both ends. The aircraft accelerated very slowly and needed approximately 14,200 feet (2.7 mi)(4.3 km) of the runway to gain enough speed to lift from the ground, the wings arching up dramatically just before take-off. During the flight, the two pilots had to deal with extremely cramped quarters. To reduce stress, the two intended to fly the plane in three-hour shifts, but this did not prove to be very successful and they became extremely fatigued.

The plane also continuously reminded the pilots of its pitch instability and fragility. They had to maneuver around bad weather numerous times, most perilously around the 600 mile (1,000 km) wide Typhoon Marge. Libya denied access to the country's airspace, forcing precious fuel to be used. As they neared California to land, a fuel pump failed and had to be replaced with its twin pumping fuel from the other side of the aircraft. The plane safely came back to earth, touching down at 8:06 AM at the same airfield. The average speed for the flight was 116 miles per hour (187 km/h).

Aircraft Development

The aircraft was first imagined by Jeana Yeager, Dick and his brother Burt Rutan as they were at lunch in 1981. The initial idea was first sketched out on the back of a napkin. Voyager was built in Mojave, California, over a period of 5 years. The Voyager was built mainly by a group of volunteers working under both the Rutan Aircraft Factory and an organization set up under the name Voyager Aircraft (it was not, as is sometimes believed, built by Scaled Composites).

The airframe, largely made of fiberglass, carbon fiber, and Kevlar, weighed 939 pounds (426 kg) when empty. However, when it was fully loaded before the historic flight, it weighed 9,694.5 pounds (4,397 kg). The aircraft had an estimated lift to drag ratio (L/D) of 27.

Voyager had front and rear propellers, powered by separate engines. The rear engine, a water-cooled Teledyne Continental IOL-200, was planned to be operated throughout the flight. The front engine, an air-cooled Teledyne Continental O-240, was operated to provide additional power for takeoff and the initial part of the flight at heavy weights.

Voyager is now on display at the Smithsonian Institution's National Air and Space Museum in Washington, DC.

Specifications

General Characteristics

- **Crew:** Two pilots
- **Length:** 29 ft 2 in (8.90 m)
- **Wingspan:** 110 ft 8 in (33.80 m)
- **Height:** 10 ft 3 in (3.10 m)
- **Empty weight:** 2250 lb (1020.6 kg)
- **Gross weight:** 9694.5 lb (4397.4 kg)
- **Powerplant:** 1 × Teledyne Continental O-240, 130 hp (100 kW) 1 × Teledyne Continental IOL-200, 110 hp (81 kW)

Performance

- **Maximum speed:** 122 mph (196 km/h)
- **Range:** 24,986 miles (42,212 km)
- **Endurance:** 216 hours

VSS ENTERPRISE

The **VSS *Enterprise*** is the first commercial spaceship being constructed for Virgin Galactic. It will also be the first ship of the SpaceShipTwo class, based on upscaling the design of SpaceShipOne. It is due to be rolled out in the middle of 2009, with test flights beginning in late 2009 and commercial service starting in 2011. The launches will occur at Virgin Galactic's launch pad located near Upham, New Mexico. The name is an acknowledgement to the USS *Enterprise* from the *Star Trek* television series.

Entrepreneur Richard Branson, head of the space tourism company Virgin Galactic, offered William Shatner, the actor who portrayed Captain Kirk in the original *Star Trek* series, a free ride into space on the inaugural space launch of the VSS *Enterprise*, with a retail value of $200,000. However, Shatner turned it down, and said, "I do want to go up but I need guarantees I'll definitely come back."

VSS VOYAGER

VSS Voyager is to be the second ship built and used as part of the Virgin Galactic Fleet. It is a SpaceShipTwo-class suborbital manned spaceplane. Like its sister craft, VSS Enterprise, it shares its name with both a fictitious Star Trek starship (USS Voyager) and a real NASA spacecraft (Voyager).

The design's first mothership (White Knight Two) is named VMS Eve, and the second is expected to be named VMS Spirit of Steve Fossett, in honour of Steve Fossett.

VMS EVE

VMS Eve is a carrier mothership for Virgin Galactic and launch platform for SpaceShipTwo-based Virgin SpaceShips. It also functions as a zero-g flight tourist plane. It is the first WhiteKnightTwo built by Scaled Composites for Virgin Galactic. The "VMS" prefix means **Virgin Mothership**.

Public Launch

The aircraft was named after Evette Branson, the mother of Richard Branson, Chairman of the Virgin Group. The jet plane has nose art of a blond woman holding the Virgin Galactic corporate flag. The image is based on how Evette Branson looked when she was younger, and is called **Galactic Girl**. The aircraft was officially launched on Monday, July 28, 2008, in Mojave, California, USA, at the Mojave Spaceport, home of Scaled Composites. On December 12, 2008 the aircraft performed first taxi tests, and a week later the maiden flight. *Eve* will be used in the Virgin Galactic testflight programme, preceding entry into commercial usage. It is expected that commercial service will start in 2010.

It is the largest all composite aircraft ever constructed, and it has the longest single-piece composite aircraft part: a 140 ft (43 m) long wingspar. Burt Rutan has dismissed fears that pressurization cycles might induce fatigue failure in the composite structure. Richard Branson has also announced that it will be highly fuel efficient.

THE SPACESHIP COMPANY

The Spaceship Company is a spacecraft manufacturing company formed by Burt Rutan and Richard Branson in mid-2005, jointly owned by Virgin Group and Scaled Composites, which will own the technology created by Scaled for Virgin Galactic's Virgin SpaceShip programme. This includes developments on the care-free reentry system and cantilevered-hybrid rocket motor, licensed from Paul Allen and Burt Rutan's Mojave Aerospace. The company will manufacture Virgin Galactic's spacecraft and will sell spacecraft to other buyers. The suborbital launch system offered will be Tier 1b, that of SpaceShipTwo and White Knight Two.

The launch customer for the company and SS2/WK2 will be Virgin Galactic, having placed an order for five SpaceShipTwos and two White Knight Twos, with a 1½-year exclusivity clause.

SCALED COMPOSITES WHITE KNIGHT

The **Scaled Composites Model 318 White Knight** is a jet-powered carrier aircraft used to launch the SpaceShipOne experimental spacecraft. It was developed by Scaled

Composites as part of their Tier One programme. The aircraft is subsequently being offered by Scaled on a contract basis as a research testbed, and was also used for drop tests of the Boeing X-37 spaceplane from June 2005 until April 2006.

History

The Scaled Composites model number for White Knight is **318**. White Knight is registered with the Federal Aviation Administration as **N318SL**.

The White Knight carrier airplane was designed around the twin afterburning J-85 engines, which were selected for their availability and low cost.

White Knight first flew on August 1, 2002. The flight was aborted shortly after takeoff due to a problem with the outboard wing spoilers. These trailing edge spoilers were designed to greatly increase the glide slope so that the White Knight vehicle could act as a flying simulator for training of SpaceShip One pilots. During the first flight, the mechanical over-center torque was insufficient to maintain the spoilers in the closed position. The spoilers deployed into the free stream and began a limit cycle forcing the pilot (Melville) to abort. The spoilers were subsequently disabled completely and the desire for a steep glide slope matching SpaceShip One was abandoned.

White Knight next flew on August 5, 2002, and this time performed well. Development proceeded over the next few months. With White Knight developed and evaluated, on April 18, 2003. White Knight and SpaceShipOne were presented to the media.

Subsequently, White Knight flew as part of the Tier One programme that won the Ansari X Prize on October 4, 2004. Afterwards White Knight was used to carry and launch DARPA's experimental X-37 spaceplane for its approach and landing tests in 2005 and 2006.

It was followed up by the White Knight 2 which have a similar but larger design.

SpaceShipOne Programme

Flights of White Knight are numbered, starting with flight 1 on August 1, 2002. Flights where SpaceShipOne is carried also get one or two appended letters. An appended **C** indicates that the flight was a captive carry, and **L** indicates that SpaceShipOne was launched. If the flight actually flown differs in category from the intended flight then two letters are appended, the first giving the intended mission and the second the mission actually performed.

White Knight flights carrying SpaceShipOne

Flight	*Date*	*Pilot*	*SpaceShipOne flight*
24C	May 20, 2003	Peter Siebold	01C
29C	July 29, 2003	Brian Binnie	02C
30L	August 7, 2003	Brian Binnie	03G
31LC	August 27, 2003	Brian Binnie	04GC
32L	August 27, 2003	Brian Binnie	05G

(Contd.)

(*Contd.*)

Flight	Date	Pilot	SpaceShipOne flight
37L	September 23, 2003	Peter Siebold	06G
38L	October 17, 2003	Peter Siebold	07G
40L	November 14, 2003	Brian Binnie	08G
41L	November 19, 2003	Brian Binnie	09G
42L	December 4, 2003	Peter Siebold	10G
43L	December 17, 2003	Peter Siebold	11P
49L	March 11, 2004	Brian Binnie	12G
53L	April 8, 2004	Brian Binnie	13P
56L	May 13, 2004	Brian Binnie	14P
60L	June 21, 2004	Mike Melvill	15P
65L	September 29, 2004	Mike Melvill	16P
66L	October 4, 2004	Brian Binnie	17P

X-37 Test Programme

White Knight was contracted to perform both captive carry and drop test flights of the DARPA/Boeing X-37. First captive carry flight was on June 21, 2005, and first drop was on April 7, 2006 (the X-37 was subsequently damaged on landing at Edwards AFB). Initially, the flights originated from Mojave, but following the landing incident, the Programme was moved to Air Force Plant 42 in Palmdale, California, and at least five subsequent flights were made there.

Adaptive Compliant Wing Test Programme

In late 2006, White Knight flew a seven-flight test programme of the Adaptive Compliant Wing developed by FlexSys Inc with funding by the Air Force Research Laboratory. A laminar flow test article was mounted vertically under White Knight's centerline pylon for the 20-flight-hour research programme that tested the flexible wing's aerodynamic characteristics.

Specifications

The aircraft was a completely new independent design. White Knight and SpaceShip One shared the same forward fuselage outer mold line (OML) to reduce development costs and with the original intent to allow for White Knight to act as a flying simulator for training SpaceShip One pilots.

General Characteristics

- **Crew:** 2
- **Capacity:** 2
- **Powerplant:** 2× General Electric J85-GE-5 afterburning turbojets

- **Payload:** 8,000 lb (3,600 kg)
- **Wingspan:** 82 ft (25 m)
- **Fuel capacity:** 6,400 lb (2,900 kg)

Performance

- **Service ceiling:** 53,000 ft plus (16,000 m)

SCALED COMPOSITES SPACESHIP THREE

The **Scaled Composites SpaceShipThree** is a proposed orbital spaceplane to be developed by Virgin Galactic and Scaled Composites if SpaceShipTwo is successful. Unlike the previous two Scaled Composites spaceplanes, this craft would be designed both to reach orbit and be capable of orbital reentry.

SPACE ISLAND PROJECT

The **Space Island Project** is a project whose goal is to create a stand-alone commercial space infrastructure supporting manned business activities in Low Earth Orbit (LEO) 400 to 500 miles above earth.

The centerpiece of this project is the Space Solar Energy Initiative which will collect energy with solar panel satellites and then beam this energy to receiving towers on Earth using "very weak microwave beams."

The Space Island Group is the organization behind this project, and plans to accomplish this through the use of technologies, vehicles and procedures developed by NASA and aerospace companies over the last 25 years.

SPACE ISLAND GROUP

Space Island Group (**SIG**) is a commercial organization based in West Covina, CA that is dedicated to the development of commerce, research, manufacturing and tourism in space. They plan to accomplish this by designing, building and operating commercial space transportation systems and destinations. Their flagship project is the Space Island Project. This will be a stand-alone commercial space infrastructure supporting manned business activities in Low Earth Orbit (LEO) 400 to 500 miles above earth. They plan to accomplish this through the use of technologies, vehicles and procedures developed by NASA and aerospace companies over the last 25 years.

Funding

One of the unique propositions outlined by the Space Island Group is their funding methodology. They argue that previous attempts at commercial space projects have had a dependency on revenue and subsidies from government agencies, but that they have a funding plan that would be viable through capitalizing on commercial markets such as solar power satellites.

PIONEER ROCKETPLANE

Pioneer Rocketplane was an aerospace design and development company intent on developing affordable manned space flight. The company is most famous for advocating a horizontal takeoff, turbo-jet and rocket propelled, aerial-refuelled, rocket plane concept called the Pathfinder. The company still exists, but is no longer operating. Pioneer's intellectual property is now owned by Rocketplane Limited, Inc., but Rocketplane Limited does not employ any of the principals of Pioneer Rocketplane.

History

Note that most of this history was developed using the Internet Archive's Way-Back-Machine www.rocketplane.com

The "Black Horse" Study

The "Black Horse" study began with a bar napkin at the White Sands Missile Range Officers' Club on May 12, 1993. The original concept was developed by then Air Force Captain Mitchell Burnside Clapp, who envisioned an aerial refuelled, rocket powered single-stage to orbit (SSTO) vehicle using jet fuel and hydrogen peroxide. This concept seemed a natural match for the Air Force's TransAtmospheric Vehicle (TAV) mission and studies began at the USAF Phillips Laboratory. Aerospace engineering legend Burt Rutan and noted aircraft designer Dan Raymer contributed input to the development of the design.

During the winter of 1993-94, the U.S. Air Force's Phillips Laboratory conducted a six-week study with WJ Schafer Associates and Conceptual Research Corporation which developed the Aerial Propellant Transfer (APT) concept further. This concept used existing components, existing tankers, landing gear, and conventional technology as much as possible.

The "Black Colt" Study

Another study of a somewhat different APT concept was done at Martin Marietta during January through May 1994, this one of a near-term suborbital X-Plane that could serve as a demonstration vehicle for the APT concept. Because the vehicle was about half the size of Black Horse, it was decided to call it "Black Colt."

This concept used an existing NK-31 RP/O2 rocket engine with two Garrett F-125 turbofans used for takeoff, loiter during aerial propellant transfer, and landing propulsion. Also, rather than push for the very high performance required to achieve true SSTO operation, the Black Colt was a suborbital vehicle, with the 1000 lb payload then being delivered to orbit by means of a Star 48V upper stage.

The Private Sector

Mitchell Burnside Clapp left the Air Force in 1996. Teaming up with Robert Zubrin (co-author of the Martin Marietta Black Colt study) and promoter Charles Lauer, he founded Pioneer Rocketplane. To help the new company get started, it allied with Dr. Zubrin's research company, Pioneer Astronautics, in Lakewood, Colorado. General Tony McPeak, now retired from the Air Force, joined the company as Chairman of the Board. During this time Pioneer Rocketplane refined the concept for the Pathfinder rocketplane. It had to require no new engine developments, which would postpone the first flight by years. It had to be built by subcontractors to avoid the time and expense of building an in-house manufacturing capability. Most importantly, it had to be able to support the requirements for the new low earth orbit communications satellites. This led to the switch from hydrogen peroxide to liquid oxygen as the preferred oxidizer, and drove an increase in overall size.

Version 2.0 of the Pathfinder concept was delivered in 1997 by Conceptual Research Corporation.

The Bantam Effort

On June 9, 1997, NASA's Marshall Space Flight Center announced Pioneer Rocketplane as one of four winners in phase one of the Bantam-X programme competition. Pioneer Rocketplane; Summa Technology, Inc. (partnered with Lockheed Martin) of Huntsville, Alabama; Aerojet-General Corp. of Sacramento, California; and Universal Space Lines of Newport Beach, California were selected. Total funding for these awards was approximately US$ 8 million.

Company Restructuring

During the Bantam effort, Pioneer Rocketplane relocated to Vandenburg Air Force Base. It also severed its relationship with Robert Zubrin's Pioneer Astronautics in Lakewood, CO. Co-founder Dr. Robert Zubrin remained President of Pioneer Astronautics, but was no longer affiliated with Pioneer Rocketplane.

Design 4.0 and 5.0

Pioneer Rocketplane completed a milestone in early September 1998 by completing a full internal systems design review with its subcontractors. The system design review revealed a very well constructed, consistent, "closed" design for Pioneer Rocketplane's Pathfinder Launch system. A "closed" design represents a good engineering solution we are sure will work when the hardware is actually built.

RASCAL Programme

In March 2002, Pioneer Rocketplane was awarded a phase one contract for the Defense Advanced Research Projects Agency's RASCAL programme. RASCAL stands for "Responsive Access, Small Cargo, Affordable Launch." This capability would provide a means for rapid launch of orbital assets for changing national security needs. In many respects, the mission requirements are similar to the Bantam effort of several years prior.

Pioneer XP

The Pioneer XP (X-Prize) was a concept for a four-seat fighter-sized vehicle powered by two jet engines and two rocket engines, enabling it to reach altitudes of 350,000 feet. This concept was developed initially as a contender for the Ansari X Prize. It has applications for passenger travel, as a research and observation platform, and as a promotional and sponsorship opportunity. The XP would operate from ordinary airfields within the well-established rules and practices for aircraft. This concept has evolved into the Rocketplane XP programme.

Rocketplane Limited

In 2001, Rocketplane Limited, Inc. was formed. Pioneer Rocketplane is a part owner of Rocketplane Limited, but ceased operations as an independent company. Rocketplane Limited purchased the intellectual property of Pioneer and put in place an all new management and engineering team to push the development of the Rocketplane XP. In 2006, it acquired Kistler Aerospace.

MIRCORP

MirCorp was a commercial space company created in 1999 by space entrepreneurs and involving the Russian space programme that successfully undertook a number of firsts in the business of space exploration by utilizing the aging Russian space station Mir as a commercial platform. Its actions were highly controversial and angered many as it created a roadblock to the planned International Space Station in creating a viable, low cost alternative.

The company achieved the following:

- First commercial lease agreement for orbiting manned space station (December, 1999)
- First privately funded manned expedition to a space station (launch April 4, 2000, return 16 June 2000)
- First privately funded cargo resupply mission in space (April 27, 2000)
- First privately funded spacewalk (May 12, 2000)
- First contract for space tourist (Dennis Tito, June 19, 2000)

In terms of business development, the company was able to launch the era of space tourism by signing American businessman Dennis Tito to his launch contract. It also signed with television producer Mark Burnett (producer of the Survivor reality show) and with NBC, to produce a reality show "Destination Mir," where the winner would travel to space. And it also was able to sign other media, entertainment and commercial space research projects. MirCorp's CEO Jeffrey Manber later stated "we failed to survive but proved the business model, and in the long term that will be just as important."

The company came to an end for a variety of reasons. It seems to have been a combination of the financial backers inability to continue funding the venture, a business model that made little sense, and pressure by NASA to de-orbit the station. NASA viewed the station as a threat to their own plans for the International Space Station. The station existed until 23 March 2001, at which point it was deliberately de-orbited, breaking apart over the Pacific Ocean.

Background

The company was formed as an idea by telecommunications and space investor Walt Anderson and space advocate Rick Tumlinson. Russia lacked the funds to upgrade and save the space station, and had concluded that it had no choice but to deorbit the station. Several ideas were floated, some absurd and some interesting, including one to hand over the Mir to the United Nations. The idea proposed by Anderson and Tumlinson was to save the Mir space station by raising it to a higher orbit to gain time and developing a "space tether" to supply power to keep the space station in orbit while further funds were raised. This plan was never implemented by the MirCorp team, as the United States government barred the export of the space tether technology until after the deorbit of the space station was announced. It was just one of many obstacles placed in front of the venture by the American government.

The founders recruited well known space entrepreneur Jeffrey Manber, who had helped negotiate the first contract between the Soviet Union and NASA on space interests, and had also represented the huge Russian space company RSC Energia in its American dealings during the 1990's. Manber created the business model for the venture which involved proving that space could be a platform for media and entertainment, as well as serious space research.

In February 2000, the agreement between the Russian space company RSC Energia, which had the commercial rights to the space station, and MirCorp, was announced in London. Present at the press conference was MirCorp CEO Jeffrey Manber and RSC Energia General Director Yuri P. Semenov. Also present at the press conference was co-investor Dr. Chirinjeev Kathuria, and Andrew Eddy, recruited from the Canadian Space Agency.

The news took senior NASA officials by surprise, and thus began the roller-coaster ride of the MirCorp efforts. Their efforts were criticized by many as a private interference with international space policies. Their desire to sell ticket to space as part of a "citizen explorers" programme was ridiculed by NASA and its supporters.

Yet, as a result of the company's backing, the RSC Energia officials boosted the Mir into a higher orbit, thus postponing the deorbit that had been agreed to by the Russian Space Agency in discussions with NASA. Manber later explained that the business model for the venture was modelled after that of air travel, where Boeing may build the planes but commercial agents such as United or British Airways sells the tickets. The intent was to have marketing experts sell the space programme, and let the space manufacturer, RSC Energia, focus on the safe operations of the station. Manber explained that in the aviation world it was not the manufacturers who sold the tickets, it was the marketing companies. MirCorp and RSC Energia were the first to use this strategy for space exploration, which has emerged again more recently with Sir Richard Branson's announcement to market Scaled Composites StarShip suborbital flights.

It was also unusual as an international venture with Russia in the 1990's in that the Russians were given the operating control of the venture, reflecting the political realities of the importance of the Mir to the Russian society. RSC Energia owned 60 per cent of MirCorp, whereas the financial investors controlled 40 per cent. Investor Anderson explained that he was comfortable letting the Russians run the space component, and his team would run the business. "A lot of this venture is based on trust, pure and simple." Anderson explained. Anderson was not so sanguine regarding NASA and used the media interest in the venture to launch many critical comments towards NASA, the planned International Space Station and even the foreign policies of the American government. This could not have but solidified opposition to the venture inside the Administration. Indeed, Anderson selected Holland as the headquarters for the company since he believed the country was far more ethical than that of his own.

Regardless of the controversy, a new era in space exploration was inaugurated on April 4, 2000, when the Soyuz TM-30, known as the MirCorp mission carried two crew members, Sergei Zalyotin and Alexandr Kaleri, to shut the Mir space station.

The two man crew returned the dormant Mir space station to life, located the source of the leak, repaired the leak, and carried on a number of commercial and basic research. Zalyotin admitted to being nervous when the hatch door was opened, not sure what exactly would be found in the station. While the mission was being undertaken, the management of MirCorp was able to announce a number of commercial contracts, including that of the agreement with NBC and Mark Burnett. NBC even began running commercials promoting its upcoming "Destination Mir" reality show.

On June 16th, on schedule, the mission came to an end. It had lasted 73 days and the crew returned in good health. Behind the scenes, the MirCorp management and Energia space officials were both surprised at the technical and commercial success, but worried that the Mir would soon have to be shut for good. On June 19, 2000, a press conference was held at the Russian Mission Control Center TSUP, at which the MirCorp president, along with RSC Energia head of International Development Alexander Derechin, announced that Dennis Tito, a former US space programme engineer, who founded Wilshire, Associated—the Santa Monica, California-based company that revolutionized the field of investment management consulting, was MirCorp's first "Citizen Explorer."

Mr. Tito would subsequently withstand intense pressure brought on him and on Russian space officials, by NASA not to undertake his mission. NASA administrator Daniel Goldin publicly rebuked MirCorp for their efforts during Congressional hearings. Tito went forward with his training and eventually, with the deorbit of the Mir, he transferred his efforts to fly on the International Space Station. With the help of RSC Energia, MirCorp and later Space Adventurers, he became the first space tourist to visit the International Space Station.

The Tito Saga

Dennis Tito was not the first "amateur" to blast into space. Previously, Japanese TV journalist Toyohiro Akiyama has flown on a commercial mission to the Russian space station Mir. What might have made his mission different was that Tito was the first to pay for his own ticket, thus earning the designation of the first space tourist.

The Tito mission also took place in the backdrop of the whole controversy regarding the decision by the major Russian space company RSC Energia to work with MirCorp to create a commercial space station, and thus, many felt, put at risk the struggling Russia's obligations on the planned International Space Station. NASA's behaviour about learning of the Tito mission was unusual. The space agency immediately cancelled planned high level meetings between the Russian and US space agencies. Their legal team declared that a bill would be sent for any damages caused by the flight of Tito.

"In November 2000, we informed NASA that we planned to launch Tito to [Alpha]," said Koptev, who did not recall NASA expressing any negative reaction at that time. That situation changed, however, as the two space powers entered into a standoff in which neither would back down. The head of the Russian Space Agency later told reporters that "Our legal advisors told us that the fine for any misdoing aboard the station, including damage to morale, could exceed the money that we had earned from Tito's contract, and could even exceed Russia's space budgetary capacity," Koptev said. The reaction after the eventual mission to the International Space Station, not to the Mir as initially planned, was harsh and personal. Dan Goldin, NASA administrator, implied that Dennis Tito was not an American patriot and US Sen. Barbara Mikulski of Maryland compared the behaviour of all those concerned with the space tourist programme to that of "pimps."

The Senator's harsh views reflected many in Washington who regarded with disdain the concept of commercialization connecting with national space programmes.

In addition, on several occasions the Russians claimed that they had not been reimbursed by MirCorp for services. MirCorp founder Walt Anderson was later charged with federal tax evasion, plead guilty, and was sentenced to nine years in federal prison.

The End Days

By the end of the 73 day MirCorp mission, the company enjoyed a $70 million backlog in customer orders. But the decision was made by Russia to yield to the American pressures and deorbit the station; in addition, the two financial investors were late on their payments and new investors were frightened off by the negative publicity from NASA.

The company remained in business even after the Mir was destroyed. It handled the efforts of *NSync boy band Lance Bass's unsuccessful effort to fly to space, as well as that of former NASA official Lori Garver (currently Deputy NASA Administrator), who also sought to use advertising as a means to be a space tourist, before finally closing the doors. MirCorp attempted to demonstrate that a private company could manage a manned space station; that a business model could be developed around an orbiting space station. However, its failure to produce sufficient revenue to pay its modest expenses and the imprisonment of one of its founders for tax evasion indicate that its efforts were unsuccessful. Today the situation has changed. Former NASA administrator Michael D. Griffin has voiced full support for commercialization of manned space activities and the Russian operated space tourist programme is fully accepted by the United States.

The space tourism programme has continued in Russia, which today enjoys far more robust funding than a decade ago. It does seem to reflect the view of the Russians that involvement of everyday people is good for the future of space exploration, and not an act of desperation, as many implied at the onset.

BLUE ORIGIN GODDARD

Blue Origin Goddard is the name of the first development vehicle in the Blue Origin New Shepard programme, which flew for the first time on November 13, 2006. Named after rocketry pioneer Robert Goddard, the vehicle is a subscale demonstrator and flew at a 285 ft altitude during its initial flight. The private spacecraft venture is being funded by the billionaire founder of Amazon.com, Jeff Bezos. He hopes that the private spacecraft could eventually bring space travel within the reach of the masses. A video of the cone-shaped Goddard vehicle shows it climbing to about 85 m (285 ft) before returning back to Earth, in a remote part of Texas.

The flight marks the first time Jeff Bezos has broken his silence on the work of his space company, Blue Origin. On the company's website, Mr Bezos said: "We're working, patiently and step-by-step, to lower the cost of spaceflight so that many people can afford to go; and so that we humans can better continue exploring the Solar System." "Accomplishing this mission will take a long time, and we're working on it methodically." Mr Bezos founded Blue Origin in 2000 with the intention of developing a vertical take-off and landing vehicle, able to take passengers to the edge of space. No timescale for commercial trips has been announced but documents released by the US Federal Aviation Administration suggest they could start as early as 2010.

The video filmed on 13 November 2006 from a site about 120 miles east of El Paso in Texas shows the first craft to launch under the New Shepard programme. The vehicle climbed for approximately 10 seconds, reaching a height of 285 ft, before starting to descend and making a controlled landing back on its feet approximately 25 seconds after take-off. The launch, described by Mr Bezos as "both useful and fun", was watched by friends, family and a team of engineers.

BLUE ORIGIN NEW SHEPARD

The **Blue Origin New Shepard** reusable launch vehicle is a manned rocket which is being developed by Blue Origin, a company owned by Amazon.com founder and billionaire Jeff Bezos, as a commercial system for suborbital space tourism. The New Shepard makes reference to the first United States astronaut in space, Alan Shepard.

The launch vehicle is assembled at the Blue Origin facility near Seattle, Washington. Blue Origin is starting the process to build an aerospace testing and operations center on a portion of the Corn Ranch, a 165,000-acre (668 km^2) land parcel Bezos purchased 40 km north of Van Horn, Texas. Blue Origin Project Manager Rob Meyerson has said that he selected Texas as the launch site particularly because of the state's historical connections to the aerospace industry, although that industry is not located near the planned launch site, and the vehicle will not be manufactured in Texas.

A sub-scale demonstration vehicle made its first flight on November 13, 2006.

Design

The New Shepard craft is planned to be a vertical take-off/vertical landing (VTOL) system. Its appearance and technical concept are similar to the DC-X. The overall shape is circular in cross-section and ogive (bullet shaped) from nose to tail, the base being somewhat rounded. It is powered by a cluster of nine engines powered by High test peroxide (HTP) and RP-1 kerosene, arranged in a 3 by 3 grid on the bottom. Four landing legs containing shock absorbers also extend from the edges of the bottom. The existing demonstrator vehicle has a diameter of 7 metres and a height of 15 metres. The total mass of the propellant is 54 tons and the thrust is 1000 kN.

In comparison to the DC-X, the New Shepard looks very "short and squat". The DC-X was designed in order to allow it to maneuver hypersonically for increased "crossrange" during re-entry, an important quality for a military mission that would be launched into a polar orbit. When such a spacecraft returns to the vicinity of its launch pad after one orbit, the Earth's rotation will have made the spacecraft seem to drift to the west, upwards of 750 miles (1,210 km) for a launch from the southern US mainland assuming a 90 minute low-Earth orbit. The DC-X's forebody was shaped to allow a lifting re-entry to maneuver back to its launch site.

A passenger and cargo spacecraft has considerably less need for cross-range. In these cases the need for a polar orbit is eliminated, and launches generally take place due east in order to take advantage of the Earth's rotation. In this case when the spacecraft returns to its launch area after one orbit, it is generally moving along the same "line" and little correction is needed. For instance, a launch directly east from the equator into a 90 minute orbit will complete in a little under 90 minutes because the launch site is rotating toward the spacecraft, and when it reaches the re-entry point the site will be directly under its flight path. For launches from the US the orbit is also "cut off" as the site rotates towards the spacecraft, but in this case the spacecraft will only return to the same north-south point after one complete orbit. This means that a small amount of cross-range maneuvering is required, but considerably less than for a polar orbit, perhaps on the order of 100 miles (200 km).

As a result, the craft is much "rounder" than the DC-X, optimized for tankage and structural benefits rather than re-entry aerodynamics. It has not been stated if the vehicle is intended to re-enter base first or nose first, but the former is most likely for a variety of reasons. For one, it reduces heat shield area, and thus weight, covering only the smaller bottom surface rather than the much larger upper portions. The area around the engines would likely require some sort of heat protection anyway, so by using the base as the heat shield the two can be combined. This re-entry attitude also has the advantage of allowing the spacecraft to descend all the way from orbit to touchdown in a base-first orientation, which would seem to offer some safety benefits as well as reducing aero-loading issues. The resulting craft looks something like a scaled-up version of the Apollo Command Module, which also used a base-first lifting re-entry profile. The rounded base may be further evidence of this re-entry mode.

None of its competitors in the nascent space tourism market have disclosed plans to use a similar design. However, it does appear to be very similar to the Japanese Rocket Society's study effort, the Kankoh-maru, which also planned to produce a

VTOL base re-entry vehicle for space tourism. The Kankoh-maru was much larger, however, with a passenger capacity of 50.

Mission

The New Shepard is expected to be launched vertically from West Texas and then perform a powered flight for about 110 s and to an altitude of 40 km. The craft's momentum would continue to carry it upward in unpowered flight and would decelerate until culminating at an altitude of about 100 km. After reaching apogee the vehicle would perform a descent and restart its main engines a few tens of seconds before vertical landing, close to its launch site. The total mission duration is planned to be 10 minutes.

The manned variant would feature a separate crew module that could separate close to peak altitude, and the propulsion module would perform a powered landing while the crew module would land under a parachute. The crew module can also separate in case of vehicle malfunction or other emergency using solid propellant separation boosters and perform a parachute landing.

Development Schedule

Initial low altitude flight testing (up to 600 m) with subscale prototypes was scheduled for the fourth quarter of 2006. This was later confirmed in a press release by Blue Origin. It could involve up to ten flights. Incremental flight testing to 100 km altitude is planned to be carried between 2007 and 2009 with increasingly larger and more capable prototypes. The full-scale vehicle is expected to be operational for revenue service in 2010, and could fly up to 50 times a year. Clearance from the FAA is needed before test flights begin, and a separate license is needed before commercial operations begin. The company held a public meeting on 15 June 2006 in Van Horn, as part of the public comment opportunity needed to secure FAA permissions. Blue Origin says that once cleared for commercial operation, they would expect to conduct a maximum rate of 52 launches per year. The RLV would carry three or more passengers per operation.

Initial Flight Tests

The first test was reported to have taken place on November 13, 2006 at 6:30 am local time (12:30 UTC); an earlier flight on the 10th being cancelled due to winds. This marks the first developmental test flights undertaken by Blue Origin. The flight was by the first prototype vehicle, known as **Goddard**. The flight to 285 feet (87 m) in altitude was successful. Videos are available on the Blue Origins website and elsewhere.

DSE-ALPHA

Deep Space Expedition Alpha (**DSE-Alpha**), is the name given to the mission planned to take the first space tourists to fly around the moon. The mission is organized by Space Adventures Ltd. who were responsible for taking the first space tourist Dennis Tito into orbit in 2001. The plans involve a modified Soyuz capsule docking with a booster rocket in Earth orbit which sends them on a free return trajectory that flies around the moon once. Tickets are expected to cost $100 million. It is hoped that launch will take place before 2010.

The use of the Soyuz spacecraft makes sense in many ways; the original Soyuz design of 1962 was specifically intended for circumlunar travel. In the late 1960s a stripped down Soyuz variant, under the name Zond, made several attempts at circumlunar flight, with eventual success.

The DSE proposal is to launch the Soyuz with one crew member and two passengers aboard; a Zenit rocket booster will then be launched carrying a rocket stage weighing up to 14.5t, to dock with the Soyuz and propel it to circumlunar velocity. On June 28, 2007 Space.com reported that two passengers have made reservations, with contract negotiations expected to be concluded by the end of the year.

Critics have argued, however, that the Zenit rocket is not powerful enough for this mission and that the larger Proton rocket will in fact be needed. The extra cost of the Proton rocket could push the total mission cost to well over US$100 m.

Another criticism that has been levied is that the unmanned Zond missions were only partially successful, with one spacecraft suffering cabin depressurisation, and all but one failing to follow the correct re-entry and landing trajectory. If the trajectory problem were to recur on a manned mission the crew would be at risk of potentially dangerous *g*-forces and a sea landing in a remote area.

COSMOPOLIS XXI

Cosmopolis XXI is a planned Russian vehicle that is billed as a space tourism vehicle, similar to Mojave Aerospace's Tier One programme. Designed and built by the Myasishchev Design Bureau, it would use the M-55X launch aircraft (derived from Myasishchev M-55), and the proposed **C-21** spaceplane or its successor the Explorer. It would be a TSTSO (Two-Stage to SubOrbit) launch platform.

The **Explorer** spaceplane is a suborbital tourist spaceplane based on the C-21 design. The plane is being developed by Space Adventures with the Russian Federal Space Agency and is designed to carry 5 passengers. It is to be air-launched by carrier aircraft from a Space Adventures spaceport. The spaceport for the Explorer is being developed with Prodea (the company of Anousheh and Amir Ansari, who funded the Ansari X-Prize) in the United Arab Emirates, the Ras Al Khaimah spaceport.

XCOR AEROSPACE

XCOR Aerospace is a private rocket engine and spaceflight development company based at the Mojave Spaceport Mojave, California. XCOR was formed by former members of the Rotary Rocket, rocket engine development team in September 1999. XCOR is headed by Jeff Greason who is the CEO.

Key People

Jeff Greason, Dan DeLong, Aleta Jackson and Doug Jones previously worked at the failed Rotary Rocket company.

Projects

Projects have included:

- EZ-Rocket, a Rutan Long-EZ homebuilt aircraft fitted with two 400 lbf (1.8 kN) thrust rocket engines replacing the normal propeller engine. EZ-Rocket has been flown at numerous airshows including the Oshkosh Airshow.
- Rocket Racer—The EZ-Rocket programme led to the rocket plane design for the Rocket Racing League. This consists of a modified Velocity SE with a 1500 lbf LOX-kerosene engine. The engine uses pressure-fed LOX and pump-fed kerosene, a combination that allows the fuel to be stored in the airplane's wing tanks while avoiding potential complications with pumping liquid oxygen.
- The Lynx, capable of carrying a pilot and a passenger or payload on flights to 65 km by 2010. Between 20 and 50 test flights of Lynx are planned, along with numerous static engine firings on the ground. A full step-by-step set of taxi tests, runway hops and full-up flights are planned to get the vehicle to a state of operational readiness. Lynx is envisaged to be roughly the size of a small private airplane. It would be capable of flying several times a day making use of reusable, non-toxic engines to help keep the space plane's operating costs low. The Lynx supersedes a previous design, the Xerus spaceplane.
- **Tea cart engine**, a 15 lbf (67 N) thrust rocket motor burning nitrous oxide and ethane, mounted on a small industrial cart. The tea cart engine has repeatedly been fired indoors at conferences and demonstrations and had accumulated over 1,837 firings and 9,039 seconds of run time by February 25, 2009.
- **LOX-methane rocket engines** in testing in 2005.
- Early LOX-methane work led to a NASA contract, jointly with ATK, to develop a 7500 lbf engine for potential use as the CEV lunar return engine. On January 16, 2007 XCOR announced the successful test firing of a preliminary "workhorse" version of this engine.
- XCOR has developed Nonburnite (tm), a cryo-compatible, inherently non-combustible composite material based on a thermoplastic fluoropolymer resin. Low coefficient of thermal expansion and inherent resistance to microcracking make it well suited to cryogenic tank use and also part of vehicle structure.

8

Major Global Organizations Associated with Space Travel and Tourism

SPACE TOURISM SOCIETY

The **Space Tourism Society** (**STS**) is a new not-for-profit society specifically focused on space tourism based in USA. STS have chapters in Japan, Norway, and the United Kingdom.

The STS is a California 501(c)3 non-profit organization whose mission is to encourage as many people to travel into Earth orbit as soon as possible for the space experience. STS aims to provide the vision and voice for the evolution of humanity off-world in a humane, fun, and beautiful direction. STS was created to inspire people to build real products for future use in space.

ASTRONAUTE CLUB EUROPÉEN

The **Astronaute Club Européen** or ACE, is a French association created on December 3, 2005 (decree of the *Journal Officiel* n°20050049), by Jean-Pierre Haigneré (cosmonaut), Laurent Gathier (director of space activities of Dassault Aviation and space pioneer) and Alain Dupas (Physicist, head of mission at CNES); and whose headquarters are located in the rooms of the Aéroclub de France in Paris.

Presentation

Its role is to promote space tourism and suborbital spaceflight in Europe and to pilot the development of private parabolic and suborbital flights, and to make them available to the general public. With this purpose, the association is promoting the design and development of the suborbital human spacecraft (VEHRA-SH).

Since it has been created, the ACE has participated in :

- the publication of space books;
- the organisation of conferences;
- many events (conferences, congresses, etc.);
- the proposal of study topics to European universities.

The VSH Project

The VSH project is part of the Aerospace Student Challenge, which allows teams of

European students, through collaborative work, to participate in the development of the project by addressing various aspects of the VSH system: propulsion, avionics, flight simulation but also maintenance, management, legal aspects, etc… while complying to the overall technical framework of the VSH, a vehicle launched from a commercial aircraft, which will reach Mach 3.5 and an altitude of 100 km, the limits of space. This VSH will be developed in close association with aeronautical and space companies such as :

- Dassault Aviation
- SAFRAN
- THALES

LIFTPORT GROUP

LiftPort Group is a privately-held Washington State corporation. It was founded in April 2003 by Michael J. Laine and is dedicated to creating cheap, reliable, and safe access to space. The company is focused on the construction of a space elevator using carbon nanotubes.

History

- April 2003: LiftPort Group founded.
- April 12, 2004: LiftPort Group cosponsored the Official Yuri's Night celebration in Seattle, Washington.
- November 12, 2004: Demonstrated a lifter at the Massachusetts Institute of Technology by having it climb up a ribbon approximately 90 metres tall, during a snowstorm.
- April 29, 2005: Announced plans for a carbon nanotube manufacturing plant, the company's first formal facility for production of the material on a commercial scale. The new facility was to serve as the regional headquarters for the company, and represent the fruition of LiftPort Group's three years of research and development efforts into carbon nanotubes, including partnering work with a variety of leading research institutions in the business and academic communities. Set to open in June 2005, LiftPort Nanotech was to be located in Millville, New Jersey.
- September 20, 2005: LiftPort Group designed and built a better lifter, longer ribbon (Tether) and load bearing Balloon to further illustrate proof of concept and progress. The lifter climbed the 1,000-foot (300 metres) ribbon which was suspended from the balloon.
- January 2006: LiftPort successfully launched an observation and communication platform a full mile (a kilometre and a half) in the air and maintained it in a stationary position for more than six hours while robotic lifters climbed up and down a ribbon attached to the platform. The platform, a proprietary system that the company has named "HALE" (High Altitude Long Endurance), was secured in place by an arrangement of high altitude balloons, which were also used to launch it. The robotic lifters measured five

feet, six inches (1.7 metres) and climbed to a height of more than 1,500 feet (460 m), surpassing its last test record by more than 500 feet (150 m).

- June 11, 2007, Slashdot reported that LiftPort was to be penalized due to an alleged illegal offering of shares of the company.
- June 2007, Michael Laine from LiftPort Group responded, explaining the issue as a paperwork mistake which resulted in a $20,000 fine.

COMMERCIAL SPACEFLIGHT FEDERATION

The **Commercial Spaceflight Federation** is a private spaceflight industry group, incorporated as an industry association for the purposes of establishing ever higher levels of safety for the commercial human spaceflight industry, sharing best practices and expertise, and promoting the growth of the industry worldwide.

Current members	
Person	**Company affiliation**
Eric Anderson	CEO of Space Adventures
John D. Carmack	President of Armadillo Aerospace
Peter Diamandis	CEO of X Prize Foundation
Frank DiBello	President of Space Florida
Art Dula	CEO of Excalibur Almaz
Jeff Greason	CEO of XCOR Aerospace
Steve Landeene	Executive Director of Spaceport America
Taber MacCallum	CEO of Paragon
David Masten	CEO of Masten Space Systems
Rob Meyerson	Programme Manager of Blue Origin
Vernon McDonald	Director of Commercial Human Spaceflight for Wyle
Bill Mitchell	CEO of Masten Space Systems
Elon Musk	CEO of SpaceX
Doug Shane	President of Scaled Composites
Mark Sirangelo	Chairman of Sierra Nevada Corporation Space Systems
Will Whitehorn	President of Virgin Galactic
Stu Witt	General Manager of Mojave Spaceport

The CSF staff includes Bretton Alexander (President), John Gedmark (Executive Director), Matthew Isakowitz (Associate Director), and James Muncy (Senior Advisor).

ASSOCIATION OF AUTONOMOUS ASTRONAUTS

The **Association of Autonomous Astronauts** is a worldwide network of community based groups dedicated to building their own spaceships. The AAA was founded on 23 April 1995. Although many of their activities were reported as serious participation in conferences or protests against the militarization of space, some were also considered art pranks, media pranks, or just an elaborate spoof. The AAA had numerous local chapters which operated independently of one another, with the AAA effectively operating as a collective pseudonym along the lines of Luther Blissett (nom de plume).

The Association's ostensible five-year mission, a reference to *Star Trek*, was to "establish a planetary network to end the monopoly of corporations, governments and the military over travel in space". Artists who became involved were often connected to the zine scene or mail art movements. The five year mission's completion was marked at the 2000 Fortean Times conference, although some chapters have continued activities to the present day.

Writer Tom Hodgkinson described them as "a loose bunch of Marxists, futurists, and revolutionaries on the dole", going on to explicate their mission as "reclaim[ing] the idea of space travel for the common man". To the AAA, he said, "space travel represented an ideal of freedom". Annick Bureaud of Leonardo/OLATS viewed their work as "space art" that "combine[d] freely space, cyberspace, raves, esoteric things, techno-music, etc.", calling attention to "how they recycle ... key images (the MIR Space Station, the astronauts on the Moon, etc.) ... mixed with science-fiction (and specially Star Trek) buzz-words or images" and then subject these "sacred icons" to "iconoclastic treatments".

The London chapter participated notably in the J18 Carnival Against Capitalism protests during that year's G8 summit, with a contingent of AAA members dressed in space suits delivering a petition against the militarisation of space to the headquarters of Lockheed. The group was particularly concerned about the Cassini-Huygens spacecraft and its RTG power source performing an earth fly-by to boost its speed toward the outer Solar System.

Timeline

- 23 April 1995: Launch of the Association of Autonomous Astronauts in the grounds of Windsor Castle, UK.
- 23 April 1996: Publication of 1st Annual Report: "Here Comes Everybody!"
- 23 April 1997: Publication of 2nd Annual Report: "Dreamtime Is Upon Us!"
- 21-22 June 1997: 1st Intergalactic Conference—Public Netbase, Vienna, Austria
- 23 April 1998: Publication of 3rd Annual Report: "Moving in Several Directions At Once!"

- 18-19 April 1998: Intergalactic Conference—Link Centre, Bologna, Italy
- 23 April 1999: Publication of 4th Annual Report: "Space Travel By Any Means Necessary!"
- 18-June 27, 1999: Space 1999: Ten Days Which Shook The Universe—various venues, London, UK. http://www.deepdisc.com/space1999/
- 23 April 2000: Publication of 5th Annual Report: "See You In Space!"
- 23 April 2007 : AAA II Wake-Up Communique: "The Dream Is Just Beginning"

AAA Groups and Links

- AAA mailing list: http://tech.groups.yahoo.com/group/aaacommunityspace Programme/
- AAA 10 Year Anniversary Video Site : http://semaphore.blogs.com/aaa/
- AAA 333 Bologna
- AAA Anzio
- AAA Vienna : http://aaa.t0.or.at
- Raido AAA : http://www.uncarved.org/aaa.html
- Nomad AAA
- AAA Glasgow Cabal
- AAA Kernow : http://www.myspace.com/bodminmoorexplorer
- Disçonaut AAA http://www.uncarved.org/disconaut/
- Dionysian AAA : http://www.angelfire.com/id/ASP/DAAA.html
- Inner City AAA
- East London AAA
- Jungle AAA : http://socialfiction.org/jungleaaa
- Oceania AAA : http://www.deepdisc.com/aaa
- AAA Aotearoa
- AAA Insurgent Cosmos
- AAA Parasol
- AAA Toronto : http://mirmnp.blogspot.com
- AAA Noordung : http://www.nskstate.com/noordung/index.php
- AAA Argentina
- AAA Paris Nord
- AAA Paris Sud
- AAA Montpellier
- AAA Amsterdam/Area 23
- Forum AAA Rosko (Fr) : http://www.rezoweb.com/forum/technologie/aaaroskoforum.shtml
- "Quitter la gravité", the AAA book in French (Editions de L'Éclat, 2001) : http://www.lyber-eclat.net/lyber/aaa/quitter_la_gravite.html
- AAA Twin Cities (Minnesota, USA)

Music

"Rave In Space" CD (2000)

EL CLUB DE LOS ASTRONAUTAS

El Club de los Astronautas is a space advocacy group of artists. They promote a manned, interstellar voyage by doing art and debating strategies that might make stand out this idea beyond fiction. Therefore a hypothetical spaceship is suggested, the Mare Nostrum Spaceship, which builds upon the following ideas and topics:

- regenerative and anti-ageing medicine, stem cell and gene therapy
- new pharmaceuticals, nootropics and adult neurogenesis
- neurally-controlled animats, biomechanics and artificial organs
- supercomputing, neurosimulation and neuronal modelling
- neurotechnolgy, brain computer interfaces and neuroprosthetics
- the metaverse and the socio-psychology of the avatar and the internet
- bioethics, technopolitics, science fanatism and human rights

El Club de los Astronautas was invited to the Museum of Science of Barcelona (Cosmocaixa), the University of Barcelona, the Centre de Cultura Contemporània de Barcelona (CCCB), to HispaCon, Sónar, Institut Fatima, etc.

9

Space Art, Fellowships and Prizes: Model Examples

SPACE ART

Space art is a general term for art emerging from knowledge and ideas associated with outer space, both as a source of inspiration and as a means for visualizing and promoting space travel. Whatever the stylistic path, the artist is generally attempting to communicate ideas somehow related to space, often including appreciation of the infinite variety and vastness which surrounds us. In some cases, artists who consider themselves space artists use more than illustration and painting to communicate scientific discoveries or works depicting space; a new breed of space artists work directly with spaceflight technology and scientists as an opportunity to expand the arts, humanities and cultural expression relative to space exploration.

Photography

The Cosmos contains many sources of visual inspiration that our growing abilities to gather and propagate has spread through the mass culture. The first photographs of the entire Earth by satellites and manned Apollo missions brought a new sense of our world as an island in empty space and promoted ideas of the essential unity of Humanity. Photographs taken by explorers on the Moon shared the experience of being on another world. The famous 'Pillars of Creation' Hubble Space Telescope and other Hubble photos often evoke intense responses from viewers, see for example Hubble's Planetary Nebula. Perhaps such images provide modern audiences with fresh visions through which the religious awe invoked by the great murals in cathedrals of earlier centuries can be experienced anew.

Modern Digital Art

Practitioners of the visual arts have for many decades explored space in their imaginations using traditional painting media and many are now using digital media toward similar ends. Science Fiction magazines and picture essay magazines were once a major outlet for space art, often featuring planets, spaceships and dramatic alien landscapes. Chesley Bonestell, R.A. Smith, Lucian Ridaux, and Ledek pesek were some of the major artists actively involved in visualizing space exploration proposals with input from experts in the infant rocketry field anxious to spread their ideas to a wider audience. A strength of particularly Bonestell's work was the portrayal of exotic worlds with their own alien beauty, often giving a sense of destination as much as of the technological means of getting there.

International Association of Astronomical Artists

The premier organization in the world for creating space art is the International Association of Astronomical Artists. Composed of over 120 members, the IAAA strives to depict the wonders of the Universe in ways to inspire the greater human population and raise awareness of space. Members of the IAAA have been creating space art in all of its myriad forms for 25 years, from traditional painting, to digital works, and 3-D zero-gravity sculpture.

The Artists

Space artists may work closely with space scientists and engineers to help them to visualize and develop their scientific and technological concepts making the dream of space exploration a reality. Other forms of pictorial space art bring the viewer to inner visions inspired directly or otherwise by the fruits of the expanding vision of Humanity. Some aspects of such art pay visual homage to outer space, popular ideas of life on other worlds including alien visitation visions, dream symbology, psychedelic imagery and other influences on contemporary visionary art.

Now that artists have experienced zero gravity conditions during many flights flown with NASA, the Russian and French Space Agencies, and with the Zero Gravity Arts Consortium as part of a hope for migration of Humanity beyond Earth, artistic expressions unknowable today will continue to unfold with new forms of microgravity expression emerging. Although such dreams await substantial opportunity, early efforts by artists to have art pieces placed in space have already been accomplished with holography, painting, microgravity mobile, floating literary works and sculpture.

Zero G Space Art

The first painting to be brought to Earth-orbit was a radiant study of the golden sunlight on a Soviet space station by Russian artist Andrei Sokolov, carried aboard the Soviet Mir space station in the mid 1980s. In 1984 Joseph McShane and in 1989 Lowery Burgess had their conceptual artworks flown aboard the Space Shuttle utilizing NASA's 'Get Away Special' programme. The first sculpture specifically designed for a human habitat in orbit was Arthur Woods' *Cosmic Dancer* which was sent to the Mir station in 1993. In 1995, Ars ad Astra—the 1st Art Exhibition in Earth orbit consisting of 20 original artworks from 20 artists and an electronic archive also took place on the Mir as a part of ESA's EUROMIR'95 mission. In 1998, Frank Pietronigro flew Research Project Number 33: Investigating The Creative Process in a Microgravity Environment where the artist drew, created 'drift paintings' and danced in microgrvity space. In 2006, the artist returned to microgravity flight to create three new works, one in collaboration with Lowry Burgess, Moments in the Infinite Absolute, Flags in Space! and a new form of microgravity mobile.

Fallen Astronaut

Small art objects have been carried on several Apollo missions, such as gold emblems and a small *Fallen Astronaut* figurine that was left on the Moon during the Apollo 15 mission. Visual observations have been recorded in drawings and commentary by earlier Cosmonauts and Astronauts of difficult to photograph phenomena such as the airglow, orbital twilight colors, and outer details of the Solar corona. An able and observant artist can record aspects of the surroundings beyond the design limitations of any particular camera system.

Astronomical Art

Astronomical art, the direct inheritor of the artistic standards of Bonestell, is an aspect of space art whose primary emphasis is in giving the viewer visual impressions of alien and exotic places in the Cosmos. As an Astronomical artist one should have a sense of why the lighting, sky color, even your chosen landscape surroundings appear as they do, and how a drastic change in a specific condition as on other worlds could alter the scene dramatically. One should have a reasonable 'grounding' in science, the nature of the sky and weather, and geology for knowing the Earth, as well as Astronomy for knowing the heavens. Such artists share with every other conceivable creative expression the vast arena containing what can be called Space Art.

Space Art Related Books

- *Space Art* Ron Miller Starlog Magazine
- *Space Art: How to draw and paint planets, moons and landscapes of alien worlds* Michael Carroll, Watson Guptill Publishers 2007
- *Infinite Worlds* Vincent Di Fate
- *Eyewitness to Space, from the Art Programme of the National Aeronautics and Space Administration* (1963 to 1969). Foreword by J. Carter Brown. Preface by Thomas O. Paine. New York: H.N. Abrams
- *Fire and Ice: A History of Comets in Art* Roberta J.M. Olsen Walker and Company, New York
- *Visions of Space* David A. Hardy Paper Tiger 1989
- *Worlds Beyond: The Art of Chesley Bonestell* Ron Miller & Frederick C. Durant, III
- *In the Stream of Stars: The Soviet-American Space Art Book* Sokolov, Miller, Myagkov, Hartmann, International Association for the Astronomical Arts
- *Blueprint for Space* Frederick I. Ordway, III & Randy Liebermann, eds
- *Visions of Spaceflight Images from the Ordway collection* Frederick I. Ordway III Four Walls Eight Windows, New York 2000

- *Celestial Visitations: The Art of Gilbert Williams* 1979 Pomegranate Artbooks
- *Cosmic Art* Ramond & Lila Piper Hawthorne Books 1975
- *Universe* Don Dixon Houghton Mifflin 1981
- *Imagining Space Achievements, Predictions, Possibilities 1950-2050* Chronicle Books 2001
- *Star Struck: One Thousand Years of the Art of Science and Astronomy* Ronald Brashear Daniel Lewis 2001, University of Washington Press
- *Futures: 50 Years in Space* David A. Hardy & Patrick Moore AAPPL 2004

Space Artists

- Chesley Bonestell
- Michael Carroll
- Don Davis
- Don Dixon
- David A. Hardy
- William K. Hartmann
- Jon Lomberg
- Ron Miller
- Rick Sternbach
- Juraj Petovsky link title

Space Art Organizations

- Association of Autonomous Astronauts
- El Club de los Astronautas
- International Association of Astronomical Artists
- Zero Gravity Arts Consortium

SPACE FELLOWSHIP

The **International Space Fellowship** (ISF) is an international news and information network dedicated to the development of the aerospace industry.

The organisation works to report and communicate aerospace news and information to its valued community. Offering a unique and fresh approach, the International Space Fellowship works alongside leading aerospace organisations with the goal of bringing space to the general public. Our online news service finds the latest aerospace news from both inside and outside our community often meaning we are the first place for breaking news.

History

In the early days the Space Fellowship was the Official X PRIZE Foundation web forum and a separate X PRIZE blog on Google's blogspot. On 12 July 2004 the X PRIZE Foundation web forum and the X PRIZE blog spot joined to form the X PRIZE News. On 18 October 2005 the X PRIZE News was renamed to the International Space Fellowship.

Members

Aerospace companies/Teams and prizes having their official forums listed on the Space Fellowship are:

- Armadillo Aerospace
- JP Aerospace
- Micro-Space
- Masten Space Systems
- Interorbital Systems
- Microlaunchers
- Cambridge University Spaceflight
- Epsilon vee
- Team Prometheus
- N-Prize

ANSARI X PRIZE

The **Ansari X PRIZE** was a space competition in which the X PRIZE Foundation offered a US$10,000,000 prize for the first non-government organization to launch a reusable manned spacecraft into space twice within two weeks. It was modelled after early 20th-century aviation prizes, and aimed to spur development of low-cost spaceflight. The prize was won on October 4, 2004, the 47th anniversary of the Sputnik 1 launch, by the Tier One project designed by Burt Rutan and financed by Microsoft co-founder Paul Allen, using the experimental spaceplane SpaceShipOne. $10 million was awarded to the winner, but more than $100 million was invested in new technologies in pursuit of the prize.

The second X PRIZE, the Archon X PRIZE, was announced in October 2006 by the X PRIZE Foundation. The third X Prize, the Progressive Insurance Automotive X Prize, was announced shortly thereafter. The fourth X Prize, the Google Lunar X Prize, was announced in September 2007.

Motivation

The X PRIZE was first proposed by Dr. Peter Diamandis in an address to the NSS International Space Development Conference in 1995. The competition goal was adopted from the SpaceCub project, demonstration of a private vehicle capable of flying a pilot to the edge of space, defined as 100 km altitude. This goal was selected to help encourage the space industry in the private sector, which is why the entries were not allowed to have any government funding. It aimed to demonstrate that spaceflight can be affordable and accessible to corporations and civilians, opening the door to commercial spaceflight and space tourism. It is also hoped that competition will breed innovation, introducing new low-cost methods of reaching Earth orbit, and ultimately pioneering low-cost space travel and unfettered human expansion into the solar system. The X PRIZE was modelled after many prizes from the early 20th century that helped prod the development of airflight, including most notably the $25,000 Orteig Prize that spurred Charles Lindbergh to make his solo flight across the Atlantic Ocean. NASA is developing a similar prize programme called Centennial Challenges to generate innovative solutions to space technology problems.

Created in May 1996 and initially called just "X PRIZE", it was renamed "Ansari X PRIZE" on May 6, 2004 following a multi-million dollar donation from entrepreneurs Anousheh Ansari and Amir Ansari.

Contestants

Twenty-six teams from around the world participated, ranging from volunteer hobbyists to large corporate-backed operations:

- Acceleration Engineering
- Advent Launch Services
- ARCASPACE
- Armadillo Aerospace
- American Astronautics Corporation
- Bristol Spaceplanes Limited
- Canadian Arrow
- The da Vinci Project—website
- Pablo de Leon & Associates
- Discraft Corporation
- Flight Exploration
- Fundamental Technology Systems
- High Altitude Research Corporation
- IL Aerospace Technologies
- Interorbital Systems
- Kelly Space and Technology
- Lone Star Space Access Corporation
- Micro-Space, Inc.
- PanAero, Inc.
- Pioneer Rocketplane
- Scaled Composites' Tier One project

Winning Team

- Space Transport Corporation
- Starchaser Industries
- Suborbital Corporation
- TGV Rockets
- Vanguard Spacecraft
- Whalen Aeronautics Inc.

This contestant list notably did not include traditional space access companies like Boeing and Lockheed, which many in the industry believe to be incapable of replacing their present space transportation vehicles with low-cost alternatives. These critics claim as evidence the companies' several failed attempts to do so, such as the X-33 project, on contract from NASA and other U.S. government agencies. However, the X PRIZE Foundation itself did not ban these companies from applying, so long as they could prove their efforts on this project would be free of government funding.

Competition Status

The Tier One project made two successful competitive flights, X1 on September 29, 2004 piloted by Mike Melvill to 102.9 km and X2 on October 4, 2004 piloted by Brian Binnie to 112 km. They thus won the prize, which was awarded on November 6, 2004. (Note: the winning team is referred to by several names at various times: Tier One, Scaled Composites, and Mojave Aerospace Ventures.)

The trophy is currently on display in the St. Louis Science Center in St. Louis, Missouri.

Flight Attempts by Teams that did not win

Although only the Tier One team actually launched a spacecraft into suborbital space, several other teams have conducted low-altitude tests or announced future plans to launch into space:

- The da Vinci Project originally announced that their first flight would be on October 2, 2004, but this was postponed indefinitely on September 23, 2004, as they were unable to obtain a few necessary components in time. They have not announced a revised timetable.
- The Canadian Arrow team conducted a successful full-power engine test in 2005 and announced on June 2, 2005, that it had received permission from the Canadian government to use Cape Rich as a future launch site.
- On August 8, 2004, Space Transport Corporation's **Rubicon 1** and Armadillo Aerospace's test vehicle, in two separate unmanned test launches, both crashed and were destroyed.
- On February 15, 2005, AERA Corporation (formerly American Astronautics) announced its plans to send seven paying passengers into space as early as 2006, a full year before the first announced speculative Virgin Galactic flight.

List of Major Donors by Order of Donation

- Anousheh Ansari and Amir Ansari
- First USA (J.P. Morgan Chase), $1,000,000
- New Spirit of St. Louis Organization
- Danforth Foundation, $500,000
- Tom Clancy, $100K-$500K
- J.S. McDonnell (McDonnell Douglas)
- Andrew Taylor (Enterprise Rent-A-Car)
- Andrew Beal (Beal Bank)
- St. Louis Science Center

Organization

With the Ansari X PRIZE, the X PRIZE Foundation (based in Santa Monica, CA) established a philanthropic model in which offering a prize for achieving a specific goal stimulates entrepreneurial investment that produces a 10 times or greater return on the prize purse and at least 100 times in follow-on investment and social benefit. The Foundation has developed into a non-profit prize institute that conceives, designs and manages public competitions for the benefit of humanity.

Spinoffs

The success of the X PRIZE competition has spurred spinoffs that are set up in the same way. There have been two major spinoffs at this point, the first of which is the

M Prize (short for Methuselah Mouse Prize), which is a prize set up by University of Cambridge biogerontologist Aubrey de Grey which will go to the scientific team that successfully extends the life or reverses the aging of mice, which would then eventually be available to humans. The second is the NASA Centennial Challenges, which consist of (among others) the Tether Challenge in which teams compete to develop superstrong tethers as a component to space elevators, and the Beam Power Challenge which encourages ideas for transmitting power wirelessly. An independent spinoff called the N-Prize was started by Cambridge Microbiologist Paul H. Dear in 2008, designed to foster research into low-cost orbital launchers.

The X PRIZE foundation itself is developing additional prizes, including one around genomics, and another around energy—the Progressive Insurance Automotive X Prize. There is also a possible "H-Prize", focused on hydrogen vehicle research, although this goal has already been addressed by H.R. 5143, an X-Prize-inspired bill passed by the House of Representatives.

10

Sex in Space: A Tourism Perspective

SEX IN SPACE

Sex in space is human sexual activity in weightless and extreme environments of space. The act of human intimacy, sexual intercourse, and procreation distinguished by the state of weightlessness (precluding artificial gravity) presents difficulties surrounding the performing of most sexual activities due to Newton's Third Law. The topic also includes conception and pregnancy in off-Earth environments.

The topic has been hotly disputed to clarify its potential impact on human beings in the isolated, confined, and hazardous environment of space. Past discussions often included attempts to determine speculations (e.g., about the STS-47 mission, on which married astronauts Mark C. Lee and Jan Davis flew), and even hoaxes, such as Document 12-571-3570.

Experts such as Princeton astrophysics professor Dr. J. Richard Gott consider humanity's expansion into space crucial to survival, but it was considered taboo for decades of space faring exploration history.

As of 2009, with NASA planning long-term missions for lunar settlements with goals to explore and colonize space, the topic has taken its respected place in life sciences. Scientist Stephen Hawking publicly concurred in 2007 that possibly human survival itself will depend on successfully contending with the extreme environments of space.

Debates

The debate of sex in space has turned from taboo to discussion of human procreation, relationships and reproduction in the extreme environments of space.

Discussions include the selection process and compatibility of crews for long-term missions, calls and ethics of testing, and the effects of conception and embryonic gestation in microgravity.

It is assumed that the nervous and vestibular systems may fail to develop properly in individuals growing up in a low or a weightless environment, and that this would have implications for space-born humans making the trip to Earth though the possibility of pregnancy in weightless environments in humans is currently uncertain.

United States

NASA has not issued any public statement as to whether or not anyone has had intercourse on space shuttle missions; a NASA spokesman (Bill Jeffs) has stated "We don't study sexuality in space, and we don't have any studies ongoing with that...If that's your specific topic, there's nothing to discuss."

Soviet Union

A Soviet research facility in the field of space medicine, the Institute of Biomedical Problems (IBP), has been involved for decades in the sex-related studies of living species in space. The Institute's interest in topic began in the early 1960s, when it noticed a difference in behaviour between two dogs that had flown in space, Veterok and Ugolyok. Ugolyok, unlike Veterok, maintained quite a healthy libido during his longer-than-average life span.

A 1976 article reported that an exposure of Wistar rats to 22 days of weightlessness and other spaceflight factors induced no morphological changes in the spermatogenic tissue or disorders in the spermatogenic process of the rats, and the offspring of the male "space rats" was normal in all aspects.

Regarding human sex, Dr. Anna Goncharova said that if crew members are just colleagues and friends, one should never impose on them any intimate relations for the sake of their psycho-emotional stability. It was rumoured that the unhappy marriage of Soviet cosmonauts Valentina Tereshkova and Andrian Nikolayev was in part instigated by the pressure of the IBP.

Effects of Microgravity on Human Anatomy

Sexual Activity

In zero gravity there is no natural convection to carry away body heat and bodily fluids tend to pool around the body. Scientists have found that people tend to perspire more in microgravity. The sweat from sexual activity could pool as floating droplets.

Although zero gravity is a boon for saggy body parts, males might notice a "slight decrease" in penis size due to the lower blood pressure that humans experience in microgravity.

Reproduction

Studies conducted on reproduction of mammals in microgravity include experiments with rats. Although the fetus developed properly, the rats that developed in microgravity lacked the ability to right themselves.

The 2Suit

The 2suit (alternately *2-Suit* or *twosuit*) is a garment designed to facilitate effortless intimacy in the weightless environments such as outer space, or on planets with low gravity. The flight garment, invented by Vanna Bonta, was one of the subjects of History Channel's *The Universe* "Sex in Space" documentary, September 13, 2008, which broke ground as the first documentary to open the topic of sex in space to a global mainstream audience.

Popular Culture

IMDB has the keyword "zero gravity sex" for movies, and the TV Tropes Wiki maintains an article on the depictions of space sex in media in general.

Spoof NASA Document

The difficulties microgravity poses for human intimacy were discussed in the anonymous fictional NASA Document 12-571-3570 in 1989, where the use of an elastic belt and an inflatable tunnel were proposed as solutions to these problems. A spoof mission patch and other documents were determined to be hoaxes.

In Science Fiction

In 1973, Isaac Asimov made conjectures about what sex would be like in the weightless environment of space. He anticipated some of the benefits of engaging in sex in an environment of microgravity.

When Apollo 11 astronaut Michael Collins published his autobiography *Carrying the Fire* in 1974, a contemporary *Time* Magazine quoted the following passage:

> "Imagine a spacecraft of the future, with a crew of a thousand ladies, off for Alpha Centauri, with 2,000 breasts bobbing beautifully and quivering delightfully in response to every weightless movement... and I am the commander of the craft, and it is Saturday morning and time for inspection, naturally."

Science fiction author Arthur C. Clarke was quick to point out in a letter to the editor that he had beaten Collins to addressing the matter in the novel *Rendezvous with Rama* (1973):

> "Some women, Commander Norton had decided long ago, should not be allowed aboard ship; weightlessness did things to their breasts that were too damn distracting. It was bad enough when they were motionless; but when they started to move, and sympathetic vibrations set in, it was more than any warm-blooded male should be asked to take. He was quite sure that at least one serious space accident had been caused by acute crew distraction, after the transit of an unbolstered lady officer through the control cabin."

The magazine followed this up by running a letter from one Sharon Smith, who agreed that the presence of breasts "bobbing weightlessly" would render spacemen unable to do their jobs and added that the space programme must safeguard itself by the painful but necessary step of excluding men.

In Film

- The sci-fi horror film *Supernova* (2000) featured sex between several of the characters in zero-gravity areas of the Medical Ship.
- Private Media Group filmed a brief scene for the space-themed pornographic film *The Uranus Experiment* in a Russian aircraft flying a parabolic track (similar to NASA's Vomit Comet). *The Uranus Experiment* features around 20 seconds of pornography actors Sylvia Saint and Nick Lang (who portray astronauts living on a space station) having sex in freefall. The scene was nominated for a Nebula Award, but did not win.
- A piece of folk music on the subject: author Diana G. Gallagher's Pegasus Award-winning *A Reconsideration of Anatomical Docking Maneuvers in a Zero-G Environment*.
- In the James Bond film *Moonraker*, James Bond (played by Roger Moore), and the Bond girl, Dr. Holly Goodhead, have sex in the cargo bay of the Moonraker 5 Space Shuttle in the final scene.
- The comedy *Moving Violations* (1985) suggests the main characters, played by actors John Murray and Jennifer Tilly, have an intimate encounter in a weightlessness simulator.
- In the novelization of *Alien*, Parker tells Brett about an episode of zero-G sex that went wrong.
- In the movie *Cube 2: Hypercube*, two of the main characters have sexual intercourse while floating in the middle of a cube room.

2SUIT

The **2suit** (alternately **2-Suit** or **twosuit**) *(abbrv.)* **2S** is a garment designed to facilitate effortless intimacy in the weightless environments such as outer space, or on planets with low gravity.

History

The 2Suit was invented by American novelist, actress and poet Vanna Bonta in 2006 after an experience in zero gravity in 2004 when she flew with the National Space Society. Bonta presented the garment design in 2006 on a panel at a New Space conference of the Space Frontier Foundation, of which Bonta is an Advocate. In 2008, the first 2Suit was manufactured and tested by a History Channel documentary for the series The Universe.

The documentary described the "2Suit is one small step for humankind colonizing the universe." The garment was presented as a utilitarian garment with general applications that serves the need for human intimacy and procreation by stabilizing physical proximity in microgravity environments.

Design

The garment is made of two components flight suits designed to be worn alone or attached to another 2S model for the purpose of intimacy or sex in space. Once attached, additional design functions are deployed, releasing ultralight fabric which transforms the 2suit into one roomy garment that keeps two people in proximity of one another without need to exert effort. It includes Velcro strips, zippers and diaphanous inner material.

The 2suit is equipped to fasten to a stable surface. The roominess within the garment is adjustable from within. It also is lined with inner harnesses for optional use that can regulate the garment to adjust proximity of various points of the bodies to one another. A quick-disrobe function removes the garments, optionally leaving harnesses in place for stabilization to a static surface.

Function and Purpose

The function of the 2suit is to stabilize human proximity, thus facilitating intimacy, tandem or adjacent tasks, recreation, or human procreation in weightless environments. Its serves general Rest and Relaxation as well as procreative functions. The 2suit also has useful thermal applications in emergency situations, as it can store body heat.

The 2suit enables lounging or work station stabilization, relieving the need to exert constant effort to prevent drifting apart that occurs in weightless and microgravity environments. The 2suit stabilizes the extremes of Newton's law of motion in zero gravity, i.e., for every action there is an equal and opposite reaction. A state of human intimacy is experienced, providing psychological benefit, by facilitating complete relaxation in close proximity, without drift upon contact, and without otherwise needing to be in confined cubicles.

The invention was a result of Bonta's personal experience in zero gravity in 2004 when empirically noting the effects of the complete lack of attraction of physical mass in weightless environments. Imagining prolonged periods in low or zero gravity environment, Bonta projected that in weightless environments, a sense of human intimacy, including reading or relaxing in close proximity, would be lacking outside of confined areas. The constant effort to maintain physical proximity could create cumulative, if low grade, stress.

Postulating "relaxed human closeness as a conditioned requisite that creates a sense of well-being," Bonta devised the 2suit. As a solution, it would eliminate constant physical struggle to remain close in microgravity, and still alternately afford open space conditions for enjoyment, in privacy or for group activities involving couples, such as movies or events.

Family versions might expand to 3 or 4suit, for use with undergarments.

2suit in Media and Pop Culture References

- Inventors Digest May 2009; Vol. 25 Issue 5—2suit Adds New Meaning to the Mother of Invention, by Jennipher Adkins
- WIRED.IT News Scienza Lo spazio, mai stato così sexy, by Giorgia Scaturro; 27 April 2009
- The Universe—Sex in Space New Era for Mankind?—History Channel premiere; 2 December 2008

- The Universe: Sex in Space Explores Human Side of Space 2 December 2008
- Tests for sex in space may begin IGN August 2008
- Sex in Space Possible but Problematic Wednesday, 20 August 2008
- Sex in space could be out of this world Metro.UK, by Fiona MacDonald
- The 400-mile high club The Sunday Times, by Richard Johnson; October 7, 2007
- Sex in space: how to do it right
- Sesso nello spazio? La Repubblica, by Benedetta Perilli, **25 July 2006**
- The Zero G Spot Outside Magazine, by Michael Behar, **December 2006**

BEST "ZERO GRAVITY SEX" TITLES

1 *Defying Gravity* (2009 TV series) Episode: Pilot
Under the command of two experienced astronauts, a relatively untested crew set off on the Antares,...

2 *Moonraker* (1979)
James Bond investigates the mid-air theft of a space shuttle and discovers a plot to commit global genocide.

3 *Dracula* (2000)
A group of thieves break into a chamber expecting to find paintings, but instead they release the count himself, who travels to New Orleans to find his nemesis' daughter, Mary Van Helsing.

4 *Falling Fire* (1997)
In the not so distant future mankind has squandered their resources. A team of specialists is sent to...

5 *Supernova* (2000)
Supernova chronicles the search and rescue patrol of a medical ship in deep space in the early 22nd...

6 *Red Shoe Diaries* (1992 TV series)
Episode: Weightless

MILE HIGH CLUB

The **mile high club** (or **MHC**) is a slang term applied collectively to individuals who have engaged in sexual intercourse while on board an aircraft in flight. There is no known formally constituted club so named. However, since "membership" of the "club" is really a matter of an individual asserting they have qualified, the qualifications for membership are open to some interpretation.

Some people attribute the allure of the club to the lower atmospheric pressure in the flight cabin, which they claim increases the intensity of orgasms. Another explanation is the vibration of the airplane, which may make arousal easier. Others say that they have fantasies about pilots or flight attendants, or a fetish about planes themselves. For many others, perhaps the majority, the appeal of joining the MHC is the thrill of doing something taboo and the thrill of the risk of being discovered.

History

A website using the name *Mile high club* humorously claims the "club's" "founder" as pilot and design engineer Lawrence Sperry along with "socialite Mrs. Waldo Polk" citing their possibly anecdotal flight in an autopilot-equipped Curtiss Flying Boat near New York in November 1916.

The American transportation authority NTSB reports a documented case in which sexual activity is at least partly responsible for an aviation accident.

In November 2007 the BBC reported a story headlined "Airline Bans A380 Mile-High Club" about a measure taken by Singapore Airlines. The airline asked their first class passengers shortly after the introduction of their new Airbus A380 to respect the law. The 12 first class cabins feature a double bed, but the cabins are not soundproofed.

Noted Instances

Some incidents of people attempting sexual activity on planes have become popularly known:

- In October 1999 two passengers of an American Airlines flight from Dallas to Manchester were arrested after engaging in "sex acts" in front of other passengers in the business class section of the aircraft. Both lost their jobs after the press storm following the incident.
- In late 2006, a couple was arrested in part for refusing to stop overt sexual activity on a flight in a case that received widespread media attention. The couple's lawyer claims that the couple was not engaging in sexual activity, but that the man was sick and resting his head on the woman's lap.

Richard Branson, the owner of Virgin Atlantic Airways and Virgin America Airways, claimed that he joined the mile high club at age 19 (c. 1969) by engaging in sex with a woman in a lavatory. He found out after that she was married, and they had no relationship beyond the encounter in the plane.

On February 11, 2007, Lisa Robertson, a Qantas flight attendant, was dismissed after having sex with actor Ralph Fiennes in a business class lavatory during a flight from Darwin to Mumbai on January 24, 2007. Robertson at first denied the allegation, but subsequently admitted the encounter in an interview with the *Daily Mail*. She also said that she had stayed with him at his Mumbai hotel. Fiennes has refused to comment on the matter.

Legality

The BBC ran an article investigating whether sex on a plane was legal. Their conclusion was that it would depend on many factors, such as whether or not the act occurred in sight of others. Also, for international flights the law could vary depending on departure and destination cities, what country(ies) was being overflown at the time, and the nation of the carrier airline.

Charter Flights

Several private charter companies offer the opportunity to book a flight for the express purpose of engaging in sexual activity. Some commercial enterprises cash in on people's interest in joining the club by offering special charter flights designed for the purpose or by selling souvenir certificates and other items. Some websites also provide resources such as historical information about the club.

GALACTIC SUITE

Galactic Suite is a planned private space station intended for use as an orbital hotel. The company behind the project, Galactic Suite Limited of Barcelona, Spain, plans to have the station operational by 2012, and says that investors have come forward to finance the station. Critics, however, have contended that the stated time-frame is unreasonable and no evidence of hardware has been produced.

History

The station began as a hobby for Xavier Claramunt, director of Galactic Suite Limited and former aerospace engineer. *Galactic Suite* entered development after an unnamed space enthusiast invested US$3 billion to build the space station. An American company with the goal of colonising Mars has invested in the project, and discussions are reportedly ongoing with additional private investors from Japan, the United States and the United Arab Emirates.

Project

Designs for *Galactic Suite* call for a central hub with four modules radiating out, providing three bedrooms for six customers at a time. Claramunt says that while it will be a challenge to design a bathroom that works in microgravity, showers may be taken in a spa room with bubbles of floating water. The issue of moving around in space will be solved by having guests wear suits of Velcro and sticking to the module walls, similar to its use in the film *2001: A Space Odyssey*. The station will orbit the Earth once every 80 minutes, providing 15 day-and-night cycles every 24 hours. Claramunt says that construction of the station will begin in October 2008, and that European company EADS Astrium will be the contractor in charge of building the modules and other equipment.

The company has stated that a three-day stay will cost US$4 million per customer. Included in this cost is an intensive eight week space training course on a tropic island. Company studies have found that 40,000 people worldwide are capable of affording such a stay.

Equip also plan to design a James Bond-style astronaut training spaceport which will be based in the Caribbean. The spaceport will also house a new launch system built with safety and the environment in mind.

Criticism

Some experts, including Thomas Bouvet (International Astronautical Federation), Mark Homnick (4Frontiers) and Juan de Dalmau (Centro Tecnológico para la Industria Aeronáutica y del Espacio) are sceptics of the project. They have raised concerns that Galactic Suite will be unable to meet the 2012 goal because no hardware has been built and tested. The stated investment to the company is an issue since they have not revealed the identity of their investor, nor does the investment seem to be enough to cover all the project's needs; for example, the suborbital shuttle proposed by EADS Astrium would cost €1 billion, and the transformation of ESA's Automated Transfer Vehicle into a craft capable of transporting people to space would cost €2.3 billion. Further, EADS Astrium claims to have no information regarding the *Galactic Suite* project.

11

Space and Spaceflight: Issues Related to Survival, Adaptation, Suit, Food, Music and Medicine

SPACE AND SURVIVAL

Space and survival is the relationship between outer space and the long-term survival of the human species and civilization. It is based on the observation that space colonization and space science could prevent many human extinction scenarios. A related observation is the limited time and resources thought by some to be available for the colonization of space.

Uses of Space Colonization

Extinction can be prevented by improving the physical barrier or increasing the mean distance between people and the potential extinction event. For example, people may survive imminent explosions by being in a bunker or evacuating. Pandemics are controlled by putting exposed people in quarantine and moving healthy people away. In the long history of animal life on Earth only lineages that diversify survive into the deep future. Our lineage, genus Homo, has reduced from several species co-existing on Earth to just one—all but our own going extinct since the start of the last Ice age. This would be a danger sign for any other large mammal genus. Space colonization, particularly of other star systems, would allow our genus to diversify and adapt to potentially new habitats.

Barrier

Life support systems that enable people to live in space may also allow them to survive hazardous events. For example, an infectious disease or biological weapon that transmits through the air could not infect a person in a closed life support system. An internal supply of air and a physical barrier exists between the person and the environment.

Location and Distance

Expanding the living area of the human species increases the mean distance between humans and any hazardous event. People closest to the event are most likely to be killed or injured; people furthest from the event are most likely to survive.

Multiple Locations

Increasing the number of places where humans live also helps to prevent extinction. For example, if a massive impact event occurred on Earth without warning, the human species could possibly become extinct; its art, culture and technology would be lost. However, if humans had previously colonized locations outside Earth, the opportunities for the survival and recovery of the species would be greater.

Opportunities for Space Colonization

Space colonies do not currently exist. It can be said, however, that humans have had a continuous space presence since 2000 due to the International Space Station. There is concern that the human species may lose its organized societies or its technological knowledge, use up required resources or even become extinct before it colonizes space.

The author Sylvia Engdahl wrote about the "Critical Stage", a period of time when a civilization has both the technology to expand into space and the technology to destroy itself. Engdahl states that the human civilization is at a Critical Stage, but that the funding for space exploration and colonization is minuscule compared to the funding for weapons of mass destruction and military forces.

NBC News space analyst James Oberg commented that "It's just a matter of waiting until we get some kind of cosmic 9/11 that will make everyone say 'why didn't we see this before,' and then we'll have enough money to afford these programmes.

Uses of Space Science

The observation and study of space protects Earth, as space hazards can be seen in advance and, if given enough time to prepare, acted against.

Near-Earth Objects

Near-Earth Objects (NEOs) are asteroids, comets and large meteoroids that come close to or collide with Earth. Spaceguard is the collective name for some of the efforts to discover and study NEOs, however these efforts are not highly funded.

Objections

Creating a backup colony in space is a very costly method, and it's likely other ways of creating an independent colony are more cost efficient. While extinctions occur on the order of tens of millions of years, major damage to the structure of the Earth itself is likely on the order of billions of years. As a result, an independent surface colony, or an oceanic or sub-terrestrial colony may be a cheaper way to obtain a similar but less robust result.

The argument for diversified human populations also depends on these populations being "human." As speciation in the *Homo* genus occurs on the order of 100,000 to a million years, an independent colony may not be "human" after a short time on a geological scale.

Far more likely, an independent colony may revolt and pursue its independent self-interest. In terrestrial civilizations, this frequently occurs on the order of 10 to 100 years. Even a loyal colony may decide that it is against its economic or political interests to aid a troubled Earth, or to recolonize Earth.

The survivability and sustainability of a colony could potentially be less than the survivability and sustainability of the Earth population, especially during a colony's infancy. Creating colonies that can reliably withstand the rigours of space and unpredictable extraterrestrial environments for thousands of years may be very expensive. The creation of a colony that not only survives, but also grows to a scale where it can support programmes to create its own new colonies is a far more difficult task.

HUMAN ADAPTATION TO SPACEFLIGHT

Human physiological adaptation to the conditions of space is a challenge faced in the development of human spaceflight.

The fundamental engineering problems of escaping Earth's gravity well and developing systems for in-space propulsion have been examined for well over a century, and millions of man-hours of research have been spent on them. In recent years there has been an increase in research into the issue of how humans can survive and work in space for extended and possibly indefinite periods of time. This question requires input from the whole gamut of physical and biological sciences and has now become the greatest challenge, other than funding, to human space exploration. A fundamental step in overcoming this challenge is trying to understand the effects and the impact long-term space travel has on the human body.

Importance

The sum of mankind's experience has resulted in the accumulation of 58 solar years in space and a much better understanding of how the human body adapts. However, in the future, industrialisation of space and exploration of inner and outer planets will require humans to endure longer and longer periods in space. A recent report has highlighted the limits to the quality and quantity of current data, which make it difficult for scientists to extrapolate all the effects of living in space long term. The majority of the data comes from missions of short duration and so some of the long-term physiological effects of living in space are still unknown. A round trip to Mars with current technology is estimated to involve at least 18 months in transit alone. How the human body reacts to such time periods in space is a vital part of the preparation for such journeys. On-board medical facilities need to be able to cope with any type of trauma or emergency as well as contain a huge variety of diagnostic and medical instruments in order to keep a crew healthy over a long period of time, as these will be the only facilities available on board a spacecraft to cope with not only trauma, but also the adaptive responses of the human body in space.

Public Perception

Public perception of living in space is generally skewed towards the TV sci-fi of *Star Trek* where gravity is artificially produced and journeys to distant stars take less than a day. The real-world difficulties of extended space travel are far more complex than those presented in most science fiction novels or movies.

Effects on Humans

The effects of space conditions on humans can be separated into two areas, the physical and the psychological.

Unprotected Effects

The environment of space is highly dangerous without appropriate protection. The greatest threat is from the lack of pressure in the vacuum environment, while temperature and radiation effects also have an influence. In the low pressure environment, gas exchange in the lungs would continue as normal but would result in the removal of all gases, including oxygen, from the bloodstream. After 9 to 12 seconds, the deoxygenated blood would reach the brain, and loss of consciousness would result. Death would gradually follow after two minutes of exposure—though the limits are uncertain. As shown in the film depiction of Arthur C. Clarke's vignette in *2001: A Space Odyssey* (1968), if actions are taken quickly, and normal pressure restored within around 90 seconds, the victim may well make a full recovery.

Humans and animals exposed to vacuum will lose consciousness after a few seconds and die of hypoxia within minutes, but the symptoms are not nearly as graphic as the imagery in the public media. Blood and other body fluids do boil when their pressure drops below 6.3 kPa (47 Torr), the vapour pressure of water at body temperature. This condition is called ebullism. The steam may bloat the body to twice its normal size and slow circulation, but tissues are elastic and porous enough to prevent rupture. Ebullism is slowed by the pressure containment of blood vessels, so some blood remains liquid. Swelling and ebullism can be reduced by containment in a flight suit. Shuttle astronauts wear a fitted elastic garment called the Crew Altitude Protection Suit (CAPS) which prevents ebullism at pressures as low as 2 kPa (15 Torr). Rapid evaporative cooling of the skin will create frost, particularly in the mouth, but this is not a significant hazard.

A short-term exposure to vacuum of up to 30 seconds is unlikely to cause permanent physical damage. Animal experiments show that rapid and complete recovery is the norm for exposures shorter than 90 seconds, while longer full-body exposures are fatal and resuscitation has never been successful. There is only a limited amount of data available from human accidents, but it is consistent with animal data. Limbs may be exposed for much longer if breathing is not impaired. Robert Boyle was the first to show in 1660 that vacuum is lethal to small animals. In 1942, in one of a series of experiments on human subjects for the Luftwaffe, the Nazi regime exposed Dachau concentration camp prisoners to vacuum in order to determine the human body's capacity to survive high-altitude conditions.

As well as experimentation with humans and monkeys, a few cases of loss of pressure have occurred in the past, especially in experimentation on spaceflight projects. One such case is discussed in a NASA technical report: *Rapid (Explosive) Decompression Emergencies in Pressure-Suited Subjects*:

> "At NASA's Manned Spacecraft Center (now renamed Johnson Space Center) we had a test subject accidentally exposed to a near vacuum (less than 1 psi) [7 kPa] in an incident involving a leaking space suit in a vacuum chamber back in '65. He remained conscious for about 14 seconds, which is about the time it takes for O_2 deprived blood to go from the lungs to the brain. The suit probably did not reach a hard vacuum, and we began repressurizing the chamber within 15 seconds. The subject regained consciousness at around 15,000 feet [4600 m] equivalent altitude. The subject later reported that he could feel and hear the air leaking out, and his last conscious memory was of the water on his tongue beginning to boil."

There has been one recorded incident of death from decompression in spaceflight, the Soyuz 11 decompression accident, in 1971.

Cold or oxygen-rich atmospheres can sustain life at pressures much lower than atmospheric, as long as the density of oxygen is similar to that of standard sea-level atmosphere. The colder air temperatures found at altitudes of up to 3 km generally compensate for the lower pressures there. Above this altitude, oxygen enrichment is necessary to prevent altitude sickness, and spacesuits are necessary to prevent ebullism above 19 km. Most spacesuits use only 20 kPa (150 Torr) of pure oxygen, just enough to sustain full consciousness. This pressure is high enough to prevent ebullism, but simple evaporation of blood, or of gases dissolved in the blood, can still cause decompression sickness (the bends) and gas embolisms if not managed.

Rapid decompression can be much more dangerous than vacuum exposure itself. Even if the victim does not hold his breath, venting through the windpipe may be too slow to prevent the fatal rupture of the delicate alveoli of the lungs. Eardrums and sinuses may be ruptured by rapid decompression, soft tissues may bruise and seep blood, and the stress of shock will accelerate oxygen consumption leading to hypoxia. Injuries caused by rapid decompression are called barotrauma, and are well known from scuba diving accidents. A pressure drop as small as 100 Torr (13 kPa), which produces no symptoms if it is gradual, may be fatal if it occurs suddenly.

In a vacuum there is no medium for removing heat from the body by conduction or convection. Loss of heat is by radiation from the 310 K person to the 3 K of outer space. This is a slow process, especially in a clothed person, so there is no danger of immediately freezing. (Evaporation of skin moisture in the vacuum would cause immediate cooling but only by a very small amount.) Exposure to the 6000 K radiation from the Sun would lead to local heating that would be well distributed by the body's conductivity and blood circulation. Other solar radiation, particularly ultraviolet rays may cause severe sunburn in a few seconds.

Protected Effects

Despite modern technology, some hazards still prove impossible to remove. The most important factor affecting human physical well-being in space is weightlessness, more accurately defined as microgravity environments. Living in this type of environment impacts on three types of human tissue:

- gravity receptors
- fluids
- weight bearing structures

Gravity Receptors

Living on earth we constantly feel the gravitational pull and our bodies react automatically to maintain posture and locomotion in a downward pulling world. In microgravity environments, these constant signals the body is adapted to are absent. The otolith organs in the middle ear sensitive to linear accelerations no longer perceive a downwards bias, muscles are no longer required to contract to maintain posture and pressure receptors in the feet and ankles no longer signal the direction of down. These changes can immediately result in visual-orientation illusions where the astronaut feels that he has flipped 180 degrees. Over time however the brain adapts and although these illusions can still occur most astronauts begin to see "down" as where the feet are. People returning to Earth after extended weightless periods initially have great difficulty maintaining their balance but recover the ability very quickly, highlighting the remarkable ability of the human body to adapt. Over half of astronauts also experience symptoms of motion sickness for the first three days of travel due to the conflict between what the body expects and what the body actually perceives.

Fluids

The second effect of weightlessness takes place in human fluids. The body is made up of 60 per cent water, much of it intra-vascular and inter-cellular. Within a few moments of entering a microgravity environment, fluid is immediately re-distributed to the upper body resulting in bulging neck veins, puffy face and sinus and nasal congestion which can last throughout the duration of the trip and is very much like the symptoms of the common cold. In space the autonomic reactions of the body to maintain blood pressure are not required and fluid is distributed more widely around the whole body. This results in a decrease in plasma (water in the blood stream) volume of around 20 per cent. These fluid shifts initiate a cascade of adaptive systemic effects that can be dangerous upon return to earth. Orthostatic intolerance results in astronauts returning to Earth after extended space missions being unable to stand unassisted for more than 10 minutes at a time without fainting. This is due in part to changes in the autonomic regulation of blood pressure and the loss of plasma volume. Although this effect becomes worse the longer the time spent in space, as yet all individuals have returned to normal within at most a few weeks of landing.

Weight Bearing Structures

The third and most worrying effect of long-term weightlessness involves bones and muscles. Without the effects of gravity, skeletal muscle is no longer required to maintain our posture and the muscle groups used in moving around in a weightless environment are very different to those required in terrestrial locomotion. Consequently some muscles atrophy rapidly. The types of muscle fibre prominent in muscles also change. Slow twitch endurance fibres used to maintain posture are replaced by fast twitch rapidly contracting fibres that are insufficient for any heavy labour. Bone metabolism also changes. Normally bone is laid down in the direction of mechanical stress, however in a microgravity environment there is very little mechanical stress. This results in a loss of bone tissue approximately 1.5 per cent per month especially from the lower vertebrae, hip and femur. Elevated blood calcium levels from the lost bone result in dangerous calcification of soft tissues and potential kidney stone formation. It is still unknown whether bone recovers completely. Loss of bone and muscle make it very difficult for humans to move and even breathe under the weight of Earth's pull upon their return. The longer the flight, the more loss will occur until it may become impossible for the individual to survive the pull of Earth's gravity for any extended period of time.

Effects of Radiation

Weightlessness is not the only factor to affect the human body in space. Without the protection of the Earth's atmosphere and magnetosphere astronauts are exposed to high levels of radiation through a steady flux of cosmic rays. A year in even low-earth orbit results in a dose of radiation 10 times that of the annual dose on earth resulting in a high risk of astronauts developing cancer. High levels of radiation can create 'chromosomal aberrations' in blood lymphocytes. These cells are heavily involved in the immune system and so any damage may contribute to the lowered immunity experienced by astronauts. Over time immunodeficiency results in the rapid spread of infection between crew members, especially in such confined areas. Radiation has also recently been linked to a higher incidence of cataracts in astronauts. Protective shielding and protective drugs may lower the risks to astronauts to an acceptable level, but data is scarce, and longer-term exposure will result in greater risks.

Sense of Taste

One effect of weightlessness on humans is that some astronauts report a change in their sense of taste in spacehttp. Some astronauts find that their food is bland, others find that their favourite foods no longer taste as good, some astronauts enjoy eating certain foods that they would not normally eat and some find no change whatsoever. The reason for this is uncertain, and several theories have been suggested:

- Congestion: Microgravity may cause fluid buildup in the sinuses, changing the taste in a similar fashion to holding one's nose while eating.
- Physical food degradation: Food in orbit is often stored for some months before being consumed. This and the stellar radiation may cause a breakdown in the groups of chemicals that give food its taste, resulting in bland food.
- Boredom: Menus for the ISS astronauts are planned on a repeating 8-day cycle, which are selected from a menu designed by NASA, and taken into

space with the astronaut. This constant repetition may lead to some astronauts getting tired of food that they had previously liked.

- Psychological changes: The loss of taste may be purely psychological.

Astronauts often choose strongly tasting food such as salsa or shrimp cocktail.

Other Physical Effects

Other physical discomforts such as back and abdominal pain are commonly experienced with no clear cause. These may be part of the asthenia syndrome reported by cosmonauts living in space over an extended period of time, but seen as anecdotal by astronauts. Fatigue, listlessness, and psychosomatic worries are also part of the syndrome. Data are inconclusive, however the syndrome does appear to exist as a manifestation of all the internal and external stress crews in space must face. The amount and quality of sleep experienced in space is poor due to highly variable light and dark cycles on flight decks and poor illumination during daytime hours in the space craft. Even the habit of looking out of the window before retiring can send the wrong messages to the brain resulting in poor sleep patterns. These disturbances in circadian rhythm have profound effects on the neurobehavioural responses of crew and aggravate the psychological stresses they already experience.

Psychological Effects

The psychological effects of living in space have not been clearly analyzed but analogies on Earth do exist, such as Arctic research stations and submarines. The enormous stress on the crew, coupled with the body adapting to other environmental changes, can result in anxiety, insomnia and depression. According to current data however astronauts and cosmonauts seem extremely resilient to psychological stresses. Interpersonal issues can have an enormous influence on a human's well-being and yet little research has been undertaken to examine crew selection issues in relation to this. The Mars Arctic Research Station and Mars Desert Research Station have examined the influence of different crew selections when living in a completely isolated environment and may provide vital data for future experiences.

Future Prospects

At the moment only rigorously tested humans have experienced the conditions of space. If off-world colonization someday begins, many types of people will be exposed to these dangers, and the effects on the elderly (except for John Glenn) and on the very young are completely unknown. Factors such as nutritional requirements and physical environments which have not been examined here will become important. Overall, there is little data on the manifold effects of living in space and this makes working to mitigate the risks during a lengthy space habitation difficult. Test beds such as the International Space Station (ISS) are presently being utilized to research some of these risks.

The environment of space is still largely unknown, and there will likely be hazards of which we are not currently aware. Meanwhile, future technologies such as artificial gravity and more complex bioregenerative life support systems may someday be capable of mitigating some hazards.

FLIGHT SUIT

A **flight suit** is a full body garment, worn while flying a powered aircraft such as military airplanes and helicopters. These suits are generally made to keep the wearer warm, as well as being practical, and durable (including fire retardant). Its appearance is usually similar to a jumpsuit. A military flight suit may also show rank insignia. It is sometimes used as a combat uniform in CQB or VBSS situations, for its practicality.

History

As aviation developed in unheated open cockpits, the need for warm clothing quickly became apparent, as did the need for multiple pockets with closures of either buttons, snaps, or zippers to prevent loss of articles during maneuvers. Various types of flight jackets and pants coverings were developed and, during World War I, leather two-piece outfits were common among pilots to ward off the chill caused by propwash and the cold of low-oxygen high altitude flying. Leather quickly became the preferred material due to its durability and the protection it offered against flying debris such as insect strikes during climb-outs and landings, and oil thrown off by the simple rotary and inline motors of the time.

By the time World War II started in earnest, electrically-heated suits were introduced for patrol and bomber crews who routinely operated at high altitudes above 30,000 feet, where air temperatures could get so cold that flesh could freeze instantly to any metal in which it came in contact. As pressurized cabins came into operation, the necessity of wearing bulky leather and shearling jackets and pants began to fade. For example, pilots, navigators, and bombardiers of a B-17 operating in Europe in 1944 would wear their officer's uniforms under an A-2 flight jacket comfortably due to the enclosed and heated cabin, but the waist gunners would have to wear electrically-heated suits as they fired their guns through open window gunports. When the B-29 Superfortress was introduced in the fight against Japan, along with remote-controlled coordinated gun turrets, the fully-pressurized crew cabin made the necessity of bulky flight gear obsolete.

Where bomber pilots could get away with wearing their dress uniforms as flight gear, fighter pilots needed a uniform that functioned in the tight confines of the typical fighter plane cockpit. The AN-S-31 flight suit was developed for the US Army Air Corps and featured two button-down breast pockets and two button-down shin pockets that could be accessed from the sitting position. The US Navy used a slightly different model that featured slanted pockets with zippers. The material used was either wool or tight-weave cotton for wind resistance and fire protection.

The need for short-duration fire protection was demonstrated early during that war. As technology advanced, the fire-protective flight suit, helmets, goggles, masks, gloves and footwear were designed and used. The footwear often could be cut to appear like civilian shoes in the country where the crew member would land if shot down.

Flaky jackets were also developed to give bomber crews some protection from flying shrapnel, though these increased the overall weight of the airplane and reduced the effective bombload that could be carried.

With the era of jet flight and improved focus on safety, however, fully fire-retardant materials were required. It was also simpler to make a one-piece suit when it would potentially have to fit over existing clothing or various types of under-garments.

Also, with the coming of jetflight came the development of the G-suit, a special kind of flight suit (worn alone or in combination with a traditional flight suit) that protected the wearer from the physical stress of acceleration by compressing the body to keep blood from pooling in the legs. As the pilot executed high-G combat maneuvers, his blood would literally be pulled from his head and shift downwards into his lower body, starving the brain of oxygen and causing a blackout. The G-suit was designed to allow some retention of blood in the pilot's head, allowing him to execute high-G turns for sustained periods of time.

In the 1950s and 1960s even more specialized suits needed to be developed for high-altitude survelliance (such as with the U-2 and SR-71 aircraft) and spaceflight. These would include full pressurization, and would be the precursor to today's space suits.

Current Standards

The current flight suit that is standard for most air forces and navies is made of Nomex, a fabric made from spun aramid that is lightweight and fire resistant. The flame retardant capabilities of this matter make it ideal for protecting aviators in case of a fire. The suit is often green or desert tan in color, with multiple pockets for specific pieces of gear (such as a clear plastic pocket on the thigh intended to house a map of the aircraft's planned flight path) but color, style, and cut vary greatly from country to country. The current model flight suit for the US military is the CWU 27/P and is available in sage green and desert tan. Commercial flight suits for civilian flying are also available, and are frequently used by helicopter crew (including non-pilots such as flight engineers and nurses), aerobatic pilots, and others who desire a practical "uniform".

The United States Marine Corps wore flight suits during most vehicle patrols and ground combat operations in Iraq and Afghanistan, because their standard camouflage utilities were not flame-resistant. Flight suits are now being phased out among ground personnel with the introduction of the Flame Resistant Organizational Gear or "FROG" suit, which resembles the standard camouflage utilities.

Spaceflight

NASA astronauts have worn one-piece flight suits when in training or on flights in their NASA T-38s. The current flight suit worn by astronauts is Royal blue, made of Nomex. The now common "shirt-sleeve" environment of the orbiting Space Shuttle and ISS has resulted in much more casual attire during spaceflight such as shorts and polo shirts. In the pre-Challenger era, shuttle crews wore light blue flight suits and an altitude helmet during launch/reentry. Apollo crews wore white 2-piece beta cloth uniforms during non-essential activities and the full A7L pressure suit during Launch, TLI, Lunar Ascent/Decent, and EVAs. Mercury and Gemini crews wore their pressure suits for the duration of the mission with the exception of Gemini 7.

Colors

Pilots and flight crews use several colors of flight suit. NASA crews, for example, wear blue flight suits as a sort of functional dress uniform during training. The orange suits that they wear during launch and reentry/landing are designed for high visibility should there be an emergency recovery. White suits are worn during space walks to control temperature. NASA non-astronaut flight crew at Langley Research Center wear blue, and crew at the Dryden Flight Research Center wear either green or desert tan, and all newer suits issued are desert tan.

SPACE FOOD

Space food are food products, specially created and processed for consumption by astronauts in outer space.

Early History

Russian

Apollo-Soyuz Test Project (1975)

The astronauts of the Apollo-Soyuz Test Project received samples of Soviet space food when the combined crew dined together. Among the foods provided by Soyuz 19 were canned beef tongue, packaged Riga bread, and tubes of borscht and caviar. The borscht was labelled "vodka" as a joke.

United States

One of John Glenn's many tasks, as the first American to orbit Earth in 1962, was to experiment with eating in weightless conditions. Some experts had been concerned that weightlessness would impair swallowing. Glenn experienced no difficulties, however, and it was determined that microgravity did not affect the natural swallowing process.

Project Mercury (1959-1963)

Astronauts in later Mercury missions disliked the food that was provided. They ate bite-sized cubes, freeze-dried powders, and tubes of semiliquids. The astronauts found it unappetizing, experienced difficulties in rehydrating the freeze-dried foods, and didn't like having to squeeze tubes or collect crumbs.

Project Gemini (1965-1966)

Several of the food issues from the Mercury missions were addressed for the later Gemini missions. Tubes (often heavier than the foods they contained) were abandoned. Gelatin coatings helped to prevent bite-sized cubes from crumbling. Simpler rehydration methods were developed. The menus also expanded to include items such as shrimp cocktail, chicken and vegetables, toast squares, butterscotch pudding, and apple juice.

The crew of Gemini III snuck a corned beef sandwich on their spaceflight. Mission Commander Gus Grissom loved corned beef sandwiches, so Pilot John Young brought one along, having been encouraged by fellow astronaut Walter Schirra. However, Young was supposed to only eat approved food, and Grissom wasn't supposed to eat anything. Floating pieces of bread posed a potential problem, causing Grissom to put the sandwich away (although he did enjoy it) and the astronauts were mildly rebuked by NASA for the act. A congressional hearing was called, forcing the NASA deputy administrator George Mueller to promise no repeats. NASA took special care about what astronauts brought along on future missions.

Apollo Programme (1961-1975)

The variety of food options continued to expand for the Apollo missions. The new availability of hot water made rehydrating freeze-dried foods simpler, and produced a more appetizing result. The "spoon-bowl" allowed more normal eating practices. Food could be kept in special plastic zip-closure containers, and its moisture allowed it to stick to a spoon.

Skylab (1973-1974)

Larger living areas on the Skylab space station allowed for an on-board refrigerator and freezer, which allowed perishable and frozen items to be stored and made the microgravity the primary obstacle. When Skylab's solar panels were damaged during its launch and the station had to rely on minimal power from the Apollo Telescope Mount until Skylab 2 crew members performed repairs, the refrigerator and freezer were among the systems that Mission Control kept operational. Menus included items such as processed meat products and ice cream. A dining room table and chairs, fastened to the floor and fitted with foot and thigh restraints, allowed for a more normal eating experience. The trays used could warm the food, and had magnets to hold eating utensils and scissors to open food containers.

Modern

Today, fruits and vegetables that can be safely stored at room temperature are eaten on spaceflights. Astronauts also have a greater variety of entrées to choose from, and many request personalized menus from lists of available foods including items like fruit salad and spaghetti. Astronauts sometimes request beef jerky for flights, as it is lightweight, nutritious, and can be utilized in orbit without packaging or other changes.

Cultural Favourites

Korean

In April 2008, South Korea's first astronaut, Yi So-yeon, was a crew member on the International Space Station and brought a special version of Korea's national dish, kimchi. It took three research institutes several years and millions of dollars to create a version of the fermented cabbage dish that was suitable for space travel.

Jewish

In June 2008, Gregory Chamitoff brought bagels into space for the first time. He was on STS-124 for ISS Expedition 17, and brought with him 18 sesame seed Montreal-style bagels from his cousin's bakery.

Processing

Designing food for consumption in space is difficult. Foods must meet a number of criteria to be considered fit for space; first, the food must be physiologically appropriate, specifically, it must be nutritious, easily digestible, and palatable. Second, the food must be engineered for consumption in a zero gravity environment. As such, the food should be light, well packaged, quick to serve, and easy to clean up (foods that tend to leave crumbs, for example, are ill-suited for space). Finally, foods must require a minimum of energy expenditure throughout their use, i.e., they should store well, open easily, and leave little waste behind.

Carbonated drinks have been tried in space, but are not favoured due to changes in burping caused by microgravity. Coca-Cola and Pepsi were first carried on STS-51-F in 1985. Coca-Cola has flown on subsequent missions in a specially-designed dispenser that utilizes BioServe Space Technologies hardware used for biochemical experiments. Space Station Mir carried cans of Pepsi in 1996.

Packaging

Packaging for space food serves the primary purposes of preserving and containing the food. The packaging however should also be light-weight, easy to dispose, and help in the preparation of the food for consumption. The packaging also includes a bar-coded label, which allows for the tracking of an astronaut's diet. The labels also specify the food's preparation instructions in both English and Russian.

Many foods from the Russian space programme are packaged in cans and tins. These are heated through electro-resistive (ohmic) methods, opened with a can-opener, and the food inside consumed directly. Russian soups are hydrated and consumed directly from their packages.

NASA space foods are packaged in composite retorts similar to that found in US Army MREs. They are also packaged in sealed containers which fit into trays to keep them in place. The trays include straps on the underside, allowing astronauts to attach the tray to an anchor point such as their legs or a wall surface and include clips for retaining a beverage pouch or utensils in the microgravity environment.

Types

There are several classifications for food that is sent into space:

- *Beverages (B)*–Various rehydratable drinks.
- *Fresh Foods (FF)*–Foods that spoil quickly that needs to be eaten within the first two days of flight to prevent spoilage.
- *Irradiated (I) Meat*–Beef steak that is specially packaged and sterilized with ionizing radiation.
- *Intermediate Moisture (IM)*–Foods that have some moisture but not enough to cause immediate spoilage.
- *Natural Form (NF)*–Mostly unprocessed foods such as nuts, cookies and granola bars that are ready to eat.
- *Rehydratable (R) Foods*–Foods that have been dehydrated and allowed to rehydrate in hot water prior to consumption.
- *Thermostabilized (T)*–Foods that have been processed with heat to destroy microorganisms and enzymes that may cause spoilage.

More common staples and condiments do not have a classification and are known simply by the item name:

- *Shelf Stable Tortillas*–Tortillas that have been heat treated and specially packaged in an oxygen free nitrogen atmosphere to prevent the growth of mold.
- *Condiments*–Liquid salt solution, oily pepper paste, mayonnaise, ketchup, and mustard.

Consumer Derivatives

Capitalizing on the popularity of the Apollo space missions, Pillsbury marketed "Food Sticks" (also known as "Space Food Sticks") for the consumer market in the early 1970's. Fourteen individually-packaged sticks were included in a box, and came in six flavours such as peanut butter, caramel, and chocolate. Food Sticks were marketed as a "nutritionally balanced between meal snack".

Tang, originally marketed in 1959, also saw an increase in popularity during this era due to its inclusion on the manned spaceflights.

SPACE-THEMED MUSIC

Space-themed music is any music, from any genre or style, with lyrics or titles relating to outer space or space travel.

Songs or other musical forms influenced by the concept of outer space have appeared in music throughout history, both in instrumental and vocal pieces with lyrics. As early as Ancient Greece, Pythagoras believed in something called the "harmony of the spheres". He believed that since planets and the stars all moved in the universe according to mathematical equations that these mathematical equations could be translated into musical notes and thus produce a symphony. This idea was explored further throughout Western history under the theories of Musica universalis. Some more recent and widely different examples are *The Planets* by Gustav Holst, and the song "Space Oddity" by David Bowie. Outer space also appears as a theme in "space age" retro pop music, such as Stereolab's *Space-Age Bachelor Pad Music.*

Music about outer space attracts enthusiastic listeners from all walks of life. Some have created webpages to share their interests. NASA, JPL, and the US Governmental Centennial of Flight Commission even have a webpages showcasing and discussing music about outer space.

Music about Outer Space

In 1958, Karl-Birger Blomdahl composed an opera Aniara to a libretto by Erik Lindegren based on the poem Aniara by Harry Martinson, a tragedy set aboard a spaceship.

The Japanese musician Isao Tomita has produced many albums with space-based themes, such as *The Planets* (1976), his version of Holst's suite; *Kosmos* (1978); *Bermuda Triangle* (1979); *Dawn Chorus (Canon of the Three Stars)* (1984); *Space Walk—Impressions of An Astronaut* (compilation, 1984); *Mind of the Universe—Live at Linz* (1985); *Back to the Earth—Live in New York* (1988); and *Nasca Fantasy* (supporting Kodo, 1994).

The Vangelis album *Albedo 0.39* (1976) is entirely devoted to space, while a segment of *Heaven and Hell* (1975) was used as the theme to the PBS television series *Cosmos* by Carl Sagan. His work *Mythodea: Music for NASA's Mars Odyssey Mission* is reflective of his interest in space exploration.

Mike Oldfield's 1994 album *The Songs of Distant Earth* was based on Arthur C. Clarke's SF novel *Songs of Distant Earth.* Pop songs also mention outer space, such as Chris de Burgh's "A Spaceman Came Travelling," the Bonzo Dog Band's "I'm the Urban Spaceman," David Bowie's "Space Oddity," Elton John's "Rocket Man," and Deep Purple's "Space Truckin'."

Several albums have featured music inspired by the Apollo space programme. In 1983, Brian Eno with his brother Roger Eno and producer/recording artist Daniel Lanois, composed the score for the film *For All Mankind,* a documentary of NASA's Apollo programme; an album of the music, *Apollo: Atmospheres and Soundtracks,* was later released. On The Orb's 1991 two-disc debut album, *Adventures Beyond the Ultraworld,* disc one of features an ambient musical simulation of the Apollo 11 moon journey, including excerpts of NASA recordings of the radio conversations between Mission Control and the astronauts in space.

The filk anthology albums *Minus Ten and Counting* (1983) and *To Touch the Stars* (2003) celebrate and promote the exploration of outer space.

Author and classical music critic David Hurwitz describes Joseph Haydn's choral and chamber orchestra piece, *The Creation,* composed in 1798, as space music, both in the sense of the sound of the music, ("a genuine piece of 'space music' featuring softly pulsating high violins and winds above low cellos and basses, with nothing at all in the middle ... The space music gradually drifts towards a return to the movement's opening gesture ... "); and in the manner of its composition, relating that Haydn conceived *The Creation* after discussing music and astronomy with William Herschel, oboist and astronomer (discoverer of the planet Uranus).

Another band to use space as musical inspiration is the Christian "Astro-Rock" group Brave Saint Saturn, whose three albums, *So Far from Home, The Light of Things Hoped For,* and *Anti-Meridian,* form a trilogy that chronicles the journey of the fictional spaceship, the *USS Gloria,* on a trip to survey the moons of Saturn. The music uses space narratives, lingo, samples and quotes to portray the journey.

Soundtracks for Movies and TV Shows about Outer Space

Soundtracks of science fiction movies and television and radio series often feature music associated with outer space, such as *Star Wars, Star Trek, Doctor Who, The Hitchhiker's Guide to the Galaxy, Red Dwarf, The X-Files,* and others.

Music Played in Planetariums and Observatories

Many forms of music are used Observatory and Planetarium shows, particularly genres such as Electronic music, classical music, Space music, and Space rock. Some artists, such as Geodesium, specialize in creating custom music for Planetariums.

During the 1970s, IMAX's OMNIMAX (now IMAX Dome) film system was conceived to operate on planetarium screens. More recently, some planetariums have re-branded themselves as "dome theaters," with broader offerings including wide-screen or "wraparound" films, fulldome video, and laser shows that combine music with laser-drawn patterns.

Music Made with Sounds of Outer Space

Energy sources in the atmosphere, such as lightning, can produce sounds (*sferics, tweeks,* and *whistlers*) in the very low frequency (VLF) radio band.

Objects in space—the Sun, planets, stars, quasars, pulsars, galaxies, and active galaxies—all produce signals that, if received (usually through radio astronomy dishes and processed), can be used by a musician as the basis for any kind of composition imaginable.

Scientists with an interest in space-based sounds include:

- Don Gurnett.
- Stephen P. McGreevy.
- Alexander Kosovichev, a Stanford scientist whose researches into the sun's oscillations (and who uploaded the sounds to the net) encouraged Stephen Taylor to create his album.

- Dr. Fiorella Terenzi has created several works that use sounds derived from celestial radio signals homepage, *Space.com* entry.
- NASA produced a CD in 1992 from Voyager 1 & 2 recordings of electromagnetic fields processed with digital sampling techniques.

Artists/bands who have included such sounds in their works include:

- Terry Riley, along with the Kronos Quartet, in their album *Sun Rings*, which used "sounds of the planets recorded by the Voyager mission on its journey to deep space".
- Stephen Taylor, in the album *The Heart of the Sun*.
- Robert Schroeder's album *Galaxie Cygnus-A* used interstellar noise from the distant galaxy in the title.

SPACE MEDICINE

Space medicine is the practice of medicine on astronauts in outer space whereas astronautical hygiene is the application of science and technology to the prevention or control of exposure to the hazards that may cause astronaut ill health. Both these sciences work together to ensure that astronauts work in a safe environment. The main thing is to discover how well and for how long people can survive the extreme conditions in space, and how fast they can adapt to the earth's environment after coming back from space.

History

Hubertus Strughold (1898-1987), a former Nazi physician and physiologist, was brought to the United States after World War II as part of Operation Paperclip. He first coined the term "space medicine" in 1948 and was the first and only Professor of Space Medicine at the School of Aviation Medicine (SAM) at Randolph Air Force Base, Texas. In 1949 Strughold was made director of the Department of Space Medicine at the SAM (which is now the U.S. Air Force School of Aerospace Medicine (USAFSAM) at Brooks Air Force Base, Texas). He played an important role in developing the pressure suit worn by early American astronauts. He was a co-founder of the Space Medicine Branch of the Aerospace Medical Association in 1950. The aeromedical library at Brooks AFB was named after him in 1977, but later renamed because documents from the Nuremberg War Crimes Tribunal linked Strughold to medical experiments in which inmates of the Dachau concentration camp were tortured and killed.

Who Benefits from Space Medicine Research?

Astronauts are not the only ones who benefit from space medicine research. Several medical products have been developed that are space spinoffs, that is practical applications for the field of medicine arising out of the space programme. Because of joint research efforts between NASA, the National Institutes on Aging (a part of the National Institutes of Health), and other aging-related organizations, space exploration has benefited a particular segment of society, seniors. Evidence of aging related medical research conducted in space was most publicly noticeable during STS-95.

Medical Space Spinoffs from the Early Space Exploration Years (Pre-Mercury Through Apollo Projects)

- Radiation therapy for the treatment of cancer. In conjunction with Cleveland Clinic, the cyclotron at NASA's center in Cleveland, Ohio—which had been utilized for testing nuclear propulsion systems for air and spacecraft—was used in the first clinical trials for the treatment and evaluation of neutron radiation therapy for cancer patients.
- Foldable walkers. Made from a lightweight metal material developed by NASA for aircraft and spacecraft, foldable walkers are portable and easy to manage.
- Personal alert systems. These are emergency alert devices that can be worn by individuals who may require emergency medical or safety assistance. When a button is pushed, the device sends a signal to a remote location for help. To send the signal, the device relies on telemetry technology developed at NASA.
- CAT Scans and MRIs. These devices are used by hospitals to see inside the human body. Their development would not have been possible without the technology provided by NASA after it found a way to take better pictures of the Earth's moon.
- Muscle stimulator device. This device is used for ½ hour per day to prevent muscle atrophy in paralyzed individuals. It provides electrical stimulation to muscles which is equal to jogging three miles per week. Christopher Reeves used these in his therapy.
- Orthopedic evaluation tools. Equipment to evaluate posture, gait, and balance disturbances was developed at NASA, along with a radiation-free way to measure bone flexibility using vibration.
- Diabetic foot mapping. This technique was developed at NASA's center in Cleveland, Ohio to help monitor the effects of diabetes in feet. These efforts helped.
- Foam cushioning. Special foam used for cushioning astronauts during liftoff is used in pillows and mattresses at many nursing homes and hospitals to help prevent ulcers, relieve pressure, and provide a better night's sleep.
- Kidney dialysis machines. These machines rely on technology developed by NASA in order to process and remove toxic waste from used dialysis fluid.
- Talking wheelchairs. Paralyzed individuals who have difficulty in speaking may use a talking feature on their wheelchairs which was developed by NASA to create synthesized speech for aircraft.
- Collapsible, lightweight wheelchairs. These wheelchairs are designed for

portability and can be folded and put into trunks of cars. They rely on synthetic materials that NASA developed for its air and spacecraft.

- Surgically implantable heart pacemaker. These devices depend on technologies developed by NASA for use with satellites. They communicate information about the activity of the pacemaker, such as how much time remains before the batteries need to be replaced.
- Implantable heart defibrillator. This tool continuously monitors heart activity and can deliver an electric shock to restore heartbeat regularity.
- EMS Communications. Technology used to communicate telemetry between Earth and space was developed by NASA to monitor the health of astronauts in space from the ground. Ambulances use this same technology to send information—like EKG readings—from patients in transport to hospitals. This allows faster and better treatment.
- Weightlessness. While not an invention *per se,* the weightlessness of space one day may allow individuals with limited mobility on Earth—even those normally confined to wheelchairs—the freedom to move about with ease. A notable individual to take advantage of weightlessness in the "Vomit Comet" during 2007 was physicist Stephen Hawking.

Major Historical Medical Investigations in Space during the Space Shuttle Era

STS-95

John Glenn, the first American astronaut to orbit the Earth, returned with much fanfare to space once again at 77 years of age to confront the physiological challenges preventing long-term space travel for astronauts—loss of bone density, loss of muscle mass, balance disorders, sleep disturbances, cardiovascular changes, and immune system depression—all of which are problems confronting aging people as well as astronauts. Once again Glenn stepped forward to play an historic role in the future of space exploration, but this time he would provide new medical research in the field of gerontology as well.

Decompression Sickness

Decompression Illness in Spaceflight

In space, astronauts use a space suit, essentially a self-contained individual spacecraft, to do spacewalks, or extra-vehicular activities (EVAs). Space suits are generally inflated with 100 per cent oxygen at a total pressure that is less than a third of normal atmospheric pressure. Eliminating inert atmospheric components such as nitrogen allows the astronaut to breathe comfortably, but also have the mobility to use their hands, arms, and legs to complete required work, which would be more difficult in a higher pressure suit.

After the astronaut dons the space suit, air is replaced by 100 per cent oxygen in a process called a "nitrogen purge". In order to reduce the risk of decompression sickness, the astronaut must spend several hours "pre-breathing" at an intermediate nitrogen partial pressure, in order to let their body tissues outgas nitrogen slowly enough that bubbles are not formed. When the astronaut returns to the "shirt sleeve" environment of the spacecraft after an EVA, pressure is restored to whatever the operating pressure of that spacecraft may be, generally normal atmospheric pressure. Decompression illness in spaceflight consists of decompression sickness (DCS) and other injuries due to uncompensated changes in pressure, or barotrauma.

Decompression Sickness

Decompression sickness is the injury to the tissues of the body resulting from the presence of nitrogen bubbles in the tissues and blood. This occurs due to a rapid reduction in ambient pressure causing the dissolved nitrogen to come out of solution as gas bubbles. In space the risk of DCS is significantly reduced by using a technique to wash out the nitrogen in the body's tissues. This is achieved by breathing 100 per cent oxygen for a specified period of time before donning the space suit, and is continued after a nitrogen purge. DCS may result from inadequate or interrupted pre-oxygenation time, or other factors including the astronaut's level of hydration, physical conditioning, prior injuries and age. Other risks of DCS include inadequate nitrogen purge in the EMU, a strenuous or excessively prolonged EVA, or a loss of suit pressure. Non-EVA crew members may also be at risk for DCS if there is a loss of spacecraft cabin pressure.

Symptoms of DCS in space may include chest pain, shortness of breath, cough or pain with a deep breath, unusual fatigue, lightheadedness, dizziness, headache, unexplained musculoskeletal pain, tingling or numbness, extremities weakness, or visual abnormalities.

Primary treatment principles consist of in-suit repressurization to re-dissolve nitrogen bubbles, 100 per cent oxygen to re-oxygenate tissues, and hydration to improve the circulation to injured tissues.

To date there have been no reported cases of DCS in the NASA space programme.

Barotrauma

Barotrauma is the injury to the tissues of air filled spaces in the body as a result of differences in pressure between the body spaces and the ambient atmospheric pressure. Air filled spaces include the middle ears, parananal sinuses, lungs and gastrointestinal tract. One would be predisposed by a pre-existing upper respiratory infection, nasal allergies, recurrent changing pressures, dehydration, or a poor equalizing technique.

Positive pressure in the air filled spaces results from reduced barometric pressure during the depressurization phase of an EVA. It can cause abdominal distension, ear or sinus pain, decreased hearing, and dental or jaw pain. Abdominal distension can be treated with extending the abdomen, gentle massage and encourage passing flatus. Ear and sinus pressure can be relieved with passive release of positive pressure.

Pretreatment for susceptible individuals can include oral and nasal decongestants, or oral and nasal steroids.

Negative pressure in air fill spaces results from increased barometric pressure during repressurization after an EVA or following a planned restoration of a reduced cabin pressure. Common symptoms include ear or sinus pain, decreased hearing, and tooth or jaw pain.

Treatment may include active positive pressure equalization of ears and sinuses, oral and nasal decongestants, or oral and nasal steroids, and appropriate pain medication if needed.

Decreased Immune System Functioning

Astronauts in space have weakened immune systems, which means that in addition to increased vulnerability to new exposures, viruses already present in the body—which would normally be suppressed—become active. In space, T-cells (a part of white blood cells that produces antibodies) do not reproduce properly. T-cells that do exist are less able to fight off infection. NASA research is measuring the change in the immune systems of its astronauts as well as performing experiments with T-cells in space.

Loss of Balance

Leaving and returning to Earth's gravity causes "space sickness," dizziness, and loss of balance in astronauts. By studying how changes can affect balance in the human body—involving the senses, the brain, the inner ear, and blood pressure—NASA hopes to develop treatments that can be used on Earth and in space to correct balance disorders. Until then, NASA's astronauts must rely on a medication called Midodrine (an "anti-dizzy" pill that temporarily increases blood pressure) to help carry out the tasks they need to do to return home safely.

Loss of Bone Density

Unlike people with osteoporosis, astronauts eventually regain their bone density. After a 3-4 month trip into space, it takes about 2-3 years to regain lost bone density. New techniques are being developed to help astronauts recover faster. Research in the following areas holds the potential to aid the process of growing new bone:

- Diet and exercise changes may reduce osteoporosis.
- Vibration therapy may stimulate bone growth.
- Medication could trigger the body to produce more of the protein responsible for bone growth and formation.

Loss of Muscle Mass

In space, muscles in the legs, back, spine, and heart weaken and waste away because they no longer are needed to overcome gravity, just as people lose muscle when they age due to reduced physical activity. Astronauts rely on research in the following areas to build muscle and maintain body mass:

- Exercise may build muscle if at least two hours a day is spent doing resistance training routines.
- Hormone supplements (hGH) may be a way to tap into the body's natural growth signals.
- Medication may trigger the body into producing muscle growth proteins.

Man-Machine Interface

Orthostatic Intolerance

In space, astronauts lose fluid volume—including up to 22 per cent of their blood volume. Because it has less blood to pump, the heart will atrophy. A weakened heart results in low blood pressure and can produce a problem with "orthostatic tolerance," or the body's ability to send enough oxygen to the brain without fainting or becoming dizzy. "Under the effects of the earth's gravity, blood and other body fluids are pulled towards the lower body. When gravity is taken away or reduced during space exploration, the blood tends to collect in the upper body instead, resulting in facial edema and other unwelcome side effects. Upon return to earth, the blood begins to pool in the lower extremities again, resulting in orthostatic hypotension."

Psychological Factors

Radiation Effects

Soviet cosmonaut Valentin Lebedev, who spent 221 days in the orbit in 1982 (an absolute record for stay in Earth's orbit), loses his eyesight to progressive cataract. Lebedev stated: "I suffered from a lot of radiation in space. It was all concealed back then, during the Soviet years, but now I can say that I caused damage to my health because of that flight."

Sleep Disorders

Fifty per cent of space shuttle astronauts take sleeping pills and still get two hours less sleep. NASA is researching two areas which may provide the keys to a better night's sleep, as improved sleep decreases fatigue and increases daytime productivity:

- Environmental cues and practices may be able to retrain the body's circadian rhythm.
- Medication could improve sleep by increasing the production of melatonin, a sleep hormone.

Medical Interventions

- Exercise to maintain muscle strength and function
- Sleep cap
- Medication, including hormone replacement therapy

How Does One Prepare for a Career in Space Medicine?

Educational Programmes

- Naval Operations Medical Institute (NAMI)—Pensacola, Florida
- U.S. Air Force School of Aerospace Medicine—Brooks City-Base, San Antonio, Texas
- University of Texas Medical Branch at Galveston (UTMB)—Aerospace Medicine Residency programme
- Wright State University School of Medicine—Dayton, Ohio
- Vanderbilt Center for Space Physiology and Medicine—(Dr. David Robertson)
- Space Studies Department at the University of North Dakota

Related Degrees, Areas of Specialization, and Certifications

- Aeromedical Certification
- Aerospace Medicine
- Aerospace Studies
- Emergency Medicine
- Family Practice
- Internal Medicine
- Occupational and Preventive Medicine
- Ophthalmology
- Otolaryngology
- Public Health

Professional Organizations

- Aerospace Human Factors Association
- Aerospace Medical Association
- Air Medical Physician Association
- American Psychological Association
- Association of Air Medical Services
- Aviation & Aerospace Medicine
- Federal Aviation Administration Office of Aerospace Medicine
- Human Factors & Ergonomics Society
- Human Performance in Extreme Environments

Commercial Spaceflight Medicine

Three major institutions teamed up to investigate space medicine applications in commercial spaceflight. The directors of these programmes are listed.

- Mayo Clinic Scottsdale—(Dr. Jan Stepanek)
- University of Texas Medical Branch at Galveston (UTMB)—(Dr. Richard Jennings)
- Wyle Laboratories Commercial Spaceflight Service Unit—(Dr. Vernon McDonald)
- National Space Biomedical Research Institute (NSBRI) Space Medicine Liaison at Baylor College of Medicine—(Dr. Jonathan Clark)

Bibliography

Abitzsch, S, Eilingsfeld, F. "The prospects for space tourism: investigation of the economic and technological feasibility of commercial passenger transportation into Low Earth Orbit (LEO)." *IAF, International Astronautical Congress, 43rd, Washington, Aug. 28-Sept. 5, 1992.*

Albert A. Harrison, Yvonne A. Clearwater, Christopher P. McKay (eds.). *From Antarctica to outer space. life in isolation and confinement.* Conference entitled "The human experience in Antarctica: applications to life in space". Papers. 1987 Aug. Sunnyvale, CA. New York: Springer-Verlag. 1991.

Alford, Henry "Out Of This World". *Travel & leisure.* No. 12 vol. 29 (1999): p. 132.

Analysis of potential alternatives to reduce NASA's cost of human access to space. Hawthorne, Krauss and Associates, LLC, 1998.

Aoki, H., *et al.* "A study of orientation in a zero gravity environment by means of virtual reality simulation". *Journal of Gravitational Physiology.* No. 2 Vol. 7 (July 2000): pp. 93-94.

Arnopoulos, Paris. *Cosmopolitics. public policy of outer space.* Toronto. Lancaster: Guernica. 1998.

Ashford, David "How Soon Will Space Tourism Start?". *Architectural Design.* No. 2 vol. 70 (2000): p. 10.

Beardsley, Tim "The Way To Go In Space". *Scientific American.* No. 2 vol. 280 (1999): p. 80.

Benson, J.W. "Commercial space development needs cheap launchers". STAIF international forum 1998. New York: AIP, 1998.

Bertol, Daniela. *Designing digital space. an architect's guide to virtual reality.* New York. Chichester: Wiley, c1997.

Billings, Marcus D., *et al.* "Impact test and simulation of energy absorbing concepts for Earth entrey vehicles". *AIAA / ASME / ASCE / AHS / ASC structures structural dynamics and materials conference and exhibit, 42nd, Seattle, WA, Apr. 16-19, 2001.*

Budden, Nancy Ann. "Virtual presence: one step beyond reality. Ad Astra: *To the Stars.* pp. 30-35, 1997.

Charles M. Reynerson. "An engineering and cost concept design model for space tourism platforms using data from prior human spacecraft missions" Johnson, Stewart W. (ed.). *Space 2000.* proceedings of Space 2000: the seventh international conference. Reston, VA: ASCE, 2000. pp. 617-623.

Cheng. Chia-Jui (ed.). *The use of airspace and outer space for all mankind in the 21st century.*The Hague. London: Kluwer Law International, c1995.

Collins, P. "Passenger space travel: the normalization of space activities". *Space access and utilization beyond 2000; proceedings of the symposium, Washington, DC, Feb. 18, 2000 (A01-22266 05-12).* San Diego: Univelt, 2001. (Science and technology series. Vol. 101): pp. 151-158.

Collins, P. "Public choice economics and space policy: realizing space tourism" *Acta Astronautica* No 5-12 Vol. 48: pp. 921-950.

Collins, P., *et al.* "Design and construction of zero-gravity gymnasium" *Journal of Aerospace Engineering* No. 2 Vol. 10 (April 1997): pp. 94-98.

Collins, Patrick "Space Tourism - the Key to the Coming Economic Boom". *Architectural Design.* No. 2 vol. 70 (2000): pp. 18.

Collins, Patrick "The space tourism industry in 2030". *Space 2000.* proceedings of Space 2000: the seventh international conference. Reston, VA: ASCE, 2000. pp. 594-603.

Collins, Patrick "Tourism in Low Earth Orbit: The Trigger for Commercial Lunar Development?". Galloway, Rodney G. (ed.) Lokaj, Stanley(ed.). *Space 1998.* proceedings of Space 2000: the sixth international conference. Reston, VA: ASCE, 1998. pp. 752-756.

Collins, Patrick Kuwahara, Sunao Nishimura, Tsuyoshi "Artificial Gravity Swimming Pool". Galloway, Rodney G. (ed.) Lokaj, Stanley(ed.). *Space 1998.* proceedings of Space 2000: the sixth international conference. Reston, VA: ASCE, 1998. pp. 744-751.

Corby, Thomas James Patrick. *The disappearing frame. a practice-based investigation into the composition of virtual environment artworks.* Open University, 2000

Curran, Douglas. *In advance of the landing: folk concepts of outer space.* New York: Abbeville Press, 1985.

Dasch, Pat; Smith, George "The NASA-STA Space Tourism Study: Results". *Ad astra.* No. 3 vol. 10 (1998): p. 20.

Downie, D. B., Schmid, T. "Space transportation and risk management from an insurance perspective". *International symposium on space technology and science, 22nd, Morioka, Japan, May 28-June 4, 2000; Proceedings.* Vol. 2, Tokyo, Japan, Japan Society for Aeronautical and Space Sciences and 22nd ISTS Organizing Committee (2000): pp. 2260-2269.

Durlach, N., *et al.* "Virtual environments and the enhancement of spatial behaviour: towards a comprehensive research agenda." *Presence, teleoperators and virtual environments.* No. 6 Vol. 9 (December 2000): pp. 593-615.

Eilingsfeld, F., Schaetzler, D. "The cost of capital for space tourism ventures". *IAF International Astronautical Congress, 51st, Rio de Janeiro, Brazil, Oct. 2-6, 2000.*

Finch, Edward. *Astrobusiness: a guide to the commerce and law of outer space.* New York: Praeger, 1985.

Funatsu, Y. "Legal framework for space travel". *International symposium on space technology and science, 22nd, Morioka, Japan, May 28-June 4, 2000; Proceedings.* Vol. 2, Tokyo, Japan, Japan Society for Aeronautical and Space Sciences and 22nd ISTS Organizing Committee (2000): pp. 2256-2259.

Gaubatz, W. A., *et al.* "SpaceClipper tourist vehicle". *International symposium on space technology and science, 22nd, Morioka, Japan, May 28-June 4, 2000; Proceedings.* Vol. 2, Tokyo, Japan, Japan Society for Aeronautical and Space Sciences and 22nd ISTS Organizing Committee (2000): pp. 2232-2237.

Gavert, R.B. "Three near term commercial markets in space and their potential role in space exploration". *STAIF international forum 2001*. New York: AIP, 2001.

Goodrich, Jonathan N.. *The commercialization of outer space. opportunities and obstacles for American business*. Quorum Books. 1989.

Graham-Rowe, D. "Chef's special: fresh fish will top astronaut's menu, thanks to an on-board biosphere" *New Scientist* No. 2319 Vol. 172 (1st of December 2001): p. 20.

Greber, Bettie (ed.). *Space manufacturing*. AIAA.

Haines, Richard F.. *Space station proximity operations windows*. Moffet Field: NASA, 1987.

Haltermann, Bob "New Space Travel and Tourism Division Added to the Space Transportation Association". *Space energy and transportation*. No. 1 vol. 3 (1998): p. 1.

Hansson, A."Astronautics: the need for organizational entrepreneurs". *Earth Space Review* No 4 Vol. 9: pp. 36-39. Journal held in the library.

Hansson, Anders "Virtual Space Tourism". *Architectural Design*. No. 2 vol. 70 (2000): p. 26.

Harland, David Michael. *The space shuttke: roles, missions and accomplishments*. Chichester, Wiley, 1998.

Hollister, W.M. "Castles in space". *Acta Astronautica* (1967).

Hujsak, Edward. *The future of U.S. rocketry*. La Jolla: Mina-Helwig, 1994.

International air transport and activities in outer space. legal, political, economic and financial aspects. Latin American conference. Papers and programme. Leiden: International Institute of Air and Space Law, Leiden University, 1989.

Isozaki, K., *et al*. "Considerations on vehicle design criteria for space tourism" *Acta Astronautica* No. 5-12 Vol. 37: pp. 223-237.

Iwama, K. "The requirement of rocket engines for space tour vehicles". *International symposium on space technology and science, 22nd, Morioka, Japan, May 28-June 4, 2000; Proceedings*. Vol. 2, Tokyo, Japan, Japan Society for Aeronautical and Space Sciences and 22nd ISTS Organizing Committee (2000): pp. 2290-2295.

Jasani, Bhupendra (ed.). *Outer space. a source of conflict or co-operation?* United Nations University, 1991. Information furnished in conformity with the Convention on Registration of Objects Launched into Outer. United Nations, 1994.

Jodra, Serge. "Vive le tourisme virtuel". *Ciel et Espace* No. 375 (August 2001): pp. 34 38.

Johnson, Stewart W. *Engineering, Construction, and Operations in Space*. Proceedings of the Fifth International Conference on Space '96 held in Albuquerque, New Mexico, June 1-6, 1996. New York: ASCE, 1996.

Karl-Heinz Boeckstiegel (ed.). *Environmental aspects of activities in outer space. state of the law and measures of protection*. International colloquium. Papers. Koeln: C. Heymanns. c1990.

Kauffman, James L.. *Selling outer space. Kennedy, the media, and funding for Project Apollo, 1961-1963*.Tuscaloosa. London: University of Alabama Press, c1994.

Kinnersley, M. Shefold, K. " The ROCKOT vehicle qualified for commercial launches". El-Genk, Mohamed S. (ed.). *STAIF international forum 2001*. New York: AIP, 2001.

Koelle, D.E. "A cost engineered launch vehicle for space tourism". *Acta astronautica*. No. 7/12 vol. 44 (1999): p. 649.

Koelle, Dietrich E. *Handbook of cost engineering for space transportation systems with TRANSCOST 7.0*. Ottobrunn: TransCostSystems, 2000.

Kreisel, J. "Optional approaches for venture-backing of new space ventures". *IAF International Astronautical Congress, 51st, Rio de Janeiro, Brazil, Oct. 2-6, 2000.*

Lau, Lydia M.S. *Use of Virtual Science Park resource rooms to support group work in a learning environment.* University of Leeds, School of Computer Studies, 1999.

Lindskold, Anders. Space tourism and its effects on space commercialization. Individual Project Report.1999

Markham. Annette N. *Life online. researching real experience in virtual space.* Walnut Creek, Calif., London: Altamira Press, c1998.

Maryniak, G.E. "Space Resources for Space Tourism". *Space Resources Roundtable II: held November 8-10, 2000, in Golden, Colorado.* LPI Contribution No. 1070, Lunar and Planetary Institute, Houston, 2000., p. 33.

Maryniak, G.E. *Space resources roundtable II.* X PRIZE Foundation, 2000.

Marzwell, N. "Financial, economic, business planning, and market requirements to start a viable space tourism business". *General public space travel and tourism.* Pasadena:California Institute of Technology, 1999. vol. 2:pp 40-46.

Mendell, Wendell. "Space 2010...and beyond". *Earth Space Review* No 1, Vol. 10 (2001): p. 39

Mirabito, Michael M. *Exploration of outer space with cameras. A history of the NASA unmanned spacecraft missions.* Jefferson: Mcfarland, 1983.

Miyahara, A. "A study of safety standard for space tour vehicle: structural design requirements". *International symposium on space technology and science, 22nd, Morioka, Japan, May 28-June 4, 2000; Proceedings.* Vol. 2, Tokyo, Japan, Japan Society for Aeronautical and Space Sciences and 22nd ISTS Organizing Committee (2000): pp. 2276-2281.

Motion perception, eye movements, and orientation in real and virtual space. first joint Swiss-Japanese scientific seminar. Blackwell, 2000.

Nagatomo, M. "A Japanese perspective on research and development of reusable rockets". *Space access and utilization beyond 2000; proceedings of the symposium, Washington, DC, Feb. 18, 2000 (A01-22266 05-12).* San Diego: Univelt, 2001. (Science and technology series. Vol. 101): pp. 31-39.

Nagatomo, Makoto. "Start of space tourism" *Society of MEdical Research for Space Station, the MERSS 5th symposium on space medicine: medical and physiological experiment utilizing parabolic flight.*

Nagel, David J. "Pervasive sensing". *Integrated command environments, proceedings of the conference, San Diego, CA, 31 July 2000 (A01-24676 05-54).* Bellingham, WA: Society of Photo-Optical Instrumentation Engineers (SPIE proceedings): pp. 71-82.

Nozaki, K., *et al.* "Concept for functionally-distributed space hotel". *International symposium on space technology and science, 22nd, Morioka, Japan, May 28-June 4, 2000; Proceedings.* Vol. 2, Tokyo, Japan, Japan Society for Aeronautical and Space Sciences and 22nd ISTS Organizing Committee (2000): pp. 2245-2249.

Olds, John R. Investigation of vehicle requirements and options for future space tourism. Georgia Inst. of Tech., 2001.

ONeil, Daniel, Bekey, Ivan, Mankins, John, Rogers, Thomas F., Stallmer, Eric W.. *General Public Space Travel and Tourism.* NASA/NP-1998-03-11-MSFC/VOL1. California Inst. of Tech. (Pasadena, CA United States), 1999.

ONeil, Daniel, Bekey, Ivan, Mankins, John, Rogers, Thomas F., Stallmer, Eric W.. *General Public Space Travel and Tourism.* NASA/CP-1999-209146/VOL2. California Inst. of Tech. (Pasadena, CA United States), 1999.

O'Neill. D. *General public space travel and tourism. one year report.* CP-209146. National Aeronautics and Space Administration, 1999.

Pearlman, Robert "Space Tourism: A Consumer's Guide". *Ad astra.* No. 3 vol. 10 (1998): pp. 22.

Penn, Jay P. Lindley, Charles A. "Space tourism optimized reusable spaceplane design". El-Genk, Mohamed S. (ed.) *STAIF international forum 1997.* New York: AIP, 1997.

Pinkus, B. [*et al.*]. *Engineering ethics: balancing cost, schedule, and risk-lessons learned from the space shuttle.* Cambridge: Cambridge University Press, 1997.

Randerson, J. "In space, no one gets to sleep" *New Scientist* No 2319 Vol. 172 (1st of December 2001): pp. 16.

Reggestad, V., *et al.* "Space tourism: from dream to reality". *IAF International Astronautical Congress, 51st, Rio de Janeiro, Brazil, Oct.2-6, 2000.*

Reichert, M. "The future of space tourism." *Earth Space Review* No 2 Vol. 9: pp. 45-52.

Reijnen, Gijsbertha Cornelia Maria. *The pollution of outer space: in particular of the geostationary orbit: scientific, policy, and legal aspects.* Dordrecht: Martinus Nijhoff, 1989.

Reijnen, Gijsbertha Cornelia Maria. Utilization of outer space and international law. Amsterdam: Elsevier, 1981.

Roberts, M. "Inflatable Habitation for the Lunar Base". Mendell, W.W. (ed.). The Second Conference on Lunar Bases and Space Activities of the 21st Century, Proceedings from a conference held in Houston, TX, April 5-7, 1988.

Rogers, T. "Space tourism: a response to continuing decay in US civil space financial support". *Space policy.* No. 2 vol. 14 (1998): pp 79.

Rogers, T.F. "Space Tourism" - Its Importance, Its History, and A Recent Extraordinary Development" *Space Energy and Transportation.* No. 3 vol. 5 (2000): pp.4-11.

Rogers, T.F. "Space tourism, its importance, its history, and a recent extraordinary development". *Acta Astronautica* No 3-10 Vol. 49 (August-November 2001): pp. 537-550.

Rogers, T.F. "The NASA-STA cooperative space tourism study. *Space 98, Proceedings of the sixth international conference and exposition on engineering, construction, and operations in space, held in Albuquerque, NM, 26-30 April, 1998.* Reston: American Society of Civil Engineers (1998): p. 688.

Rogers, T.F. *Space resources utilization roundtable.* Space Transportation Association, 1999.

Rycroft, Michael (ed.). *The space transportation market: evolution or revolution?*. Dordrecht: Kluwer, 2000.

Sachdeva, G.S. "Space Tourism: Some Legal Implications". *The Indian journal of international law.* No. 1 vol. 39 (1999): p. 47.

Samuel, E. "Lost in space: how do you find the way out when there's no up or down?" *New Scientist.* No 2315 (3rd of November 2001): p. 24.

Savage, P.-D., Smith, J.-D. "Utilization of virtual environments for astronaut crew training". *International Conference on Environmental Systems (ICES), 30th, Toulouse, France, July 10-13, 2000; Proceedings.*

Scott Jr., Richard W. "Policy/Legal Framework for Space Tourism Regulation". *Journal of space law.* No. 1 vol. 28 (2000): pp1.

Seboldt, W. Reichert, M. Hanowski, N. ...[*et al.*] "Long term scenarios for space exploration and utilization". Johnson, Stewart W. (ed.). *Space 2000.* proceedings of Space 2000: the seventh international conference. Reston, VA: ASCE, 2000. pp. 14-23.

Sietzen, F. "Alpha: mixing science and commerce." *Aerospace America* No 4 Vol. 39 (April 2001): pp. 28-32.

Smitherman, D.V., Jr.. *New space industries for the next millennium.* NASA Marshall Space Flight Center, 1998.

Stone, Barbara A. "Space tourism: a flight of fantasy or the next major space product?" *Thirty-first space congress, Cocoa Beach, FL, 26-29 April, 1994, proceedings.*

Tarzwell, R. "The Medical Implications of Space Tourism". *Aviation Space and Environmental Medicine.* No. 6 vol. 71 (2000): p. 649.

Thompson, Milton O., Peebles, Curtis. *Flying without wings.* Washington: Smithsonian Institution Press, 1999.

Traa-Engelman, Hanneke Louise van. *Commercial utilization of outer space. law and practice.* Dordrecht. London: Martinus Nijhoff, c1993.

W.W. Mendell. *Lunar bases and space activities of the 21st century.* Houston: Lunar and Planetary Institute, 1992.

Waller, D. "Factors affecting the perception of interobject distances in virtual environments. *Presence.* No. 6 Vol. 8 (December 1999): pp. 657-670.

Weber, Derek. "Space station Mir: the first hotel for space tourists". *Space 98, Proceedings of the sixth international conference and exposition on engineering, construction, and operations in space, held in Albuquerque, NM, 26-30 April, 1998.* Reston: American Society of Civil Engineers (1998): p. 325.

Wei, Wu, *et al.* "Forecasting display technique of human in network virtual environment". *Journal of Harbin Institute of technology* No. 3, Vol. 8 (September 2001): pp. 207-211.

Weishar, Peter. *Digital space. designing virtual environments.* New York: McGraw-Hill, 1998.

Westwood, James D. (ed.). *Medicine meets virtual reality 2001. outer space, inner space, virtual space.* IOS Press. Ohmsha, 2001.

Wheeler, Alison. *Virtual primitives for the representation of features and objects in a remote telepresence environment.* University of Surrey, 2000.

White, Frank. *The overview effect: space exploration and human evolution.* Reston, AIAA, 1998.

Wichman. H., Gaubatz, W. "Space tourist research". *International symposium on space technology and science, 22nd, Morioka, Japan, May 28-June 4, 2000; Proceedings.* Vol. 2, Tokyo, Japan, Japan Society for Aeronautical and Space Sciences and 22nd ISTS Organizing Committee (2000): pp. 2250-2255.

Winter, Frank H. *Rockets into space.* Cambridge: Harvard University Press, 1990.

Yajima, Kazuyoshi "A New Era of Space Medicine for Space Tourism". *Architectural Design.* No. 2 vol. 70 (2000): p. 21.

Index

Acrobatic airplanes, 5
Active Space Missions, 16
Aerobraking, 55, 103, 111, 208
Aerospace, 71, 94, 192, 197, 229, 258, 264
  companies, 257, 279
  plane, 207-8
  vehicles, 207
Air breathing engines, 207
Akiyama, 2, 131, 135
Allen, Paul, 179, 196, 198-99, 215, 218-19, 236, 241, 249, 251, 254
Almaz space station, 65, 127, 175
Altitude Gain, 89, 90
American aerospace company, 177
American Rocket Company, 199, 235
American space transport company, 202
America's Space Prize, 6, 127, 178
Anderson, 261-62
Ansari, Amir, 226-27, 267, 280
Ansari, Anousheh, 3, 7, 8, 131, 192, 226
Ansari, Hamid, 226
Apollo, 46, 76, 83, 116, 118, 130-31, 140, 156, 192, 277, 285, 306
Apollo-Soyuz Test Project, 302
Arianespace, 123-24
Asteroids, 10, 21-23, 26, 29, 30, 32, 36-38, 108-9, 127, 199, 293
Astrium, 167-68, 170, 173
Astronaut Badge, 133
Astronaut Corps, 129
Astronaut Safety and Mission Assurance Department, 203
Astronaute Club Européen, 269
Astronomy, 13, 15, 68, 69, 226-27, 235, 277, 307
Avionics, 165, 244, 248, 270

Beal Aerospace, 126
Benson Space Company, 199, 201, 234-36
Bigelow Aerospace, 6, 125, 127, 163-66, 211-14
Biosphere, 30, 32, 39
Blue Origin New Shepard, 264
Boeing International Space Station, 166
Bone density, 120, 310, 312
Branson, Sir Richard, 4, 125, 186-88, 217-19, 261
British Aerospace, 169

California, 1, 60, 83, 86, 90, 101, 177, 198, 201-2, 229, 252, 254, 256, 259, 267
Canadian Arrow, 184
Canadian radio station, 191
Canadian Space Agency, 68, 261
Cape Canaveral, 6, 204-5
Carbonaceous chondrites, 109
Celestial bodies, 9, 99, 100
Chemical rockets, 54, 112
Chinese space programme, 47, 129
CHIPSat, science mission, 235
Cislunar space, 36, 56
Civilian Aerospace Test Center Test Programmes, 88
Civilian space agencies, 128, 133
Civilian Space eXploration Team, 99, 215
Clementine mission, 51
Closed orbit, 99, 206
Combustion engine, internal, 89, 90
Commercial astronauts, 4, 128, 133-34
Commercial flights, 6, 105, 167, 188
Commercial Human Spaceflight, 230
Commercial space
  flight, 60, 125
  Launch Act, 123, 133
  Launch Amendments Act, 5, 125, 133
  station, 6, 263
  transportation, 60, 122, 124

Commercial Spaceflight
  Federation, 271
  Medicine, 314
Crew
  Altitude Protection Suit, 10, 295
  cabin, 156, 158, 242, 247
  capsule, 165, 177
  module, 266
  rotation, 81
CTN, 245

D-2 mission, 210
DASA, 169
Decompression
  rapid, 11, 296
  sickness, 11, 296, 310-11
Deimos, 30, 31, 35
Deorbiting spacecraft, 12
Docking, failed, 65
Dragon, 202, 204
Dream Chaser, 199-201

EADS Astrium, 113, 167-68, 291
Earth altitude, 122
Earth-based astronauts, 108
Earth gravity, 34
Earth-Launched Spaceflight, 99
Earth observation satellite, 60, 63, 98
Earth's rotation, 265
Ebullism, 10, 11, 295-96
Electromagnetic radiation, 9
Elliptic orbit, 104
Enceladus, 36
Escape velocity, 12, 34, 99, 100
European Aeronautic Defence and Space Company, 167, 169-70
European aerospace company, 169
European Space Agency, 2, 47, 68, 77, 81, 123, 129, 134, 227

FAA, 5, 60, 86, 133, 215, 266
Failed Spaceflight Ventures, 126
Falcon, 6, 126-27, 164, 200, 202-5
Federal Space Agency, 3, 227
First Human Spaceflights, 98, 117, 125, 236
First Orbital Launches, List of, 18
First test flights, 125, 251

Flight
  atmospheric, 104, 208
  bag, 192
  commercial orbital space tourism, 200
  funded space, 215
  independent, 209, 215
  initial, 168, 201, 264
  respective space, 3
  sequence, 154, 156, 158, 160
  simulator, 218, 248
  space tourist, 192
  suborbital space tourism, 4
  sub-orbital tourist, 105, 250
  trajectory, 185, 208
Fuel
  casing, 242, 245
  cells, 54
  extra, 55, 113
  solid, 157, 245, 247
Fuzzy orbit, 111

Galactic Suite, 290-91
Ganymede, 35
Gates, Bill, 223-24
Gemini missions, 303
GeneSat missions, 212
Geostationary orbit, 83, 102, 110, 197
Global Projects, 241
Gott, Richard, 40, 42, 283

HAAS, 154-55
Habitation, 15, 34, 36, 37
Hohmann transfer orbits, 110-11, 113
Hubble Space Telescope, 13, 42, 166, 275
Human intimacy, 283, 285-87
Human launches, 82, 84
Human spaceflight, 15, 39, 69, 83, 116-19, 128, 138, 206, 241, 251, 294
  achieved, 133
  conducted, 18
  launches, 119
  launching, 118
  longest single, 118
  missions, 117-18, 120
  private, 119
  programmes, 118, 128, 178
  safe, 236
Hybrid rocket motors, 198-99, 215, 235-36, 241, 244

Hydrogen, 30, 35, 47, 51, 113, 115, 246
Hypoxia, 10, 11, 295-96

ICBMs, 103, 105-6
Inertial Vertical Flight, 156, 160
Intellectual property, 179, 198, 235, 251, 258, 260
Intergalactic space, 9, 14
International Space Station, 1, 3, 8, 68-71, 78, 79, 124-25, 175-76, 183-84, 192, 195, 200-2, 221-22, 224-27, 229-30, 261-63
Interplanetary Spaceflight, 108
Interplanetary travel, 13, 98, 108-9
Interstellar space, 13, 14
ISS, 3, 6, 8, 29, 64, 68-72, 74-81, 119, 124-25, 131, 192-95, 204, 224-27, 229-30, 232
ISC Kosmotras Dnepr rocket, 211, 213
ISS crew, 79, 80

JIMO mission, 112
Johnson Space Center, 132, 230
Jumpstart mission, 200
Jupiter, 29, 34, 35, 108-9, 114

Kathuria, Chirinjeev, 183-84, 261
Kazakhstan, 83, 193, 224, 227, 232, 238
Kennedy Space Center, 60, 83
Korean Astronaut, 134-35

Launch pads, 82, 100, 154, 161-62, 253, 265
Launch sites, 60, 83, 100, 179, 183, 191, 205, 220, 264-66
Launcher, 118, 195, 202, 204
Low-cost orbital launcher, 282
Low-earth orbit, 12-13, 29, 59, 60, 68, 69, 106, 110, 115, 120, 186, 199, 203, 257, 265
Low gravity, 35, 50, 57, 58, 70, 286
Lunar base, 45-47, 53, 55
Lunar Mission, 193
Lunar space elevators, 31, 55, 114
Lunar surface, 46, 54-56, 58, 83, 98, 139, 155

Magnetosphere, 13, 35
Manned
  space station, 263
  spaceflight, 15, 116-17, 158, 305
  Sub-orbital Spaceflights, 107
Martin, Lockheed, 124, 126, 164-65, 169, 184, 259
McAuliffe, Christa, 2, 3, 132, 134
Melvill, Mike, 89, 90, 131, 216, 218, 280
Mercury missions, 302-3
Microgravity, 70, 75, 76, 106, 120, 283-85, 287, 290, 302-4
Military-use space station, 64
Mir Space Station, 125, 130, 184, 260-62, 272
Mojave Aerospace, 179, 215, 219, 241, 250-51, 254, 267, 280
MONODS, 247
Moon and Near Earth Asteroids, 29
Most Spacewalks, 140

NASA's
  astronauts, 131, 301
  Commercial Orbital Transportation Services, 202
  DeepSpaceOne, 112
  Johnson Space Center, 193
  Mars Odyssey Mission, 306
  Marshall Space Flight Center, 259
  missions, 202
  Orion spacecraft, 54
  Space Shuttle, 68, 123
  space shuttles, 5, 58, 184
  SpaceFlight, 185
  Transhab design, 211, 213
National Space Society, 21, 286
Nautilus space station, 6
Near-Earth
  asteroids, 35, 37, 199
  objects, 30, 293
Neptune, 108, 178
Nevada space technology startup company, 163
New Jersey, 190, 223, 225-26
New Shepard, 166-67, 264-66
Nitrogen, 22, 23, 30, 35, 36, 115, 246, 310-11
Non-rocket spacelaunch, 102
Nuclear thermal rockets, 113

Occupied Space Stations, List of, 66
Olsen, Gregory, 3, 7, 131, 138, 192, 225-26
Orbit
  high Earth, 37
  low, 34, 154
  near-Earth, 197
  space-colony, 21
  stable, 12, 102

Orbital
colonies, 20, 36, 37
craft, 185, 217, 219, 250
flights, 5, 82, 101, 106, 117, 155, 250
launch capabilities, 18
launch systems, List of, 150
launches, 18, 94, 102
Mission Explorers Circle, 194
mission, 194
Sciences Corporation, 86, 180
space tourism, 2, 122
spacecraft, 200-1
spaceflight, 12, 99, 101-4, 166, 186, 194, 206
spaceplanes, 184, 208-9, 257
spaceship, 198
speeds, 103, 219
stationkeeping, 24
velocities, 5, 102, 110
Orbiting Space shuttle, 301
Orbiting space station, 106, 263
ORIZONT vehicle, 159
Ottawa Treaty, 174
Outer space, 9, 10, 13, 15, 22, 26, 58, 63, 70, 98, 99, 117, 275-76, 284, 286, 292, 305-8
Oxidiser tank, 207, 244-45, 247
Oxidiser, 207, 245

Parachutes, 101, 157-58, 175, 177, 184, 266
Personal Spaceflight Federation, 1, 60, 235
Photon radiation, 10
Pioneer Rocketplane, 258-60
Planetariums, 307
PlanetSpace, 183-84
Polar orbit, 83, 265
Pressurised modules, 68, 72
Private Spaceflight Companies Offering Services in Space and Space Tourism, 149
Private Spaceflight Companies, 124, 149
Privately-funded missions, 131
PRIZE Foundation, 227, 279-81
Proton rocket, 68, 72, 267
Publicly-Funded Space Tourism, 195

QUID, 61

Radiation, 24, 34, 47, 52, 112, 115, 121, 165, 197, 296, 298, 313
damage, 121, 197
detection, 214
-induced cancer, 115
pressure, 10, 13, 112
-proof louvres, 24
protection, 20, 30, 32, 43
sickness, 121
Radiators, 24
Return flight, 224, 228
Reusable spacecraft, 6, 86, 101
Robotic missions, 15, 78
Rocket booster, 156-58
Rocket engines, 5, 89, 90, 102-3, 157, 160-61, 168, 178, 184-85, 201, 207, 246, 258, 260
monopropellant, 157
Rocket launch sites, 82, 83
Rocket launches, 98, 113
Rocket motors, safe hybrid, 199, 201, 236
Rocket spaceplanes, 206
Rocketplane Limited, 4, 185, 187, 258, 260
Romanian Space Agency, 162
Rotary Rocket, 86, 126, 185, 267
RSC Energia, 123, 184, 261-62
Rubicon, 196
Russian Federal Space Agency, 68, 116, 129, 134-35, 224, 230, 267
Russian Mission Control Center, 262
Russian Soyuz, 3, 8, 125, 193, 221, 228, 230
Russian Space Agency, 1, 3, 60, 226, 261, 263
Russian space company RSC Energia, 261, 263
Russian space programme, 60, 226, 228, 260, 304
Russian space station Mir, 71, 262
Rutan, Burt, 4, 89, 90, 125, 179, 196, 215-16, 219, 235, 241-42, 245, 250-51, 254, 279

Satellite manufacturing, 58, 59
Scientific suborbital flights, 106
SEPI, 173
Sexual activity, 283-84, 289-90
Sheerin, Geoff, 183-84
Shepard's spaceflight, 238
Shuttle mission STS-93 in July, 117
Shuttle mission, 80, 134
Shuttleworth, Mark, 3, 7, 8, 130-31, 192-93, 220-22, 226
Sierra Nevada Corporation, 198
Silver Dart, 184
Simonyi, Charles, 3, 7, 131, 192-93, 222, 224
Singapore Spaceport, 91, 92
Skylab, 63, 64, 192, 230, 303

SMART-1 mission, 54
Solar arrays, 72, 74, 75, 212-14
Solar energy, 15, 22, 29, 30, 45, 51, 53, 54
Solar power satellites, 21, 30, 58, 257
Solar radiation, 114, 296
Solar thermal rockets, 31, 113
Solar wind, 10, 12-14, 52, 57, 197
Sounding rockets, 103, 106, 178
Soyuz rocket, 1, 68, 72, 81, 124, 138, 192, 221, 267
Soyuz TMA-9 mission, 227
Space Adventures, 1, 3, 4, 8, 91, 93, 136, 187, 192-96, 221, 224-26, 231-32, 266, 267
Space advocacy, 26
Space agencies, 16, 39, 68, 71, 81, 116, 118, 263
Space art, 272, 275-77
Space colonies, 20, 29, 36, 39, 40, 42, 44, 56, 293
Space Colonization and Commercialization, 29
Space colonization, 21, 29, 31, 33, 35, 39-41, 45, 69, 292-93
Space elevators, 31, 35, 65, 100, 113, 127-28, 270, 282
Space environment, 15, 121, 197, 295, 300
Space exploration, 1, 15-17, 26-28, 44-46, 71, 78, 98, 101, 108, 124, 195, 200, 260-62, 275-76, 309-10
Space Flights, 26, 79, 216
Space Frontier Foundation, 7, 286
Space habitats, 20-23, 36-39, 65
Space hazards, 165, 293
Space hotels, 1, 5, 6
Space industry development, 86
Space infrastructure, 43, 62
Space Island Group, 6, 257
Space Island Project, 257
Space jet, 168
Space launcher capabilities, 18
Space launchers, 18
  commercial, 20
  inherited, 18
Space medicine, 284, 308, 314
Space missions, extended, 297
  favoured manned, 112
  robotic, 206
  travel aboard, 134
Space music, 306-7
Space Oddity, 306
Space Odyssey, 1, 290, 295
Space programmes, 2, 41, 62, 118, 122, 131-34, 195, 228, 261, 285, 308
Space Race, 1, 19, 45, 62
Space radiation, 24
Space settlements, 29-31
Space shuttle
  astronauts, 176, 313
  mission, 70, 80, 81, 210, 284
Space sickness, 130, 312
Space station projects, 70, 71
Space stations, 2, 6, 7, 15, 20, 36, 63-65, 68, 71, 77, 79, 82, 126, 175, 228, 261
Space technology, 15, 62, 63, 98, 210, 235
Space tourism, 1, 3, 5, 7-9, 60, 84, 98, 127, 129, 134, 137, 149, 164, 241, 269
  commercial, 7, 234, 236
  industry, 1, 7-9, 60, 84, 116, 137, 179-80, 185
  preliminary manned suborbital, 176
  trips, 136
Space tourists, 3, 4, 7, 8, 15, 61, 118, 125, 138, 184, 192-93, 195, 218, 222, 224, 227, 262-63
  self-funded, 131, 135, 220, 226
Space Transport Corporation, 196
Space vehicles, 64, 114, 137, 149, 199, 202
  manufacturers of, 149
Spacecraft, 12, 13, 46, 47, 81-83, 98, 99, 101-5, 110-13, 116-21, 127-30, 164-66, 175-77, 186-87, 206, 211-16, 243-44, 265
  design, 176-77, 197
  electrostatic, 197
  interplanetary, 69
  launching, 82
  piloted, 241
  rocket, 194
  rocket-powered, 176
  sub-orbital, 106
SpaceDev Dream Chaser, 198-200, 235
Spaceflight, 4, 62, 98, 100-1, 103-5, 116-17, 130-31, 133, 227, 230-32, 238, 250, 292, 301-3, 310-11
  amateur, 99
  commercial, 83, 105, 198, 229, 251, 279, 314
  complete, 239
  extended, 121
  low-cost, 279
  missions, 122, 136, 192
  participants, list of, 135
  private, 122, 126, 232

records, list of, 138
single, 64
sub-orbital tourist, 83
surrounding private, 125
Spaceplanes, 101, 185, 200-1, 206-7, 209-11, 215,
flying suborbital, 122
horizontally-launched, 208
rocket-propelled, 5
suborbital tourist, 267
Spaceport America, 93-95, 220
Spaceport Singapore, 93, 194
Spaceport tax, 95
Spaceports, commercial, 60, 94, 194-95
Space-related activities, 26, 153
Spaceship Company, 179-80, 217-19, 251, 254
SpaceShipOne, 4, 83, 86, 89, 90, 99, 103, 106, 119, 125-26, 178, 215-19, 235-36, 243-44, 246-51, 253-55
Spacetourist, 206, 231
Spacewalks, 7, 117, 128, 194, 310
SpaceX Dragon, 127, 203-4
SpaceX Falcon, 101, 164
STABILO, 155-58
STS-47 mission, 283
STS-9, space shuttle mission, 230
Sub-orbital spaceflight, 83, 99, 119, 194, 211, 250, 269
achieved human, 84
funded human, 86
inaugural, 188
low-altitude, 178
mile apogee, 178
minimal, 99
Scaled Composites StarShip, 261
semi-ballistic, 106
Sub-orbital trajectory, 99, 101, 103, 105, 184, 209

T-cells, 312
Technological demonstrator, 161
Test flights, 98, 125, 167, 217-18, 220, 248-49, 253, 256, 266
Test pilots, 131, 218
Testflights, 6
Tito mission, 263
Tito, Dennis, 3, 7, 125, 131, 184, 193, 226, 229-30, 262-63
Trailblazer, 200

United Launch Alliance, 124, 200
Unmanned Jupiter missions, 112

Vertical flights, 104-5
Vinci Project, 176
Virgin Balloon Flights, 191
Virgin Blue, 189
Virgin Galactic, 4, 5, 7, 94, 95, 106, 125, 179, 186-87, 217-18, 220, 241, 251, 253-54
Virgin SpaceShips, 179, 187, 248, 251, 254
Vostok missions, 238
Voyager, 108, 206, 252-53

Weightless environments, 6, 121, 283-87, 297
White Knight, 186-87, 216, 218, 244, 246-48, 250-51, 254-56

XCOR Aerospace, 4, 86, 125, 201-2, 267

Yasny Launch Base in Siberia, 164-65

Zero-gravity, 23, 50, 57, 76, 232, 284, 286-87
Zero-Gravity flights, 192-93
Zond missions, 267